The Social Origins of the Welfare State

Studies in Childhood and Family in Canada

Studies in Childhood and Family in Canada is a multidisciplinary series devoted to new perspectives on these subjects as they evolve. The series features studies that focus on the intersections of age, class, race, gender, and region as they contribute to a Canadian understanding of childhood and family, both historically and currently.

Series Editor
Cynthia Comacchio
Department of History
Wilfrid Laurier University

Manuscripts to be sent to
Brian Henderson, Director
Wilfrid Laurier University Press
75 University Avenue West
Waterloo, Ontario, Canada, N2L 3C5

The Social Origins of the Welfare State

Québec Families, Compulsory Education, and Family Allowances, 1940–1955

Dominique Marshall

Translated by Nicola Doone Danby

Wilfrid Laurier University Press

We acknowledge the support of the Canada Council for the Arts for our publishing program. We acknowledge the financial support of the Government of Canada through the Book Publishing Industry Development Program for our publishing activities.

Canada Council for the Arts | Conseil des Arts du Canada

Library and Archives Canada Cataloguing in Publication

Marshall, Dominique, 1961–
The social origins of the welfare state : Québec families, compulsory education, and family allowances, 1940–1955 / Dominique Marshall; translated by Nicola Doone Danby.

(Studies in childhood and family in Canada)
Translation of : Aux origines sociales de l'État-providence.
Includes bibliographical references and index.
ISBN-13: 978-0-88920-452-2
ISBN-10: 0-88920-452-7

1. Welfare state. 2. Family policy—Québec (Province). 3. Family—Québec (Province)—History—20th century. 4. Education, Compulsory—Québec (Province)—History—20th century. 5. Family allowances—Québec (Province)—History—20th century. 6. Child labor—Québec (Province)—History—20th century. I. Danby, Nicola Doone, 1974– . II. Title. III. Series.

HV109.Q84M3713 2006 361.6'50971409044 C2006-903991-7

Waterloo, Ontario, Canada
www.wlupress.wlu.ca

Cover design by P.J. Woodland. Front cover photograph—originally from the National Film Board—from the National Archives of Canada, Official Publications, National Library of Canada negative NL15302, Department of National Health and Welfare, *Allocations familiales: Charte de l'enfance* (Ottawa: King's Printer, 1945–1946), published in *La Presse*, 25 February 1944. Reproduced with the permission of *La Presse* and the Department of Public Works and Government Services Canada. Author photo by Graphics, Oxford-Brookes University. Text design by Catharine Bonas-Taylor.

This book is printed on Ancient Forest Friendly paper (100% post-consumer recycled).

Printed in Canada

To my husband, Andrew, with all my gratitude

Contents

Introduction

During the Second World War, the federal and provincial governments made generous promises to Québec's poor children. In 1943, the prime minister of Québec, Liberal Adélard Godbout, recognized their right to a minimum level of education. Four years of power had allowed him to put an end to the half-century of quarrelling between the province's Catholic clergy and Liberal reformists over the State's role in education. Radio and newspapers informed parents, children, teachers, and school commissioners that, beginning in September 1943, school would be both free and compulsory until the age of fourteen or until grade seven, inclusively. This policy earned Godbout and his ministers the reputation of having been the precursors to the Quiet Revolution. With the aim of modernizing the province's economy, they effectively strove to extend the social grip over public institutions, a task that would be taken up by the "équipe du tonnerre" of another Liberal, Jean Lesage, in 1960.

In 1944, a year after Québec's adoption of this law on compulsory education, Canadian prime minister William Lyon Mackenzie King announced that all children aged sixteen and under would have the right to a "minimum of welfare" and, to this end, monthly family allowances in the amount of four to nine dollars would be disbursed to all mothers. The necessities of war production and the approaching general elections led Mackenzie King to establish the country's first universal social program, one of the foundations of the Canadian Welfare State.

The two laws dictated that parents were responsible for their children's physical security at least until the age of fourteen, permitting these youths to acquire a minimum of intellectual development. It became illegal for children to work instead of attend school, and the State commit-

Notes to introduction start on p. 195.

ted itself to guaranteeing that none of them shoulder the material obligation to achieve this objective. This policy was not altogether new; previously, children aged sixteen and under who wished to work for a manufacturer or distributor needed to obtain a permit from the Québec Department of Labour (QDL), a measure that prevented them from compromising their education too seriously. Without this permit they risked putting their employers in an illegal position, which was all the more likely since the war had breathed new zeal into the labour inspectors. In addition to this permit system, the Catholic parish priests observed a custom of waiting for children to reach grade seven before admitting them to solemn communion. In certain cities in the 1920s—Montréal in particular—parents and children were already dealing with truancy officers and the school boards' enumerators. And finally, starting in 1936, the poor mothers who could help local authorities to recognize the honesty of their situation received a modest "Needy Mothers' Assistance" from the provincial government, which occasionally allowed them to keep a child in school. Later, to facilitate military recruitment, the federal government undertook to pay out a relatively generous "Soldiers' Dependants' Allowance" for children under sixteen years of age.

What was new in the war years was that the social safety net the two States had woven together affected all children. Family historians agree that the State's increased intervention in the domains of education and welfare was a major change in twentieth-century Western households. The system for educating children multiplied relationships between families and State representatives. At the same time, precise models of childhood and family life were attached to the institutional structure, becoming omnipresent in subsequent decades. What is less clear is how, in which direction, and to what degree these changes influenced the lives of poor families. It is possible to examine in closer detail the documents where politicians and officials left traces of their projects, of their efforts and frustrations; where fathers, mothers, daughters, and sons talked about school and their mutual responsibilities, about their views of the working world; where observers saw those families summon officials and public servants, either to obey or to protest against them, and finally where families attempted to change the public authorities' perceptions of the society in which they were about to intervene.

The interest in the history of family allowances, compulsory education, and child labour laws does not end with the families these programs were meant to help. For those historians studying the politics of Québec and Canada, the adoption of these policies was a turning point in the history of the State. These laws thus merit further study, particularly since fifty years later, the Welfare State is in a state of crisis. The increase in social spending is alarming, the mid-century's mature and broad social programs seem to have fallen short of expectations (the issue of school dropout rates is one example, or even the question of children who do not like school), and the provinces—even the "regions" within these provinces—denounce the centralism of the laws promising a minimum standard of living. Many ask if they should not renounce the Welfare State, and in 1992 family allowances were replaced with non-universal tax credits. At the same time, however, those citizens interviewed in polls repeat that life is good in Canada and that social programs are largely responsible for their satisfaction. Is the crisis the effect of incomplete reforms, and should the generosity of the Welfare State increase? Or should the debate on the State's desired degree of intervention become a broader interrogation of the relations between State and society?

When the moment comes to decide what we want to conserve and what we are ready to question, it is often refreshing to know that institutions do not last forever. They have their own inertia, certainly, but the rigidity of the Welfare State's regulations, the assurances of its advertisements and pamphlets, its inspectors' confidence, the solidity of its buildings, or even the anonymity of its cheques are not the products of simple and inevitable advances. Rather, they are the result of painstaking meetings among multiple groups of the larger society with varying degrees of influence. From the moment of these social programs' implementation, the compromise they represented was threatened.

Who exactly contributed to the inauguration of this Welfare State and with whose interests in mind, in the name of which values and, ultimately, with what success? The following pages tell the story of these laws, from a variety of angles.

This book is part of a renewal in the study of the history of the State, which examines public institutions while keeping in mind above all the nature of the society in which the State takes shape. Based on the work that has been done in social history over the last few decades, the supporters of the "new political history" wish to distinguish themselves from a type of history they deem elitist and too close to the nationalist projects of the nineteenth century. Belonging to the latter school of thought, the first histories of the Welfare State and of education served as a vehicle for the ideas put forward in official reports or in reports written by members of professions connected with the programs' implementation. The new movement extends beyond the study of elections, political parties, or State employees' activities and includes all relations of power within a society. In turn, these relations contribute to the creation (and perpetuation) of the large categories of social relations, studied in the new history, among classes, genres, generations, regions, nations, and ethnicities.[1]

This movement is especially concerned with the slow construction of public institutions. It takes into account the socio-economic situation of all the actors present at the heart of public administration and the ways by which they relate to civil society. The history of social policy has always drawn considerably on the study of public administration. Because social policies have a tendency to remain in the shadow of parliamentary debates, their history is often to be found in the "corridors."[2] But beyond the public officials to whom traditional administrative histories have accustomed us, the new history proposes looking at the society to which they belong and react. The idea of neutral "social needs" belongs to technocratic fictions, whose history it is important to retrace by paying close attention to the demands of interest groups and classes that supported social measures, and by noting requests that were both accepted by officials and refused by them.[3]

Institutions of education and welfare provide environments in which power relations can be observed between the central and the peripheral, as well as among the authorities of local societies.[4] The local struggles and respites, in which parents and children play a major role, add to the efforts from the centre to reorient the practices of teachers, social workers, school principals, students, and parents. This history of public education and the Welfare State draws on the history of the family to examine the relative autonomy of household workings and understand their internal logic.[5] The history of labour is also examined in an attempt to determine the reasons behind the growing decline of the juvenile labour market in the twentieth century and to gauge the impact of the strengthened legislation in the context of other economic and cultural developments.[6]

Similarly, the scholars of the "new political economy," while continuing to view the State as the tool of accumulation for the dominant class, see it further as a relatively autonomous and sufficiently heterogeneous entity to be the subject of focused study. According to them, the State can be seen as a place where temporary compromises are developed with economically disadvantaged groups, with the aim of obtaining the legitimacy necessary to maintain a certain social harmony. The various actors hiding behind the unique label of the State—the government, public servants, public institutions—have different responsibilities, values, and interests.[7] Studies of historical sociology have developed fruitful analytical methods based on the idea that the State acts as an agent of cultural revolution. Seen this way, the history of the Welfare State can become the "process of simultaneous production both of the collective good and of the community."[8]

The first four chapters of this book are largely inspired by this historiography. Chapter 1 reviews the diverse legislative policies, retracing the major social realities the authors of bills in Québec and in Canada faced, and introducing the political groups who influenced these officials. Chapter 2 goes on to explore the laws themselves where they were implemented—in the offices of public servants and inspectors. The practices of these State agents reveal not only their professional ethics and their corporatist interests but also their pragmatism and openness to the world, which were essential for the daily tasks of administration and allowed clients of the Welfare State to hold a certain amount of power. Chapter 3 examines the State's intentions regarding children and parents. The officials' values, as they related to the family and to poverty, are discussed, as are the foundations of the conviction that the State needed to intervene in the families' decisions regarding the length and cost of children's education. These ideas refer in turn to the culture of the elites, to the sources of their inspiration, and to their individual histories.

To what degree were the original objectives attained? Chapters 4 and 5, centred on families, attempt to answer this question. Assessments of the first twenty years of the field of the history of the family often mention the lack of studies looking at the links between families and other social authorities. Historians examining the exterior of the family too often ask only unidirectional questions concerning the impact of major social changes such as industrialization or migration on families. In the other direction, relatively little is known about the family's influence on the creation of institutions.[9] Family sociologists have long studied the relationship between the history of the household and the history of social change. Many have sought to show how the family's primary function of "socialization" has been progressively taken up by the State in the twentieth century. However, these studies often suffer from the narrowness of functionalist theories, which offer as an explanation only the general logic of the diversification of modern societies. Their critics prompt us to determine the precise circumstances surrounding changes, to research phenomena other than this simple transfer of roles, to challenge the rigidity of this broad theory in order to propose more specific laws, and to explain particular practices and institutions.[10]

Choosing to analyze the family can lead to the underestimation of the particularities of its individual members, as demonstrated in the simplistic use of the "family strategy" concept, which presupposes that all members pursue the same goal: the family's continued reproduction. In order to integrate the power struggles between the sexes and generations into an analysis of the relations between families and other institutions, we can view the family as a "system within a system," a unit of power relations also involved in larger political relations and the dynamics they experience.[11] Recent studies on the history of women have revealed the gendered character of public institutions and of family relations, and they have attempted to analyze the connection between the two orders of phenomena. Works dealing with generational conflicts, on the manner in which "politics structure the transition to adulthood," lead to the same type of study.[12]

The final group of difficulties put forward in recent historiographies of the family concerns discourses about families; more specifically, critics warn against the tendency among historians to confuse images of families created by the elite with the actual opinions of family members. Similarly, they point at the danger of confusing the laws' intentions with the real effects of the policies once implemented and confusing the officials' views of the laws' impacts with the critical examination of their effects.[13] Such confusion occurs in works that adhere to the theory of an authoritarian State gradually depriving families of their traditional responsibilities while inculcating them with the State's morals[14] or works that assume the political relations in a democracy to be consensual. In their opinion, if the Welfare State assumed at once the new responsibilities created by urban and industrial society and the traditional responsibilities that families could no longer perform, it was because different groups in society requested it and the needs of the population were evolving, just as was the capacity of the State's and of the economy's capacities to respond to such request.[15] However, the history of the conditions in which the elite's ideas on poor families developed is worth further investigation. We can then consider the variety of values attached to families while keeping in mind the differences of class, ethnicity, and region.[16]

All too often, studies of family practices and values are carried out separately. To escape the impasse created by the parallel development of approaches interested in "sentiment" and "family economy," it is necessary to analyze the relations of families with other institutions.[17] Similarly, when discussing the State, we must keep in mind the history of ideas on the State. Increasingly, histories of the Welfare State take into account contemporary political theories, the history of their creation, and the basis of their legitimacy.[18]

Using the methods of the history of the family and its recent orientation, chapter 4 focuses on the study of the family's economic and cultural circumstances. It begins by establishing that the reformists succeeded in extending the school-leaving age for a certain number of children and in giving parents sufficient means to provide them with a more comfortable childhood. This discussion is followed by an exploration of families' motives for accepting the new public policies. Chapter 5 examines the minority of children who remained on the margins of the new promises of citizenship and further attempts to determine what caused these exclusions: the programs' limitations and the moral and economic requirements of families confronted with a capitalist market, the effects of which the Welfare State could not completely correct.

When considering the political role of families, many specialists of socio-economic history study the population's response to the State's controlling attempts. They investigate, in the culture of various social groups, the elements leading to an explanation of this resistance with the aim of discovering its origins. Critical reviewers suggest that the relationships between the State and families need to be addressed in a more flexible manner, taking into account that they are two mutually influenced complex and dynamic systems and that they depend, in turn, on larger trends of society. The state can reflect social inequality without being the exclusive instrument of the economic elite; and it is possible that the interests of poorer families and of the state may temporarily coincide. In this regard, poorer families may do more than simply resist—they may become forces of social change.[19] They must be included in explanations of the transformations of large socio-economic indicators and of policies. The sociologists studying "State formation" as "cultural revolution" have sketched out a way to account for this double shift.

In this vein, chapter 6 returns to the question of policy to show how in the following two decades the laws studied here altered the relationships among the State, families, and special interest groups and shaped their hopes and demands. It opens up perspectives for the analysis of the creation of social policy in Québec during the Quiet Revolution.

A final word on the nature of this study, on its sources, and its chronological and spatial limits: the sources constituting the main corpus are documents issued by public administration. These include annual reports and administrative archives from ministers and public institutions responsible for the implementation of three laws: the federal Department of Public Health and Welfare and, in Québec, the Department of Labour and the Department of Public Instruction.[20] Concerning the Compulsory School Attendance Act and the decentralized implementation of the policy, I consulted the sources of a few local school boards chosen for their resemblance to the 2,000 boards of the province.[21] The records of those prosecuted for not obeying compulsory school attendance in Montreal complete this general picture.[22] Regarding the Family Allowances Act, the Québec Regional Office archives complement those of the Ottawa head office.[23]

On the whole, the collections of governmental and institutional archives bring together the projects, objections, and demands of a variety of Québec's social actors. Moreover, these administrative sources capture them at the moment of their meeting. They reveal, among other things, previously unnoticed aspects of child labour that these same laws strove to abolish. Ironically, the more child labour is investigated, the more visible it becomes. As the sources are the product of the very same process we seek to comprehend, an important bias requires our attention. The production of information related to the administration of the laws is studied in one section of this work, where the documentary basis of the thesis is examined critically.

This collection of documents contains important clues about the values and actions of not only officials, experts, and special interest groups but also, due to the universal character of compulsory education and family allowances, of hundreds of families. As preliminary census returns from this period are not yet available, the results collected by public administration offer an alternative, a reconstitution of the collective biographies at an intermediate scale.

Why the period 1940–55? Family historians have yet to rigorously address twentieth-century changes. A major component of this history is the birth of the Welfare State.[24] The spatiotemporal constraints of the present work were, by and large, imposed by the extent of the analytic interrogation. Moreover, for this project of observing families through the prism of the State, the period of time examined is more justified by the rhythm of the State than by that of the families. Given the shortness of the period, it is difficult to examine overall changes in family life over the long term; however, it is long enough to permit the observation of the complete cycle of these three laws. The story begins in the early 1940s, a time of upheaval in Canada and Québec in economic, political, and social matters. It ends twenty years later with Paul Sauvé's arrival in power in Québec and the inauguration of a new era of governmental development. If the terrain explored corresponds to that of other provinces, as with many recent histories of the Welfare State, it is because in the history of social laws, the strength and relative homogeneity of provincial structures and traditions, is remarkable.[25] The exclusion of the country's other provinces and territories has the drawback of denying a comparison of different political entities. However, through an examination of family allowances, this study incorporates the relationship between the citizens of Québec and the federal government, too often neglected by historians studying contemporary Québec. From another viewpoint, this geographic choice permits the simultaneous analysis of different social groups in Québec, and the province offers ample material to ponder explanations of changes in families and in politics according to social class, religion, and ethnicity. This is all the more interesting, since the history of the family suffers from an overexposure to urban populations and to central Québec, which works on the Saguenay and the Lower St. Lawrence regions insufficiently counterbalance.[26]

The three laws examined do not represent the totality of the government's public intervention in the realm of childhood between 1940 and 1955. However, they are the laws affecting the largest number of children, and they all concern the period of youth's entrance into the labour market. Not examined, for reasons of practicality, are the act of 1945 assisting apprentices and a number of policies affecting families less exclusively in areas such as income taxes, private insurance, and the regulation of wages. Moreover, certain aspects of the history of compulsory education and family allowances have not been considered. Given their unique circumstances, the domain of the protection of childhood and the relations between the State and First Nations families require their own studies.

This book is based on research I carried out while writing my doctoral thesis in history between 1985 and 1989, during which time I benefited from Social Sciences and Humanities Research Council (SSHRC) and fonds pour la formation des chercheurs et l'aide à la recherche (FCAR) grants. I pursued this research during a post-doctoral apprenticeship thanks to these same granting councils and to the Fondation du prêt d'honneur. An internal grant from Carleton University allowed me to complete my work. I would also like to thank my professors: Bettina Bradbury, who directed my doctoral work; René Durocher, with whom I planned this project; Hal Benenson, Sam Warner, Winnifred Rothenberg, Jacques Rouillard, and Jane Lewis, who helped me to define the particular elements of study. I would also like to thank all those colleagues who read and commented on different portions of my work: Bruce Curtis, Robert Goheen, Jim Kenny, Paul-André Linteau, Blair Neatby, Nicole Neatby, and Shirley Tillotson. I am thankful to many archivists and librarians for having assisted me in my efforts to retrace documents: John Taylor, of the old Department of National Health and Welfare; Benneth McCardle, former head of the archives of the Department of National Health and Welfare; Sheila Pawls, who replaced her; and the head of the Archives de la Commission scolaire régionale des Vieilles-Forges. Nicola Doone Danby wrote the translation, and Carroll Klein patiently oversaw the production at Wilfrid Laurier University Press as Maryse Labrecque had done at the Presse de l'Université de Montréal. Cheryl A. Lemmens provided a particularly helpful index. Finally, my thanks go to Yvan Dupuis, who edited the French manuscript, and to Jodi Lewchuk, who edited the English translation.

Abbreviations

A…	Archives of…
ACSSMCM	Archives de la Commission scolaire de Sainte-Marthe-du-Cap-de-la-Madeleine
ALN	Action libérale nationale
ANQQ	Archives nationales du Québec à Québec
AR…	*Annual Report of…* (*RA…: Rapport annuel de…*)
ARQDL	*Annual Report of the Québec Department of Labour*
ARSPI	*Report of the Superintendent of Education*
ASHRT	Archives de la Société historique de la région de Terrebonne
ASJCF	Archives de la Société de Jésus, province du Canada français
CCF	Co-operative Commonwealth Federation
CCPIC	Catholic Committee to the Public Instruction Council
CDSA	Centre de documents semi-actifs des Archives nationales du Québec à Québec
CNEA	Canada and Newfoundland Education Association
CSC	Commission scolaire de Champlain
CSCM	Commission scolaire de Cap-de-la-Madeleine
CSNDV	Commission scolaire Notre-Dame-de-la-Visitation
CSRVF	Commission scolaire régionale des Vieilles-Forges
CSSLF	Comission scolaire Saint-Louis-de-France
CSSMCM	Commission scolaire de Sainte-Marthe-du-Cap-de-la-Madeleine
CTCC	Confédération des travailleurs catholiques du Canada
DLGRQ	*Department of Labour General Report Québec*
DNHW	Department of National Health and Welfare
DPI	Department of Public Instruction
FCS	Fédération des commissions scolaires
FNSJB	Fédération nationale Saint-Jean-Baptiste
FPTQ	Fédération professionnelle des travailleurs du Québec

JOC	Jeunesse ouvrière catholique
LOC	Ligue ouvrière catholique
M…	Minutes from…(PV…: Procès-verbal de…)
MCSC	Montréal Catholic School Commission
MSWC	Montréal Social Welfare Court (called Juvenile Court until 1950)
NAC	National Archives of Canada
NAC/NFTSA	National Film, Television, and Sound Archives
NFB	National Film Board
NSS	National Selective Service
PCPIC	Protestant Committee to the Public Instruction Council
PBSCCM	Protestant Board of School Commissioners of the City of Montréal
PSBGM	Protestant School Board of Greater Montréal
QDL	Québec Department of Labour
QRO	Québec Regional Office (Family Allowances)
RACA	*Rapport annuel des contrôleurs d'absences*
RAMSNBES	*Rapport annuel du Ministère de la Santé nationale et du Bien-être social*
RGMTQ	*Rapport général du Ministère du Travail du Québec*
RSQ	*Revised Statutes of Québec*
SC	*Statutes of Canada*
SPI	Superintendent of Public Instruction
SQ	*Statutes of Québec*
SWSQRO	Social Welfare Service, Québec Regional Office (Family Allowances)
UCC	Union des cultivateurs catholiques

1

The Drafting of Laws

Social Movements and Legislation

The 1943 provincial Compulsory School Attendance Act and the 1945 federal Family Allowances Act were the first pieces of legislation from both levels of government to guarantee the universal rights of children. The announcement of the drafting of these laws was surrounded by declarations on equality. In his 1943 throne speech, the prime minister of Québec, Adélard Godbout, declared that "Canadians, be they English or French, have the right to education and none should be deprived of future opportunities" and that "inspired by children's best interests, this law... will thus permit them to acquire the minimum education necessary in these times."[1] As for the Family Allowances Act, it had to ensure a minimum standard of living to every child under the age of sixteen: it would "grant to all our children the equal opportunity to succeed" and constitute no less than a "charter of childhood." Acting as a "step toward the abolition of misery and fear," it would "put all Canadians, coast to coast, on equal footing."[2]

Officials often claimed they were responding promptly to the demands of the population, and it is tempting for historians to explain the adoption of social laws by the new needs of the population. This type of causal explanation is not without precedent, but this reason alone accounts neither for the chronology of the policies' adoption nor for the particular form the promises of equal opportunity took during those years of conflict. At the end of the nineteenth century, most workers' unions had asked that the State make it possible for working-class children to stay in school; as for the improvement of the families' standard of living, it was one of the unions' raisons d'être.[3] Why is it that the political elite did not seriously consider these questions until the Second World War? And what were their goals in creating these first universal social programs?

Notes to chapter 1 start on p. 199.

The history of the adoption of these laws begins with the workers' movement, which, in exceptional circumstances due to the war, was given unparalleled power of negotiation. In times of war, political leaders and business people have often been the proponents of minimal policies towards workers in order to conserve the legitimacy of their power. In the longer term, the sudden creation of new institutions ensuring a minimum of education and welfare provided politicians with the opportunity, principally under the pressure of major economic interests, to carry out a kind of catch-up, to address the broader aspects of the economy that had been put on the back burner in the wake of the market crash of 1929, namely the transformation of industrial labour and urbanization. In this manner, the changes in the country's economic structure, just as those in the evolution of the power relations between the employers' groups and the workers' unions, led officials to support the idea of the State's increased role in education and child welfare. The federal and provincial elite did not always react to these economic changes in the same manner as the elite of other Western countries facing the same wide-reaching changes. The economic problems as well as their associated social relationships in Canada and in Québec bore a distinctive character. Officials were in the habit of dealing with certain State structures, and these particularities would have a profound effect on the social programs of the first Welfare State.

Adélard Godbout and the Provincial Compulsory School Attendance Act of 1943: Liberal Reformism, "Managerial Reformism," and Clerical Agriculturalism

The history of the Compulsory School Attendance Act is above all the result of the renegotiation of an old agreement between the political and clerical elite, whose interests were rapidly evolving. On one hand, the war had permitted the election of a reformist government, one that was more open than ever to the city dwellers' demands: among the provincial Liberal Party, French-Canadian business people, and the clergy, there was a general desire to better the education of workers and farmers. On the other hand, the Catholic clergy's opposition to the State was being crushed under the influence of a modernized agriculturalism and Social Catholicism.

In Québec, on the eve of the Second World War, the Church still controlled education. In the middle of the nineteenth century, while anglophone provinces had established a governmental system of primary education, Québec (Canada East) had gone a different route. The combination of the country's failed revolutions of 1836–37, and the ultramontanism of the whole Catholic world had given the Québec clergy a controlling grip over the management of the teaching network financed by the province and mandatory property taxes collected at the municipal level. Québec's political elite had gradually come to accept this concession of State power to a "competing structure of power over the people." Increasingly concerned with developing the country's industry, by attracting large companies as well as improving the province's industrial structure, they adhered to "English [Liberalism], champion of Parliamentary sovereignty," and the growing conservatism in the social sphere made it necessary for them to consider the Church as an inexpensive agency of control.[4]

The employers themselves, insofar as teaching was concerned, had shared the opinions of the clerics, and this situation lasted until the end of the 1920s. Since the beginning of the twentieth century, important groups of larger employers had been open to the notion of compulsory education. If they were satisfied with the more limited scope of education reforms, it was because the province's industries still only required a minimal proportion of people with more than primary education. In the 1910s and 1920s, most notably, it was for the labour force's acquisition of more qualifications that the Montréal Catholic School Commission (MCSC) had centralized its structure and extended primary education beyond grade seven, under the influence of the "Fordist" trend that had become prevalent in the province's urban centres during the 1920s.[5] Closer to the culture of larger companies, the Protestant network of public education, not pledged to a jealous Church, but perpetually disappointed in its efforts to introduce compulsory education, had undertaken not only structural centralization but also the implementation of an integrated high-school network.

For their part, Lomer Gouin's and Louis-Alexandre Taschereau's successive Liberal governments had preferred to devote a larger portion of the booming provincial purse to public works rather than to education. To them, highway infrastructure was more pressing than improving the labour force's competency. However, they had created technical schools that offered high-school-level education and technical institutes for university-level education. They had also supported the opening of additional levels to prolong primary school. Thus, the officials had ensured that a minority of workers could improve their qualifications, but they did not believe the time had come to fundamentally redesign primary-school teaching. The economy's slowdown, provoked by the 1929 crash, did nothing to help change the structure of the labour force.[6] Since the end of the nineteenth century, the same lukewarm commitment to the education of the masses had led the provincial government to adopt a series of laws prohibiting children from working in factories and commercial establishments. This type of law, as we will see later on, constituted little more than a protective half measure for the poor that would change according to economic conditions.

The workers' unions had therefore called for compulsory education in vain, anxious though they were to improve their status through an increase in their level of education and to protect their members against the competing force of cheap labour. History was then repeating itself when, in 1941 and 1942, the new Québec Federation of Labour, bringing together most of the workers' unions affiliated with American labour bodies, proclaimed that "students generally leave school toward grade seven, sometimes even grade six, not yet sufficiently prepared for the struggle for existence and forever condemned to a lower standard of work."[7]

During the war, and for reasons that had little to do with its social programs, a relatively reformist government had been elected in Québec. Fearing conscription, Québec voters chose the Liberal team to govern the province. Their trust in Adélard Godbout, and the close ties between the provincial and federal branches of the Liberal Party, signified the end of Maurice Duplessis' Union Nationale government. The Liberal Canadian prime minister, Liberal William Lyon Mackenzie King, had declared that a vote for Godbout was a vote against conscription. Any other choice would be seen by the other provinces as a repudiation of Mackenzie King's decision to wage war without conscription and, eventually, Mackenzie King would lose power. The Québécois would then have to expect the worst. Since 1917, in every federal or provincial election, a strong French-Canadian majority had remembered the connection between the Conservative Party and conscription, helping the Liberal Party to maintain power in Québec. Many Québécois voters had waited until 1936 to break this habit, while a new provincial Conservative Party leader, Maurice Duplessis, sporting the reformist colours of a resigning group of the Liberal Party, the Action libérale nationale, had raised the standard of nationalism and of provincial autonomy in response to the general confusion caused by the 1929 crash. The reformed party had adopted a new name, the Union nationale, to more clearly distinguish it from the federal party, the source of a burdensome and negative association. But in 1939, the same autonomist attitude would lead Duplessis to defeat: 55 per cent voted for the Liberals and only 36 per cent for his Union nationale.[8]

Compulsory education was not part of the Québec Liberal agenda in 1939 but, in the three years it had spent in opposition, the party had regained a reformist enthusiasm. In the course of five years, Godbout's team would address not only the issues of primary school but also of women's suffrage, the quality of civil service, health insurance, and orphans. Having arrived in power owing to international events over which he had no control, he was faced with the colossal tasks of rebuilding a party divided by the problems of reform and increasing its support with urban voters, who were least likely to be seduced by Duplessis' traditionalist nationalism.

In one respect, Godbout intended to address workers' management, as their participation in the war effort had provided them with new political levers. "Why," asked *Le Monde ouvrier* writers in a virulent editorial favouring compulsory education, "in circumstances in which our fate hangs in the balance, would we want to continue whittling away at something which so deeply affects the progress and safety of the people?"[9] Officials also worried that more radical movements would sway the population. In 1944, for instance, women's volunteer agencies drew the provincial secretary's attention to "the communist wave sweeping over our metropolis" and asked that the Compulsory School Attendance Act be more strictly enforced.[10] The law was presented on the radio as a "godsend for the worker" that would "favour the education of the working masses."[11]

Godbout also benefited from the support of the suffragettes, who had always associated political power with social reform. Invited to the first ever Liberal Party Convention in 1938, they had proposed to include compulsory education in the agenda, immediately following women's right to vote, as well as free and standardized books. Though this principle was not officially adopted by the meeting, it was nonetheless well received. Likewise, at its 1941 convention, the League of Women's Rights of the province had declared itself in favour of compulsory education.[12]

Furthermore, the war had reinstated the fight against juvenile delinquency as the order of the day, one of the oldest and most popular Western reformist battle cries. More and more, the solution that surfaced was compulsory education. In the spring of 1943, a journalist from the *Standard* alarmed the Montréal public by reporting that juvenile delinquency had increased by at least 100 per cent:

> Schools in war-factory districts are reporting an increasing number of Latchkey scholars, meaning students who come to school with their key on a string round their neck because their mother is at work in the factory their father is away at war. A school principal said that it wouldn't be half bad it we were sure that children were attending school, but they only come half the time and we're not sure that they're getting proper meals. We don't have the tools necessary to keep an adequate eye on them.

The journalist's conclusion was to reaffirm the necessity of compulsory education.[13] Furthermore, studies in the social sciences seemed to confirm the close connection between crime and a lack of education, a conclusion many early-twentieth-century reformists had foreseen. Delinquent children risked becoming criminals if they were not reformed. It is difficult to determine if these worries corresponded to a real increase in youth misdemeanours. What is certain, however, is that a context of large-scale social changes, like that of the war effort, increased awareness of such social problems.[14] In any case, middle-class reformists supporting Godbout increasingly believed compulsory education was the best way to detect, control, and reform future criminals.

The prime minister's reasons for subscribing to compulsory education were also shared by the most influential members of his party. His receptive attitude to employers' demands was no different from those of the previous provincial prime minister, but the business people's demands had changed, and with them the Liberal government's view on public education. If the prime minister had wanted Québec to have "the best-educated working class in the world," it was, in his own words, because "in a rapidly changing world, in which new discoveries are constantly made, the new ways of producing and working, a people which does not wish to be left behind must keep up. The most comprehensive primary education possible, given to all children in positive conditions facilitating the parents' task, that is the first condition of this progress."[15]

In 1943, there were two new issues in the employers' demands. On one hand, since 1939, the war factories' significant needs had increased large businesses' demands for educated and competent staff. This, in turn, had accelerated the reorganization of the government's interests, making the development of secondary education a priority. The prime minister of Québec quickly understood that there would be a great need for qualified workers. "In a few months," he proclaimed in 1940, "we will need fifty thousand expert labourers in the province of Québec and two hundred fifty thousand across Canada. Where will we find them?"[16] The global conflict had presented employers with another preoccupation. As in 1914, the 1939 mobilization had shed light on the soldiers' low level of education: the president of the Canadian army's educational services stated that a significant portion of them did not even know how to read.[17]

In fact, the war uncovered longer-term general phenomena that the stock-market crash had helped to hide. Catholic sociologists had already noticed it: larger businesses with greater needs for more qualified labour were now controlling the province's economic activity, and they had a more dynamic view of the State's role in the training and monitoring of the labour force.[18] Similar considerations had brought the Catholic labour unions to distance themselves from the clerical authorities on the issue of compulsory education. Consisting of workers with few qualifications, the Confédération des travailleurs catholiques du Canada (CTCC) had been slower than other unions to establish the connection between future career and education. But the war had accelerated industrial development and the demand for increased technical competence to the point of convincing the most skeptical of the need for better-trained workers.[19] In 1941, for example, a joint inquiry of the Ligue ouvrière catholique (LOC) and the Jeunesse ouvrière catholique (JOC) drew attention to young Catholic workers' low level of education. Hiring children in war factories only served to aggravate the problem, even in the eyes of the bishops: "The easier jobs businesses and factories are offering boys and girls are poisoned bait," they wrote in a letter to the clergy, "but should not allow parents to forget the higher need of providing their children with adequate education."[20]

Another indication of the rise in demand for educated workers was that the majority of small- and medium-sized business owners had joined the upper middle class in accepting, even defending, compulsory education. In August 1940, the Montréal Board of Trade declared itself in favour of compulsory school attendance, and half of Québec's boards of trade fell into step in the autumn of 1942. During the 1920s and 1930s, the groups of local entrepreneurs who wanted to improve education had not been strong enough to persuade Taschereau to undertake major reforms. By the early 1940s, the number and activity of these associations, which constituted the main channel of communication of business people and manufacturers with politicians, had grown considerably. Unlike the associations from the upper middle class, they included a large number of French Canadians and held both business productivity and the provincial economy close to their hearts. The Saguenay Chamber of Commerce organized an "Education Week" in conjunction with the theme "Education is an investment" for the individual, the family, and society alike.[21]

These changes in economic interests brought to an end the controversy, over half a century old, regarding the respective roles of the government, the market, and individuals. Members of the elite concerned with securing a stable environment in which business could be better conducted had progressively adopted a "reformist" liberalism, more "managerial" than "progressive," which accepted more government intervention in corporate affairs, as in other Western countries.[22] Primary education was thus no longer the responsibility of the individual; rather, it was a civic responsibility, the State having to guarantee access to all.

As soon as he came into office, Godbout demonstrated his support of the "managerial" reform trend by putting individuals connected to the MCSC and the business world into the superintendent positions. Victor Doré, professor at the École des Hautes Études Commerciales of Montreal, had already been the director of the MCSC. The new director of public education in the cabinet, Provincial Secretary Hector Perrier, belonged to the same movement: a private-practice lawyer, he had been head of the MCSC, where he and Doré had met. Perrier had also been a member of the Catholic Committee to the Public Instruction Council (CCPIC) for seven years. A professor at the Université de Montréal with a degree in social sciences, Perrier spent some time as a politician in the Godbout government. Adélard Godbout had come from the opposite direction. Trained as an agronomist, he was member of a profession that had long hoped for teaching to be modernized outside the cities. An educator himself, his wish was for the government to ensure that primary school give young people from the countryside a greater appetite to learn. It was because of his skills and education that he had occupied the position of minister of agriculture in Taschereau's government during its final years. No longer the republicans of long ago, whose anticlericalism had always deterred the clergy, the supporters of State intervention now had more opportunities to attract the CCPIC's favour. And it was precisely on this issue of country schools that certain members of the province's upper clergy were preparing themselves to change their perspective.

The Liberal Party knew that it would have to confront the strong opposition of the Catholic Church. In 1940, to win the Terrebonne County by-elections, the party had even assured the electorate that the changes coming with regards to education would be effected with the clergy's approval and that there would be no Department of Education.[23] Since 1901, the episcopacy had undermined every legislative project on compulsory education thanks to its hold over the most powerful element in the educational field: the Catholic Committee to the Public Instruction Council.[24] Meanwhile, in October 1939, when Godbout came into office, a few breaches opened in the wall of clerical opposition, and he knew to make the best of it. For many Catholic officials, the fear of seeing French-Canadian society lose its rural character had finally overridden the idea that compulsory education was a foreign institution, threatening to religion.[25]

Since 1929, the pope had acknowledged that compulsory education could serve the Church's ends. But this change in political philosophy was not sufficient in convincing the upper clergy to abandon its position. In May 1939, when the Protestant Committee to the Public Instruction Council (PCPIC) had again invited the Catholic Committee to consider the idea, the members responded that they did not believe it to be "appropriate to make up their mind...on compulsory education."[26] How to explain the upper clergy's opposition to the State's intervention while the pope himself was in favour of it? In Québec, the Church had taken on the role of guardian of the French-Canadian culture, and most nationalist lay people supported its goal. For the majority of these nationalists and clerks, compulsory education had its roots in the Protestant, anglophone world.

It appears that, in the end, these same worries connected with the nation's survival and the maintenance of the Church's role in national development, overcame the best of the clergy's opposition to compulsory education. The upper clergy had always been interested in encouraging school attendance in the countryside, as the Church provided most of its teaching in schools. In the past, religious authorities had used many methods to support and prolong rural children's stay in school: encouragement, propaganda, program improvement, financial assistance to school boards based on the number of students registered, and an obligation for all parents of children between the ages of seven and fourteen, to pay a monthly fee to the school whether their children attended or not. Taxes were also imposed on all proprietors regardless of their children's school attendance, and pupils were encouraged to attend through a kind of reward system, with a certificate awarded at the end of primary school. There was even the possibility of exempting less-fortunate parents from paying school fees.[27] In the 1920s, the Liberal government had approached the issue with a similar series of policies. Louis-Alexandre Taschereau and Provincial Secretary Athanase David believed that the education of rural dwellers was the key to the survival of agriculture, as better-educated farmers would practise more scientific and viable agriculture. In 1922, politicians and clerks had developed a new program for primary schools that took rural needs into account.[28]

In the mid-1930s, the Church was deeply concerned to see most farmers' sons leaving school after grade five and quickly losing what little education they had acquired. It had never adopted the Liberal vision of an industrial Québec, and with a group of lay nationalists it emphasized colonization and agriculture as remedies for French Canada's economic problems. The Church feared that young people would be tempted by urban life and hoped that in keeping boys in school longer, the desertion of both the countryside and farming—phenomena that seemed to them to threaten French-Canadian culture as well as its own position—could be prevented. In these times of economic crisis, the clergy had intensified its nationalist stance. There was particular concern over its propaganda to return to the soil, which had not produced satisfactory results. The episcopacy had therefore pushed for a "country renaissance." It attempted to revive the farming profession by using two different sources of influence already at its disposal: professional organizations and one-room schoolhouses, which it hoped to "ruralize." At the suggestion of Monseigneur Courchesne, bishop of Rimouski, the Congrès de l'enseignement agricole held in Québec in October 1937 had expressed the hope "that a survey be carried out in our rural areas with the aim of keeping our boys in school up to and including grade seven." The same year, the bishops published a letter urging the faithful to re-evaluate the one-room schoolhouse by improving teachers' wages and seeking to convince the country dwellers to leave their children in school until grade six and, if possible, until grade eight.[29]

In the spring of 1939, determined to find alternate means, the clergy entrusted the finances and legislation commission of the Catholic Committee with an inquiry "with the purpose of elucidating the causes of irregular and brief primary school attendance." The conclusions of its April 1940 report to the Catholic Committee were alarming. Over the course of the 1938–39 school year, more than 41,000 children between the ages of seven and fourteen had not attended school at all; 27,382 children had left without finishing primary school. As for the 432,296 who were registered, the absentee rate was up to 15 per cent, corresponding to an average of one day per week per student. The new government used the same numbers to paint a more complete picture of the Catholic schools' problems and submitted its report to that same commission seven months later. In the agriculturalist spirit that continued to drive it, the Catholic Committee responded with a recommendation for special winter schools for country boys, which schedule would not interfere with their farm work. Moreover, members requested that the "superintendent supply them with documentation as complete as possible regarding compulsory attendance and monitoring practices in other provinces."[30] Thus accepting to relegate to the back burner the theological and political debates on the respective duties of the individual, the Church, and the State, which had up to then fuelled the quarrels between them, the province's upper clergy was appropriating the pragmatic worries of the Liberal government, and making the teaching of the greatest possible number of children the fundamental characteristic of its social policy. The topic of the debates about respective duties of Church, State, and the individual is explored further in chapter 3.

Meanwhile, newspapers were already reporting the rumour that "the Godbout government, under the guidance of Messrs. Hector Perrier and Victor Doré, would soon propose the following reforms: compulsory education and career orientation system," but the cabinet did not wish to act without the support of the Catholic Committee, and it was still difficult to determine what the two in fact could agree upon.[31]

In the spring of 1941, the superintendent of public instruction (SPI) had brought the question of compulsory education to the Catholic Committee upon presentation of his first annual report. To him, the situation seemed sufficiently distressing for the Catholic Committee to implement compulsory school attendance gradually, as local school boards became ready. Victor Doré knew that he was facing an organization divided on the issue. Through individual meetings and a variety of propositions, he believed that he could help the defenders of compulsory education to be heard and find the necessary tools to change the clergy's general position. The archdioceses of Québec and Montréal were already fully supportive of the idea, but the fear of losing the religious prerogatives was still too strong in many sectors of the clergy, notably with those directing the classical colleges. These individuals looked beyond compulsory education and foresaw a complete reform of secondary education, which threatened their monopoly. That year, Doré was forced to remove the paragraph addressing compulsory education from his report, but he added a segment outlining the extent of his powers, a way of reminding them of his right to act without the approval of the Catholic Committee.[32]

The Catholic hierarchy once again attempted to take the leading role in the development of the reforms. Cardinal Rodrigue Villeneuve, head of the Québec Church, put his efforts into developing his own methods for compulsory education: in the summer of 1941, he reminded those at his parish visits of "parents' serious duty regarding school attendance" until the end of primary school. Moreover, he continued to explore the possibility of compulsory education: in September 1941, he announced to the Catholic Committee that before adopting compulsory education, it needed to study the causes of, and solutions to, the problem of insufficient registration and irregular attendance. The committee therefore held a conference on education, where it re-examined the entire primary-school structure.[33] Provincial Secretary Hector Perrier seized the opportunity and prepared "a questionnaire... destined for all of the province's schools with the aim of obtaining the most specific statistics possible on school attendance," which he submitted to the bishops in December 1941. When he announced to them that the results would be discussed at the education conference, it was clear that they could no longer refuse. But the bishops feared that a conference at which such specific statistics would be discussed could only inflame the supporters of compulsory education, and therefore at its 24 January session, the Catholic Committee decided to abandon the idea of a conference altogether.[34] Instead it chose to extend the study to include all problems involved with primary school and invited all the provincial education officials to submit reports on the subject. On the bishops' agenda, school attendance ranked fourth only, coming after the school, its pedagogical organization, and its administrative organization but before the financial problems. Thus, the committee attempted to draw the public's attention away from compulsory education towards the improvement of the teaching network, as it had successfully done since the beginning of the century.

The results of the school survey took longer than expected and had only a limited scope. But such a survey had succeeded in opening an important channel of communication between the Catholic Committee and the hundreds of teachers and administrators in the public instruction system. Now that the upper clergy announced that it was ready to study the principle of compulsory education, teachers who had previously been wary of going against the Church were free to discuss the issue. Moreover, since the committee had requested reports on primary education, Victor Doré now had in hand new and legitimate means with which to gather behind him an opinion base, which he knew to be largely in favour of his bill. Already in 1940, the Alliance catholique des professeurs de Montréal had carried out its own survey on primary education reforms, and 94 per cent of its members were in favour of compulsory education. Doré published a notice in the newspapers calling for all those interested to submit a report on primary schools; furthermore, the Department of Public Instruction (DPI) organized conferences and study sessions in which the provincial secretary enthusiastically pushed for compulsory education, program reform, increased attendance, and raises in teachers' wages.[35]

Bishops, school boards, inspectors, and teachers' assemblies answered the call: in all, the department received over 110 reports. They dealt mostly with education problems, as the bishops had hoped, but a quarter of them considered school attendance to be one of the system's weakest points. Among them, 14 believed the time had come for compulsory education. In reading the synthesis of the reports prepared by the department in November 1942, the members of the Catholic Committee learned that "the State's proposal for students still of the age of compulsory education comes from all sides, from the ecclesiastical to the layman. School attendance should be compulsory for the first eight years of primary school, according to some; until the age of sixteen, according to others."[36]

During this time, the DPI's research on compulsory education practices in other provinces and countries was coming to a successful close, and the results became further arguments against nationalist opposition. This outcome added an outdated quality to Québec singularity; its trait of originality no longer seemed to be the symbol of national identity, but rather a disadvantage for the future of the French-Canadian culture:

> "If we do not wish to be left behind, as an ethnic group," wrote the secretary of the Department upon his return from the annual meeting of the Canadian and Newfoundland Education association in September 1942, "we must without delay resort to the reforms implemented in our school

> legislation. It is useless to discuss the subject of primary school, useless to endlessly reorganize the programs, useless to hope to make up for all of the lost time; we must not shrink from the two following points: centralization and compulsory attendance until grade nine."[37]

"'The popular opinion to be drawn from these reports,' explained the superintendent to members of the Catholic Committee, 'is that if compulsory attendance is not the only solution, it is still the best means to ensure the progress of education for the masses.'"[38]

By the end of 1942, the majority of bishops were ready to accept the principle of compulsory education. It is difficult to know to what extent they felt their hand had been forced. What is certain is that they endeavoured to minimize the meaning of this revolution in the school system and that they would launch other projects to maintain their power. The Catholic Committee stated that it recognized the extent of the attendance problem revealed by the surveys and that none of the primary teaching changes requested in the reports were possible if the minimum length of children's study remained unknown. The main advantage of a compulsory attendance law would therefore be the possibility of a serious study of the reasons behind school non-attendance: "'the planned law,' declared Cardinal Villeneuve, 'will provide the opportunity to study the root of the problem and to intervene with the most effective means.'"[39] Based on the same "educational" logic that had led it to undertake the study, the committee thus made compulsory education a prerequisite for educational reforms. In this view, it focused immediately on preparing a new program. When school began in the fall of 1943, the episcopacy was careful to diminish the meaning of the law. It presented compulsory schooling as another medium available to clerics for reaching their previous objectives and took care to emphasize that compulsory education did not mean that schools were run by the State.[40]

Victor Doré and Hector Perrier used New Brunswick's law as their model. Four months after its approval by the Catholic Committee, Perrier submitted the text to the legislative assembly and reported on the seriousness of the absenteeism issue in Montréal and Québec, as well as the experiences of other countries.[41] In 1944, the assembly abolished school fees until grade nine. On this occasion it took a significant and new step towards free and standard books: the DPI offered to reimburse 75 per cent of the cost of books to schools who would not charge students for them and 90 per cent if the textbooks were recommended by the government. Perrier hoped that all books would be free to students within three years. Furthermore, the department promised financial assistance to parents who carried out their new legal responsibilities regarding education.[42]

The Failure of the 1943 Provincial Family Allowances Act

The history behind family allowances finds its origins in wartime labour relations and belongs to the legacy of a different government. In fact, many of the participants who had led Adélard Godbout's government to adopt the Compulsory School Attendance Act no longer held their appointments when the time came to argue in favour of the institution of provincial family allowances. To be sure, there were women's groups, Catholic unions, farmers' groups, and a reformist clergy who argued in favour of the implementation of provincial family allowances. However, some key elements were missing. On one hand, the provincial government's "managerial" reformists and the bishops did not seem to share the same level of enthusiasm or the same energy as they had for the other issue. On the other hand, the employers' organizations finally left the family allowances issue up to the federal government, which the war had infused with unparalleled dynamism. Finally, the federal government had become the main interlocutor for the international unions and women's groups.

On the eve of the Second World War, the Québec clerical authorities subscribed in relatively large numbers to the Social Catholicism Leo XIII had sanctioned in 1891. According to the Social Doctrine of the Catholic Church, the main solution for urban poverty should be a "family wage" and, to this end, Catholic, labour, and employers' associations combined in a corporate framework to oversee labour relations, which was preferable to the State's doing so. It had been necessary to wait until the 1910s for the movement to develop a certain degree of popularity in the province. Organized mainly by the Jesuits, annual meetings on social topics (the Semaines sociales du Canada) and a publishing house (the École sociale populaire) had attempted to sensitize the religious elite and lay people to the concepts of Social Catholicism. Among other accomplishments, their efforts had resulted in the creation of a central Catholic labour body.[43]

In 1941, the bishops could easily declare that the "family wage" was essential for the improvement of the living conditions of the province's families and, furthermore, that they were ready to plan the implementation of family allowances, though the form the allowances would take was not yet determined. According to the episcopate, the initiative should have been the employers'.[44] Among the Church, the debates recalled the Liberal discussions on the State's and the individual's roles in a wage economy. The upper clergy was hostile to the possibility of expanding "social justice," something that should be the State's concern, to the detriment of "charity," which depended on individual's initiatives, and which the clergy heavily supervised. Thus, the most visible theologian on the subject of compulsory education, Father Hermas Lalande, invited the poor parents who wanted to give their children an education to call on the government for assistance within the parameter of private charity: "There are no grounds for [parents] to ask the government to force them, but rather to simply encourage them; that is, help them and facilitate their children's education."[45]

It was in this spirit that in 1940 the Conseil central de la Société Saint-Vincent-de-Paul de Montréal had agreed, with the MCSC, to assist with the attendance of students who did not attend school because of a lack of proper clothing and shoes, or because of their parents' wishes.[46] The bishops' lack of zeal regarding family allowances contrasted with the energy and common sense the upper clergy demonstrated with school reforms in the 1940s. Above all, this half-heartedness was proof of agriculture's central position in their social thinking; they feared that overly generous social programs for urbanites would increase the rural exodus.[47]

Meanwhile, the episcopacy's weak interest in the principle of a family wage, promoted by Rome, had left sufficient space for other Catholics to lead a relatively effective campaign on the subject. Since the 1920s, Jesuit Léon Lebel had begun to hold conferences and publish brochures on family allowances. He had updated a version of the Social Doctrine of the Catholic Church, more precise than the bishops' version, and notably different. For him, the idea of a standardized family wage could not justly be applied to large families: only a "minimum living wage" coupled with family allowances was equitable and realistic. This is how Lebel and his religious brothers had come to interpret the encyclicals' view of "reasonable wage." This solution would be less costly than a "reasonable" universal salary, and combined with the "family wage," the family allowances advantageous to larger families would constitute a pro-natalist policy.[48]

Father Lebel was opposed to the allowances being handled by isolated groups of employers and employees. Less worried by the State than the episcopacy was, he had pleaded energetically for compulsory and uniform allowances to be paid out by public authorities. He claimed that otherwise, as demonstrated by the French example, employers would fear competition with their neighbours, and the program would be compromised before the majority of workers were able to benefit from it. Furthermore, autonomous labourers, in particular the farmers to whom Lebel paid particular attention in his capacity as chaplain for the Union des cultivateurs catholiques, would never be included in an optional program.[49] Every year, since 1923, the CTCC had called for provincial allowances from the government based on Lebel's model. The Catholic labour body was gaining in influence; in 1936, it represented 37 per cent of the province's union members, the largest proportion yet. The 1929 crash had lent some credibility to its criticism of capitalism and, in the cities and businesses outside of Montréal, where American-style trade unionism was unpopular, the strength of Catholic trade unions had seen a marked increase.[50]

During this time, Québec's nationalist clerics had come to associate poverty with large families without a thorough investigation of wage levels in the province. We have seen how the fate of city dwellers was judged to be less worrisome than that of rural dwellers, and that relatively little was known about urban poverty. What concerned these clerics, however, was the fertility of French-Canadian women, and it was often with this nationalist preoccupation in mind that they had come to accept the idea of a family wage and to tacitly approve Lebel's family allowances campaign. In fact, for Lebel, the allowances were a means of preventing at once the rural exodus, a fall in the birth rate, and immigration to the United States. The payments should also, for the same reasons, begin at the third child and increase after the birth of each new child.[51] In 1941, the province's bishops announced that without the family salary, "our influence will shrink along with our numbers. We will be fated to rapid extinction. We will have failed the mission entrusted to us by providence."[52] Maximilien Caron, then the vice-dean of the Faculty of Law at the Université de Montréal, expressed doubt as to the effects of family allowances on the birth rate: "experience shows that in countries where family allowances are paid out, they do not result in an increased birth rate. In my opinion, our demand for them must be based exclusively on the necessities of the public good."[53] Already the federal government had adopted a stance distant from pronatalism: its allowances program for soldiers' dependants had set a maximum of forty-eight dollars of full benefits for the children of each family—meaning twelve dollars per child in a family of four children—in accordance with the Canadian average, a decision that had been denounced by the Fédération nationale Saint-Jean-Baptiste (FNSJB).[54]

For bishops and lay nationalists alike, a fall in the birth rate would decrease the political weight carried by French Canadians. Their demographic strength was dependent upon a strong birth rate, which counterbalanced the effects of immigration, more advantageous to the English-speaking parts of the country. This phenomenon had also often been invoked in former campaigns for the establishment of family policies in the provinve of Québec.[55]

Interpreted somewhat differently by the religious and nationalist worlds, the whole of the corporatist project made some headway within official policy. Lebel had met with enough success that in Ottawa in 1929, the House of Commons Committee on Industrial Relations invited him to

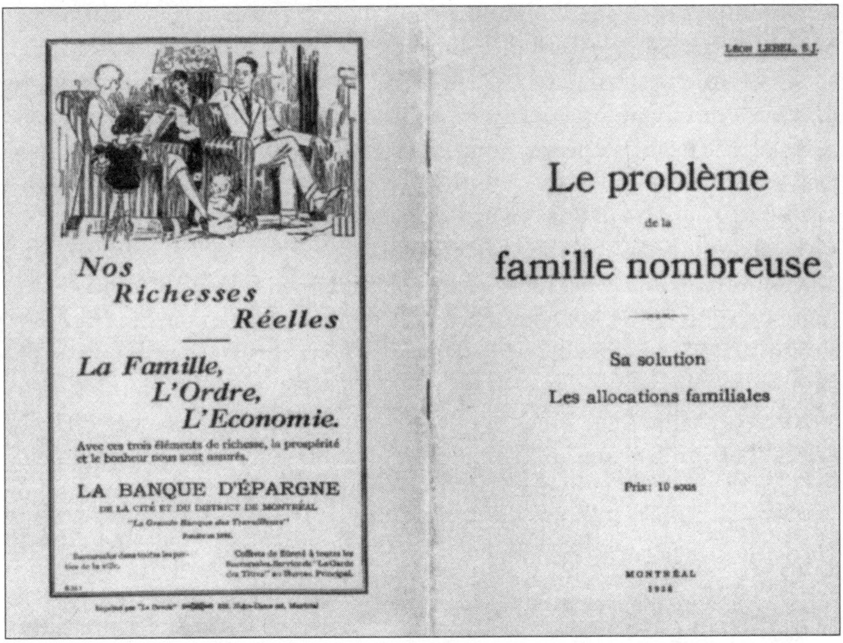

Figure 1. The coexistence of two attitudes with regard to the birth rate in Québec is most aptly represented in Léon Lebel's 1928 brochure entitled *Les allocations familiales: Solution du problème des familles nombreuses*, in which a French-Canadian bank's advertisement, on the back cover, features a "nuclear" family.

Source: Léon Lebel, *Les allocations familiales: Solution du problème des familles nombreuses* (Montréal: *Le Devoir*, 1928). (Reproduced with the permission of *Le Devoir*.)

take part in its hearings. But his hopes were dashed: Mackenzie King's government was not in any rush to adopt social policies, its excuse being the pitfalls of the many disputes between the provinces and the Dominion. That same year, the Québec Conservative Party convention had included Lebel's propositions of allowances for large families in their audacious social reform program, aimed at satisfying the demands of Montréal workers brought to the party by its new leader, Camillien Houde.[56] Louis-Alexandre Taschereau's provincial government was also affected by corporatism: in 1924, a law on professional unions had favoured the development of the CTCC; in 1931, Gérard Tremblay, secretary of the CTCC's Conseil central de Montréal since 1921 and union secretary general since 1930, had become the deputy minister of labour; and in 1934, the provincial government had adopted a collective-agreement law that encouraged the creation of "comités paritaires" of employers and workers.[57]

During the war, pressure from women and from nationalists antagonized by the federal government's centralism gave more weight to the arguments of those defending provincial allowances in the spirit of the Social Doctrine of the Catholic Church. Since women would be voting for the first time in provincial elections in 1944, all parties were careful to develop a family policy. Moreover, in 1943, numerous Catholic reformist associations led a campaign for provincial family allowances with the help of the FNSJB.[58]

Strong because of such support, Adélard Godbout's government picked up the labour legislation thread where Taschereau's Liberal government had left off in 1936. But the steps it took remained relatively limited with regard to the CTCC's demands, as Godbout's government feared that employers would show a much stronger opposition to the State's intervention in labour relations than they had previously done in relation to compulsory education. Not only did these types of policies more directly affect their profits and internal affairs, but other corporatist provincial policies threatened to damage their competitiveness by burdening them with responsibilities employers would not have in the rest of Canada.[59] In 1940, the provincial labour minister, Edgar Rochette, established the Superior Labour Council, consisting of four equally important groups representing labourers, employers, economists or sociologists, and representatives of the government. It thus took the step towards "intercorporative assembly" the CTCC had called for, but it was only a single step, as it made certain that role of the council would be limited to that of consultant.[60] In the summer of 1943, the minister created a family allowances program, encouraging the "comité paritaires" to pay family allowances.

This optional program would suffer an even worse fate than Lebel had foreseen. None of the eighty existing committees took advantage of the law. The majority of employers who had supported compulsory education were largely Protestant and were not interested in the family allowances project's corporatist character. Furthermore, the war's tax levies had pulled the rug out from under the feet of the provincial legislators, removing any desire on the part of Québec's employers to spend further.[61]

In fact, only limited numbers of the French-Canadian small-scale businesses who could have paid for family allowances under Godbout's program had joined Church-supported Catholic employers' associations. Even the employers who had joined the Professional Association of Industrialists gave little consideration to the Social Doctrine of the Catholic Church, biased as they were by their interests as employers. Indeed, according to the Professional Association of Industrialists, small- and medium-sized businesses did not possess the necessary capital to establish social security policies. Similarly, the Montréal Chamber of Commerce declined all responsibility regarding hired labourers' standard of living. It chose to blame "the economic organization in general" for the fact that "a large number of families [were] not in the position to carry out [their educational duties]."[62] This reorientation of the Social Doctrine of the Catholic Church was even easier to accomplish, as the members of the upper clergy disagreed on the issue: the archbishop of Québec supported this conservative attitude, while the archbishop of Montréal distanced himself from his colleagues' position on the issue in 1950.[63] A Jesuit magazine editorial reported on the dissatisfaction social Catholics showed about the Provincial Family Allowances Act:

> The war-time-like atmosphere where all achievements are carried out on such a large scale, almost monstrous at times, had prepared the country, the province, for large-scale implementation. It is here that the bill[,]...announced with such fanfare, has had its disconcerting timidity revealed. It essentially tells a small group of employers: "You are authorized to organize family allowances." In current taxation circumstances, with competition and employers' psychology, it can be concluded that if a few new words are inserted into laws, none of the facts will change. Québec City has not given the province family allowances.[64]

In the months that would follow, labour shortages and urgent calls for wage increases might have brought Catholic employers to use the provincial law, as French and Belgian Catholic employers were doing in similar circumstances.[65] But the federal government prevented any such possibility, as it was preparing to launch its own program, which was of quite a different breed.

Mackenzie King and the 1945 Federal Family Allowances Act

International labour unions had always rejected the idea of family allowances out of the fear that they would serve as a pretext for wage reduction.[66] Indeed, those who had supported compulsory education were now absent from Godbout's group of supporters of provincial allowances, and they contributed to the failure of the program. Ironically, the pressures of the very same group indirectly led to the establishment of the universal family allowance system at the federal level. With the war, the dramatic increase in production had precipitated a radical drop in unemployment rates, which gave the labour unions unexpected leverage. Since the end of 1941, the government had reserved the right to set wage levels and had established a price-and-wage-monitoring policy to contain the inflation entailed by increased production. Due to this veritable nationalization of working conditions, the central government had taken on the role of the unions' main interlocutor. In 1943, when a wave of discontent spread through the Canadian labour world, the central labour bodies called for the lowest wages to be excluded from the federal price-and-wage-monitoring policy. Québec salaries had been set at the lowest level out of all the Canadian provinces, and the cost of living had increased by 16 per cent since the beginning of the war. In 1943, J.-H. Leclerc, the MP for Shefford, denounced the position of low-paid Quebecers under a monitoring system that penalized Québec. Shortly thereafter, *Le Droit*, the Ottawa-based French daily, published a virulent attack of the federal policies in the name of Québec families:

> In a Granby factory (Shefford), which employs a significant number of workers, the average weekly salary is $17.82, including the cost of a living increase bonus.... How can a worker be expected to properly raise children on wages of famine?... In many cases, the mother must also go the factory route and leave her children in the hands of some housemaid, in order to supplement her husband's income. Often, in these families, the children leave school early to look for work in the factories at any wage possible to increase the father's income. Such a system will undoubtedly lead to the disintegration of the family and of society.[67]

The federal authorities did not meet these demands, and tensions mounted. The National War Labour Board suggested family allowances as a means of keeping wages low without harming the federal wage policy. It was, according to the board, the only alternative to the deregulation of wages under 50 cents per hour, which would cost the government between $400 million and $700 million. The minister of finance, having learned the details surrounding these numbers, had no trouble convincing employers that the $175 million cost of family allowances would in fact be a sizable savings.[68]

Thus, the immediate result of federal family allowances was to quell the discontented workers; but in order to fully achieve this end, it had been necessary that a series of reforms give the workers more rights in the institutions managing the war economy. The 1944 Order in Council forced war-factory employers to negotiate collective agreements.[69] In the House of Commons, Mackenzie King presented family allowances as a policy that would solve the urban workers' problem of insufficient salaries: "In the case of large families, the children's allowance will help to increase their standard of living... above the bare necessities, at least, as the amount often depreciates because of the small amount reaching the head of the family in relation to his number of obligations, meaning the number of children."[70] The central labour bodies were not duped by the government's attempts to dissociate the policy from its wage-regulation measure, and they continued to oppose family allowances. For the moment, however, Mackenzie King's reforms seemed to succeed in quelling labour unrest.

The direction of wartime economy coupled with the federal government's close ties with the Canadian upper class gave Mackenzie King a unique advantage in his attempts to solicit the support of employers, the very same elite whose support Godbout had feared losing over compulsory family allowances and had greeted his optional program with mere indifference. Beyond helping them settle wage issues, Mackenzie King assured them that family allowances would guarantee a prosperous future. Entrepreneurs dreaded the eventual change in demand for their products in the transition to a peacetime economy. They envisioned a return to increased unemployment and the same slowdown in production that had followed the First World War, between 1919 and 1922. Furthermore, there was little preventing the belief that there would be a repeat performance of the disastrous economic conditions of the 1930s. By injecting $200 million per year into the Canadian economy, Mackenzie King's advisors planned to maintain the demand for goods, thus stabilizing the economy and preventing a collapse of national revenue. Maintaining the same level of demand was even more important given that, since the end of the 1920s, consumption per capita had become a determining factor for Canadian industry. Cabinet members believed that the allowances transferred the earnings of higher-income households with a low marginal propensity to spend to poorer households with a relatively high propensity to spend. "I believe that almost all the money in the form of family allowances will be spent on commodities produced or manufactured in our country," declared Mackenzie King in the House.[71] In supporting this particular means of maintaining consumption, the government was doubtlessly aware that the goods destined for children (e.g., shoes, clothing) would correspond exactly to the country's fragile industries as well as those that had been mobilized to full capacity to meet the needs of soldiers. As for the surplus, the Canadian Manufacturers' Association had publicly declared it was in favour of the government's increasing citizens' buying power. In 1943, the governor of the Bank of Canada had also indicated that the allowance would help the government curb inflation after the war, when it would have to renounce price- and wage-monitoring. Minister of Health and Welfare Brooke Claxton added J.M. Keynes to the list of government supporters: Keynes had long been in favour of family allowances, although the policy was not "Keynesian" strictly speaking, as it did not provide a flexible stabilization tool.[72]

The Liberal caucus had another advantage to offer employers. If children were considered one of the country's greatest riches, the allocations could be perceived as State subsidies to private businesses. Seen this way, family allowances were more important than universal old-age pensions, according to the Bank of Canada, which was one of the program's main promoters, since "money is spent to ensure children's minimum health and education needs are [*sic*] more likely to be a productive national investment."[73] It is possible that the Canadian government's long history of intervening in the economy had rendered the allowances more acceptable than they would have been in the United States.[74] In the case of family allowances, like that of the Compulsory School Attendance Act, many of the country's employers had accepted more State intervention to ensure labour be maintained. Only a few traditionalist nationalists now denounced this logic, when this type of reasoning would previously have been relatively unsuccessful.[75] In the end, Mackenzie King made the program easier for employers to accept, assuring them that the money would come directly from the public purse. There was nothing left of Father Lebel's drafts, in which employers and management were to contribute to a national fund, nor was there any threat of competition between provinces, which a program limited to Québec would have caused for employers. It seems that heads of Québec business had additional reasons to celebrate. In varying premiums according to number of children, the federal government would disburse more money in the province, which would further help to maintain lower wages. At least that was what Toronto MP Henry Jackman feared: "I am fairly certain that in recent years, nearly the entire moderately priced furniture industry has been established in Québec due to the lower salaries in the province. If family allowances are paid out at the stated rates...they could lead to a greater tendency to move hiring [into Québec even more]."[76] In all, this "Fordist" openness to the State's intervention can also be explained by the growing concentration of businesses, by their reticence and increasing incapacity to ensure their employees' standard of living for each of their local concerns.[77]

But the history of strikes in 1943 and the relations between employers and Mackenzie King do not explain why Mackenzie King and his advisors held on to the idea of family allowances. The cabinet had also concluded that universal benefits to mothers with families would satisfy, in a more egalitarian way, the mounting demands for state intervention in social affairs.[78]

Mackenzie King expected that sooner or later he would have to respond to a deeper movement than the one behind recent strikes, which favoured more general social laws. The popularity of the Co-operative Commonwealth Federation (CCF) was growing, and the members of his own political party, united in September 1943 on the occasion of the convention of the National Liberal Federation of Canada, had opted for a social security platform in which allowances played a major role.[79] Gone was the time when "the rich man took a basket of necessaries to the poorer people in his city," he announced. "[This] will not be accepted by the people of Canada."[80] The Marsh *Report on Social Security for Canada*, ordered during the war by the cabinet's Advisory Committee on Reconstruction, had predicted that, out of pride, poor parents would not take advantage of allowances paid only to disadvantaged people. Furthermore, so that everyone would have the right to the family allowances, they would not be contributory (they would come out of the country's consolidated revenue, to which citizens already contributed, depending on their income);[81] this universal system was different from social insurance plans such as the 1940 unemployment insurance program and the provincial workers' compensation program begun in the 1910s and 1920s, which had not included those members of the labour force who did not receive a wage or who had irregular work patterns.

Since the beginning of the war, the general atmosphere of mobilization had added positive grounds to the rejection of partial and discretionary programs. The requirements of participating in a global conflict had led many countries, including Canada, to launch campaigns for "minimum income," "social security," and the struggle against poverty. It was in this climate that Canada signed the Atlantic Charter in 1942, committing to watch over its inhabitants' welfare: citizenship did not simply entail the current patriotic duties; after the war it would also include new social rights to accompany the existing civil and political rights. This shift of patriotism into internal policy was not necessarily a result of the passage from wartime to peacetime. It was also the product of a long-term transformation of the foundation of Western nationalism from military loyalties towards loyalties centred on social programs. Indeed, family allowances would later become a significant vehicle for Canadian nationalism, next to the country's most significant international autonomy gained throughout the 1920s and 1930s, Crown societies, and the creation of new national symbols.[82] In the wake of these engagements, the Marsh Report had proposed an employment program, a universal unemployment insurance program, a universal wage, and assistance and insurance policies for illness and for seniors and invalids.

Thus, in promising to send money to 1,400,000 homes one month after the 1945 election, the government could easily prove its aim was to avoid returning to the pre-war standard of living, an eventuality that worried the public. Adopting this single policy also allowed Mackenzie King to continue to be vague on the time frame of the other policies. On the eve of the 11 June 1945 general federal election, Mackenzie King's team would be able to campaign with increased credibility on the theme of "a new social order for Canada," since the new allowances program was scheduled to begin 1 July. One of the Liberal electorate's propaganda brochures was entitled *Liberal Family Allowances*. The Progressive Conservative Party MPs, who recognized the manoeuvre, made, in vain, an attempt to redirect it: Mackenzie King had not been elected to decide on postwar social policies, they said, and they called for a referendum on the issue. Armed with a new progressive platform, they found themselves in the paradoxical position of having to vote in favour of a policy whose election-minded character they had denounced.[83] In fact, no other party dared to prevent its ratification. The CCF MPs had included the allowances in their program since 1942; they were part of a collection of policies aimed at improving the lot of low-paid workers and making the country's standard living conditions uniform. Not least among these policies was the creation of a national wage scale. The CCF lost some of their originality as they became aware of the effect their rapid rise to popularity was having on Mackenzie King. Even the Social Credit Party members of the House compared the policy with the social dividends their party had proposed.[84]

The fusion of the two streams of reformism, "executive" and "progressive," could not have been accomplished outside the crucible of cabinet headquarters—that is, without the high-ranking officials and Liberal ministers, who had believed in the benefits of increased State intervention in economic planning since the late 1930s. In this respect, the federal government's advance on the provincial government was undeniable despite Adélard Godbout's efforts to improve the status of civil service. Meanwhile, mandarins in the federal government did not all agree on social policy. A minority endorsed the Marsh Report, in which family allowances would exist only to prevent the rates of other social programs from being adjusted in relation to family size. But the report did not have any other direct influence on the cabinet than to define more clearly the problem of insufficient wages, a question the politicians had battled since the wave of labour conflicts.[85] In fact, the more powerful federal government experts, those with the Economic Advisory Committee, and its president, Deputy Minister of Finance Clifford Clark, had not received the proposals for a universal social security system warmly. They had eliminated the possibility for direct involvement in the economy as the CCF socialists had wanted and Marsh himself had wished for when he ensured that his plan would not work unless the government also committed itself to guaranteeing a higher percentage of employment. For the federal bureaucrats, family allowances represented the lowest possible cost to the government en route to settling ongoing industrial conflicts. It was in this way that family allowances acted as a shop window for the implementation of a welfare state that was well under the expectations of reformists during the war. The workers' and farmers' associations and women's groups had never doubted that the emancipation of their members would require improvements to education and children's welfare. Where legislators differ from them was in choosing to give precedence to this type of policy at the cost of other social policies.

Meanwhile, a climate of worry about the size of the Canadian population was also facilitating the connection between poverty and the fact of having children.[86] In the House of Commons, many MPs who were concerned about the lowered birth rate of Canadian women hoped that the allowances would resolve the problem: children would become a "source of joy and satisfaction, as it should be," instead of too often being a source of worry, and a burden.[87] The legislators referred to the pro-natalist position of British economist and government advisor on social policies, William Beveridge. This opinion was shared beyond the borders of the governmental party. "The problem of the subsistence of large families is certainly more complicated than that of a nuclear family," declared the head of the CCF in the House. "If this were not so, I think families would be much larger."[88] Most MPs were probably informed that the decline in fertility rate also touched francophones, a fact that had been made clear in the 1931 census monographs on the family. The author of one of the monographs had already indicated that the allowances would possibly cancel out this demographic movement: "If the worker felt reasonably sure that he could always provide for his children he would doubtlessly be inclined to have more."[89] Nationalist feminists in the province also knew how to use this concern in their social demands for reconstruction.[90]

Mackenzie King's cabinet endeavoured to justify its relunctance to endorse vast reconstruction plans by alleging that the main reason for poverty was the size of families. This reasoning was not new: at a time when families were typically large, children actually constituted the largest age group among the poor, and studies showed that the incomes of larger families were inferior to those of smaller families. The ministers rushed to reach the next step, in which they admitted that the improvement of the disadvantageous circumstances of the 19 per cent of employees raising 84 per cent of the country's children constituted the main solution to poverty.[91] This attitude set them apart from the long-time supporters of family allowances who had insisted on limiting the role of family allowances to simple wage supplements and united their demands for family allowances with other pressures to raise wage levels. When the ministers declared that the allowances offered the correction of "this anomaly [by which] wages are paid for completed work and not according to the breadwinner's number of children," they presumed that the "salary for work completed" was sufficient. In Godbout's cabinet, in the educational sectors, as in many Catholic reformist associations, many shared this tendency of grouping together the categories of poor parents and parents of large families.[92]

In launching the allowances program, the federal government aimed to promote the domestic role of women. "With the example of this policy," declared Minister Paul Martin, "the House...is also implicitly paying long-deserved homage to Canadian mothers."[93] The Restigouche-Madawaska MP went further: "These allowances are granted to the mothers of families as a wage to help them better feed and house their children."[94] Many women's groups supported the policy, and a disproportionate number of women MPs spoke during the House of Commons debates on family allowances. Until then, unlike their British and Australian counterparts, Canadian women's groups had concentrated their family policy demands on allowances for needy mothers who were without a husband's revenue. Social science writings in the 1930s, which raised awareness about the general insufficient wages problem, had helped to spread the popularity of standardized family allowances. In addition, numerous feminist associations deemed that women's domestic work should be better recognized.[95] They also hoped, as the promoters of allowances for needy mothers had previously done, that the allowances would prevent certain children from being placed in orphanages or in foster homes. In his project for the complete post-war social security system, Leonard Marsh had insisted on the fact that the payments to mothers proposed by the majority of the proponents of family allowances constituted a veritable recognition of mothers' work and rights.

For the women's movement, as for the workers movement, the federal government had become the main interlocutor. Women had not only had the right to vote in federal elections since 1919, but the women's movement had also, since the beginning of the war, maintained a close relationship with the federal government. In exchange for their support of the war effort and the campaign to bring married women into the paid labour market, numerous women's groups worked in public organizations, such as one of the cabinet's many expert group committees on planning reconstruction. The federal government did not adopt the main conclusion reached by the 1944 report on women and reconstruction, a call for the creation of a climate in which mothers would be given the choice to stay at home or to work outside it without negative effects on their children's well-being.[96] Thus, the Family Allowances Act only did "pay homage to women" in its contribution to children's well-being. However, wartime women workers held a specific bargaining power to which Mackenzie King was not immune. More than simply sharing Marsh's belief that family allowances included in a larger collection of social policies would help eliminate poverty, the report also emphasized that mothers encouraged to work on salary during the conflict would more willingly renounce their income at the end of the war if they themselves received payments destined to ensure their children's well-being. The number of married Canadian women who had taken on jobs had climbed from 10 per cent in 1939 to 35 per cent in 1944 and, from the very beginning of the war, the federal government had put in place a collection of policies to ensure that they would return home at the end of the conflict.[97]

Maurice Duplessis, Provincial Autonomy, and Social Policies

Maurice Duplessis' return to the province's leadership in 1944 would begin the erosion of the consensus between "Fordist" employers, "managerial" Liberal reformists, egalitarian workers' unions, and middle-class reformists. The prime minister's Conservative nationalism clashed with compulsory education and family allowances in more ways than one. His opposition to the federal law would never amount to much, but he did manage to give Godbout's new education system a serious shake. The examination of his policy not only provides a view of power relations between Québec and Ottawa but also permits further study of the notion of welfare held by the French-Canadian political and clerical elite. The nationalists focused their attacks on pro-natalism, the legal status of mothers and their right to receive family allowances cheques, and the various forms of institutional protection for children favoured by the Church.

Even before Duplessis' arrival, Adélard Godbout had already attempted to dilute the federal government's centralism. Early in 1944, when Mackenzie King had exposed his federal plan for universal family allowances in detail, Godbout had distanced himself from the corporatist model he had supported until then. The combined influence of the federal precedents and of the ideological changes among the defenders of Social Catholicism had made him open up to a new type of public policy.[98] In fact, in April 1944, a committee of the Superior Labour Council had drafted a report on family allowances, assisted by a team of researchers from Université Laval. These experts were closely linked to an intellectual movement led by Dominican Father Georges-Henri Lévesque, who in turn was strongly influenced by a radical current of Catholic European social action and wanted to change the province's social legislation. One month later, the report endorsed universal allowances announcing the same advantages the National War Labour Board had indicated to Mackenzie King one year earlier: universal benefits could be less costly than wage increases and a solution to labour strife less damaging to the freedom of the labour market. Furthermore, the employers would not need to fear competition from the other provinces. Meanwhile, the CTCC itself had changed its plans. Even if it had been opposed to Mackenzie King during the 1942 referendum on conscription, it approved his labour legislation.[99]

Godbout asked Mackenzie King to give up decreasing rates for large families—a measure to be discussed later on—and to consider the provinces' autonomy: provincial experts from the Superior Labour Council had advised him to ensure that a combined program recognize the federal initiative while attempting to preserve the provincial jurisdiction in the matter of welfare. Such a system would be jointly administered by the two levels of government, in the same manner as the old-age-pension system created by the federal government in 1927 and introduced to Québec by the Taschereau government in 1936. However, in August 1944, Godbout placed his support with the federally administered program, affirming instead that it was the product of collaboration between his government and the Dominion authorities "for the good of Québec and of Canada."[100] Determined to preserve the initiative, Mackenzie King had developed a way to avoid a legal conflict between the provinces and the central government by giving the allowances a non-contributive character and invoking the federal spending power.[101]

Why did the province lose its leading status on the family allowances issue? It is possible that because of the provincial elections, which were supposed to take place in October 1944, Godbout had believed—as had Taschereau in 1936 with regard to old-age pensions—that the popularity of Mackenzie King's project was a safer bet than speaking out against federal prerogatives. According to the Ottawa Conservatives, the law was even the product of an agreement between Godbout and Mackenzie King to ensure Godbout's return to power after Mackenzie King had seriously compromised Godbout's chances for re-election by adopting conscription (Mackenzie King later denied being aware of the date of the provincial vote at the time of his throne speech on allowances and having "discussed family allowances with the Prime Minister of Québec").[102] Be that as it may, it is certain that Mackenzie King's assurances were founded on the federal State's responsibilities and methods in managing the wartime economy. The rationale for centralization was self-sustaining: as the federal government announced new prerogatives, it would attract demands from unions, employers, and then from the electorate, reinforcing the centripetal movement.[103]

Once returned to power, Duplessis immediately addressed the threat of centralization he believed was implied in the federal family allowances project. He entrusted the task of proving the law unconstitutional to three lawyers, and they set to it diligently, invoking the provincial jurisdiction over civil rights. Instead of taking the law before the courts, he made a proposal to the federal cabinet "for the establishment of a family allowances system in accordance with the province's constitutional interest and rights."[104] On 22 February 1945, the legislative assembly sanctioned a family allowances law authorizing Duplessis to negotiate based on this reservation, after four sessions devoted almost entirely to the issue. The head of the Québec government went so far as to declare that if he was not able to obtain an agreement, the province itself would be responsible for the program.[105] After an unsuccessful meeting with the Department of National Health and Welfare (DNHW) in April, he abandoned his strategy of negotiation. Nevertheless, Duplessis did not want to establish an equivalent social program himself. Indeed, the head of the Union Nationale did not wish to encourage the growth of the provincial family allowances program created by Godbout in 1943; he had rejected it as being a weak defence against federal intervention and he did not want to reinforce the clout of a corporatist network that gave the workers too much power.[106] The policy he adopted in response to the federal intrusion was much weaker than his announced counterattack. He backed down on a single adjustment of the needy mothers' allowances rates, a program he had established during the 1929 crash and from which only 30 per cent of family allowances beneficiaries could profit.

Godbout's Liberal Party, now the Opposition, found itself in the ironic position of contesting the federal family allowances law, invoking the province's autonomy in matters of education and family life.[107] In Ottawa, the French-Canadian MPs were largely unsuccessful in their attempts to put their own nationalist bent on the family allowances law, whether by encouraging large families, reinforcing paternal authority, or even promoting a greater respect for the autonomy of the Church and the province in the administrations of schools and charitable institutions.

In the end, the Canadian Family Allowances Act was not to be pro-natalist, contrary to the hopes of French-Canadian nationalists, who reaffirmed some of Léon Lebel's ideas in the House.[108] The different birth rates between the country's anglophones and francophones had compromised all special treatment of large families (see figures 2 and 3). Many anglophone caucus members realized pro-natalist policies would not be a disadvantage for the anglophone population. But some anglophone MPs accused Mackenzie King of paying "baby bonuses" to his francophone vot-

Figures 2 and 3. From the large "revenge of the cradle" family of Québec to the "nuclear family" of Canadian family allowances.

Sources: Gérard Forcier, o.m.i., *Les allocations familiales: Savez-vous ce qu'elles sont?* (Ottawa: Centre social de l'Université d'Ottawa, 1944); National Library of Canada, negatives NL19345 and NL19347, Canada, DNHW, *Rapport annuel*, 1950 (Ottawa: King's Printer), 96. (Reproduced with the permission of the University of Ottawa and the Department of Public Works and Government Services Canada, 1997.)

ers, and their anxiety contributed to their animosity towards French Canadians, which had been provoked by the latter's opposition to conscription. Herbert Bruce, a Conservative MP, summarized this point of view: "The money will not go to those provinces who have suffered the greatest losses of soldiers."[109]

Thus, facing a potentially explosive debate, Mackenzie King's government developed the idea of a decreasing allowance rate after the birth of the fourth child.[110] To avoid debates degenerating yet again into ethnic conflicts, the prime minister, who in other situations had confirmed that family size was a major cause of poverty, explained that "as a family grows, there are many costs which do not repeat themselves...I can scarcely speak from personal experience, but I remember that when I was a child, it was thus." Furthermore, the principle had already been written into the law governing allowances to soldiers' dependants.[111] Mackenzie King had specified that regardless, large families would benefit from appreciable advantages,

> which will mean that for a household of seven or eight children a supplementary cheque of forty or fifty dollars per month. Everything is relative. For a man whose income is one thousand or twelve hundred dollars, an extra contribution of four, five or six hundred dollars means a lot and will permit such a family to obtain articles which it would otherwise have had to go without.[112]

Duplessis and numerous nationalist politicians also contested what they saw as the federal government's intrusion into education through the Family Allowances Act.[113] Education was Québec's concern and one of the Prime Minister's most closely guarded projects. The allowance ceased to be paid when a child "over six years old and physically able to attend school,...does not attend or does not receive equivalent instruction as prescribed by the law."[114] Many provincial allowances programs for needy mothers already included clauses regarding children's school attendance.[115] The federal government was thus taking the greatest advantage possible of its share of constitutional powers. In 1945, the federal government was forced to back down a little in the face of pressures from Duplessis and the other provinces. It decided to suspend allowances only if children did not meet their province's education laws, but if the province refused to cooperate, the federal government reserved the right to see to it that the law was applied.[116] Furthermore, it reserved the right to suspend disbursements in cases where a child worked without pay. Thus, incapable of direct involvement with the prickly domain of public instruction, the federal government had to be content to influence education in an indirect manner.[117]

One final subject worried the nationalists: their mistrust of the federal government regarding orphans. The Family Allowances Act did not foresee helping children living in charitable establishments, but it did include adoptive families, parents managing foster homes, and all other individuals caring for children.[118] Thus, the charitable establishments desiring to receive allowances for their residents were forced to place the institution under the management of a placing agency that would employ a social worker. Once they had acquired the co-operation of such an organization, any person or establishment able to prove that it spent over five dollars per month on the child's welfare could receive allowances.[119] The federal law reflected the practices of the anglophone provinces and Québec's anglophone community. In the Québec francophone communities of 1945, such placing agencies were rare, and the federal government sought to support their development. The favour of foster families fell into place with the dominant belief of social workers and of francophone sociologists and, more widely, with an international movement for the care of children in families.[120] In 1944, this belief had dominated the works of the Québec Health Insurance Commission (the Garneau Commission) and led Godbout to adopt a law similar to the North American model of the Children's Aid Society. Duplessis quickly abolished the policy, as the clerical elite had little trouble convincing him to return to the institutional model.

In short, Mackenzie King believed that he could draw more Québec votes without conceding to the nationalist pressures. He courted the province's workers in particular, who had the largest families and the lowest wages. The allowances would even provide them with a solid material basis for demanding wage increases. To direct the flow of popular recognition to the proper channels, the cheques and accompanying pamphlets would amply remind the recipients that "the family allowances are paid by the federal government."[121] Accepted reluctantly by Duplessis, lacking the nationalist regulations many of the House's Francophones would have wanted included, the Family Allowances Act was to become one of the main tools in the increase of federal jurisdiction. Montréal jurist Maximilien Caron informed his fellow citizens of the trend in March 1945, in a radio interview during which he still defended the idea of a program administered by the provincial government:

> If the federal budget finds it is struggling with an annual commitment of up to two hundred million, because of the family allowances, the provinces will have trouble recuperating their sources of income, left during wartime, and will find themselves financially incapable to carry out the responsibilities involved with social security in the coming peacetime, responsibilities bestowed upon them by the British North America Act.[122]

At the provincial level, Duplessis' withdrawals proved more successful. Many elements of the Compulsory School Attendance Act were abandoned after Godbout's departure. The Union Nationale government did little to apply a law that it had previously opposed. It went so far as to abolish the policies put in place by the previous government to help families send their children to school: gone were free tuition, a portion of the assistance program for free books, and assistance in the form of clothing for poor families. As well as invoking the interests of poor families, Duplessis feared that applying the Compulsory School Attendance Act would upset parents, thus damaging his political support.[123]

Instead, he adopted a law in 1946 "to ensure the future of education," one meant to improve educational equipment with the injection of new funds into the educational network. From that moment on, the government assumed all the school boards' debts and converted them to lower rates, and an "education fund" of $20 million was created, of which a portion would come from the 2 per cent sales tax instituted in 1940 by the Godbout government. To sustain this fund, Duplessis established new taxes on natural resources.[124] According to Omer Côté, the provincial secretary present at the project's inception, these subsidies would favour school attendance better than any law on compulsory education. Duplessis was also able to decrease the provincial government's contribution to free books. In 1949 he lowered the provincial government's contributions from 90 to 50 per cent, aiming to save part of the $450,000 the program for books cost him.[125] He also re-established school fees. In 1949, the school boards became "free" to impose a monthly uniform cost not exceeding 50 cents for elementary education and $1 for those in grades eight and nine.[126] The decision came partly from the prime minister's conservatism: school fees made parents more responsible. It was also a budgetary precaution: the elimination of the monthly fees in 1944 had cost the Treasury an annual sum of approximately $500,000. Finally, the issue of returning to the monthly fee belongs to, although indirectly, the history of Duplessis' resistance to the encroachment of the federal government. In 1946, a commission of inquiry on the distribution of municipal and school taxes had already seen the reestablishment of school and book fees as a means of recovering federal money through education:

> Since the law awarding free books and imposing children's school attendance was passed, the federal government enacted a law aiming to establish family allowances.... If we preach to the people about their dignity, their rights, their ways, we must also preach about their responsibilities and their duties. Your school board suggests that the Department of Public Instruction consider the provincial government's option of deducting

this part of the family allowance at source, according to the spirit and the letter of the law reserved for children's' education.[127]

The Industrial and Commercial Establishments Act

During the war, the exceptionally high demand for labour pushed politicians to encourage the increase of universal education, it also enticed many young people to leave school early. Unions, churches, social workers' associations, women's groups, youth groups, and school boards all organized campaigns against child labour. Dozens of letters lamented the fact that, taking advantage of the temporary financial situation, thousands of children were leaving school for work, signing away their health and their future.[128] More often, reformists wanted the State to oblige students to stay in school. The Compulsory School Attendance Act for children under fourteen had solved part of the problem, but the Liberal cabinet was not ready to extend compulsory education to fourteen and fifteen years of age.[129]

The reformists hoped that the existing law on youth welfare, which outlawed hiring children under sixteen in certain sectors, would be called upon.[130] They also put the Industrial and Commercial Establishments Act back on the public agenda. They called for medical examinations of children by social workers before their hiring, for adequate career counselling, and for work permits to be issued more selectively in industrial and commercial establishments, being mindful of children's economic situation and of the nature of the work being done.

As it had done for the first forty years of the twentieth century, the government would again adjust its young labourers' education policy to market fluctuations. In the early twentieth century, when the demand for juvenile workers in manufacturing was increasing, the provincial government knew to turn a deaf ear on the propositions to reform the labour laws by limiting children's admission to industrial establishments. It took the Depression following the Great War to institute a proper inspection system, but once prosperity had returned, the new work permits served only to sanction the hiring of adolescents and even of children. The provincial Liberals' constancy on the subject is even less surprising, when one realizes that the assistant deputy of labour in Adélard Godbout's government, Gérard Tremblay, had played the same role in Louis-Alexandre Taschereau's government.

From 1939 to 1945, the Québec Department of Labour (QDL) responded to demands concerning the ban on work for children fourteen and fifteen years of age by putting off promoting their education until after the war. Reformist requests to prevent employers from turning to juvenile labour were ignored. The labour minister also refused to take advantage of the Youth Protection Act, alleging that, for the moment, young people were particularly needed for delivery jobs; the minister would only use the act later, in the case of unemployment.[131] He did not strengthen his policy on issuing work permits either. In his annual report at the beginning of the war, the deputy minister of labour justified issuing triple the number of work permits than had been issued over the previous year by "the entrance of youth fourteen to sixteen years old, for whom work is necessary, into the war factories."[132] But he was aware of the controversy surrounding his inaction when he attempted to explain that since "the majority of registrations having taken place at the beginning of the holidays, it would be [...] the worst time to presume that the certificate holders had definitely left school to pursue paid work." In reality, only between 40 and 60 per cent of these permits had been approved for summer work only.[133]

This inaction was not only the product of a submission to market forces. Since the beginning of global hostilities, the provincial government was no longer the only captain of the ship on the matter of labour, its prerogatives having recessed in the face of the federal government's focus on the war economy. Thus, events outside Canada's control reoriented the central government's manner of conducting internal affairs, a position provincial governments had difficulty countering. Adélard Godbout opposed this redistribution very little, due to the fact that he owed his 1939 victory to his federal Liberal colleagues. Relationships of mutual assistance between the two levels of government in labour matters were nothing new, but the war, as we have seen, had heightened them. In this context, the ambivalence of the QDL towards child labour appears to have been an echo of the hesitation of its counterpart at the federal level.

What was happening at the Department of Labour in Ottawa? Similarly to Godbout's cabinet, Mackenzie King's ministers approved the principle of prolonging the education of poor children. Over the course of the conflict, the federal government also distinguished itself by making a number of declarations of good intentions regarding juvenile labour. At the beginning of the war, for instance, it was decided not to include children under sixteen in the potential labour lists created by the National Selective Service (NSS), "given that children from 14 to 16 are not considered to be a resource the service could call on should the need arise" and that the provincial governments protected children of this age.[134] In 1944, the federal Department of Labour toyed with the idea that the NSS should look after the fourteen- and fifteen-year-olds, with the aim of keeping track of their whereabouts at the very least. But it drew back from this position as soon as its Québécois counterpart declared that children were the responsibility of the province. The federal officials thus decided that children under sixteen coming to them would be sent to the provincial inspection service.[135] Given the ability with which Mackenzie King had manipulated the Constitution at the time of the adoption of the Family Allowances Act, it is possible that this measure could have simply been a careful pretext. In fact, the federal government was not inclined to legislate for children from fourteen to sixteen years old, as demonstrated in Minister Brooke Claxton's response to the head of the CCF, who asked that family allowances be extended until the age of eighteen to keep children away from the labour market: "If I am not mistaken, everywhere [other than New Zealand], there is a definite limit set; no child over 15 receives the allowance because, ordinarily, it is the maximum age to be in school and many children begin to earn their living at that age."[136]

With the war coming to an end, the fear that children would be competition for adult labourers returning from the front amplified the calls to extend children's education. This time, legislators concerned about labour conflicts as large as those of 1919 complied with the demands. The heads of the Provincial Employment Service decided that "the official may not issue a permit if the youth...is asking for work in a city where there is rampant unemployment."[137] The same fear of seeing an employment crisis had added to the popularity of family allowances. The allowances could decongest the labour market by keeping children in school, as was stated in the House by the head of the CCF, M.J. Coldwell.[138]

In 1945, Maurice Duplessis honoured several promises on the matter of child labour made by his predecessor during the war, adding his own particular blend of protection against the intervention of the federal government.[139] In April of that year, he changed the intent of the "age and study certificate" to make it an instrument of protection for young workers. Developed with advice from the Youth Bureau, an organization bringing together the Junior League of Montreal, the Ligue de la jeunesse féminine, and the Jewish Junior Welfare League, the system anticipated new "work permits" that would authorize only the work described on the official document and have to be renewed if the child changed employers. As a result, "there would be an automatic monitoring of juvenile labour, ensuring that young boys and young girls are placed in jobs befitting their ages, gender, and physical abilities."[140] To these changes, the labour minister added a professional training plan for fourteen- and fifteen-year-old workers. At the same time, the department updated its professional training programs. New training schools and employment agencies could equip children to take on specialized jobs.[141] But the Industrial and Commercial Establishments Act did not require the medical examination called for by the unions and by some officials since the beginning of the century, as well as by the Montpetit Commission in the 1930s, despite the fact that, since 1946, international labour conventions were supposed to guarantee such an examination.[142]

In short, the new law regulating children's labour had to satisfy many interests—those of workers' unions, who were not only protecting their children but also aiming to prevent a wage decrease for themselves; those of veterans and officials, who were worried about the impact of the soldiers' return to the labour market; those of reformists and journalists, who were hoping to correct the abuses of the industrial system; and finally, those of the political and economic elite, who wanted to improve labourers' level of education when economic conditions allowed them to go without their services for the time being.

In conclusion, the Compulsory School Attendance Act and the Family Allowances Act "cannot be attributed to the deliberate action of any particular legislator."[143] These laws, as well as the emergence of a regime of universal rights, were called for by different social groups engaged in the pursuit of highly varied interests. Through these social policies, a democratization of political life was also made manifest. They can be seen as the long-term product of the extension of suffrage to poor men and to all women.[144] They are also the product of a shift in votes from the country to the cities, which was far from completion in 1940. The political stage had been expanding, making room for a variety of public groups with different aims.[145] To accommodate these newcomers into the political sphere, Liberal reformists had pushed the frontiers of the public sphere out little by little, creating a social sector in the State where the fate of children received special attention.[146] Between 1880 and 1925, labour unions and "managerial" Liberal reformists from professional and economic backgrounds had contributed to the organization of laws regulating child labour and a series of policies for the technical training of a minority of farmers' and workers' sons. The 1929 crash had cooled the ardour of reformists and the needs of entrepreneurs alike. But, in the context of war, strengthened by the support of labour unions, women's groups, and the progressive Catholic layty and benefiting from the slowdown of the Catholic rural renaissance and from the contradictions within the upper clergy, Adélard Godbout took on the task of modernizing the State's social role by establishing women's suffrage, provincial family allowances, and, most important, compulsory school attendance. In Ottawa, the drive to direct the economy and wartime labour relations permitted Mackenzie King to lead the transformation of the social role of the State. More powerful than Godbout, he would become the focus of egalitarian demands from labourers, progressive employers, reformist groups, and social science experts, which led him to establish universal family allowances. Once Duplessis returned to power in Québec and the war ended, there was no Québec nationalist reformist group powerful enough to counter the federal initiative.

When describing social policy during the war years, it is fairly common to talk about "consensus." But we must be careful to note its limits. Neither the unifying rhetoric of war patriotism nor the phenomenon of the convergence of the aims of many public groups should obscure the fact that they were all involved in "conflicts of distribution." The employers were the first to sketch the borders of social policy, its "managerial" reformism accepting very little of the wealth redistribution proposed by the international unions' "progressive" reformists and, increasingly, by the Catholic unions. Godbout and Québec's employers' associations shared Mackenzie King's convictions on the subject, as did the majority of the mandarins and a goodly portion of the heads of business. Moreover, the reservations of the episcopacy regarding the State's intervention and, in its wake, the reservations of large portions of the province's electorate as well as that of small- to medium-sized cities, all slowed Godbout's legislation. The Union Nationale's return brought the reach of the reformist consensus down a notch. Maurice Duplessis' efforts were centred mostly on the improvement of living conditions for farmers, who were his main voters, through a large rural electrification program as well as agricultural credit. For city voters, he stood for anti-statism seeking as he was the support of the upper clergy. Finally, if he was concerned in the same way Godbout had been about pleasing employers, he certainly didn't respond with the same universal view on national education and its role in the economy.[147] We can therefore view the birth of the Welfare State as an "unwanted result," a phenomenon of "emergence," or a consensus "of composition," whose creation was facilitated by economic conditions and technological advances.[148]

2

Implementing the New Laws

Institutionalization of New Rights

The meaning of children's new universal rights would depend on how the Compulsory School Attendance Act and the Family Allowances Act were applied. An examination of the institutions, both new and old, through which the officials would act allows further discovery of the players whose interests would affect the laws in their own particular ways. By analyzing the structure and the workings of these transmission systems, we are also able to revisit the legislators' intentions, to examine them even more closely.[1]

The Consolidation of the Department of Public Instruction: Statistics and Centralization

Setting up the Compulsory School Attendance Act was one of the main aspects of a much larger project, which was to rationalize and extend the function of the provincial State. Adélard Godbout's purpose was to modify the role and status of the province's public service. To this end, he planned to recruit experts who would be shielded from public pressures. In order to hire State employees according to "meritocratic" criteria, he created the Public Service Commission, an innovation that distinguished him from the previous Liberal leader, Louis-Alexandre Taschereau, who had a reputation for being contemptuous of officials.[2]

The extended size and prerogatives of the educational administration took a variety of forms, the most significant being to open information channels between schools and the Department of Public Instruction (DPI). Determined to learn more about the province's families, the superintendent of public instruction (SPI) encouraged the population to contact him

Notes to chapter 2 start on p. 215.

directly with their worries and difficulties regarding the new Compulsory School Attendance Act. He received hundreds of letters from parents about the new law, and Victor Doré established a relatively respectful rapport with those who wrote to him.[3]

Meanwhile, most of the collection efforts focused on developing provincial statistics. The first priority of many authors of the Compulsory School Attendance Act, as we have seen, was to amass information on the subject of school attendance; many maintained the typical liberal reformist faith in social science as a means to solve social problems.[4] The concentration of power thus brought a centralization of knowledge about families, as was the case in the development of most modern States. Assembled, standardized, and publicized in a new format, the information could rattle the stability of local figures and regulations in the very places where the information had been collected.[5]

Before 1943, school inspectors were bound to carry out the annual enumeration based on elementary-school teachers' registers, and every year the school-board secretary-treasurers had to enumerate all their municipality's children between the ages of six and seventeen.[6] But the quality of these censuses was dubious, and school boards in big cities rarely completed the task. However, it was possible to ascertain approximately how many children were not registered in school every ten years by comparing the number of students enumerated by inspectors with the number of children in the federal census. This method held a certain significance on the provincial scale, but it was impossible to analyze the results on a local level, as many attended school in a district different from the one in which they were counted.

In the end, the most precise statistics from the DPI were those examining the number of children enrolled in each grade, and the supporters of compulsory education had not failed to use them to emphasize the decrease in the number of children from one level to the next. But they still lamented the impossibility of counting those who were not registered, and during the early-century debates on compulsory education in the legislative assembly, their efforts to obtain solid figures on school attendance rates had been in vain.[7] During the 1910s and 1920s, they had succeeded in influencing the DPI to improve its collection methods a little, but the lack of precise methods to calculate attendance allowed the defenders of the status quo to draw an idyllic picture of education in Québec.[8]

Thus, in 1938, when the Hepburn Commission studying the problems of Protestant teaching uncovered flagrant anomalies in the school census from the 1930s, and when the radical liberal daily paper *Le Jour,* wishing to understand the Catholic state of affairs, called for a general inquiry into the educational system and attendance, a minor improvement of statistical techniques could have been expected. Indeed, thanks to the figures provided by two of the most conscientious municipalities, the Hepburn Commission had unveiled the worrisome situation that an accurate poll would reveal: in Brome County, 8 per cent of Protestant children between the ages of six and thirteen did not attend any school at all; in the other municipality, near Montréal, 17 per cent of children of the same age were not even registered in a school.[9]

But the change in the method of school data collection was to come from elsewhere: the Catholic Church call for an inquiry into the situation in the countryside. At that time there were high officials in the provincial administration who were knowledgeable enough about the urban reformists' education perspectives that they expanded the rural inquiry's range to include city districts. In fact, in 1939, before Godbout came into power, inspector general of elementary schools C.-J. Miller and DPI secretary B.-O. Filteau had had census forms for children aged seven to thirteen inclusively sent to school inspectors in each school district they would visit that fall. To "know as precisely as possible the reasons leading children, boys in particular, to leave school so early," inspectors had to inquire about the quantity and motives of those who had left school, in the view of teachers, school commissioners, or even district priests.[10] From August 1940, the new government used this preliminary work for its task of persuading the clergy. Provincial Secretary Hector Perrier and SPI Victor Doré reviewed the inquiry figures of their predecessors to prepare a more complete report on the problem of Catholic education, with the help of six employees from the DPI.[11] The remainder of this story lead up to the adoption of compulsory education, and was recounted earlier in this work.

Subsequently, the provincial leaders attempted to implement the Compulsory School Attendance Act as they had advertised: by means of "definite facts." In the "managerial" reformist spirit of Godbout's cabinet, the continuous collection of "official scientifically established statistics" was at the foundation of efficient management, a credo the superintendent was borrowing explicitly from the business world:

> We must not be surprised by the apparent multiplicity of the facts to be collected. Any administrator of a well-run business must be able, at any time, by means of perfectly kept records, to ascertain the exact state of affairs. Children's time in school is a valuable asset and those managing it must be as careful in tracking the losses and causes as if they were accountants in a commercial business.[12]

Inspired by the techniques perfected at the Montréal Catholic School Commission (MCSC) over the two previous decades, Doré created the

Statistical Research Service of the DPI, which he established in Montréal, first on Avenue du Mont-Royal and later on Avenue du Parc-Lafontaine.

Hector Perrier entrusted the management of the service to a Jesuit, Paul-Émile Beaudoin, who was completing his theological studies in Montréal and also taught part time for the MCSC. A professor of chemistry, algebra, and physics, he had pursued an interest in educational statistics as an autodidact.[13] His passion for statistics as a means for improving education did not differ much from the Jesuits' concern for education: he later concluded a brochure from the DPI with the slogan "Étude, propagande, action" [Study, propaganda, action], recalling the motto of the Jeunesse étudiante catholique, who had also been led by the Jesuits. On a larger scale, Jesuits used statistics to lead their campaigns of Catholic reformism. The provincial secretary did not fail to emphasize the interests his cabinet shared with the Jesuits when he wrote to Beaudoin's superior to ask his permission to keep the former on as director longer.[14]

The statistician created uniform collection tools, which the boards were to use systematically. To ensure the high quality of local work, and to attract competent individuals who would complete their tasks as responsibly as possible, the department invited the school municipalities to pay their census-takers.[15] The MCSC had already offered a payment of five cents per child to the priests who were counting children during their parish visits.[16] In the Cap-de-la-Madeleine Board, statistics had been remarkably well maintained since 1932, when the property owners who hadn't the means to pay their school taxes had been offered complete debt forgiveness in exchange for their participation in the census.[17] To improve the quality of the research service's figures, Beaudoin also perfected tools suitable for helping educators and managers understand the workings of school administration. He showed an unprecedented care for the clarity of his tables, and he instructed his readers on the principles of statistical analysis.[18]

The interest in precise statistics snowballed for the directors at the DPI. Many educators recognized the usefulness of the figures as soon as they were published: "From now on," wrote the inspector from the urban district of Saint-Vincent-de-Paul, "these statistics signify something: they are rapidly proving to be both interesting and useful."[19]

The superintendent and the statistician encouraged the inspectors to "track and even anticipate the evolution of numbers of people of various ages living in a given territory."[20] These projections of educational clientele would then permit the State to build schools and put programs in place. Furthermore, the new attendance and assiduity statistics would serve to defend the department's aims. "From now on," Beaudoin wrote in the preface of his first census, "the department will be able to answer both our own questions, and the questions of others. It will set in motion a healthy propaganda."[21] Journalists would support his efforts as they impatiently awaited the publication of the results, to make them known. The Statistical Research Service even used these numbers as a public-relations tool for the province: "Those who immediately conclude that Québec parents or children scorn education, or even that they are Canada's most negligent," read the census introduction, "proceed unscientifically, and worse still, proceed in error." The service endeavoured to show, for example, that Québec's performance in education was superior to that of other provinces when taking into account the effect of large family sizes on school statistics.[22]

The department's propaganda sought to justify its activities in front of domestic opponents. In the fall of 1944, 3,500 copies of the previous year's census results were sent to MPs, school boards, dioceses, rectories, and teachers' colleges: "Without the help of the statistics," Beaudoin clearly admitted, "any provincial educational administration is...rendered powerless to the stir caused by the 'pressure groups.' A scrupulously researched report, it is able to justify its decisions: conservations, refusals, innovations."[23] In a society dominated by the business world, such measurements of the education system's effectiveness doubtlessly helped school administrators explain their demands and defend their budgets.[24]

In the first few years of the Compulsory School Attendance Act's implementation, two original works were published: *Recensements scolaires* and *Rapports de juin*. A "rich subject for further study is available for the first time to specialists and to all those interested in the progress of education in the province," read the preface of *Recensements scolaires*. Father Beaudoin compiled the results meticulously, organizing them by region and school board, and new information was introduced on the motives for non-registration, for example, or on students' attendance. He created "age-degree" tables, which provided a comprehensive mapping of the students' progress according to grade, a methodological innovation authorizing the evaluation of the "needs to be met" in "normal" circumstances. He also went so far as to propose statistical correlations between levels of education and wages.[25]

On the local scale, the census established by the DPI in 1943 was a refined tool that could be used to track down children not attending school. It required verification of school registrations at private institutions or outside the municipality, and the enumeration date was moved from January to September for the information to be useful from the beginning of the school year. The census-takers also had to keep their lists updated by keeping a record of all the families moving within the municipality during the year. The department required that a register and absence-monitoring forms be used to track each student's daily schedule. The teacher had to check for attendance irregularities twice a day and inquire about their cause immediately or forward the case to the school principal and the truant officer. When recording an absence, the teacher now had twelve categories to choose from. Then the teacher completed a series of forms, inspired by the MCSC, such as the "parents' first warning," which asked parents to provide an explanation for the absence "immediately," as well as the date of the child's planned return. The form ended on an unambiguous tone: "Unless there is a serious reason for this absence, please see that your child returns to school immediately." Upon returning to school, the child would present a note from home, allowing the teacher to assess the reason for the absence. If the absence was longer than six days, it became the business of the truant officers, to whom the teacher forwarded the student's information by means of a "weekly report." The inquiry then began by telephone, mail, or with a visit, depending on the officer's judgment. Finally, teachers and officers had to record children's movements between school boards by means of a "transfer advisory," found on the last page of the province's new monthly report cards.[26]

The rationalization Godbout had sought quickly met some sizable obstacles, initially created by the politicians themselves. Between justifying the department's activities and describing the problems of the educational system, the balance would soon tip towards vindication. From the second publication of the census onwards, statisticians did not approach the subject of poverty anymore, except to refute its importance: "The proportion of these types of cases is minute, all thanks to our parish and charity diocesan organizations."[27] The game of exposure had apparently become too dangerous.

Another kind of problem emerged when some inexperienced or incompetent officials had trouble keeping their promises. In addition, the added strain of the war on the State's human and financial resources normally earmarked for civil projects significantly slowed the collection and synthesis of statistics. Already during the school census adventure of 1942, the department's intentions had come up against the scarcity of resources at its disposal, an obstacle that would soon cool the enthusiasm of officials in charge of the implementation of compulsory education. The 1942 inquiry had been scheduled to begin in January of that year, but such large quantities of the eighty-page notebooks had to be printed that, given the restrictions imposed by the war, the paper manufacturers were not able to provide the necessary materials until March. Beginning in April, the task awaiting those in charge of the compilation "went far beyond what they had expected," for rather than providing them with its own compilation services, the department had chosen to use the Dominion Bureau of Statistics, where the necessary expertise and technology were more readily available. The federal body had agreed to collaborate on the project, but it was eight months behind in its own work, the war having reduced the number of employees involved in the national census compilation by one-third. In the fall of 1942, the DPI still had not produced a single figure from the survey, and it was plain that the supporters of the Compulsory School Attendance Act would have to proceed without the department. Some compilations were published later, but in the meantime, the Statistical Research Service was not able to analyze the results. Father Beaudoin used these compilations in subsequent publications regardless and provided the most realistic and faithful portraits of school attendance before compulsory education.[28]

The new DPI experts also came up against some resistance from senior officials. Until then, the inspectors' reports and the secretary-treasurers' censuses had been compiled by the Québec Bureau of Statistics, a branch of the Department of Industry and Commerce. Such responsibility was not surprising given the provincial State's concern for industrial promotion. The head of the Québec Bureau of Statistics, aiming to maintain his privileges, insisted to the cabinet on the Bureau's legal foundation and on the quality of his technical equipment. Moreover, he questioned the legitimacy of the new department's work: though he recognized the quality of the results of Father Beaudoin, he judged that the department should be content with carrying out a limited number of inquiries.[29] The delay in the Jesuit's research work seemed to support this perspective: as Beaudoin had not been able to complete his compilation of the teachers' absence forms within the three-month deadline, the Québec Bureau of Statistics was forced to publish the 1943–44 *Statistiques de l'éducation* three years late.[30]

The new officials attempted to promote their own "services" and to encourage political leaders to increase the number of their colleagues. Planned development, in their opinion, required centralized and qualified leadership:

> More than ever, we must emphasize the collaboration between family and school, laymen and clergy, parish and municipality or diocese. These diverse collaborations, essential for the greater good of our youth, require constant precision, and a highly active impetus on the part of our entire education system's nervous system, the Department of Public Instruction.[31]

To reach this aim, Father Beaudoin was ambitious. He suggested new administrative services be created: a board for publicity and parents' education as well as a service for the protection of children, among others.[32] But the impasse that ended a study on student health shows how Adélard Godbout's administrative reform had not been solid enough to survive the Liberals' brief rule of Québec. In order to study the role of sickness in absenteeism, Doré had asked teachers to record children's heights and weights three times a year and to include these measurements in their monthly report cards and school registers in order to indicate a yearly progression and establish the proportion of students whose measurements were outside the norm. Not only had the department not foreseen the scarcity of scales across the province, it had not foreseen any immediate use for the results, on either the local or the national scale. The only published results were, in *Rapport de juin 1945*, a "look at the health of the school population by analyzing the weight–height correlation," which used the figures of the urban schools that had a scale at their disposal. As far as we know, the data were never used to track sick children nor to indicate which regions were disadvantaged.[33]

In 1945, Victor Doré attempted to show the province's new secretary, Unionist Omer Côté, that "the work accomplished in anticipating the next six years' enrollment [is of] great importance." Doré affirmed that "the emerging conclusions will rally all efforts to quickly achieve the solutions we have already sketched."[34] But with Maurice Duplessis in power, the existence of the scientific planning system, based on school statistics implemented for the Compulsory School Attendance Act, was being compromised. The new government saw it only as a useless exercise: "The Liberals will have discussed [our education problems] to the point of discouraging us; we will have simply resolved them!" boasted Omer Côté.[35] Duplessis transferred the Statistical Research Service from Montréal to Québec City, allegedly to bring it closer to the department and speed up the compilation of the results, but the manoeuvre ended up abolishing the service. The publication of the school census results was interrupted after the second year compromising further study of general causes of truancy. The synthesis of the figures contained in the school registers was never published after 1945; the compilations themselves seem to have ceased after 1946. In 1950, the government settled the conflict about the responsibility for statistical analysis in favour of the original Québec Bureau of Statistics. From 1944–45 to 1945–46, the Statistical Research Service budget decreased from $34,000 to $22,000, and the number of its personnel was reduced by one-half.[36] After 1950, the DPI statistics became scanty at best. The new superintendent chose to publish the absentee figures no longer.

However, he kept the "age-degree" tables to provide the public with indications of the effectiveness of the educational system. The honeymoon of higher-education administration experts and political power was over.

There was another means by which the statistics could be used by the DPI to control the management of the schools: the centralization of school structures. Between 1939 and 1944, Adélard Godbout strengthened the DPI by increasing its budget from $7 million to $18 million.[37] His main tool for increasing the province's hold on the school apparatus would be, he hoped, the group of some 100 school inspectors working for the superintendant. In July 1943, on the eve of the first school year under the regime of compulsory education, Victor Doré brought them all together to communicate the new set of instructions. Since the Compulsory School Attendance Act had liberated the inspectors from the job of collecting statistics on attendance and assiduity, he relied upon them to carry out the new task of informing school staff of the government's will. He called upon them to bring together the teachers in their districts for pedagogical conferences in September, in order to pass on the new instructions. These instructions were to be repeated upon the inspector's biannual school visits. They were also to invite the school-board members to information assemblies. Many carried out their tasks diligently. Their ideas on education were, in some cases, similar to the Liberals' and some of them had even campaigned for compulsory education.[38] Others took a more passive attitude, especially when the government's demands conflicted with the views of taxpayers in their districts. In the Champlain District, the inspectors, who were both taxpayers of that area, neglected their duties by tolerating the board's failure to offer classes for girls. Finally, some protested against aspects of the law that, in their opinion, could not be implemented, reminding high officials of the situation of parents: "It is not enough to convince people to send their children to school," a Saguenay inspector regretfully informed them, "but we must also create circumstances in which it is possible for them to do so."[39] Later, Duplessis did lessen these aspects of inspectors' work, but it seems that he also wanted to win their favour: in the year 1946–47, their salaries went from $1,800 to $3,000.[40]

After the inspectors came the teachers. In the long term, Doré assured them, the Compulsory School Attendance Act would bring them recognition and would allow them to conserve their energy. Godbout's cabinet had also undertaken to improve their training, recruitment, and pay conditions. Further, it had prepared a new program specifying the nature of the pedagogic changes accompanying the compulsory education regime, but the reforms were not yet ready in 1943.[41] In the meantime, the implementation of the new law called for "some additional work" from teachers—secretarial work, for one: they were asked to keep new attendance records and to inform the truant officers about unjustified absences. There was some pedagogical work as well, to "keep students so interested in schoolwork that they will not miss a single day if they can help it."[42] Doré's demands added to an already considerable workload for the teachers, who were mostly young, underpaid women—many from the country, with little education—at the mercy of the arbitrary authority of school boards and responsible for oversized classes. Moreover, during the war years, there had been a lack of teachers, since the factories offered much higher wages.[43]

If a large number of teachers took up the new office tasks, such as those of the MCSC, many did not enforce the Compulsory School Attendance Act. The avalanche of new forms interfered with their pedagogical work, and some could see only bureaucratic chaos, unrelated to education. A good many of them did not complete the absence reports; others did not send them, citing the postage costs they had to pay themselves. Some went so far as to resign: "When they were forced to do the required tasks, [two of the four teachers in Sainte-Hélène, in Abitibi,] gave up their classes."[44] Generally, if "the school teachers and principals had taken great care in preparing the June report cards," some teachers would refuse to fill the role of "commercial business accountant," as the superintendent asked. They rejected compiling figures, not seeing their immediate use, and called for a return to the old forms, the Matane teachers even threatening to enter false numbers by writing whatever "came into their heads."[45] In emphasizing the futility of these statistical exercises, these teachers were not completely wrong. They could refer to the failure of the 1942 inquiry, for which they had worked hard, when they had believed that they would have a "profound and lasting influence on the improvement of [their] status as well as that of the province's students" the department promised them.[46] To respond within the ten-day deadline, they had worked frantically: there were questions on points as precise as the detailed inventory of school resources and the wages of the brothers and sisters of children who had left school. Among the 24,675 teachers in Québec, 23,048 of them, or 93 per cent, had done their duty.[47]

As for the education renewal, which was meant to increase students' interest in school and thus facilitate the task of enforcing attendance, the November 1943 report indicated that the new principles had not yet penetrated the schools due to a lack of resources and teacher knowledge. The instructions had been included in the educational directives of that year, but teachers continued to fail students regardless of their abilities, to strengthen their authority or to keep their own record unblemished. School was still not interesting, according to Inspector Gagnon, and that would have far more influence than compulsory education on increasing assiduity. Still, in 1947, many teachers did not see the use of "proceeding slowly and surely, taking concrete steps, using situations children understand well."[48] In the view of Outaouais District Inspector Alain, in neighbourhoods where the teacher was not qualified enough, "all the personnel's competence and commitment to enforce the law in place could never succeed."[49] The new program, according to him, was officially implemented in 1947–48. But the delay in publishing the manuals for the new philosophy, the difficult ratio of a single instructor to seven different grades in a school with only one room, and the burden of numerous classes continued to slow the movement towards individual teaching. For instance, in 1949, sixteen of the eighty-two classes of the Cap-de-la-Madeleine school board had more than fifty students.[50]

The department proved to be severe with recalcitrant instructors. Those who did not implement the instructions for monitoring absences had to face the inspectors' reprimands. In the case of two instructors from Sainte-Hélène, for example, the DPI's Catholic secretary advised the inspector to retain their paycheques until the end of the school year. Regarding the Matane instructors, Doré considered their complaints to be unfounded and expressed surprise at their "little willingness to improve" education.[51] Where Adélard Godbout had at least attempted to regulate teachers' working conditions, Maurice Duplessis put the question entirely back into the school boards' hands. "This new trend of grants," declared his provincial secretary, "puts an end to the teachers' financial and political blackmail. It puts them back into the position of being solely and completely dependent upon the local authorities."[52]

School Boards, the Department of Labour Inspectors, and the Montréal Juvenile Court

In order to enforce the elementary school principle universally, Victor Doré prepared to use the resources of 200 school boards. But he was doing it reluctantly, because many supporters of the Adélard Godbout government would have preferred that the initiatives to centralize the urban school boards, which had gotten underway at the beginning of the century, be extended across the entire province. The DPI's Catholic secretary valued and supported this administrative reform as much as the Compulsory School Attendance Act itself. Having come from a centralized MCSC, the principal authors of the Compulsory School Attendance Act shared this view. The anglophone reformists had also, during their 1942 campaign, demanded a "complete administrative reform"; in their view, the boards' financial difficulties, would add to the commissioners' narrowness of spirit to compromise compulsory attendance's success. In fact, school boards had often participated in thwarting reformists' projects since the beginning of the twentieth century.[53]

Centralization ideals were subject to the same technocratic imperatives as the statistical ideal discussed earlier. Cabinet members estimated that centralized boards would respond more readily to the department's demands by maintaining a certain distance between the local administration and the voters. In Montréal, for example, all the commissioners were selected by the different authorities connected with education. Elsewhere, meanwhile, commissioners were elected by male landowners, making them subject to the power of taxpayers with potentially different interests than those of the elite, particularly in the countryside, where a low enough property qualification allowed the majority of men to vote. In 1942, Hector Perrier was ready to answer feminist demands to allow women to be commissioners in Montréal. These women, however, would still belong to his socio-economic class, and it was in vain that the supporters of a more egalitarian liberalism called for the right of all parents to vote in school elections. It is easy to grasp Doré's reservations with regard to this electorate when reading his 1943 *Instructions* to the commissioners: he recommended that they behave as an enlightened elite and establish their authority based on their own understanding of their local conditions.[54] That the Liberals had fought for the recognition of the universal right to a minimum level of education should not cloud their hierarchical view of school administration.

The promoters of school board integration confronted great opposition. First, the upper clergy's support of the legal principle of the boards' autonomy was even greater than its opposition to compulsory education.[55] Church authorities cited the autonomy of parents, who were technically represented by the commissioners, and the autonomy of the Church as well: without this kind of independence, education would end up being managed by the State or would become atheist. It would appear that the upholding of current local structures had been the result of a compromise: so that the Catholic Committee to the Public Instruction Council (CCPIC) would adopt the Compulsory School Attendance Act, Godbout's team had to assure the bishops that a Ministry of Education would not be created. In addition, outside urban centres, school commissioners shared the views of the episcopacy. Ever since Adélard Godbout had been voted into office, school boards had fought any step towards centralization of education. This opposition motivated the creation of the Fédération des commissions scolaires du Québec (FCS), which was to lead the movement against centralization during the entire period studied.[56] Still, in 1953, J.-L. Baribeau, president of the Legislative Council, declared: "There is perhaps no country in the world where local school boards are as free and autonomous as they are in this province, and where they consequently bear just as much responsibility."[57] These defenders of the status quo argued that only relatively autonomous boards could offer teaching adapted to local conditions. They drew their inspiration from the tradition that assimilated democracy and local control.[58]

In the eyes of rural boards, the 1943 compromise was made necessary by the fact that most boards took on 80 per cent of the cost of teaching in their territories, drawing their income from the property taxes they collected. The commissioners had owed their power to this right to collect local taxes for more than a century. The provincial government's portion came in the form of subsidies for specific ends: elementary-school teachers' wage premium, advanced-level primary school, and grants to needy municipalities. For a thrifty government that had just recently transferred its taxation powers to federal leaders because of the war effort, the kind of shift in the budgetary equilibrium centralization would effect was difficult to accept, even more so since the boards had incurred some sizable debts.[59] During the 1930s Depression, the implementation of superior primary courses, the increase of school population, and the general lowering of taxable income had worsened the school boards' situations. Rural boards were at an even greater disadvantage, as most of them could not depend on income from industrial and commercial business taxes. During the 1944–45 school year, their total debt reached $82 million in liabilities and $6 million in diverse forms of loans.[60]

The Compulsory School Attendance Act brought with it a considerable increase in workload for the commissioners. In return, as it had done for teachers, the department only assured the commissioners that the work was in their own best interests. Doré attempted to demonstrate the savings resulting from a comprehensive enforcement of the law: when regular attendance was wanting, the benefit of many initiatives was jeopardized. He provided absence-monitoring forms to all the boards, as we have seen, and recommended that they adopt internal rules in accordance with the new law. The list of new tasks was extensive: the commissioners had to carry out the school census; select one or many truant officers; make the school environment more attractive by choosing teaching staff carefully; renovate schools according to modern requirements ("school furnishings, libraries and playgrounds"); and provide the schools with suitable lighting. Doré further encouraged them to ensure that children living far from school had adequate transportation, to reward more assiduous students, and to provide good examples themselves when they had children of their own.[61] The only new funds they received represented compensations for lost income. The following year, boards were forced to abolish the monthly payments in exchange for a special grant from the DPI; they were also offered a substantial reimbursement on the price of books if they were distributed to the students at no cost.

Despite the savings Doré had envisioned, the implementation of compulsory education was often slowed by the interests of each individual school board. Based on geographic placement, the extent of available resources, and their members' philosophies, these administrative entities were considerably distinct from one to the next, and attitudes varied widely regarding the new law.[62] The censuses suffered due to such lack of willingness and limited local resources: 108 Catholic and 41 Protestant municipalities did not carry out the census in the first year, namely 6 per cent and 11 per cent of the total, respectively; in the year 1944–45, 88 school municipalities did not answer the call.[63] In Montréal, it had not been possible to finish the enumeration before the legal deadline of 15 October; only 80 per cent of the work had been accomplished in November, and the MCSC did not send its complete reports the following spring.[64] The cost of the operation went a long way toward explaining the large cities' reticence to the project: in Montréal, the 1943 census had cost $20,000.[65] There was more to their unease than financial problems: the census-takers hesitated to pin the categories of reasons for non-attendance provided by the Statistical Research Services on a complex reality. In 1943, to the statisticians' dismay, they did not select a unique reason to account for each child who did not attend school. Moreover, looking only at the example of the Sainte-Marthe-du-Cap-de-la-Madeleine census figures, the overall work of tracking of unregistered children was carried out much less systematically after 1943.[66]

The boards' accomplishment of their duty of selecting their truant officers was to depend on their organizational administrative skills, their means, and the convictions of their members. The MCSC, which had already had seven officers since 1928, selected two more to especially study the non-attendance cases, something no law had previously permitted.[67] Doré, as we have seen, had hoped for a certain professionalization of local administration to ensure the quality of its new system: the truant officers would act primarily as social workers and "the wages should be sufficient to encourage them…to properly complete this important task."[68] In towns of 10,000–40,000 inhabitants, the budgetary efforts varied considerably, not necessarily in relation to the boards' revenues or the size of their school populations. In 1950, with a school population of 6,806 children, Sherbrooke had only one truant officer, who received $360 per year, while the Arvida board, with half the number of students, retained two truant officers it paid nearly $2,000 per year; the two municipalities' revenues were relatively comparable, though Sherbrooke's debt was slightly higher than Arvida's.[69] In many smaller urban boards and in the majority of rural boards that, because of their small size, could not employ a truant officer full time, the secretary-treasurer accepted the responsibility on top of the other duties attached to the position, which was permitted according to the DPI's *Instructions.*[70] But some boards, Catholic and Protestant alike, selected no truant officer at all. Furthermore, among the boards with only one position, many paid little or nothing, or they appointed the official in name only.[71] In this way, whereas the delegation of responsibilities to the school boards had budgetary advantages, it also threatened the Godbout government's aim of uniformity. Before the power of the boards, the Liberal administration seemed powerless: Hector Perrier had hesitated until the last minute to entrust boards with the task of appointing a truant officer. The law may have authorized the department to appoint an officer on the board's behalf if it had not done so already, but the threat never seemed to be put into action. The department's attempt to remedy the inequality of situations by issuing an ordinance to standardize officers' salaries went unheeded.[72]

Doré had thought he could depend on the truant officers' zeal, and many proved him right. "A world of possibility," he announced in 1943, "is available to the conscientious officer who seeks to improve the fate of today's children and of tomorrow's men." If he worked hard, the new hero "would save the young from ignorance."[73] Compelled by their faith in the virtue of compulsory education, many truant officers educated parents and were congratulated by inspectors from the DPI. Some took their monitoring task as far as establishing an individual file for each student in the municipality. Such was the case with Inspector Compton, who created 1,038 files.[74]

In towns with more stable staffing, the truant officers became increasingly competent based on their growing familiarity with the law, or on their higher pay:

> There are towns where the duties of attendance officers have been carried out since the inception of the Compulsory School Attendance Act, in 1944, by the same individuals who have established an excellent system to insure the regularity of attendance and who have earned a splendid reputation for their work. In these localities, illegal absences are almost unknown[,] since reports of absence are received each morning by the attendance officer who readily investigate [*sic*] the causes of the absences.[75]

At the MCSC there was already an absence-monitoring service, to which the Compulsory School Attendance Act simply gave legal recognition. Progressive truant officers had even become members of the United States National League to Promote School Attendance. Doré was so interested in the enforcement of the law in cities that he hired an inspector to monitor its impact on the metropolitan region.[76]

The absence-monitoring situation was no different in certain rural regions and small towns. For the priests and the secretary-treasurers, it was often a question of carrying on a tradition: already in 1938, members of the Hepburn Commission on Protestant primary school had observed that "occasionally a secretary-treasurer was at pains to persuade heedless parents to send their children to school."[77] For instance, in the early 1940s, in Nazareth, Rimouski County, a thirteen-year-old summer labourer had written to the minister of labour that "the foreman we work for won't take us before the holidays because the priest won't let him."[78] However, in other smaller school boards, the lack of money discouraged conscientious employees, and the work could only be thrown together hurriedly by those who would do it for a lower price: "I am harvesting," an inspector had to explain to the superintendent, "and my long days prevent me from finishing my work on time."[79] In this context, the nomination of a woman or a priest sometimes provided a solution, since they would do a better job for less pay.[80]

In smaller towns, attendance work sometimes came into conflict of interest with another job, as one of the district inspectors reported: "Most of the officials in that office are employees of the municipal council or school board and all collect annual salaries, which is their only security. It goes without saying that the officer would never want to upset anyone for fear of losing their position, which pays much more than the inspectors' wages."[81] Furthermore, the commissioners were concerned about being accountable for their actions to taxpayers. This pushed them not only to keep their spending low but also to refrain from offending parents' sensibilities. Officers who had refused to issue an absence permit sometimes had to go back on their decision, as "some notables (religious figures, MPs, school commissioners, etc.) interceded to obtain a tempering in favour of certain families."[82] These irregularities were such that, according to the Eastern Townships' regional inspector, they threatened the survival of the law: "The incompetence of certain truant officers will perhaps allow it to fall into abeyance through error or negligence."[83]

The same budgetary problems came with the implementation of the 1944 law on free education and books. Previously, school boards had been able to request between five and fifty cents per month from parents of each elementary school student.[84] Compulsory education caused a slight decrease in school boards' income, with the department reimbursing only 75 per cent of the losses resulting from the abolition of retribution.[85] The majority of boards had consented to abolish parents' contributions, but some continued to accept contributions from parents.[86] When Maurice Duplessis re-established boards' rights to make parents pay, all indications are that many did so out of necessity.[87]

Only half the boards took advantage of the law on free books.[88] The variety of the textbooks on the market added to the problem: each year, the Public Instruction Council authorized the use of a wide range of books, and even the boards hesitated to impose any standardization. In addition, many boards believed that parents would not take care of the books if they hadn't paid for them at least in part.[89] However, the movement in favour of free books would have gained momentum if Duplessis' government had not reduced the provincial government's contribution by 50 per cent in 1949, with the aim of saving the Treasury part of the $450,000 the predecessor's 90 per cent reimbursement program was costing. In 1952, still only half the boards prided themselves on their free textbooks.[90]

In January 1944, the DPI set about directly helping a few families who could not send their children to school for lack of money. The DPI had refused to help until then, explaining that the legislative assembly had not voted to approve any credit for this purpose. Apparently, parents' letters of complaint succeeded in persuading Doré to "provide clothes to students of school age whose parents were destitute."[91] The superintendent also attempted to remedy the shortage on children's clothing in certain regions of the province by interceding on the families' behalf at the Wartime Prices and Trade Board. He wrote to its president:

> Parents from various parts of the Province have been writing to this Department stating that they are unable to find in stores the clothing especially underwear and rubbers, which they need for their children. A number have mentioned in their complaints that because of this shortage their children will be unable to attend School. It is readily understood that because of urgent war needs curtailment in the manufacture of certain essentials became necessary in the past. However, now that the demand for some war products has lessened may I suggest that the making of suitable children's clothing be given greater priority?[92]

These remained exceptional cases. For the children who needed clothing, the superintendent counted mainly on the local charitable or social welfare associations he had asked the truant officers to alert.[93] He also attempted to extend to the entire province the MCSC experiment begun under his leadership during the Depression, where canteen- and clothing-distribution programs had been established for poor children in collaboration with charitable organizations.[94] Turning to charitable agencies continued after the Union nationale's return, as demonstrated by Superintendent Omer-Jules Desaulniers's suggestion in 1949, to a Montréal widow who could not afford to pay for her children's books: "I can only advise you to come to an arrangement on the subject with the authorities of the institutions your children attend, and seek to benefit from all the advantages offered by child welfare services."[95] Neither the boards nor the charitable agencies received any financial compensation for this aspect of the law's implementation.

Between the demands of the department and of taxpayers, many school boards soon found themselves caught in a stranglehold, just as Bienville's elected officials would complain to the superintendent: "We will probably need to open new classes and hire elementary school teachers, as well as furnish the classrooms, which will involve considerable costs.... Our fees rate is of 80 cents on one hundred dollars and taxpayers find that to be too high."[96] Many of the law's critics had already suggested that, due to their precarious financial situation, school boards would not be able to provide the necessary equipment for the new school population. They could not overlook the reality that the lack of qualified elementary-school teachers was reaching an alarming level because of the better wages offered to young women in the war factories. Detractors of compulsory education—of whom Maurice Duplessis was at the head—were correct in their objection that the measure would be useless as long as these types of problems were left unresolved: "The act could be harmful," warned, for example, a 1943 Jesuit magazine editorialist, "if the educational, financial and material problems raised do not receive a preliminary or concomitant solution, if the law does not plan for a degree of implementation based on local situations: it would otherwise end in impasses and tremendous messes."[97] Because the Compulsory School Attendance Act brought in more students, it contributed to the overcrowding of an already overextended school system. A variety of factors had combined over past decades to bring about this state of affairs: delays in the construction of new buildings during the Depression; the general movement to extend education; the increased birth rate; and the postwar immigration and migration towards cities and industrial centres. The DPI's statisticians informed the government of a possible crisis as early as 1944: "The increase in birth rate coupled with the educational complications point to an increase of over one-third of the primary school population for 1952. This increase will require, as of 1949, considerable financial and personnel resources. Until then, we have four years to settle debts, prepare staff and organize essential services to improve academic success."[98] "From 1952 until 1962," they wrote two years later, "young peoples' arrival on the labour market will increase by 33%," and they had to be prepared in new ways that would take into account the future economic needs.[99]

In the fall of 1943, some truant officers warned the department that it would be impossible to follow its instructions faithfully due to the increased number of students in schools. In some boards, the sudden growth in class size forced them to resort to short-term measures: in Chicoutimi, La Tuque, and Sainte-Adélaïde-de-Pabos, for example, the elementary-school teachers taught one group in the morning and another in the afternoon. In the Cap-de-la-Madeleine in 1953, 44 of the 136 classes were taught wherever space was available.[100] In urban areas that received the renewed rural exodus, the problem doubled, as was pointed out by the inspector in charge of schools on Montréal's South Shore:

> The affluence of new families creates a serious problem for the school boards. Arriving by the hundreds over the summer season, their children quickly filled all available classes. In some municipalities, some spaces had to be converted into classrooms: here, the church hall or basement; there, hallways, school rooms or cellars; elsewhere, cellars in private homes; somewhere else, an unfinished store. And, despite all this, hundreds of children have not been able to enroll in school this year. Even among those who have been able to enroll, many were not able to attend in the morning or the afternoon.... 23 additional classes are needed for fall 1947 for the municipality of Longueuil alone, and..., if the population continues to grow at the current rate, those 23 classes will not be enough in two or three years.... Lack of classrooms prevents the opening of workshops for manual work for boys and of housekeeping classes for girls. And those currently running would soon have to be transformed into regular classrooms.[101]

Another of the Compulsory School Attendance Act's objectives was to extend children's education beyond elementary school, but the higher-level classes were lacking. At times, one-room schoolhouses did not even offer the required minimum of grade seven. Beyond that, the supply was lower still; few boards provided the full range of grades, the highest being grade twelve, since most did not have a sufficient population pool. Advanced level upper-grade courses often overflowed with students. The fifteen years studied saw grades seven, eight, nine, and ten classes open, and sometimes close—a process varying from board to board, depending on the level of pressure from parents, students, and inspectors. The problem was to find classrooms, to hire more elementary school teachers, and to order, as was the case in Champlain, larger furnishings to accommodate older children.

Incapable of amassing the necessary resources, many boards began to pay for their students' education in classical colleges.[102]

Pressured by citizens, priests, or school principals, many commissioners wanted to build new schools, and the DPI was flooded with requests for funding. In 1944, Victor Doré increased elementary-school funding to help boards build and repair schools, something that had not been done since 1926.[103] The "education funds" Maurice Duplessis created in 1946 would partially meet the construction problems. Statistician Paul-Émile Beaudoin, a participant in the development of the project, showed ambition comparable with that he had previously demonstrated under Godbout's regime. He appeared to champion the cause: the law would permit, he believed, many more schools to be built and place Québec at the vanguard of school expansion.[104]

From then on, the provincial government's financial efforts in matters of education would augment prodigiously, which would translate into increased general subsidies to school boards and construction subsidies for building schools. Education spending went from 8 per cent of the province's budget in the year 1940–41 to 20 per cent in the year 1950–51, and then to 24 per cent in the year 1960–61. From 1948 to 1949, $13.5 million was allocated to school construction, and $33.8 million from 1954 to 1955; between 300 and 400 new schools were built each year, the majority of which were one-room schoolhouses. Nevertheless, the law ensuring the continued progress of education was but a temporary solution: in the year 1950–51, the debt level reached that of the year 1944–45, and it only continued to increase.[105]

Apart from the school boards, juvenile courts were called upon in Montréal and in Verdun. The law recognized a new category of offence, missing school, and, beginning in the fall of 1943, cases of repeated absences recorded by the Montréal Protestant and Catholic School Boards ended up in the Montréal Juvenile Court, which would become the Social Welfare Court in 1950. In this indirect way, the juvenile court's philosophy was grafted to the Compulsory School Attendance Act. This addition matched the hopes that city reformists, alarmed by juvenile delinquency, had pushed for compulsory schooling earlier. Truant officers and school principals began to point out to the court, among children who did not attend school regularly, those who encouraged others to miss school or those who, in their eyes, were beginning to follow a path of delinquency. A situation of this nature led a school principal in Pointe-Saint-Charles to make the following statement to the chief truant officer of the Montréal Protestant School Board:

> I find myself in the ridiculous situation of being laughed at by the neighborhood because a grade two pupil is able to be out of school for approximately 140 days so far this year....In a school of this type it takes a situation like this to ruin all my efforts in popularizing regular attendance. In fact, some of the pupils who had been attendance cases in the past are returning now to their somewhat delinquent attitudes towards school.

The same inspector went further in a letter to the chief judge of the juvenile court: "The law must be carried out or it will have a very bad effect on the delinquency situation in this city." The officers mostly used the court when parents refused to co-operate.[106]

Families who appeared in court met with a special MCSC agent who tried to convince them to abide by the law: "a good scare may do some good," explained Inspector Brown to Judge Nicholson.[107] Recalcitrant families had to see the judge; if they did not attend the meeting, a warrant for the child's arrest was issued. The child was then brought to the court by police and appeared immediately before the judge, a threshold crossed in the first two years of the law's implementation by 237 and 335 children, respectively. The judges informed them of the consequences of missing school and did not hesitate to brandish the threat of placing children with different families to force parents and children to modify their behaviour. At least two-thirds of them assiduously returned to school at that stage of the proceedings.[108] The other families found themselves entangled in the web of probation officers' social inquiries, investigations that extended to the entire situation of the families.[109] The officers visited the families of children who were absent illegally, inquired about their needs, and attempted to make use of all the child care available to ensure their return to school. Children and members of their families underwent medical and psychological examinations at the Mental Health Institute or in its child-care clinic.

In some cases, probation officers were able to open teachers' and principals' eyes to the pupil's family situation; they helped families obtain financial aid from charitable organizations, the municipality, or the provincial State, or even assistance for the mother at home.[110] We can therefore say that in some way, they ensured that there would be a link between families in urban communities—of the same kind that elementary-school teachers in the country could create on their own. But the social inquiry was a double-edged sword.

The court reserved a more dramatic fate for some children, placing them in reform schools, most often for a period of three years, or in foster families; annually, their numbers oscillated between eighty-eight the first year and twenty per year afterwards, until 1951, when the annual number dropped to one or two individuals—apparently because the reformatories not lacked space. Parents were responsible for these children's living expenses, except if they were too poor, in which case it was the City of Montréal that bore the costs.[111] The court therefore had its own logic, which forwarded some of these legal proceedings in directions the Godbout government had neither foreseen nor authorized.

In contrast to the Compulsory School Attendance Act, the Industrial and Commercial Establishments Act had never been enforced with the kind of systematic thoroughness applied to universal laws. It was only during their annual inspections of industrial and commercial buildings that the Department of Labour's officials made sure that the ban on children under fourteen years of age working was observed, and that fourteen- and fifteen-year-old children had a certificate. Each year, they discovered approximately one hundred children without permits and a small number of children under fourteen (between two and twenty-three) in this way.[112] Furthermore, they conducted special enquiries when workers under fourteen were pointed out to them, asking employers to remedy the situation by dismissing the child, which most did. They imposed a "penalty" for those individuals who neglected or refused to follow the law. At most, they could prosecute the employers, and the fines ranged between $10 and $4,200. For non-payment, the Industrial and Commercial Establishments Act's provision was a jail term not exceeding twelve months.[113] Officials had the task of carrying out the general business inspections, and their responsibility in terms of child labour was connected to a policy several decades old, which aimed to prevent work injuries.

Once school attendance became compulsory for children under fourteen, the certification system for children fourteen and fifteen years of age remained the only legal way of inciting them to attend school, but with it came major flaws. Some labour inspectors were neglectful: in Trois-Rivières, "some permits were awarded to children under 14, since the labour inspector did not request a birth certificate," wrote the Secretary of Public Instruction in 1943. "I am told that in other towns as well, the situation is much the same."[114] The number of children aged fourteen and fifteen working without permits remained rather large until the end of the period studied, despite the low demand for labour and increased State monitoring. A more in-depth study, carried out by the Department of Labour's inspectors and officers from the Shawinigan region employment agency, shows to what degree juvenile workers could slip through their fingers. They discovered that 46 of the 235 children (19.7 per cent) working in Wabasso factories did not have permits. Furthermore, 12 children aged fourteen to fifteen were working without permits in the region's 571 businesses and small factories. In 1953, the Department of Labour once again admitted the difficulty of monitoring the labourers under sixteen in the industrial and commercial establishments, "especially in the countryside, where young people can work over summer vacation."[115] Furthermore, to children aged fourteen and fifteen who visited the Department of Labour offices, work outside the home was rarely denied. In fact, based on the 1953–54 statistics, 75 per cent of children requesting a permit succeeded in establishing their need to work.[116]

The Institution of Family Allowances and the Federal Government's "Administrative Revenge"

The Department of National Health and Welfare (DNHW) devoted itself to renewing the public service and implementing an almost entirely new bureaucracy. Unlike Adélard Godbout, William Lyon Mackenzie King had colossal financial and human resources at his disposal with which he could quickly establish a universal family allowances program. His management of the war effort provided him with sizable budgets and educated personnel. In 1945, many resources from war programs were redirected towards the administration of family allowances. To establish the tremendous organization needed for cheque distribution, high officials were able to call on the female volunteer war personnel. They drew on the techniques and equipment from the soldiers' dependants allowance program and also on the knowledge of the social workers connected with it. The task of teaching parents was accomplished by numerous experts who had led the imposing propaganda machine of the domestic front during the course of the conflict, and the Wartime Information Board contributed to the program's launch in 1945. Finally, officers back from the front would occupy an important place in the new civil service.[117]

Mackenzie King could count on a twenty-year-old tradition of public administration. If we imagine the State as a Janus with one face turned towards the interior of the country and the other turned towards external relations, we can say that the absence of the Québécois State's international face contributed to the reinforcement of the federal advancement of the civil service.[118] In fact, the direction of international relations beyond the British lap had fuelled the transformation of federal administration since the beginning of the 1920s. In Québec, the number of civil-service professionals who were able to help Godbout was negligible. Most of these professionals had gained their management experience working in the field (as was the case with educators from the DPI and union leaders from the Department of Labour), and they had acquired their knowledge of statistics as autodidacts, through personal interest, often as amateurs.[119]

Only some came from social-science faculties, which had just recently been opened in Catholic and francophone regions. Here again, Mackenzie King was already way ahead. The educational elite's anti-statism had delayed the creation of social-science faculties, which were also important in the history of the development of both the civil service and Canada's social work. Furthermore, it is possible that Social Catholicism had not prepared Québec's francophone elite for public duty as well as the Social Gospel doctrine, which envisaged a career in civil service with a religious aspect. The federal State was partly responsible for this state of affairs, as its own demand for civil servants had constituted an important factor in the growth of anglophone universities.[120]

The implementation of the Family Allowances Act required that families be eligible, and that the information they provided be verified. The department established a "family allowances list," with individual files and machines to organize and cross-reference data on individual families, keeping it updated and integrated. The updated list was maintained by the "regional offices" in each provincial capital, and in Ottawa for the Yukon and the Northwest Territories. At the Québec regional office in 1960, there were 374 employees. At that point the system was so efficient that, in 1952, the federal government was able to use the list to find children born on the day of Queen Elizabeth's coronation and offer them a silver spoon.[121]

It was not only a question of proper cheque distribution. In the same manner as at the provincial level, politicians and high civil servants hoped to "bring the Government of Canada closer to the population."[122] Beyond opening regional offices to respond diligently to the requests from the public, they attempted to increase their knowledge about families to ensure the new social minimums and used the emerging popular social-science techniques to do so. Sociologists, social workers and regular officials conducted general surveys on how families spent their allowances. In the program's first few years, the Québec Regional Office for Family Allowances (QRO) led selective surveys with a sampling of families, to which the officials would deliver cheques in person. For its part, the DNHW led a large number of studies on the manner in which the family allowances were used, with good results.[123] The information on children's residence and economic status became very precise thanks to parents' financial interest in providing the necessary details. The general surveys on the spending of the allowances provided a wealth of information on hundreds of families' behaviours and opinions. However, the rigour of their methodological practices varied, as did their sampling criteria. The studies rarely took account of family size, income level, parents' ethnic origins, or the family's distribution by age or gender. Furthermore, many studies deliberately excluded families in which the mother or the father was absent.

Here also, the accumulation and scientific management of information would serve not only to administer the program but also to legitimize the State's interventions. In Canada, as in Australia, "the very need to know more about the civilian population, as well as to mobilize its support, seems to have been a crucial component in social policy."[124] In fact, the statistics compiled each year from the allowances files were used time and time again by officials, who affirmed that the program helped Canadian families and contributed to Canada's post-war economic rebirth. With a "vast educational propaganda program," the DHNW sought also to "win and maintain the public's comprehension and support of the measures."[125] Between 1949 and 1950, for example, an announcement was sent out with the family allowances cheques, advertising that the brochure on family allowances, jobs, family budget, children's hygiene, and education entitled *Nos enfants* was available at no cost to whoever requested it. Also, a film clip, *Parlons des allocations familiales*; a film, *Peppo*; leaflets mailed out with the cheques; posters; and displays for conferences and regional exhibits gave advice on the wisest ways to spend the allowances. The DNHW's public information director hoped that these would be useful, even to the point of being "the family's main reference."[126]

One clause in the Family Allowances Act authorized the suspension of allowances when they were not being put towards the care of children, a measure that allowed administrators to exert close monitoring of poor families. The cases of wrongful use were examined by a team made up of seven social workers and a dozen assistants from the welfare sector of the QRO. Institutions, individuals, or family members reported such families to private or public agencies whose objective was to protect children's welfare. Some cases were entrusted to private agencies, which received five dollars per investigation. In general, an exhaustive investigation procedure meant that a QRO employee would have to visit, on average, six different people for each case of negligence. If the allegation was founded, the allowance was sent to a third party; that is, to an agency or a citizen the officials trusted. When sickness, death, or separation changed the family's configuration, another person within the family was designated as recipient. If the official discovered "a very poor sense of household administration," the family could be referred to local welfare agency social workers, or even receive special recommendations. Often the mother had to submit periodical reports on the allotment of the allocation over a certain period of time.[127]

In order to increase its knowledge about families, and as it had done in a good many other areas during the war, the federal government intended to profit from the collaboration with provincial governments, whose information networks were older. This necessitated the adoption of a decentralized management model.[128] In Québec, the administration of family allowances came up against a resistance stronger than anywhere else in Canada. The QRO would have liked to have access to the Québec Bureau of Statistics' files in order to verify systematically children's date of birth and to be updated on deaths, but Duplessis prevented it from doing so for two years under the guise of protesting the federal government's intrusion into the field of primary education. Parents were hostages of this jurisdictional conflict, as many received amounts that the QRO would later recover from them. The verification was not completed until 1950. In the same way, the regional office hoped to entrust the investigations of suspect families to the province's welfare agencies, such as the "needy mothers, old-age pensions inspection services, [or] private city agencies," but the provincial government, with its exclusive jurisdiction over the investigations, did not want the federal government to profit from its inspection systems. Conscious of the constitutional problems this created, the federal DNHW hesitated to lead its own inspections until 1950, when, at the end of some negotiations followed closely by the country's and province's prime ministers, the provincial government finally authorized the collaboration between the Québec Regional Office and child-care organizations.[130]

The same problems awaited the QRO officials in charge of ensuring that children eligible for allowances maintained regular school attendance. In principle, they had to co-operate with the provinces' truant officers to keep informed about the delinquent children under their respective compulsory education laws. The federal government attempted to establish direct contact with parents or with intermediary agents. In some cases, the federal government succeeded in establishing information channels of superior quality. To keep track of any given family, for example, the allowances file constituted a more effective tool than the Compulsory School Attendance Act's transfer system on students' monthly report cards. Also hoping to profit from these advantages, the MCSC approached federal officials in 1952 with the aim of establishing a system of perpetual enumeration, as "all the previous censuses have proven to be incomplete, insufficient and, to a certain point, because of the frequent moving, impossible to use."[131] But when it came to school attendance, the threat of unconstitutionality hovered. The civil servant assigned to school attendance in the QRO, P.-A. Fournier, attempted to obtain aid from the province by any means possible: the strength of his determination was rivalled only by that of Duplessis' refusal.

Duplessis had first attempted to prevent the federal government from punishing school non-attendance with the suspension of family allowances. Once this measure was put in place, regardless, DPI Special Agent Charles Bilodeau pressured the Mackenzie King government to participate in the development of rules so that the article's enforcement on education did not provoke frictions with the province. This tactic having failed, Duplessis withdrew, categorically refusing to co-operate with the Québec Regional Office of Family Allowances. He ordered the DPI to withhold all information on children not attending school, even though all other provincial education ministries had agreed to provide this data. Québec's prime minister saw to it personally that the educators from his own constituency refused to help any federal official.[132]

Elsewhere, in the wings of the DPI and in Québec school boards, a history of collaboration was born. Unable to officially approach the DPI's personnel, and conscious of having to treat Duplessis' leanings with care, federal officials came in "by the back door."[133] There they found high officials ready to help behind the prime minister's back. Many of them were anxious to ensure the future of the Compulsory School Attendance Act they had worked so hard to create: B.-O. Filteau, who was still the Catholic secretary of the department; Omer-Jules Desaulniers, superintendent since 1948; Special Agent C.-O. Bilodeau, an inspector in the Godbout regime; and statistician P.-É. Beaudoin.[134] The federal Family Allowances Act seemed to them to be a means of escape from the financial impasse in which the DPI had found itself in the implementation of compulsory schooling. The DPI's secretary believed that the allowances offered parents a compensation his government had not been able to provide: "The Department…, until now, has had utmost tolerance to best explain the good cause to parents; but from now, with all the good the Family Allowances will bring to each family, none will be forgiven should it deny its child the right to education."[135]

J.-P. Labarre, Victor Doré's successor in the post of superintendent in 1946, welcomed this legislative disposition with a discrete relief. He discussed it with officers who were looking for ways to punish delinquent parents: "Hasn't the suspension of family allowances induced parents to better supervise their children?"[136] "It is tacitly understood," explained the head of school attendance at the Québec Regional Office of Family Allowances in 1950, "that the Superintendent of Public Education has knowledge of our work in the field of S. A. [School Attendance] but cannot admit this openly and would not like to see it become a political issue."[137]

As for the school boards' truant officers, they valued this means of influencing children to attend. Very early on, the following method became common practice: They began by threatening parents with allowance suspension, and then asked the QRO to send letters of warning to delinquent parents, who were then to send proof that the child attended school regularly by return mail. Between 1951 and 1952, the number of these requests reached a total of 730. Generally, officers had to content themselves with establishing some precedents they could rely upon later.[138] In exchange, the federal officials were able to call on truant officers to inspect the cases further when cases of non-attendance were signalled to them by those other than school personnel. Strengthened by this collaboration, the QRO succeeded in uncovering tens of thousands of children absent from school each year.[139]

Thus the Regional Office of Family Allowances became the new seat of enforcement of the Compulsory School Attendance Act when, after 1946, the provincial government tried to cancel its impact. In order to do so, federal officials benefited not only from the tacit approval of many of the DPI's high officials but, more importantly, from the co-operation of the Federation of School Boards, which was, like the QRO, at once more reformist than Duplessis and opposed to the concentration of power in his hands.

Paul-André Fournier continued the work towards the truant officers that Doré had undertaken with the DPI's school inspectors' help. Each year starting in 1949, he wrote letters to the province's secretary-treasurers to inform them of the advantages the family allowances could offer them in accomplishing their tasks and to ask them who the truant officers were, an exercise that often had the simple effect of reminding the commissioners of their duties.[140] He travelled throughout the province to meet the truant officers and give conferences for the commissioners on the importance of good attendance and the role of the allowances in the pursuit of this goal. "The fact that a number of school officers had never heard of the School Attendance Act and its application shall not be overlooked," Fournier wrote in 1948. "The Department of Quebec Education has not done much publicity in this field." He even undertook to "educate recalcitrant officers."[141] Fournier became a member of the National League to Promote School Attendance which was mainly active in other provinces. He hoped for a similar movement in Québec, and so that the officers would form an association to this end, he involved the FCS in the project.

Since 1950, he had earned himself the respect of the province's officers: "I am looked upon by most S.A. officers, with whom I have contact, as a guide, an adviser and a counselor in matters of S.A. They often ask for advice in cases they do not see fit to refer to the Provincial School Authorities."[142] The federal Family Allowances Act agents won the commissioners' trust so completely that they were able to be promoted to higher-ranking directorial positions at the centre of Québec's FCS. They also received the co-operation of the Provincial Association of Protestant School Boards, which headed up 75 per cent of the boards claiming to be Protestant.[143] Their combined efforts had a determining effect on the control of school attendance in Québec:

> For a large number of commissioners present [at the Fédération des commissions scolaires urbaines 1950 conference], the words of Mr. Fournier were a veritable revelation: it was the first time they had heard absence monitoring be discussed so effectively and clearly.... [W]e sincerely wish that Mr. Fournier's uniformization of absence monitoring methods be carried out.... [W]ithout a doubt the commissioners present will be inspired by [his] description and the methods advocated when they will have to deal with absence monitoring.[144]

This achievement is even more remarkable given that the FCS was officially opposed to any intervention by the federal government in education matters.

The joint work could not have been possible without the support of the main guarantors of the school boards' autonomy, the province's bishops. On the occasion of their annual visit to each parish, the bishops met the members of the school boards, whom they asked to increase school attendance and to maintain contact with the Quebec Regional Office. "Every single one expresses his admiration for what the Department has been doing in the field of school attendance," the head of family allowances in Québec declared in 1956.[145] Further, the allowances permitted the encouragement of regular attendance and attendance in places where the Compulsory School Attendance Act was having little effect: private schools, Native reserves, and territories not organized into school boards.[146] Lastly, the federal officials undertook a campaign to educate parents—a more systematic plan than the one implemented by Godbout's government—with the insertion of a leaflet into the cheque envelopes that reminded parents of their duty when school began again in the fall.[147]

A comparable adventure occurred in the case of orphans. The federal program succeeded in encouraging the creation of child-placement agencies while permitting the Church to maintain an important role in their development. They received the support of the province's first social workers, religious reformists, and Catholic administrators more concerned with solving the institutions' financial problems than conserving the exclusive territory over dependant childhood, and the secret support of the provincial reformist officials. Over fifteen years family allowances employees carried out the changes Adélard Godbout had wanted in 1944. At the end of 1950, they were able to invite the ecclesiastical authorities to the table and to plan the diocesan placement agencies, which would employ social workers. In 1951, twelve of the organizations were in existence already and the director of the QRO was able to declare: "It is very noticeable in practically all areas of the Province of Québec that agencies are being organized to meet the demands and needs in the Child Welfare Field. This is widely due to Family Allowances and the constant work of the authorities of our Department in Ottawa and [their] representatives at the regional level."[148] It is possible that increased rates of federal income tax helped bring the church under federal influence: indeed, the advance of federal tax was making it more difficult to collect charity from the rich, according to private welfare agencies. Besides, influenced by the ideas of Anglo-Canadian social workers, the Family Allowances Act became one of the major means of professionalizing the protection of children and one of the main factors in the expansion of social work in the province.[149]

Following a conflict over jurisdiction, the provincial State had abdicated its education and care responsibilities, creating a hole that the federal State rushed to fill. The moment Duplessis was no longer interested in the Compulsory School Attendance Act, the decentralized character of the measure, whose implementation had already slowed under Godbout, favoured a much more vigorous application. In short, with regard to the federal officials from the Québec Family Allowances Office, we can easily talk about an "administrative revenge" against Duplessis' obstruction policy.[150] In 1951, the DNHW concluded that the government's egalitarian and centralizing objectives had been reached:

> Each month, since the establishment of these allowances, we have given parents…sums which, among other benefits, have ensured more educational opportunities than ever before.…I maintain that contributing to teaching with the constitutional means at our disposal, family allowances provide us with the best possible means to increase and equalize the opportunities to be educated in Canada.[151]

In short, Adélard Godbout and Mackenzie King accomplished considerable changes in their respective States. The professionalization of employees and the production of homogeneous statistics authorized a movement extending and centralizing public institutions. From then on, the federal government maintained monthly contact with Canadian families. Poorer in expertise and in money, Adélard Godbout's brief administration succeeded in laying the foundation for a more professional organization of primary education in the province, one at least solid enough that once Maurice Duplessis had returned to power with his more personalized management style, officials continued Godbout's work.

Nevertheless, the scientific knowledge connected with public administrations bore the signs of officials' social origins. The data, which were meant to attract and conserve the support of the economic elite by convincing them of the effectiveness and profitability of the new programs—that is, those concerning the financial and technical aspects of public institutions—received the lion's share of attention.[152] As for the information linked to the monitoring of delinquent families, it was the focus of very precise attention and led to intrusions in families more serious than early political debates had ever suggested.

This process was not without its failures. Godbout's centralization ardour was compromised by the state of the school apparatus he had inherited, by the explosion of school population, and by the the loss of the provincial elections of 1944. He had himself contributed to the birth of some of the difficulties by exhibiting a budgetary conservatism meant to please the economic elite and the federal government that denied him the financial means to incite the educational personnel to perform and new tasks to help poor parents materially. He also harboured a certain respect for the more rigid preoccupations of the Catholic Church and an accommodating attitude towards the central government's interference in provincial jurisdictions. Québec also demonstrated a delay in the training of social-science experts that Godbout could not recover alone and more generally, the war favoured the development of federal administration. Furthermore, large local civil-service offices contested the legitimacy of centralization pressures. The federal State had a great deal of trouble circumventing the provincial State, and the latter faced school boards drawing strength not only from their good knowledge of school families and the local elite but also from the interest that certain concurrent powers had to keep local institutions in place: the Catholic Church, which worried about preventing the secularization of teaching, and the federal government itself.

Whatever the problems, the adopted laws well and truly permitted the institution of "a series of routine institutional practices of a neutral, natural, and evident appearance, which presented themselves as the legitimate means of administration" of the province and of the country.[153]

3

The Significance of Children's Universal Rights

Official Views on Poverty and the Family

Compulsory education and family allowances marked the arrival of the language of universal rights in legislation and institutions. Within such a system, where laws address the population as a whole, rather than an underprivileged group, the work of "social control" would give way to "regulation" by norms.[1] This chapter offers a moment to pause in the study of government officials and employees, to analyze the significance they attributed to children's rights, to see how exactly this notion represented a change of public norms, and to identify its relation to a number of ideological traditions. This chapter also seeks to understand the conflicts and alliances accompanying the construction, the contestation, and the solidification of the norms' meaning.

Poverty and Collective Responsibility

If the choice to bring the first universal social security program to the country for young people had appeared to be particularly enticing to wartime officials struggling with another set of difficulties, it was because in a number of population sectors, the idea of increasing aid to children carried a large degree of legitimacy. On one hand, it implied a concept of equality, according to which "the *conditions of departure* for competing individuals [should be] equal."[2] A speech by Mackenzie King aimed at convincing his cabinet of the necessity of creating a universal allowances system provides proof of this meritocratic ideal: "I thought the Creator intended that all persons born should have equal opportunities. Equal opportunity started in the days of infancy and the first thing, at least, was to see that the children got the essentials of life...."[3] In a preliminary work on the same program, the officials of the Department of Finance, aiming

Notes to chapter 3 start on p. 229.

Figures 4 (above) and 5 (opposite). The federal government took up one of the Canadian reformists' ideas: to found equality projects focused on children.

Sources: Canada, DNHW, *Santé et Bien-être au Canada*, 3, 10 (July 1948, supplement on family allowances), p. 1; ABRQ, 40-9, vol. 1, *Family Allowances and Income Tax* (undated, publicity insert sent to parents), 4. (Reproduced with the permission of the University of Ottawa and the Department of Public Works and Government Services Canada, 1997.)

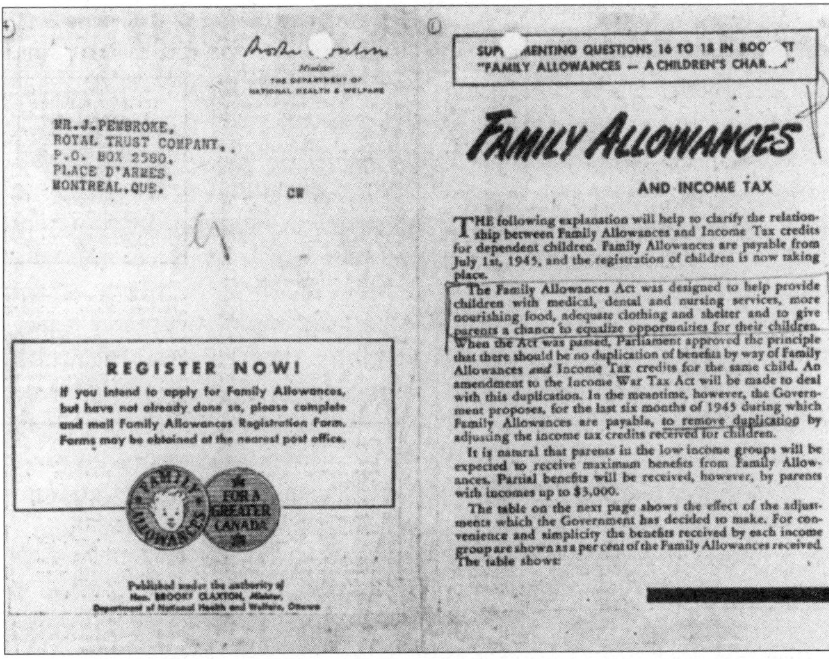

Minister
THE DEPARTMENT OF
NATIONAL HEALTH & WELFARE

MR. J. PEMBROKE,
ROYAL TRUST COMPANY,
P.O. BOX 2580,
PLACE D'ARMES,
MONTREAL, QUE.

REGISTER NOW!

If you intend to apply for Family Allowances, but have not already done so, please complete and mail Family Allowances Registration Form. Forms may be obtained at the nearest post office.

FAMILY ALLOWANCES

FOR A GREATER CANADA

Published under the authority of Hon. BROOKE CLAXTON, Minister, Department of National Health and Welfare, Ottawa

SUP[illegible]MENTING QUESTIONS 16 TO 18 IN BOO[illegible]T "FAMILY ALLOWANCES — A CHILDREN'S CHAR[illegible]"

FAMILY ALLOWANCES

AND INCOME TAX

THE following explanation will help to clarify the relationship between Family Allowances and Income Tax credits for dependent children. Family Allowances are payable from July 1st, 1945, and the registration of children is now taking place.

The Family Allowances Act was designed to help provide children with medical, dental and nursing services, more nourishing food, adequate clothing and shelter and to give parents a chance to equalize opportunities for their children. When the Act was passed, Parliament approved the principle that there should be no duplication of benefits by way of Family Allowances *and* Income Tax credits for the same child. An amendment to the Income War Tax Act will be made to deal with this duplication. In the meantime, however, the Government proposes, for the last six months of 1945 during which Family Allowances are payable, to remove duplication by adjusting the income tax credits received for children.

It is natural that parents in the low income groups will be expected to receive maximum benefits from Family Allowances. Partial benefits will be received, however, by parents with incomes up to $3,000.

The table on the next page shows the effect of the adjustments which the Government has decided to make. For convenience and simplicity the benefits received by each income group are shown as a per cent of the Family Allowances received. The table shows:

to make the population and the cabinet accept a policy they saw as essential to the stability of the post-war economy, were also of the opinion that the program could "allow even one Canadian Milton, Pasteur or Edison to realize the possibilities that might otherwise have been frustrated by the accident of his father's income."[4] Once the program had been launched, the designers from the Information Service at the Department of National Health and Welfare (DNHW) capitalized on this connection between the country's vitality and the expansion of a child's future possibilities in illustrations such as those in figures 4 and 5.

The notion of carrying the promises of equality forward for the next generation had been, for the preceding half-century, at the centre of the movement behind public health campaigns as well as movements to safeguard children. The joint declaration from fifty of the province's public bodies, which met in February 1944 at the invitation of the Ligue de la jeunesse féminine, demonstrates how widespread this point of view had become: "The problems created by the war and the changes in lifestyle, particularly in larger centres, have become increasingly difficult. Childhood does not escape these either and those individuals interested in social organizations turn to them more and more."[5] These reformists' interest in children was the result of a variety of concerns. First, there was a very real medical emergency in that many of the most dangerous illnesses were affecting children.[6] This problem was connected to a biological fact: since children are not as strong as adults, and since their bodies are still developing, work that was too taxing ran the risk of affecting their future health; their fragility in fact constituted the oldest argument against juvenile labour. Finally, this concern for children proceeded from the need to compensate for the loss of lives during wartime, which was greater among young people.

The promotion of economic rights for all children was the direct legacy of this movement for child welfare. By taking responsibility for the health of destitute children, professionals, volunteers, and officials had started on the path to something greater. Normally opposed to the State's direct intervention, many had come to see that the improvement of children's health required a struggle against poverty. The head of pediatrics at Montréal's Sainte-Justine hospital, Gaston Lapierre, explained as much:

> For many, the lack of funds prevents the establishment of adequate diets for children. Eloquent voices can give as many talks on calories and vitamins as they want, but it will do no good if we haven't the means to buy oranges, cod liver oil, vegetables, milk, enough eggs, etc. These talks will most often be commended by those with full bellies, and life will go on for the poverty-stricken. Special allowances would be necessary to fulfill the goals of the conferences.[7]

The mandatory vaccination campaign and the provincial needy mothers' allowance programs begun in the early 1920s were early stages of this process.

The Depression of the 1930s had jeopardized this movement, however, by cutting back budgets and reserving the little money available for emergency measures. But the Second World War would help resume these revisions. In fact, medical examinations of soldiers in 1939 had uncovered the poor state of Canadian health. In 1942, the armed forces had declared 27 per cent of conscripts unfit for service because of their poor state of health. Two years later, the percentage had increased to 52 per cent.[8] Twenty years after the statistics on the Great War recruits had first revealed these problems, it was agreed that subsequent campaigns centred on the change and prevention of bad hygiene habits had failed. The Governor General of Canada alluded directly to this history when he announced the family allowances program in the 1944 inaugural address to the House of Commons:

> During the current war, the army's examining doctors have found that in no uncertain terms the number of young people unfit for military serv-

> ice was considerably higher in poor and working classes than [in] wealthier families. Family allowances and social security will correct a social inequality suffered the most by children from poor families, and will provide the means to grow physically and morally for these little beings, to whom fate has not been generous.[9]

Aside from these meritocratic elements, another "requirement for equality" came into play, which helps to explain the emphasis on children: a moral concern for the poor "involuntarily out of work," even among those who took inequalities of income for granted. Even among those who "reject[ed morality] in the sphere of private life," there often existed a parallel belief in a "moral reserve meant to supply the [political] system, coming from religion, family, and charitable organizations."[10] The prevalence of this "philanthropic" spirit explains for the most part why the first social programs were dedicated to those who were clearly poor in spite of themselves, such as widows and children. Conservative historian Robert Rumilly's 1968 writings on Maurice Duplessis' intentions regarding youth are typical: "it concerns children: for him, it is irresistible. Skepticism—for some scornful bitterness—which generates commerce with other men, just like us, is tempered, for this old boy, by a constantly renewed illusion about childhood, presumed to be innocent."[11] The 1943 report on women and reconstruction ordered by the cabinet gave priority to children's aid with a comparable rationalization:

> The reconstruction policies of the government must adequately protect from want those individuals who are unable to obtain gainful employment through no fault of their own and, as an integral measure of social security in the broadest sense, the children of Canada should be protected from malnutrition and inadequate educational opportunities.... To strive for more would unduly complicate the problem: to content ourselves with less would belie the professions of faith embodied in the Atlantic charter and all the pronouncements that have followed it.[12]

But family allowances and free and compulsory schooling did more than implement old meritocratic and philanthropic notions. The authors of the universal social policies distinguished themselves from their predecessors by admitting that economic difficulties beyond the control of many healthy adults could prevent them from ensuring their children with a minimum of welfare and education. We have seen that the labour organizations had forced the federal officials into a partial acceptance of the idea that economic conditions were responsible for poverty, underlining the impossibility of raising children on wartime wages, where the levels were established by the State. Similarly, reporting on the difficulty of feeding a large family on a self-sufficient farm, small farmers had led provincial clerks to accept the idea that the evolution of the economy and general demography, rather than faults of individuals, had been responsible for the rural exodus. Moreover, the particular circumstances of the war, which meant that thousands of soldiers' families were deprived of their usual income because of the most legitimate motives of all, contributed to the recognition of poverty's structural dimension by the elite.[13] By 1944, the government had come to think that the population would accept nothing less than universal aid policies:

> We soon found an increasing resistance on the part of the public to the idea that any person, social worker or not, should presume to decide who is a deserving case and who isn't a deserving case. We got to the stage where people began to demand that legislation be written down in specific terms to provide as a matter of right certain benefits to people under clearly defined conditions that were prescribed in the law rather than left to the judgment of some individual.[14]

The idea of collective responsibility for the economic conditions of adults was making some headway and, with it, the proposition that the State should guarantee equal opportunity. "If need is not the individual's fault but the fault of the industrial system," declared Mackenzie King in the House during the debates on family allowances, "the State must overcome it one way or another."[15] In Ottawa, the shift of dominant ideas on the causes of poverty was made clearer during a debate on modes of payment. The Liberals extolled the merits of a program offered to all citizens without the State first judging the morality of the beneficiaries, while, in the view of the Conservatives, the government could not be sure that the allowances would be spent on children. There were some members of the federal cabinet who believed that the cash allowances would encourage laziness and have a counter-effect on war-production efficiency. This belief was not warranted, according to the defenders of cash allowances, because immoral and lazy parents were a very small minority. Universal allowances to soldiers' families had demonstrated that the mothers were trustworthy.[16]

The fact that two groups of the population who hadn't the right to vote had been excluded from the new citizenship benefits, confirms that the recognition of the structural causes of poverty could largely be traced back to electioneering. A minority of the "nomad Indians," and the majority of the "Eskimos," would receive their payments in kind until 1953. The treatment of the First Nations and the Inuit was denounced by the Selkirk, Manitoba, Co-operative Commonwealth Federation (CCF) MP, who in his plea invoked their status as the first Canadian inhabitants and their participation in the armed forces to claim their right to full citizenship: "If these men are fighting for us, they should be able to receive this money at the post office or where it will be paid without having to go through the Indians' agents.... The Indian is a Canadian in the very sense of the word. He is the real Canadian. We will certainly not pay an allowance to someone else if he is good enough to go fighting."[17] But the government explained that only half of Native children received direct cash allowances, as "all the Indians...do [not have] the same degree of intelligence and it would be useless to issue a cheque to people who could not cash it."[18] Minister of National Health and Welfare Brooke Claxton declared that the payments in kind had an educational role. The education he referred to was an initiation into the consumer products of white society desired by the head of Indian Affairs Branch. Equal treatment of Natives was further hampered by the fact the Branch was jealous of its privileges and guarded its assimilation projects closely. The list of authorized objects spoke for itself: powdered milk and baby cereal were practically obligatory, while other alimentary products had to be introduced gradually by the agents responsible for the distribution of the allowances to the First Nations populations. The authorization of children's clothing followed. Sending cash allowances would depend on the "degree of responsibility exercised by the parents."[19]

The Family Allowances Act subjected newly arrived immigrants to a three-year residence clause. "We believed," explained the minister of justice when the policy was adopted, "that strangers should not benefit from the allowances simply by having crossed our borders. A certain amount of time must pass as proof of their intention to stay in our country."[20] This position angered some members of parliament, who thought that paying the allowances shortly after the immigrants' arrival would help to attract and keep them in Canada.[21]

Québec's Compulsory School Attendance Act also demonstrated the progression of the idea of the collective responsibility for poverty. Many conservatives were still pushing the idea that parents' apathy and their desire for immediate material gain explained why children were leaving school: "The easy jobs offered to boys and girls by businesses and the war industry are a tempting and grievous bait, but should not let parents forget the greater need of ensuring their children's education."[22]

However, the Liberal government was now stating that there were more general economic causes for school desertion and that it was the State's responsibility to put an end to the phenomenon. Like their colleagues from public health campaigns discussed earlier, many reformists from the education field had prepared the groundwork for this effort, including instructor Joseph P. Poulin, who had led an inquiry examining the trend of playing truant in a Montréal working-class neighbourhood in 1942:

> These children do not leave school out of capriciousness, not even less out of pleasure-seeking, but simply out of necessity.... [The] parents who do not see the value of school because they themselves were not able to benefit from it encourage their children to begin work at a tender age...make up a small part of them. Most of them, on the contrary, wish to give their children a more complete education and it is only forced by inhumane living conditions that they regretfully consent to take their children out of school. Thus it is not fair to blame them lightly.[23]

In short, at the heart of the two legislative bodies, the evolution of egalitarian philanthropy and meritocratic traditions led to projects for equality among adults for which only the State could be responsible. Few were ready to adopt the idea of "equality of outcomes." Rather the notion of children's rights had offered a way out to officials desiring to avoid the question of adults' economic rights brought up by labour unions or that of "workers' rights" brought up by the most radical of Social Catholics. However reduced, this project of equality of chances now allowed for systematic efforts to reduce the inequalities between children and, to this end, to alleviate the inequalities between the adults who were their parents.

The Question of Children's Autonomy

Childhood is a difficult subject to discuss, as opinions on the young involve ideological quarrels between adults that stretch far beyond the issues of children's fate.[24] With this caveat in mind, it remains possible to examine significant ideological changes relating to childhood in conjunction with the new laws. The notion of children's rights brought about an increase in individual sovereignty of youths. It marked a point of emancipation, from childhood on, of a "core of consciousness and will."[25] The idea of awarding children greater autonomy came in turn, from new psychological trends that emphasized identity problems resulting from children's development to explain social behaviour. These schools had turned their attention away from exceptional children and towards the normal ones. Meanwhile, during the 1930s, the majority of North American education theorists had come to focus on what they called the "whole child"; recognizing "individual differences," they favoured attention to children over attention to subject matters."[26] In the same spirit, many school inspectors who had been invited to speak on the state of Québec school attendance in 1942 considered children as individuals with tastes, emotions, aptitudes, and individual needs: if they left school or attended irregularly, it was because they "lacked interest"; the fault was thus of "overloaded and badly adapted programs," the "uniform mold," and "discipline of adults."[27]

Taking up these views in the 1943 *Instructions concernant le Loi de fréquentation scolaire obligatoire,* the Superintendent of Public Instruction (SPI), Victor Doré, invited elementary-school teachers to "adapt the work to the abilities and characteristics of each student." As we have seen, teachers had to "keep children so interested in school work that they would not want to miss a single day." A new program, whose development was intimately linked to the adoption of the principle of compulsory education by the Catholic Committee to the Public Instruction Council (CCPIC), had in practice the same philosophy.[28] Based on the same image of children with their own individual tastes and interests, city reformists had called for career advice for students in transition from school to work force, with the aim of obtaining for them an attractive first job. Indeed, the Ligue ouvrière catholique (LOC) reacted with indignation when it learned, through its own poll of workers, that "54% of female workers, 58% of male workers [had] started working in a situation which carried no appeal for them whatsoever."[29] Lastly, the artists who created the yearly "back to school" leaflets that would accompany the August family allowances cheque for over a decade, represented these new doctrines with a depiction of children running joyfully towards school (see figure 6).

By acknowledging each child's "particularity," or certain independence, political leaders and, behind them, numerous professional groups eroded the notion of children's submission to their parents. In doing so they were also increasing their own potential for domination. It was not the first time the idea of children with their own interests had been used to set aside the principle of the father's authority. Since the beginning of the century, the promotion of children's rights had been used to further social workers' hold over troubled youth in Canada and the United States. In the early 1920s, for example, the League of Nations had adopted a Declaration of the Rights of Children, which the Canadian Council on Child Welfare, the bastion for the development of social work in Canada that had close links to the League, had hastened to circulate throughout the country.[30] But the children concerned did not constitute the majority. The categories of children—abandoned, delinquent, or industrial labourers—pointed to a group of parents who, in principle, had already lost a considerable part of their legitimate authority by not fully exercising their responsibilities.

With compulsory education and family allowances, the rhetoric of children's rights applied to all parents, which rendered the issue of their prerogatives more delicate. To bypass the principle of the father's authority while using the language of liberal democracy, legislators put forward the idea of children's consent. It was a practical fiction as children only obtained

Figure 6. The image of children running towards school of their own free will represented the attribution of more autonomy to youth while circumventing tricky questions about their playing hooky and the punishment of parents who did not want to conform to the new norms.

Source: ABRQ, 8-0, vol. 2, Canada, DNHW, leaflet inserted in the envelopes containing family allowance cheques. (Reproduced with the permission of the University of Ottawa and the Department of Public Works and Government Services Canada, 1997.)

their "political rights" progressively, and rarely participated in associations that would convey their demands to public authorities. They had not taken part in the establishment of their new rights and could not verify that they were enforced.[31] Thus the progress made in the recognition of children's individual sovereignty brought about decreased parental protection, making it possible for "a continuous growth of endeavours aiming at the target thus made prominent."[32]

This process of isolating children in the public sphere corresponded with an internal isolation process, an emerging perspective of childhood not in control of its own actions. The idea that children were responsible for their own morality and religion had progressively faded since the eighteenth century.[33] The movements to protect abandoned children of the early twentieth century had been the first to insist that children not carry the responsibility for their own condition; similarly, Canadian law on delinquent children had created the image of a poorly educated child in need of help and encouragement. The professionals of the first few decades of the twentieth century had given this theory a new scope by presenting themselves as experts on normal childhood. In fact, doctors had started to change the concepts of infant consciousness by using at once the exclusivity of their practices, the State's propaganda channels, and the optional public health programs. They had provided children with a certain individual will—they talked about bringing children to "an intelligent understanding of acceptable behaviours" while reducing the expanse of their free will to a minimum: to mothers, they suggested training techniques and definite habits that would prevent children from being exposed to any other way of conducting themselves. Confronted with studies which from the 1930s on, however, connected the rise of European fascism with similar parenting methods, they had entrusted mothers with the additional task of distinguishing between their children's legitimate awareness of their interests and their false instincts.[34]

The effect of the advent of children's universal rights was to increase the tension between emancipation and the growth of "intimate servitude." On one hand, the universal laws gave experts on normal childhood the legal means to reach all the country's children. On the other hand, they submitted these professionals to a State control they had until then eagerly attempted to avoid. This meeting of experts' advice with democratic requirements is perhaps not without relation to the temperance of the disciplinary regime mothers were taught to impose on the children we observe during the 1940s, a temperance that had been long hoped for in many sectors of Canadian society.[35] It is also possible that their ambition "to move completely outside of society to ensure a complete hold over it" had led the doctors to research universal means only the Welfare State could provide. To be able to employ these means, however, they would have reluctantly accepted a measure of democratic responsibility that obliged them to renounce in part the authoritarianism of their relationship with the mothers and the authoritarianism of the parent–child relationship they advocated.

Though weakened, the postulate of children's irresponsibility had not disappeared completely from official plans, and it slowed the actual advance of youths' individual sovereignty. Ideal children would be those who would submit to their parents and the requirements of school authorities on their own. They should not do as they pleased, as was the case with the boy the

Juvenile Court's psychiatrist lamented had "[an] obvious will of conducting his own affairs in his own way." Similarly they should not be too influenced by their friends. Spare time spent without supervision seemed especially dangerous, and the court repeatedly recommended that children participate in organized clubs and be registered in summer camp programs.[36]

The old official belief, stating that poor children left to their own devices would tend to follow the easier path, outlived the arrival of universal rights. The images of less-fortunate children preferring simple pleasures to an extended education continued to flourish. Here, for example, is the December 1943 declaration of the Canadian National Association for Advancement in Education on the growth of juvenile labour during the war: "Regardless of school-leaving age requirements, many boys and girls are giving up their studies to take jobs that are lucrative now but which will prove blind alleys in the future. With the return of peace time conditions these young people will hardly be disposed to submit again to the discipline of school life in order to complete their education."[37] The theory that the poor children would be inclined to seek out immediate gratification while children from more affluent families understood that they should save such pleasures for later in life received a new impetus from North American sociologists who advanced the idea of a "culture of poverty." As with legislators, they had a tendency to minimize the size of material advantages offered straightaway to wealthier children, who grew up in environments affluent enough to allow them to put off their search for a paid job until later in life.[38]

The Autonomy of Poor Parents

From the moment of their institution, universal children's rights encompassed ambiguities with significant consequences for adults. The same principles that would help families materially would justify actions limiting their choices and priorities.[39] Suspicious attitudes towards poor parents had not disappeared, but to deprive individuals of the new benefits of citizenship and to conserve a certain legitimacy, it would be necessary to create a series of justifications. At the heart of the new governmental institutions, the supporters of the idea of less-fortunate parents' faulty morality created a new basis from which they continued to shake the solidity of universal economic rights. Monitoring policies and old regulations could then resurface while new exclusion techniques emerged.

From the start, the decision to respond to the trade unions' demands on behalf of the most poorly paid workers with a public law directed at all of "families" constituted a limitation to promises of equal rights. To be sure, as we have seen, the unions had justified their demands for higher wages in war factories on the inadequacy of the lowest wages to raise a family. But the officials had deflected the attention away from disadvantaged workers to an undifferentiated group of "parents." The new economic advantages were thus accompanied with an innovation of rhetoric. Officials took the initiative to depict the image of universal parents not clearly belonging to any socio-economic class, with which few citizens had chosen to identify themselves in the first place. By "building a public" of isolated individuals, officials had been able to abandon, in principle, the field of labour relations.

At once liberated and isolated by the new government standards, it was now possible for parents to become the target for "endeavours of transformation." In official thinking, the diagnosis of "ignorance" in normal parents replaced that of the lack of morality in poor parents. The members of Adélard Godbout's cabinet attributed most of the school attendance problems to parents' own lack of education. The provincial secretary believed such ignorance to be more alarming than the families' economic situation and hoped that efforts to persuade, by truancy officers and parents' associations, together with statistics on children's success according to the level of their education, would open the parents' eyes to their duties. Even once converted to the principle of compulsory education, the CCPIC continued to believe that the Compulsory School Attendance Act's main objective should be to "conquer parents' apathy.... Easy jobs available to boys and girls in businesses and in the war industry are a grievous temptation, and should not allow parents to forget the greater need to provide their children with a suitable education."[40] The SPI went further: "the education of the public" would be a primary task of the political leaders. "To avoid being ineffective," he promised from the beginning, "the required legislation [should] be at the origins of a relatively smooth flexibility. With time and with as much goodwill as possible, it will finish by a full achievement of its goal."[41] His directives to the new truancy officers could be summed up in the following directive: they would act as social workers, not police, and they would use persuasion above all.[42]

Federal authorities also attached a great deal of importance to the idea of parents' ignorance. The education campaign led by way of the brochures inserted in the family allowances cheques is proof of this. There were no longer any preliminary surveys of the claimants' morality, but in the eyes of the members of cabinet, the payment of allowances was not sufficient in itself to confer new economic rights on children. "We would like to do everything possible to incite parents to spend this money on children as much as possible," declared Minister Brooke Claxton. He relied on the opinion of the Canadian Council of Child Welfare that the supervision of spending was a fundamental condition for ensuring the success of family allowances.[43] In Ottawa as in Québec, officials were, however, careful to separate themselves from the monitoring policies of before, and an education campaign geared towards family allowances beneficiaries would replace older techniques of family supervision and policing.[44] Within intermediary institutions, school inspectors, elementary school teachers, and experts also agreed on the need to make parents "better understand" their obligations.[45]

The consensus on this diagnosis of ignorance in parents encompassed a variety of contradictory opinions. Socialist members of parliament, for example, believed that many parents were not ill intentioned but ill informed: "In cases where the amount of family allowances is not spent judiciously,..." affirmed Dorise Nielsen, "it will not be due to an intentional waste by the beneficiary, but rather a lack of judgment managing the sum, using it for the child's most pressing needs."[46] The attitude of officials also found support from groups representing recipients, such as the Union des cultivateurs catholiques (UCC), the Confédération des travailleurs catholiques du Canada (CTCC), and women's groups.[47]

The authors of informational material for parents attempted to maintain the undifferentiated image of parents, while approaching the question of the unequal standard of living by painting enticing pictures of social mobility. *You and Your Family,* a guide for family allowances beneficiaries published in 1949, encouraged poor households to increase their standard of living by saving money. The publication considered budgetary planning as a remedy for poverty: "It may mean that you do without new shoes for another month, or that the family eats more baked beans and less meat, but somehow find the money within your means for entertainment and do not let the children do without something they really need just to make this extravagance possible."[48] The Québec Regional Office for Family Allowances (QRO) even created savings tables for parents that presented the sum they would need to save on a regular basis to afford higher education for their children.[49] Thus the authors of the informational material related, in practical ways, the universality of allowance amounts to equal opportunity in education.

Conversely, propaganda warned affluent families that their fate could become similar to that of the disadvantaged families. It indicated that middle classes were not safe from periods of economic uncertainty. Information services used a 1937–38 survey conducted by the Dominion Bureau of Statistics on family incomes and spending that determined anyone could suffer from malnutrition to explain that its nutritional advice concerned all families.[50] By emphasizing the downward direction of social mobility, the language of normalcy also contributed to the isolation of middle-class parents.

Once this equality of opportunity had been established, governmental propaganda aimed at parents would emphasize recommendations for all. The brochures inserted in the family allowances envelopes entrusted parents with teaching moderation and foresight to their own children. They encouraged habits of planned consumption with the progressive management of allowances as children grew older. Having learned that "things have value and that dolls' carriages and baseball bats, chesterfields and motor cars do not grow on trees... [s]ome one has to earn them," young citizens would be ready to prepare their own family budgets one day.[51] Public authorities appeared to rate this ability among the most important of those required to build a family, as demonstrated in figure 7. By equating economic rights with money management, the government was bringing citizenship and consumption together, in a way that refers to the major role the Canadian Manufacturers' Association and the Bank of Canada had played in the adoption of the Family Allowances Act discussed earlier.[52]

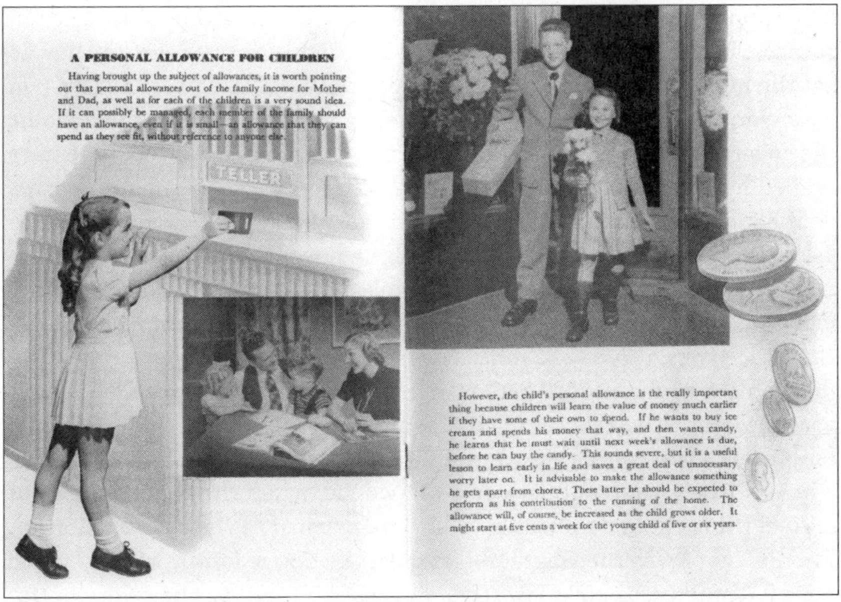
A PERSONAL ALLOWANCE FOR CHILDREN

Having brought up the subject of allowances, it is worth pointing out that personal allowances out of the family income for Mother and Dad, as well as for each of the children is a very sound idea. If it can possibly be managed, each member of the family should have an allowance, even if it is small—an allowance that they can spend as they see fit, without reference to anyone else.

However, the child's personal allowance is the really important thing because children will learn the value of money much earlier if they have some of their own to spend. If he wants to buy ice cream and spends his money that way, and then wants candy, he learns that he must wait until next week's allowance is due, before he can buy the candy. This sounds severe, but it is a useful lesson to learn early in life and saves a great deal of unnecessary worry later on. It is advisable to make the allowance something he gets apart from chores. These latter he should be expected to perform as his contribution to the running of the home. The allowance will, of course, be increased as the child grows older. It might start at five cents a week for the young child of five or six years.

Figure 7. Educating children of all classes about consumption according to the federal State: a way out of poverty or, conversely, a way to avoid a fall in social status.

Source: NAC, Official Publications, National Library of Canada negative NL15300, Canada, DNHW, *You and Your Family* (Ottawa: King's Printer, 1949), 24–25. (Reproduced with the permison of Department of Public Works and Government Services Canada, 1997.)

The problem of what happened to the children's new rights in situations of extreme poverty was circumvented. The Welfare State's propaganda took these rights for granted. It depicted uniform children, never showing differences in their means, while the charitable organizations or previous means-tested programs had used an abundance of images of poor children. Figures 8 and 9 illustrate these types of attitudes.[53]

For the same reasons, the DNHW's Information Service avoided using images of older children. Favouring images of infants, it turned attention away from the economic tensions that arose from the new norms of transition between school and work. The popularized version of the family allowances rules for new parents turned the ban on child labour into a joke with the introduction of a fictive family, the Archibalds: "It was pointed out that if a child wanted to leave school in order to earn a wage or a salary, she would not get the allowance. (Mr. and Mrs. Archibald were a little amused at reading this as they look at their week old child! The idea of her prancing about earning her living seemed very remote!)"[54]

State imagery, nevertheless, accepted the idea of a certain diversity between parents' means. The Information Service's purchasing suggestions sent to parents established a distinction between lower-income households and others. Each should use the allowances according to its circumstances. Families experiencing economic difficulties were shown "how to get the most value out of your family allowances," how to spend the sum wisely, and "how to get more for your money." For the benefit of this group, the government accentuated the importance of goods that were necessary immediately as well as occasional urgent spending, such as doctor visits, dentist appointments, and medicine. In contrast, the education campaign asked more affluent families to invest the new "income supplement" in an enrichment of family life with piano lessons, bicycles, sporting equipment, or summer camp registration.[55] One of the government's brochures, *En parlant des allocations familiales,* introduced the reader to the Gagnier family, which used the allowances to give their children vitamin D vaccinations, to buy skates for their son Jean, and to send their daughter Suzanne to the country for a holiday. Their neighbour, widow Leduc, needed "every penny of her son's allowance; when the cheque does not arrive, things get complicated"—she spent most of the sum on clothes. Finally, there was the Gagniers' friends, the Sauvé family, which "could not give much of their allowances to these things," as they were exclusively concerned with their children's development and spent the money on milk, school supplies for the oldest girl, dentist appointments, and only rarely on piano lessons for their talented son (see figure 10).[56] Below the surface of this rhetoric of difference, it is evident that the authors of the

Figures 8 and 9. From the image of the destitute children of selective programs and private charitable organizations to the normal children of universal programs.

Sources: *La Presse*, 25 February 1944, p. 19; NAC, Official Publications (image from the NFB), National Library of Canada negative NL15302, Canada, DNHW, *Allocations familiales: Charte de l'enfance* (Ottawa: King's Printer, 1945–1946). (Reproduced with the permission of *La Presse* and the Department of Public Works and Government Services Canada, 1997.)

Figure 10. Concerned with maintaining their legitimacy in the eyes of the beneficiaries, the family allowance propagandists were prepared to recognize a certain diversity in household revenues. The contrast in experiences between the fictive families (Gagnier, Sauvé, and the widow Leduc) moved away from the usual stereotypical representations, without including poorer families.

Source: ABRQ, vol. 1, Canada, DNHW, *En parlant des allocations familiales* (Ottawa: King's Printer, 1950), 12, 13, 17. (Reproduced with the permission of the Department of Public Works and Government Services Canada, 1997.)

educational brochures were seeking to capture an audience by presenting families in situations similar to the readers' own.[57]

Besides such ambiguous education campaigns, the official adoption of the principle of universal children's rights justified a public project of unparalleled reach and character to locate and monitor the poor. At the provincial and federal levels, there was a common belief that to maintain the rights the State had just conferred upon children, parents needed to be supervised to allow the identification of guilty parties. "A government such as ours," wrote the head of the welfare section of the Québec Regional Office for Family Allowances in his 1955 annual report, "being in the position to 'peep in' [on] such a large number of families and put 'our thumb' on so many unhappy situations, can do a lot to assist Canadians to live a more useful and satisfying life."[58] Thus the egalitarianism "instituted a sort of *tutelage*" for the very people it was supposed to free.... "Close monitoring [would determine] the categories 'of those deserving' and permit the extension of what Alexis de Tocqueville called 'the immense and tutelary despotism' of public administration."[59]

The right to a minimum of education and welfare bore "a compulsory character in that the individuals for whom they [had been] created [did not have] the latitude to renounce them."[60] As a high provincial official explained in 1942, Western laws generally recognized that "parents [had not] the freedom to deprive their children of elementary education, and if they [attempted it] voluntarily, the State [had] the right to intervene and prevent this injustice."[61] Thus, "imposing a uniform rule [came with] a reduction of certain individuals' freedom of initiative"; one of the "expressions [of the egalitarian ideal came] very close to colliding with the others."[62]

Provincial legislators expected to find "parents deliberately denying their children an education" for "worthless reasons." They expected these adults to be creators of "false excuses and vain promises" who would refuse to make the necessary sacrifices. This justified the harsh dealings of the truancy officers. Victor Doré confirmed that these were rare cases and that he would show them no mercy. The policy, he wrote, "aims above all to protect school children and we must maintain them rigorously only in extreme cases in which the violation is a denial of justice for their children and for their rights to an education."[63]

The Family Allowances Act brought on numerous parental obligations as well. Registration in the program was optional, but the law established that parents who received the allowances were required to devote the cheque in its entirety to the care of their children. It conferred upon the DNHW the right to interrupt payment in the case of misuse. The leaflet *You and Your Family* was firm: "'There now,' said John to his wife, 'if anyone catches you buying a new hat with Mary Olivia's allowance, they may report you and then you won't get the allowance anymore.'"[64] The threat of suspension also applied to parents who took their children out of school before the province's required age, or to those who made their children work before the provinces required legal age. Regulating clauses, similar to those of the previous programs of needy mothers' allowances, had thus survived into the era of universal rights.

This tension inherent in the idea of equality was often overlooked by officials in the name of more pressing political and material concerns. Mackenzie King and Adélard Godbout had been wary of clearly defining the minimum they promised to poor children. Family allowances were kept at a lower level than the minimum foreseen in the reconstruction plans. Such restrictions were typical of the Liberals from the C.D. Howe school: Howe, like the Conservatives, believed that higher amounts could discourage parents from working or incite them to procreate for money. So did an official from the DNHW who declared during a radio program, "With the monthly cheque's low purchasing power, production [of children] will continue to be inspired by pleasure rather than profit."[65] This suspicion also manifested itself in the implementation of the law. The family allowances investigators were vested with discretionary powers, which they often used to the detriment of poor families. Social workers connected with the QRO were able to arbitrarily scrutinize the spending habits of families. In this way, a child who had no clothes to wear to school but many toys was suspect in their eyes.[66]

The Compulsory School Attendance Act's categories for monitoring truancy constituted a ragbag; it was difficult to distinguish a boundary between general economic difficulties and individual moral errors. "The illegal or abnormal causes [listed in the official forms were]: parents' negligence, refusal to attend, poverty, labour unauthorized by the officers, at home or outside; moving (exceeding the authorized length of time); other invalid reasons: travel, store purchases, illegitimate sickness, etc." Poverty was considered at once to be a legal cause for non-registration and an "abnormal" cause for absences, an inconsistency that revealed the diversity of the administrators' perspectives. In the view of Victor Doré, the level of federal family allowances was sufficient for sending children to school. Once the federal program was in place, he attempted to reinforce the monitoring of parents: "The Department…, until now, has exercised the greatest tolerance in order to make parents better understand the cause's worthiness; but at present, with all the good the family allowances bring to each family, no one will be excused for denying a child the education which is their right."[67]

The "negligent parents" category gave rise to numerous arbitrary deeds. In principle, it referred to "a family environment, or an individual state of mind or mentality, favouring laziness, dislike of study, the lack of discipline or assiduousness" beyond economic considerations.[68] In reality, a curious mix of a lack of concern and economic need were evident, as in this list of negligent situations compiled by the truancy officer from Sainte-Thérèse de Beauport:

> ...helping one's aunt, doing the laundry, watching the house, ironing, going to town to buy a coat, cording wood, helping at butchering, harvesting vegetables and potatoes when it is known that the parents are not farmers, plowing, uncle's commemorative funeral service, weddings (2 children missed two days of school to attend a wedding), going to town to buy clothes when they could have done it on Saturday, weekly holiday, refusal to attend, chopping wood in the case of an 11-year-old child, which is a bit much, the cold (when all the other children did not miss school), going to town to get a "perm," sleeping because the night before the child went to a wedding, toothache, earache.[69]

Moreover, the categories used by juvenile court officials left little room for economic explanations and for family structures that could prevent household members from adopting the legislators' desired attitudes. Among "unhealthy environments" were those in which material comforts were lacking due to sickness, an insufficient salary, a mother working outside the home, widowhood, or the father's absence, and few attempts were made to determine if the difficulties attributed to psychology had caused poverty or were the unhappy result of it. Their files rather mentioned "emotionally unstable" fathers and mothers "conducting themselves with questionable morality." Court officers also examined the parents' degree of authority and supervision, sometimes blaming them for their "immaturity." Inversely, parental "overprotection" was also a problem.[70] In the long run, the lack of systematic means to help poor parents probably helped to spread these forms of suspicion.

In August 1943, the superintendent of public instruction who believed it was the father's responsibility to ensure that his child attended school, inquired if there was any recourse to be taken against a child who refused to do so.[71] The juvenile court had initially been selected only as a means of bringing back to school those children who refused to go in spite of their parents' admonitions. "The judge could do little else but ground the child," confirmed the superintendent, "but it is probable that such a reprimand would leave an impression on the student and would lead them to respect the law."[72] But eventually contemporary principles for the rehabilitation of young delinquents would allow judges to remove children from their families, as did Judge Nicholson in Montreal: "The family is desperately poor and the three boys actually did not have sufficient clothing and food. They are not very much to blame for breaking school law…I felt obliged to send them to reform school so that they would have sufficient clothes and food and obtain education."[73] In this way, families who were prevented from respecting the law for economic reasons paid to access the minimum of education promised to all with the loss of their integrity.

In affirming that the State could act in "children's best interests," Premier Adélard Godbout distinguished himself from his successor Maurice Duplessis, who would declare that the "State [unduly] monopoliz[ed] the role of the family" since the parents had the right to be primary caregivers for their children.[74] Duplessis stood by the traditional Liberal notion that children's only political involvement was through their parents, who had at once to represent their children and to prepare them for their future role, by supervising a progressive learning of autonomy in a climate of protection.[75] He adhered to a doctrine that Rome had enforced up until the early twentieth century and that the province's upper clergy had maintained for even longer. Indeed, official Catholic ideology had long maintained a rigid opposition to the State's intervention based on the idea that only the father of family held immediate and direct rights over his children's education and welfare. The father then had to turn to the Church for help in fulfilling his duty. The Church also reserved direct rights over children because of the sacred relationship between parents and children. In return, the Church was responsible for ensuring that the schools carry out children's religious education. Until 1929, Catholic morality had not accepted that education could fall under the jurisdiction of civil rights. Only the domain of justice belonged to the State: "Education constitut[ing] a 'duty of charity' based on moral requirements, it could not be a 'duty of justice,' neither for the children themselves, nor for the society to which they belonged."[76] The papacy was opposed to parents delegating a portion of their rights to the State. The French and American Revolutions, together with the popularity of the left-wing secular movements of the nineteenth century, had led Rome to believe that the establishment of a secular State would bring about the end of Christianity.[77]

In the early 1930s, however, socio-economic changes had rendered compulsory education important enough in the Pope's eyes to prevail over his fear of secularization and to consider cultural and material minima as a matter of "justice": "The State can demand and consequently require that all citizens have a degree of cultural, moral and physical intellect which, considering the conditions of our time, is a veritable requirement for the common good."[78] The superintendent had to remind defenders of the older theology of this current position of the Pope. He hastened to ensure them that the intervention in public life would nevertheless respect the private domain and that far from wishing to abolish individual rights, the officials were about to help secure them.

In general, representatives from the poorest classes rarely took part in the debates concerning the frontier "between the encouragement of family autonomy and its limitation" created by universal rights.[79] There were a few exceptions. In the House of Commons, the CCF denounced the clauses of the Family Allowances Act linked to the regulation of families' morality: "It is an insult to the poor to continuously repeat that they will spend this money disorderly, in bars, at the movies or elsewhere."[80] The report on women and reconstruction also recalled that rich families had not been the subject of surveillance when tax deductions for children were established in 1919.[81]

Yet during the course of the debate on compulsory education, the leaders of Québec's international trade unions mentioned the threat of State monitoring of family practices only to deny its significance. By speaking of the "duty, so rewarding in the end, to force [one's] progeny to attend school until the age of 14," they were content to emphasize that generous educational and social policies announced by the officials should not be comprised by misplaced defences of the principle of individual rights.[82] The editorial writer of a daily paper with Liberal sympathies similarly turned the question of individual rights around: if parents were not opposed to school attendance, the punitive clauses were only there out of principle and should not be a cause for concern.[83]

Criticism came instead from conservative corners. For the elite fearing the policy's socializing character, Mackenzie King was careful to assure that the law still belonged to a liberal ethic. Federal politicians insisted that they would continue to recognize families' autonomy with the same tenacity as their provincial counterparts. Cash payments would ensure the parents' autonomy, a belief Mackenzie King's cabinet shared with Leonard Marsh:

> Canadians believe not only in the family, but in a strong measure of individuality. There must be reasonable leeway for parent's [*sic*] decision in the expenditure of the budget for their children. It is an impossible situation to imagine that all guidance and all services should be provided by non-family authorities. The virtue of a standard endowment of benefit in cash is that it becomes part of the normal family income, which is left to the parent to extend.[84]

One year after Marsh, Laval sociologists had defended the same opinion in their report to the Québec government on family allowances: cash payments had the advantage over payments in service or in kind of preserving the superiority of family services provided to children. Better yet, family allowances favoured parental initiative.[85] In short, in this reformist light, the inclusion of citizens' economic rights to the list of the State's responsibilities appeared to be an update of the liberal credo for individual responsibility rather than a step backwards for these same responsibilities.

Forced to refine his doctrine, Mackenzie King confirmed that he recognized for richer parents a right to protect their private lives that was not available to poorer families. Indeed, when members of the Opposition reminded him about tax deductions established in 1919 for children, with no corresponding scrutiny of family budgets, he answered, in a spirit the Conservatives would have trouble denouncing, that "citizens contributing to the public purse surely have the right to considerations which can not be claimed, at the very least in the same degree, to those who do not pay taxes."[86]

In the end, only the parents fulfilling their responsibilities regarding their children would enjoy the right of being trusted by the authors of universal social laws. In other words, to be the best guarantors of children's social and economic rights, parents had to have the same conception of "normal" parenting as the legislators. Parents shirking their responsibilities as educators for reasons deemed invalid by the official powers would be a small minority, but they could lose their prerogatives to the profit of the State. Organizations representing poorer families rarely took on the task of defending the integrity of families who were in the right. Thus, the officials, once they had succeeded in quieting the Conservatives' pleas in favour of parents' rights, were able to exclude considerations of political philosophy from the public discussions. In so doing, they had changed the stakes of political debates.

4

The Evolution of the Status of Children

Between the New Official Norms, Market Changes, and the Cultural World of Parents

Fathers, mothers, and children learned of the existence of the two new universal laws through the post, newspapers, radio, newsreels, displays, neighbours, and hospitals, and received news from school boards (which occasionally held special public meetings on church steps), school inspectors, and even school enumerators when the Compulsory School Attendance Act officially took effect.[1] The two Montréal school boards vaunted the legal provision's "benefits," its strong and far-reaching impact and, more generally, educational historians have emphasized the positive aspects of both these laws.[2] The great majority of children already benefited from the minimum of education and standard of living guaranteed by law. Only 10 per cent of children did not meet the official standards of welfare and education promised by the law and, in these less-affluent families, the practice of sending children under sixteen years of age to work decreased over the fifteen years studied. It is difficult to isolate the precise role of the laws in the improvement of children's status from the other favourable conditions that contributed to this change. For the same reason, even the Superintendent of Public Instruction (SPI) hesitated to measure the effect of his law statistically.[3]

The focus of this chapter will be to examine the subject of families' practices and beliefs in further detail in order to characterize the State's role in the general movement to extend the economic and cultural citizenship of the country's youth. First, we will study the avenues by which the universal social programs' advent permitted children to obtain more education and a better standard of living. Our focus will then move to the transformation of family roles at the time the policies were introduced into homes, especially the alleviation of parents' and children's responsi-

Notes to chapter 4 start on p. 234.

bilities, the rise in individual autonomy, and the standardization of experiences in the direction of the typical family featured in official speeches. This is in some way an effort to determine how the politicians fulfilled their promises before moving on, in the next chapter, to the history of the less-visible and -foreseeable effects of compulsory education and family allowances.

The Progress of Schooling

In certain situations, the two new laws pushed parents and children to change their school attendance habits, as was the case for a father in Saint-Sauveur whose eldest son went "to school because of the regulation." Many truancy officers sent encouraging figures to their superiors: in Thetford-Mines, "last year there were 109 students between the ages of 6 and 14 who refused to attend school, and out of that number, many had given up school two years ago.... In the end we were able to send all of these students back to school." The increase caused school expansion or even new schools to be built, as was the case in Gaspésie in the summer of 1944.[4] Enrollment increased: in the province's Protestant schools, the rate of compulsory education–aged children registered in school rose by 1.9 per cent between June 1945 and June 1947, and in Cap-de-la-Madeleine, the rate of unregistered children decreased by more than half between September 1943 and September 1944. In September 1943, school enumerators had counted 1,523 boys and 1,036 girls of school age not registered at any school and working "illegally." The following year, despite the high demand for labour, only half this number of children found themselves in the same situation. Over a longer period, between 1951 and 1961, the proportion of children of the whole province aged ten to fourteen attending school would rise from 89.5 per cent to 96.5 per cent, bringing Quebec up to the Canadian average. The law seemed to have some effect on those beyond the compulsory school age: between September 1943 and September 1944, the number of fifteen-year-old children attending school had gone up by approximately 4 per cent:[5] "The constantly increasing number of registrations for the Certificat d'études [after grade seven]," stated the Outaouais regional inspector in 1949, "amply demonstrates that it is enough to maintain school attendance until a determined age so that a large proportion of children, who would otherwise have left school, continue of their own volition."[6]

Educators also attributed the increase in assiduity to the law.[7] In Montréal's elementary schools, attendance grew rapidly over the years immediately following the law's implementation, decreased later, and then settled at a level slightly higher than that before September 1943. In Mégantic, average attendance had gone from 89 per cent in the year 1942–43 to 96 per cent in the year 1943–44. On a much longer timeline, the "chronic hooky-playing" had been almost completely curbed, and the elementary-school teachers' and officers' monitoring brought with it a decrease in the phenomenon of leaving school early in the school year.[8]

The truancy officers often concluded that these changes were the result of the new monitoring. With these methods in place, 130 people promised the Mégantic officer to follow the law after he had convinced them it was for their children's good. "Parents are beginning to understand," the Saint-Clément officer reported: "I have managed to convince parents to send 10 of their children back to school," was the Saint-Fortunat officer's report.[9] However, upon closer examination of the conformists' motivation, deeper causes can explain their obedience to officers.

It would seem that the laws had a specific impact on the behaviour of families who were poor or those who had recently established themselves in a city. In Jacques-Cartier, a suburb in full development on Montréal's south shore, the Family Allowances Quebec Regional Office, in connection with the school boards and truancy officers, brought 848 unregistered children back to school; supplementary classes had to be opened, and the operation was called "the hit of the year."[10] In 1940 in Drummondville, American sociologist Everett Hughes had observed that children of families who had recently arrived from the country, had to work not only because of their families' poverty but also because of their cultural traditions, which were from a different economic environment. In addition, the desire to work took on a particular intensity with children whose parents had left their farms following economic problems. In such cases, officers would probably have been able to persuade parents concerned with re-creating a stable environment to use school as a remedy for the inconvenience of geographic mobility. By inculcating these families of rural origins in the norms developed by urban reformists, it is possible that the universal laws contributed to urban adaptation.[11]

For parents obeying the law, the fear of sanctions played a significant role: "School worries me," a Montréal mother wrote to the Department of Public Instruction (DPI). "They constantly come by... looking [for my thirteen-year-old son] threatening me [he could be arrested] if I don't send him...." A large number of parents made sure files were in order in front of school authorities and the Regional Office of the Family Allowances, requesting absence permits and notifying both of the entry of a son or daughter into the labour market. "I am writing to you," explained a Gaspesian mother to the SPI, "to save me some trouble when the investigators visit."[12]

The economic incentives linked to compulsory education facilitated officers' work with many of the parents who did not need to be "persuaded" any more about the benefits of education. Free education, books, and the distribution of clothing, all elements in the enforcement of these complementary policies, were deciding factors, as indicated by the inspector general of Protestant schools in 1946: "Free books for all students until grade ten led most parents to provide their children with the recommended books. And this...effectively resulted in a larger number of students than before moving on to higher education."[13] With regard to material aid, it is the Family Allowances Act that seems to have had the greatest impact. When school began in September 1945, shortly after the allowances had begun to be paid out, the increase in rates of children registering for school was as high as it had been for the Compulsory School Attendance Act's first year of implementation, and its effects were far more long lasting. Furthermore, once the Family Allowances Act was in place, the definitive departures during the school year, motivated by material needs, were fewer.[14] In Québec, as was the case elsewhere, the allowances added enough to parents' incomes to encourage school attendance. According to another province's minister of education

> Generally, we must be satisfied with how the family allowances have worked, with better economic conditions in our homes and the increase of the standard of living in the province. Today children are well fed and better dressed. As a rule, both their physical and mental health has improved. All this has resulted in making schoolwork more interesting and supported the advancement of education itself.[15]

Some families set aside a part of the allowances for costs directly linked to children's education: from one survey to the next, the proportion of parents indicating that this was the case varied between 7 per cent and 29 per cent, not including the numerous parents who saved for education.[16] Social workers conducting surveys on the effects of the allowances found families for whom the allowances were directly responsible for extending education, as in this case, in Quebec City, where, "allowances have contributed to keep the children in school. The eldest girl will discontinue her studies next September because she will not receive allowances."[17]

The threat of suspending allowances became the officers' best weapon in all of Canada. Officials noted that "the fear of being deprived of family allowances, the suspension of family allowances, is highly beneficial, efficient, almost magical."[18] In 1949, 20 per cent of the truancy officers mentioned this enforcement method's direct influence. "I received a difficult case," reported, for example, the Saint-Jean-Port-Joli officer, "but with a warning from me saying I could have their allowances withheld, the case has completely returned to normal."[19] In 1953, three bishops added their voices to the concert of praise: "[They] have openly expressed the opinion that the enforcement of the Family Allowances Act has been the primary factor to increase school attendance," reported the director of the Family Allowances' Quebec Regional Office to his superior.[20] Over the fifteen years following the program's implementation, the Regional Office suspended the payments of between 963 and 1,872 children each year who were illegally absent from school, and a nearly equivalent number regained admission to the program, demonstrating the efficiency of payment suspension.[21]

In short, compulsory education changed the educational future of a minority of Québec children, and it seems that the accompanying measures aiming to guarantee parents the economic possibility to send a member of the family to school for longer period of time were at the origin of this evolution. Aside from these material guarantees, the need for "educating parents," a task to which reformists and legislators attached great importance, was marginal, as most parents were already convinced of the necessity of having educational norms at least as high as those specified by law.

The Decline of Juvenile Labour in Industry and Commerce

In all types of labour carried out by children, factory work was the most strongly outlawed. In fact, the Compulsory School Attendance Act and Family Allowances Act added an army of truancy officers and social workers to the Department of Labour's team of inspectors, which tracked down juvenile labourers under the age of fourteen working in urban companies.

Children under fourteen working in commercial and industrial establishments were already no more than an infrequent phenomenon, and compulsory education made it absolutely rare: in September 1943, enumerators had discovered 256 boys and 140 girls working illegally outside the home; in 1944, that number was halved. The inauguration of family allowances also seems to have brought about a decrease: in the year 1944–45, 264 children had left school to work illegally; in the year 1945–46, only 48 did so.[22] This type of work was also rare for older children, of fourteen and fifteen years of age, who were beyond the officers' reach. However, it did not decrease during the 1940s and 1950s as it did for the group of younger children, despite the tightening of the Industrial and Commercial Establishments Act, the availability of family allowances for children of fourteen and fifteen, and the will of the authors of the Compulsory School Attendance Act to see children of that age continue their studies.

In the families of wage earners, tradition and the security of a regular income favoured the education of children under fourteen. Fathers working in the factories who did not have their own businesses were not inclined to pull their younger children out of school: close to 33 per cent of fathers in Québec worked in the secondary sector during the 1940s and 1950s, while their children constituted only 10 per cent of the working fourteen-year-olds. The general inquiry led by the DPI in 1942 had found only 192 sons and 350 daughters of factory workers and 65 boys and 78 girls of merchants in this situation.[23] Demand for young workers in factories was so rare that families whose main breadwinner held a position in an industrial establishment looked outside the factory for work for children under fourteen: their sons looked towards trade (194 boys and 15 girls in 1942) and their daughters towards personnel services (37 boys and 163 girls in the same year).[24]

The image of "ignorant parents" who did not see much value in school, vaunted by many compulsory-school-attendance propagandists, was rarely confirmed in the real situations officials encountered after the law was in effect.[25] Most working-class parents already saw education as an important tool for accessing the labour market. Their opinions were, in part, influenced by the requirements of employers: in the mid-1940s, even if one could still find work with a grade-five certificate, the grade-nine certificate was increasingly being requested. Observing these changes in the nature of work, parents believed that their children would need more education. Such was the case with many lumberjacks, who stated that they could no longer teach their children their trade. Having become professionals themselves, they believed more and more that technical training was important.[26] They based these convictions on their own experiences: some educated parents realized to what degree their own educations had helped them. Others saw the schooling of their children as a way to further their own aspirations of social mobility: some parents wished to have their children educated because they themselves hadn't had the chance and understood how much they missed a better education. Many letters written by nearly illiterate parents expressing the desire for a better education for their children attest to this mindset.[27] By being educated, confided some parents in interviews, their children would have "an easier time of it," "more chances," or "more success" than they themselves had. Education was the best inheritance—if not the only one—they could offer their children. The end of the Depression of the 1930s had reinforced this hope in two ways: optimism linked to the expansion of employment added to the belief that a better education increased one's capacity to face the unexpected—"today things are going well, but it will not always be so."[28]

The considerable strength of these parents' desires is revealed when we consider their efforts to ensure school attendance: "We are doing everything we can for our children's education," they said in Saint-Léon-le-Grand, "since we understand its value." They also sought to accommodate their families' economic needs with regard to children's education, whether it was attending night classes, sending children to school during the slow time of the farming season, or even placing a child of a country road family in a village family to allow him to increase his education, all of which were partial solutions, which rarely pleased the officials.[29] Many parents sought out "lighter jobs" for their children or promised that they would return to school as soon as circumstances permitted. The clause of "equivalent instruction" offered another possibility: if parents proved that their son or daughter received at least one hour of education per day, they could override the law. The law's implementation gave rise to a growth in the realm of private schooling.[30] Finally, some parents attempted to make their children work during the summer, which did not compromise schoolwork: "Every day parents visit our office," noted Department of Labour officials, "to obtain permission, over summer holidays, to have their children work under age."[31]

During the course of the debates in the House of Commons on family allowances, Mackenzie King had wanted the allowances to replace children's work, as it seemed more and more that, for children, work was a liability.[32] In 1943, legislators, officials, and provincial experts agreed on the reality that children under the age of fourteen "are not good employees due to their lack of competence and their inefficiency at work." Even most employers now wanted their employees to have a full elementary education.[33] Over the 1940s and 1950s, almost no employers openly contested the legislative standards on juvenile labour and its underlying principles. The insistence on industrial and commercial work must also be examined in the context of the strength of the demands made by skilled workers' unions, which took up the cause of compulsory education not only to improve the fate of younger generations of their class but also to open up to adults those particular sectors of the economy in which children were competing with their members.

Moreover, in their struggle against child labour, middle-class reformists had always focused on the denunciation of the most visible and impersonal tasks. Middle-class urban adults working in businesses also pitied the vulnerable children who worked with them, and without parental supervision, as is demonstrated in a citizen's letter to the provincial secretary in 1941, which described the physical and moral dangers involved in the work of delivering groceries:

> Grocery stores are keeping open late in the evenings for the sale only of beer, which is delivered by young lads on bicycles in all weather, and during the Winter as late as 11 p.m. If you could only see these miserable half fed boys, I feel sure you would get something done to prohibit beer delivered at night. These young lads are very poorly paid, have to supply their own bicycles, keep up their own repairs and pay for breakages. They are half clad and it just looks to the writer to be a crime that they should be employed, particularly in the Winter time, bringing around beer for people who could easily arrange to have their supplies delivered earlier in the evening. Trusting you will...get something done for the uplifting of these young lads...[34]

One mother who wrote to the minister of labour in March 1945 used the argument of moral danger more explicitly. Commenting on a newspaper article reporting the assault of an eleven-year-old pharmacy delivery boy, she asked: "Why do you allow a child of eleven years old to work in a pharmacy as a courier and expose him to the fate this little boy has just suffered. If you visited pharmacies, groceries, manufacturers, you would see thousands of boys and even girls of 10, 11, 12, 13, 14 years old without any protection. Who supervises children's work? Who is paid to do this?"[35] And so, in the mid-1940s, the chief inspector of the Québec Department of Labour (QDL) announced the reform of the work permits for children fourteen and fifteen years old in language that recognized children's physical vulnerability. Permits that could be used with a single employer would allow a child to perform only restricted duties and instructed that a child should not, "without notifying us first, carry out functions which often endanger his safety and his life. Incidentally, I cite the case of young Robert McKenzie, crushed to death while working for an ice merchant."[36]

At the time, recent work in humanities and social sciences had provided new theoretical bases for the reformists who pleaded in favour of an increase in labour qualifications. The connection between a low level of education and unemployment was established: in Montréal in 1937, the McGill Social Science Research Project had investigated a group of unemployed individuals between the ages of twenty-seven and thirty-two and concluded that those who had no elementary education earned, on average, twenty-one dollars less a month than those who had benefited from a secondary education.[37] These figures were taken up again by the members of the Canada and Newfoundland Education Association (CNEA), in the early 1940s: "Regardless of school-leaving age requirements, many boys and girls are giving up their studies to take jobs that are lucrative now but which will prove blind alleys in the future."[38] The systematic research Leonard Marsh and his colleagues at McGill University had led during the Depression proved what associations of workers had long denounced: there was a chasm between the level of salaries and the cost of living. The results convinced many in the political elite, who then campaigned for family allowances.[39] The family allowances, explained the brochure introducing the public to the program, became necessary when the economy went from one in which "four-fifths of the population were skilled tradespeople" to one in which "the larger part of the population work for a wage or salary."[40]

Thus, if the first legislators of the Welfare State were able to regulate with particular insistence on child labour in the industrial and commercial world, it was because the threshold of fourteen years old existed already among employers and poor parents. Strengthened by their support, the state employees would be able to successfully rebut insistent demands for exceptions from certain employers. The QDL continued to turn down those who had not yet reached fourteen years of age for work permits in industrial and commercial buildings despite an impressive expansion of the juvenile labour force during the war. In a letter dated March 1943, the chief inspector stated that "approximately 4,000 to 5,000 certificates were denied children under 14 years old."[41] It was also to no avail that parents, children, employers, notables, and priests wrote to the minister to request that exceptions be made to the rule.[42]

The officials' hard line extended into summer work, which indicated that industrial and commercial labour was in the process of becoming unacceptable in itself and not only, as before, for the school absences it required. In 1945, for example, the director of the Québec office of the Department of Labour responded negatively to a minister who requested a summer work permit for a child in his riding: "I do not dare create the precedent as this would open the door to an army of children under 14 who wish to work during the summer holidays and every day parents come to the office to obtain permission, during summer vacation, to make their underage children work."[43] Beginning in 1940, part-time work was also more closely watched and regulated. In 1941, following an investigation of delivery boys in 494 Montréal grocery stores, in which two twelve-year-olds and eighteen thirteen-year-olds were discovered working between twenty and eighty-four hours per week, the assistant deputy minister of labour had already taken the necessary measures to "fully prohibit children under 12 working" while conceding that "regarding 13-year-old children, there may be some situations in which permits may be awarded, after individual study of each case."[44]

Beginning in the fall of 1943, the QDL and DPI issued a joint directive reinforcing the prohibition of part-time work: for students of compulsory education age—that is, those who had not reached fourteen years of age before the first of July—"the [labour inspection] service refused to issue age certificates, even if only to work after school hours or on Saturday, with the aim of helping impecunious parents."[45] For the high officials at the QDL, part-time work had become reprehensible because it compromised school work, even if it was executed outside school hours. Commenting on the results of an investigation on milk deliverers between the ages of eight and fourteen in Lac-Saint-Jean, Deputy Minister Gérard Tremblay wrote that "it would be good if the parish priests would personally denounce this abuse, which is a violation of the provincial laws, exposing young people to moral dangers and preventing them from devoting their attention to their studies."[46]

The Decline of Labour for Farmers' Sons

During the 1940s, the will to systematically offer farmers' children education and a standard of living comparable with city life represented a precedent. Behind this innovation, we cannot ignore the political elite's discovery of the troubles of country life. It was a witness of rural poverty that is supposed to have led Mackenzie King to the idea of implementing the family allowances: J.W. Pickersgill, a member of the Prime Minister's Office, grew up in Manitoba, where a pension for widows of soldiers paid to his mother had allowed him to pursue his studies. Though it must be taken with a grain of salt, the account of Mackenzie King's conversion—a type of anecdote common in the history of social policies—is representative of a greater increase of awareness.[47] For a minority, the "discovery" had occurred much earlier. In 1924, the promoter of family allowances, Father Léon Lebel, had already written that "one would have to be blind not to see that the majority is far from enjoying higher standards of living than those of the workers in the cities. Outside of poets, those celebrating the charm of the countryside are scarce."[48]

The dramatic deterioration of farmers' living conditions during the 1930s crisis as well as the revival of the rural exodus with the beginning of the war had been necessary to dispel the numerous illusions political leaders had about wealth in the countryside. In the early 1940s, Catholic reformists had created some pressure so that family allowances would help to increase farmers' revenues. Those living in the country suffered from poverty at least equal to that of manual workers and they had, on average, more children.[49] Fortified with the same understanding about poverty in rural areas, Leonard Marsh, whose research team at McGill University led thorough studies on the life in rural Canada, had promoted the idea that universal family allowances would compensate for the rural citizens' disadvantages in terms of school equipment, employment centres, and health services. In 1944, during an investigation of the nation's social services in the countryside, social worker Harry Cassidy had met in Québec "[a] prominent provincial health officer [who] expressed the view…that if adequate medical care could be provided in the rural districts to supplement the existing public health services the infant mortality rate of the Province could be soon cut in half."[50]

We have already seen how renewed desires to modernize agricultural production and check rural exodus had been deciding factors in the adoption of compulsory education by the political and religious elite of Québec. However, in the case of family allowances, the connection had been less evident. In the House, the Canadian Prime Minister's explanations bore on the lack of social services in rural regions: "Family allowances," he declared, "will ensure security in rural Canada for the first time in our history."[51] "We are in the presence of one of the first policies which grants the farmer his fair share and puts him on the same footing as the city dwellers," later affirmed Deputy G.E. Woods, who, exceptionally, deplored nutrition problems.

In this context of rural hardship, it is not surprising that the weekly publication of the Union des cultivateurs catholiques (UCC) had so readily received the news of the adoption of the Family Allowances Act:

> What is to be done with these unexpected revenues? We have already advised that accounts should be opened in children's names at the *caisse populaire* [co-operative savings and loan societies]. We will leave aside the exceptional cases: if a family lives in poverty and destitution, they cannot be reproached for immediately using the money for the common good of every member of the family. But generally speaking, family allowances will be an unexpected surplus. May they serve to better prepare the future of the children! May they wait in the *caisse populaire* in the names of those concerned until the time they are useful. In our province, family allowances should help to resolve the persistent problem of establishing the young.[52]

In fact, the universal payment would soon considerably transform the economy of a large number of farming, fishing, and lumberjacking families. It is certain that the impact of the allowances varied depending on a family's standard of living and number of children, but it is already important to note that, enjoying a modest income, the rural families interviewed saw their monetary earnings increase considerably, from 16 per cent to 18 per cent on average. Mothers were thus able to take better care of their children according to Dr. Poulin, the Beauce MP in the House of Commons:

> In practising my profession in the country, I have been able to see [...] the manner in which this money is used. Often at my office, mothers bring me their little children of all ages and ask me to examine them, even if they do not consider them to be ill, to see if there is something that can be done to improve their health. After being examined and given a prescription, if one is needed, these mothers are very proud to pull their allowance cheque out of their purse and tell me that it allows them to take good care of their child.[53]

Poulin even suggested that an increase in family allowances would have a more beneficial effect than the health-insurance project the House was then planning. In particular, the allowances would help to diversify rural children's nutrition:

> ...a general-store keeper [in a] pretty village in the North admits that he watches cases of oranges emptied, and that his clients proudly proclaim that their family allowances provide sweets for their children. Yesterday, the oranges were golden fruit for rich people, rare fruit children discovered once a year at the bottom of their sock hung up on Christmas Eve...when their bad behaviour hadn't changed it into a potato![54]

Thanks to the brochure *La mère canadienne et son enfant,* many mothers from Saint-Octave in the Gaspésie were able to have access to medical information that was, until then, not available to them, as the newly established village was lacking in social services. Social workers across Canada reported that children in the country were faring better.[55]

Family allowances also permitted some farming families to go without family labour, as anthropologist Horace Miner discovered when he came to examine the parish of Saint-Denis-de-Kamouraska for the second time in the late 1940s. To be sure, the amount of the payments did not cover the costs of caring for a student, and even less so the salary of adult farm employees, but the allowances helped to break the vicious cycle of juvenile farm work. In fact, Miner observed that the family allowances, added to other new sources of income (increased prices for agricultural commodities and other governmental programs), permitted the purchase of agricultural machinery, which resulted in the liberation of children from farm work:

> Mechanization was blocked by the large family system, as the greater efficiency of the machine could not make itself felt though decreasing the number of family farm workers. Then suddenly and with only minor alteration of the old agricultural system, cash income increased beyond the old requirements. It became possible both to mechanize the farm and to rear a large family....More children were sent to school...[56]

These surpluses of income at times served to provide sources of work to day labourers.

The decrease in boys' farm work between 1940 and 1960 is the main cause of the remarkable general decrease in boys' labour across Québec. Indeed, the number of boys between the ages of fourteen and fifteen working during the week preceding the enumeration went from 18,372 to 13,648 between 1941 and 1951. In the next decade, it continued to decrease at approximately the same rate, if we are to believe the only available statistics (to our knowledge) on fifteen-year-old children. Farm work constituted the largest employment sector for boys in the beginning of the period: it brought together 75 per cent of fourteen- to fifteen-year-old workers. Ten years later, no more than half were doing farm work. For boys born in the country, the chances of being called upon would decrease: in 1941, 46 per cent devoted most of their energy to the family business; ten years later, this proportion had decreased to 27 per cent. However, in 1951, when censuses for the first time distinguished among rural children aged fourteen and fifteen who lived on a farm, it was discovered that 42 per cent of them still worked for their fathers without pay.[57]

Can we also attribute the decrease in juvenile farm work in Québec to the Compulsory School Attendance Act? Distinguishing between the two phenomena is not easy; is it because farm work was so important that there were hesitations about regulating it, or, on the contrary, was it from the moment it was regulated that it diminished? At least one part of the decrease must be attributed to the post-war rural exodus. In fact, in Québec, the proportion of farm labourers of all ages decreased from 26 per cent to 16 per cent of the overall workforce over the course of the decade. But these explanations do not suffice since, within the farming community itself, the proportion of juvenile workers gradually diminished. In addition, over the short term, we know that the Compulsory School Attendance Act did not prevent juvenile farm work from increasing, at least for the duration of the war.

The Change in Parents' Responsibilities and Prerogatives

Politicians wasted no time in emphasizing the positive effects family allowances had on families' standard of living. For example, Paul Martin, minister of the Department of National Health and Welfare (DNHW), declared, "All available indications—increased consumption of milk, medicine, cod liver oil, et cetera—demonstrate the value of the family allowances program," in the House of Commons on the occasion of the June 1948 vote on the budget.[58] The allowances' impact on families' incomes can easily be isolated from the general trend in salary increase. Between 1945 and 1957, families received an allowance of, on average, $16.07 per month, which represented 3.5 per cent of the average family's income in the Province of Quebec.[59] In this way, the allowances contributed to the general increase in consumption that characterized the post-war years. On this primary material level, it is difficult to distinguish the allowances' precise influence on family practices from the influence of all Keynesian economic policies. But we can safely state that in very poor households, the arrival of the monthly cheque was determining.

In many situations, the family allowances held an essential position among other income sources, particularly for families who could not count on the father's salary. For this reason, the program achieved one if its initial goals, which was to ensure a relatively stable income for children, regardless of what the father's situation was, as evidenced by the fictional widow Leduc from the governmental propaganda. Nineteen of the 116 families interviewed in the QRO's limited surveys were in such situations. The father's illness accounted for five of the interruptions, and unemployment was behind nine others. In three cases the husband was deceased, and in another household, the father had returned to school thanks to the privileges awarded to veterans. These families said they needed "each penny of the allowance" and, from time to time, the federal government's cheque was their sole source of income—as in the case, for example, of the family of an inspector restricted to his home by illness, or the family of an unemployed stonemason. For another quarter of this group of nineteen families, the allowances provided over one-third of their income. Compared with the other sources of income that replaced the father's salary, the amount of the allowance was considerable, particularly when the family was large. The regularity of the payment was also of great importance. A family with six children under sixteen years of age, for example, received almost the same amount in allowances (forty dollars) as in unemployment insurance for the father (sixty dollars). Another household with five children under sixteen counted on an older son's monthly salary of thirty-nine dollars, and on the twenty-seven dollars in family allowances. For the three families in the *Ten Family Surveys* who already received the provincial allowances for needy mothers, and for the family who was helped by a charitable organization, the amounts of the family allowances were even more significant, as they did not humiliate the beneficiaries like the other types of help they had received so far. For a Montréal mother with four children under sixteen, for instance, the allowance represented 35 per cent of her income. Moreover, family allowances now affected some families that had been excluded by the admissibility conditions for provincial programs, as was the case for Lou: "Lou applied for a Needy Mother's [*sic*] Allowance but the uncertainty of [her husband's] illness made her ineligible.... Family Allowances of $24.00 was the only income of which she was certain. As she discussed a budget, the fact that she had it, and had a right to it, seemed to restore some of her self-assurance..."[60]

In some cases, the allowances even facilitated families' staying together. A very large proportion of children in the province's orphanages, for example, still had a parent who was alive, and the allowances made their lives a little easier, as explained by a member of the QRO in 1950:

> The institutions report that since the event of Family Allowances, the parents are happy and proud to be able to better care for their children away from home. Prior to 1945 children mostly stayed in the institutions during the Christmas and the Summer vacations. Now the institutions are literally empty. Only the orphans and abandoned children remain in the institutions during vacation time and that may represent only 10%. The institutions of Giffard and Levis have reported that before 1946, only 50 children out of 600 would spend the two months of summer holidays in their families. Now only 50 remain in the institution, the others can go home.[61]

The progress, however, was far from secure: an inquiry on the placement of children born to needy mothers, led in the city of Québec region between 1948 and 1953, confirmed the persistence of the phenomenon: "In this single region, 1,000 children could have stayed with their families and not been placed in institutions because of the mother's insufficient revenue."[62]

The allowances soon became essential for many large families. As foreseen, the amount they received was a significant portion of their income. Six mothers in the *Ten Family Surveys* insisted on the essential nature of the program: one mother expressed that she did not know what would have happened if she had not received allowances; another confided that she would have had to take on debt; and two others declared that they had never been able to balance their budgets previously.[63]

On top of helping fathers and mothers financially, the universal social programs contributed a certain amount of support for housewives and their chores. Poor urban mothers said they could not have made ends meet without the allowances. In two of the ten houses visited randomly during the QRO's monthly surveys, housewives affirmed that allowances were "more than welcome," though in two others, respondents praised the "new feeling of security" the cheques brought. A group of researchers from McGill University noted the same attitude: "The security offered by these regular cheques... was important to many families with marginal incomes. It relieved the pressure of expenses in many cases and gave families a feeling that the allowances were in some way contributing to the children's maintenance."[64]

Thanks to the informational texts included with the cheques, the family allowances program was successful in reaching one of its initial goals: to help women raise their children. The systematic availability of the universal policy to all mothers meant that they now all received information on hygiene and health, which the State had previously created for selected groups. When the educational information service of the Canadian Welfare Council practically terminated its activities the DNHW's Information Service took on the responsibility. The mothers enthusiastically read and supported the texts provided. In a single year, 375,000 Canadian women ordered a copy of the brochure entitled *Nos enfants* by way of a form inserted in the allowance envelopes—a total of one-quarter of the province's mothers who had received the offer.[65] And what should be said about the popularity of Dr. Ernest Couture's book *La mère canadienne et son enfant*? In 1949, Minister Paul Martin signed the millionth copy for a "woman of Belgian origin, who had married a Canadian soldier and had lived in the country for three years." In 1953, four million copies had been distributed. In the small village of Saint-Octave-de-L'Avenir, many mothers consulted the booklet. At a time when doctors made their patients pay or often lived far away from them, the booklets disseminated new information on hygiene and provided advice on how to care for a newborn baby, information many mothers received with relief. Journalist Albert J. Sarrazin did not hesitate to write that the booklet "was useful in serving to fight infant mortality and form a healthy race, and future generations."[66]

In addition to reassuring mothers in accomplishing their child-rearing duties, family allowances, by providing recipients with a personal income, helped increase their social status. In many cases, the receipt of money was such a novel concept that a large number of the cheques were returned by rural post offices who did not know the mothers' first names.[67] Rich or poor, mothers often received their first-ever personal income. The allowances could thus provoke a slight displacement of men's economic power over women, particularly in wealthier households. According to the *Ten Family Surveys,* most women, especially those whose husbands had higher incomes, did not know how much their husbands earned. However, the social workers at McGill University discovered that the higher a family's income, the more the father controlled its spending. One of the investigators at the Family Allowances Quebec Regional Office reported that in one particular family, where the father was a trucker who earned $1,800 per year and had six children, "the father wants to use his money to pay his income tax but the mother is opposed." This state of affairs is perhaps related to the fact that richer women had led the 1945 struggle for cheques paid to mothers, and that it was a group of middle-class men who had, in the name of paternal authority, fought against them. At the heart of each individual family, the spouses sometimes expressed different opinions on the issue, the man showing more suspicion than his wife, and affirming that he could raise his children alone since the government might be expecting something in return for the money.[68] In addition, the allowances' disbursement method corresponded to the way in which families managed their money, as described by earlier investigators. In 75 per cent of families in Québec in which the mother was present, she alone administered the budget; in one case out of seven, both spouses managed the budget.[69]

The acknowledgement of mothers' roles reflected the hope many feminists had invested in the project. At first, the Québec caucus of the federal Liberal party prevented the cheques from being sent to mothers in Québec (despite that cheques went to mothers in every other province), echoing the political and clerical elite of the Province, who had invoked the particularity of the judicial context—the civil code inherited from the French regime, according to which the father was the main administrator of family finances. Mackenzie King suspended his decision to send the cheques to mothers in order to consult the provincial authorities on the question. Maurice Duplessis immediately answered by refusing to have the federal government override the province's regime on the question of property. With his support, the bishops declared that it was "an attack on the family and on the principle of authority."[70] In the end, the QRO, which had already begun its work, had to reprint the 70,000 cheques already written in the mothers' names.

However, both Duplessis' and the bishops' perspectives on economic roles within the family were not shared unanimously in Québec society. Already in 1944, a group of researchers in humanities and social sciences from Université Laval who had been asked by the previous provincial government to reflect on the pertinence of the allowances, had advised issuing the cheques to both parents. This formula, they claimed, had the advantage of recognizing the democratic evolution of families while respecting the patriarchal character of the province's civil code.[71] The same year, the Fédération nationale Saint-Jean-Baptiste (FNSJB) toyed with the idea of recognizing a woman with "a legal right to a certain percentage of her husband's salary, in exchange for her work and for which she could receive a salary outside the home." The FNSJB had been responsible for the publication of the *Mémoire sur l'orientation du travail féminin d'après-guerre,* prepared for Adélard Godbout's Québec Economic Advisory Council by Renée Vautelet, a social worker with connections to the National Selective Service. To the federal government's considerations on "the economic necessity of putting the woman back in the home," the Vautelet Report had added nationalist, pro-natalist, and agriculturalist elements: domestic country life had to be made enticing enough so that women originally from the country and working in factories—which Vautelet estimated to be 60,000 in number—would want to return to the country. Among "the major reasons behind the rural worker staying in the cities" was

> the lack of opportunities available to them in the country which would allow them to earn and keep their own money, after the habit of receiving a paycheque, and the tendency of the man from the country to consider the money earned by his wife as a part of the common property that she may not touch without his permission....
>
> One day there will be a legal acknowledgement of wives' significant economic contribution to the family unit. This will entail a right to a certain percentage of the husband's salary, in exchange for the work she contributes and for which she could receive a salary outside the home. The time has likely not yet come for such a suggestion in Québec, regardless of the fact that it is currently the subject of some serious questions in England. It is presented here simply to emphasize the importance of the mindset that will have to be adopted regarding women's work in the family, if we do not want to see her economically inferior situation in the matrimonial environment continue to push her more and more toward paid work, and thus farther away from the care of her children and her home.[72]

In 1945, a haphazard collection of reformist, nationalist, and feminist forces—in many ways similar to that which had supported Godbout's projects described earlier—organized a campaign in favour of sending the cheques to mothers. The movement was under the leadership of one of the first suffragettes, Thérèse Casgrain. Secretary of the League of Women's Rights, she described their methods as follows: "In order to ensure that the family allowances be paid to mothers in the province of Québec in the same way as other provinces, [we] have pressured other authorities, submitting some 500 petitions, telegrams, etc., as well as radio discussions and interviews to them. We are pleased to announce that these methods have been successful."[73] Casgrain recalled later that she knew "that the mandate existed [in the general population], and that in general it was the woman of the house who administered the family budget." The movement received the support of the Union catholique des producteurs agricoles and of the Fédération des travailleurs du Québec. Casgrain also took advantage of the friendly connections between her husband and the prime minister.[74] The movement succeeded in reversing the federal government's decision, so well in fact that the QRO, which had recently completed 370,000 new files under fathers' names, had to review them all. The whole affair, in the end, caused a delay of a few weeks in the mailing of the first cheques.[75]

Family allowances also changed housework by accelerating the transfer of family work from production to consumption. The general improvement of the standard of living during the 1920s and 1930s had already shaken the economic roles of members within individual families.[76] After the war, the increase in the standard of living permitted the majority of households to buy electric household appliances. In some cases, the family allowances facilitated this acquisition: mothers receiving an income for the first time in their marriage often invested it in the purchase of appliances. Purchasing clothes with the allowances would also free them from long hours of work.[77] These results fulfilled the aims of legislators who had hoped that the allowances would solidify the new role of mothers in an economy of consumer goods. The head of the Co-operative Commonwealth Federation (CCF) believed that the mother should receive the money, since, in his words, "it is she who buys the food and the clothing."[78]

The new rhetoric of universal rights accentuated this movement. Educational brochures from the 1940s and 1950s defended the idea that the main agent of domestic economy was the mother and wife, "a wise woman [who] regards housekeeping as a profession and prepares and follows plans as carefully as an engineer draws and follows his blueprints for a bridge...she is not only the planner but the purchasing agent and the maintenance man."[79] At the end of the 1940s, anthropologist Horace Miner observed that aspirations of the young wives of Saint-Denis-de-Kamouraska had changed:

> One compelling reason for farm families to depart from the old technology is clear. There has been a growing resistance among convent-educated, unmarried girls to the assuming of the burden of bearing and rearing a family of ten while cooking, housekeeping, gardening, milking, spinning, weaving, making clothes, and helping with the harvest and threshing.... The desirability of conveniences, now available, finds wide expression today. In the present glow of economic expansion, a girl can assert her preference for an easier life.[80]

The Increase in Children's Autonomy

Most children already shared the views expressed in the new social laws. Many were aware that the laws had been established for them: inspectors, on their annual visits, verified children's knowledge of the Compulsory School Attendance Act; elementary-school teachers could ask their students to inform them about the arrival of new neighbours or even to take a notice to the parents of an absent student; and the majority of young people, particularly those in low-income households, were aware of the existence of family allowances.[81] It is difficult to know what they thought of these measures. But according to a survey led by the Canadian Youth Commission from 1943 to 1945, for which those fifteen to twenty-five years of age expressed their opinions, 95 per cent of them favoured compulsory education until the age of fourteen or fifteen; of this number, 45 per cent hoped to see the law extended to the age of sixteen or seventeen, and 33 per cent thought that school should be compulsory until eighteen and above. Opinions on the compulsory age were less frequent among interviewees of lower means, but the differences were not significant.[82]

On a more general level, the belief that extended secondary or technical education led to a good job was widespread.[83] In the year 1948–49, the heads of Québec's provincial employment offices observed that "our young people grow more and more aware every day of the need to complete their studies, to prepare themselves for the future."[84] In Cap-de-la-Madeleine, four students even wrote to their school boards to demand that the opening of grade-ten classes: "We wish to acquire more education to be better able to manage in life," said one. "It is a task which will follow you forever if you do not grant it to us. Please then provide it to those who wish to be educated," wrote another.[85] In 1941, the Jeunesse ouvrière catholique (JOC) led a survey of 700 young potential members under sixteen years of age who had left school (see table 1); most regretted not being able to be further educated.[86]

Table 1: Percentage of Children Leaving School under the Age of Sixteen, Categorized by Reason (Québec, 1941)

Boys	
"My family needed money."	50
"I was sick of school."	28
"I was sick."	12
"I had finished school."	5
"I wanted to stay home."	3
"I didn't get along with the teacher."	1.5
"I wanted to learn a trade."	1.5
Girls	
"Mummy needed me."	61
"I was sick."	21
"My family needed money."	10
"I was sick of school."	6
"I wanted to continue with private studies."	4
"I fought with the teacher."	0.5

Source: JOC, "Le problème des jeunes qui ne fréquentent plus l'école," *École sociale populaire* 351 (April 1942): 26.

Children's new right to a minimum standard of living could confer upon them autonomy and assurance. Some children received a small portion of the allowance in the form of pocket money; others received greater responsibilities when the time came for shopping: "It's your money, chose for yourself," some mothers would tell them. For those who lived in poverty and suffered as a result of the associated humiliations, the acquisition of goods thanks to the family allowances was sometimes crucial. "I bought a red[,] white and blue sweater for my son Jean who is sick of it," wrote a mother to the women's section of *Bulletin des agriculteurs.* "The others won't be able to tease him any more. Just think, with his family allowances cheque!" A little girl confided that she would like "a new dress, bought for her, the first...instead of her older sisters' hand-me-downs."[87] This relative financial autonomy may have been able to quell the feeling of urgency for earning one's own money, which, as we will see later on, often explained why so many dropped out of school.

The benefits connected with the new economic rights also permitted some children to satisfy family obligations—which could be expensive—a choice poverty had denied them, as in the case of farmers' daughters obliged to leave home to work in town while they would have preferred to stay at home to help their families.[88] The 1941 JOC survey had shown that the majority of children entered the work force to help their families. The majority of dropouts confirmed that they had left school for economic reasons: "My family needed me," explained 50 per cent of the boys and 10 per cent of the girls; "Mummy needed me," was the reason for 61 per cent of the girls, the majority of whom worked at home (see table 1). Most of these children seemed to accept the responsibilities, such as one fifteen-year-old girl "who is ready to devote herself to her parents and brothers and sisters" or another child "who would like to work in order to help his mother," though he did not express any enthusiasm for work.

By formulating most of their recommendations in terms of consumption patterns and by devising social programs in the form of monthly allowances destined to ensure the children's standard of living, politicians and federal officials may have helped individual consumption and the activities connected with it to infiltrate the world of children, a phenomenon already favoured by the evolution of the market. This was the case not only with children in more comfortable families who, as the information brochures had advised, received on average more pocket money, but also with juvenile labourers. Most of those earning a salary gave it to their mothers—the total sum or simply a part—and, over the course of the period studied, the spending habits of these children evolved towards more individuality, a transition that sociologist Gérald Fortin observed with the logging families of Sainte-Julienne between the 1930s and 1960s: "Now that the family has become a consumption unit, the working children are also consumers. As such, they have personal needs to satisfy. Therefore, instead of continuing to hand over their wages to their parents, the children keep the wages for themselves, with the understanding that they shall pay for their board and lodging."[89] At most, very young children could work with the single aim of buying themselves small things that their parents could not. When asked by the Montréal Social Welfare Court (MSWC), they testified to having left school to make "personal purchases." As noted in one case, "to get himself food and cigarettes, [a thirteen-year-old Montréal boy] worked, as a messenger [or delivery boy], for a fruit merchant. With this money, he bought himself chips, hot dogs, Polo-Pice."[90]

Some children used this regime of compulsory schooling to contest the quality of public education. Henceforth, fathers and mothers now possessed a means to keep schools open to disruptive students, which, in turn, sometimes made it difficult to find teachers. One Québec mother remarked that it should have been possible to require "a good teacher" in return for compulsory school attendance. Some parents suspected that the quality of education carried less weight than patronage or saving money in school commissioners' decision to employ elementary-school teachers. Others complained to the DPI about teachers who beat their children. They brought up the subject of individual aptitudes and their children's hopes, which fell in line with the teachings of modern education theorists. Thus, with the support of adults, children's unhappiness regarding school practices was publicly expressed.[91]

The universal programs could also liberate children from family obligations they deeply resented. Judges, probation officers, and truancy officers all found children who worked against their wishes, who would have liked to have continued attending school, but had left at the request of their parents. Some did not understand parental demands, such as the thirteen-year-old boy who would have preferred to work for his sick mother only after school. In some cases parents seemed to be worried about their children becoming better educated and drifting away from the family.[92] To the children who were prisoners of painful family situations, the universality of the laws sometimes provided a means to alert the public authorities to their situation, as with the young woman who missed school out of fear of running into a lodger who had harassed her, or a boy who was pulled between separated parents' divergent wills: "His father continues to see him," noted the officer of the court, "telling him not to go to school, to destroy his mother's dreams." For some children, school attendance became a means of pressure: a Montréal boy thirteen years of age agreed to go to school only when he was left at his father's; another, of fourteen years, wished for his family to be reunited before he returned to the classroom.[93]

In conclusion, the new laws provided the State with the responsibility to guarantee a minimum of security for the father's income, the mother's household duties, and children's education and standard of living. Once the programs were implemented, they could not only contribute to the improvement of the comfort, status, and cultural life of all family members but also lighten the load of families' mutual obligations and soothe some of the most painful aspects of their interdependence.

5

Forgotten by Education and Welfare

The New Faces of Poverty and Juvenile Labour

In 1937, at the request Dominion Bureau of Statistics, Murdoch C. MacLean had published a monograph on illiteracy and school attendance in Canada. Noting the different levels of education in different social classes in provinces with compulsory education laws, he asked, "If they are all governed by the same law, why should there be such large gaps between the social classes?"[1] The same question can be asked about the two laws in the 1940s that also left children outside of the norms they established.

This chapter focuses on the policies' limitations. It is a study of the nature and functions of the zones of exclusion from universal rights, in which a minority of citizens found themselves—poorer households affected by the fluctuations of the market or of the life cycle, as well as those running subsistence farms—and it attempts to situate these exclusions in their respective economic contexts. This discussion also enters the domain of ideologies in order to demonstrate how, each time they encountered these situations, officials developed new descriptions compatible with the atmosphere of universal rights. The chapter concludes with a demonstration of how these tolerances and their justifications influenced poorer citizens' culture as much as the formation of the Welfare State.[2]

The Failure of Government Advice and the Discarding of Abnormal Families

Governments had indicated to parents living in difficult economic situations that saving, budgeting, or turning to private charitable organizations would ensure their children's new rights. However, these means were not accessible to some families. Discovering that their intentions for the

Notes to chapter 5 start on p. 243.

program did not translate into actual practice, the political elite conceived of new ways to blame poor parents for their fate.

The surveys studying parents' hopes for the family allowances program during its early implementation indicate a strikingly high proportion of those hoping to save their allowances. In accordance with the officials' inaugural speeches, the most prevalent wish among parents was to save the sums received with the aim of preparing for their children's future: at least 25 per cent of the beneficiaries thought this way. In reality, savings and supplementary spending gave precedence to essential goods, and even the author of the savings tables for children's education could not put his own advice into practice.[3]

Urban families in Québec and across Canada allocated most of their allowances to clothing: at least two-thirds cited this type of spending even though only 13 per cent had planned to use the allowance in this way. The phenomenon was so striking that there were even travelling salespeople who would time their monthly collection with the arrival of the allowances cheques, and some went so far as to intimidate the mothers who refused to buy their products, threatening to report them to the government for spending their allowances ill-advisedly. Ten per cent of the families in southwest Montréal had opened accounts in a large store, which they paid regularly with their monthly cheques.[4] Dalfen's, a store on Queen-Mary Road in Montréal, offered a 10 per cent discount to those who paid with their cheques (see figure 11).

Though the purchase of clothing could liberate some mothers from their household duties, many continued to knit and make their own clothes or to mend old ones: in southwest Montréal, this was the case for 50 per cent of the poorest mothers and 33 per cent of the more affluent mothers. For these tasks, grandmothers, older girls, and sometimes even neighbours were called upon.[5]

Food was the second most common entry on the list of items urban families purchased with their allowances: the proportion of families who mentioned this type of purchase varied between 19 per cent and 63 per cent depending on the survey. Brochures published by the Department of National Health and Welfare (DNHW) advised spending a part of the allowances on the improvement of children's diet, but families had not considered using them for a basic diet. Again, insufficient revenues brought about unexpected uses, and it was a problem that grew in severity with family size: "In large families, the percentage of allowances spent on clothing diminished, while the proportion allocated for food increased."[6]

Thirty-three per cent of the families used a part of their allowances to pay for medical care even though, once again, very few of them had fore-

Figure 11. Conscious of families' economic difficulties, large stores and travelling salespeople attempted to attract consumers by taking advantage of the arrival of family allowances.

Source: ABRQ, 42-8, vol. 1, *La Presse*, 14 December 1950. (Reproduced with the permission of *La Presse*.)

seen using them in this way. These were purchases of medicine and curative care rather than the prevention the education campaign had advertised. Among the 116 testimonies collected during *Ten Family Surveys,* seven mothers said that they had had to pay for operations, of which four were tonsil removals; five mothers had bought medication or paid doctors' or dentists' fees when a child had been sick; eight others had used the allowances for health care of an undetermined nature. In fact, only one family mentioned a preventative measure: buying tonics. Many doctors soon became aware of this new source of income and, like the travelling salespeople, adjusted the payment of medical fees according to the allowance rates.[7]

In east Montréal, 20 per cent of mothers used a portion of the allowances to pay the rent and another 20 per cent to repay debts, options the government publicity had not mentioned: "The reason given in most [cases of debt…] was 'but there is nothing left at the end of the month, miss!'" As for the rent, poor mothers "consider[ed] that this solution [was] more practical, because they [were] always sure to receive their cheques in the middle of the month, their allowance cheque from which they immediately [kept] the sum of the rent."[8] In this way, the allowances often dictated the timing of spending. In the case of a father of three children, a prison guard at Bordeaux whose wife was ill, the probation officer from the youth court mentioned for example that "he paid for food and heating only once a month when he received the family allowance of $21.00."[9]

Thus, the homogenizing publicity on the universal child and parent provoked great hopes, but the contrast between the desires that parents expressed on the eve of the implementation of the family allowances and their real use of them demonstrates the illusory nature of the propaganda. While parents had to ensure children's right to a minimum standard of living by means of the family allowances, there were more families like the Sauvés than the Gagniers, to use the examples from the government booklet discussed in chapter 3 (see figure 10). Communist MP Fred Rose had predicted as much: "The allowance beneficiaries will not deposit them in the bank. They will not spend them on trips overseas or on luxury items. They will take them to the stores."[10]

The government still advised those who could not afford to save money that they should plan their spending carefully. But it often condemned the planning methods of poor families. In Québec City, the enumerators discovered that "the proportion of families depositing the allowance money in savings accounts was relatively higher in 'poorer' wards." That way, as with purchases on installment plans in large stores, poor households were able to save in the very short term in order to prepare for indivisible purchases, at a time when the bank did not offer credit to all its customers. Term payments, like those to doctors, salespeople, or large stores, were more appropriate means of budgetary planning for urban families. They became more popular after the First World War, and even more so following the Second World War. When income did not permit a sufficient standard of living to ensure anything beyond subsistence, there was no money left over for planning, and, in cases where the money was needed, a new term contract requesting a smaller sum often constituted both an obligation to save and a disbursement that was a little easier to make. In the family allowances, debtors found amounts that easily made this type of planning possible for their less-fortunate clients.[11]

Another significant expenditure that officials found disconcerting was insurance. Out of the sample lot of households, 33 per cent and 20 per cent of those in Québec City and Montréal respectively set aside part of their family allowances for it. Indeed, in Québec City, insurance was the second most commonly purchased item. Parents did not always invest in insurance for educational reasons; in 60 per cent of all cases in the province, they insured only their child's life. As life insurance policies could be terminated and a portion of the payments refunded once the child had reached a certain age, insurance was a form of savings plan. In another 25 per cent of these cases, pure endowment policies aiming to pay for higher education could be partially recovered when a child reached sixteen or eighteen years of age. The premiums varied between one and three dollars per child, such significant sums that they used up to 50 per cent of the allowance. Similar to the practices of shopkeepers and doctors, some insurance agencies collected at clients' homes as soon as allowances cheques had arrived, and in east Montréal, the beginning of allowances gave rise to a considerable increase in the clientele of insurance companies.[12] However, many politicians, officials, and social enumerators viewed these strategies as signs of a lack of foresight. Québec sociologists investigating the impact of the allowances denounced life insurance, claiming, "In such cases, it is the parents of the child who, if the latter dies, are financially protected."[13]

The authorities' attitude regarding insurance had less to do with their use for poor families than for the politicians' macro-economic objectives. The DNHW's changing opinion should be viewed in this light. Originally, when children's life-insurance companies wished to address their public announcements directly to the beneficiaries of the allowances cheques, the deputy minister refused:

> either in terms of high-pressure salesmanship of consumer goods or in terms of savings investments, insurance, etc.... [the announcements] will have the effect of diverting the Family Allowances moneys into unwise

> spending, or even into unwise savings and hoarding, during the deflationary period of the postwar years when the interest of the country may call for a policy of encouragement to spending rather than encouragements to saving.[14]

Four years later, once the need to increase consumer demands had abated, the practice of saving the allowances became acceptable in the eyes of the governing party. The research branch of the DNHW responded to the Bank of Montreal's request for information; the bank then prepared public announcements with the aim of inciting parents to save the allowances for their children.[15]

The federal and provincial governments alike considered it probable that in cases of hard luck or extreme poverty, truancy officers and social workers would ask charitable organizations to help affected households. Assistance from private charities sometimes fell short of what was necessary to encourage school attendance. A Montréal mother of seven whose husband was in prison received twenty dollars from the Société Saint-Vincent-de-Paul on top of family allowances, and a father of seven who earned one hundred twenty dollars per month also received twelve dollars in charitable donations, yet neither was able to keep their children from missing school.[16]

For those families who were not able to conform to the new norms, officials rarely found proof of misuse of the family allowances. Each year, fewer than one family out of seven hundred was visited by an investigator and, upon meeting the parents, the allowances were denied to fewer than one mother out of five.[17] In these cases, the money was entrusted to a third party, and in extreme cases the Royal Canadian Mounted Police was called upon and legal action for fraud could be brought (the first such case was in 1947).[18] Among the families deemed to be irresponsible, there was the case of a mother from Macaza who sent her four children to school barefoot only every second day; meanwhile, she bought makeup and cigarettes with her family allowances cheques and spent her time with a boyfriend. She became angry with the officer who visited her home. There was also a case in which a Montréal father did not send his three children to school, instead spending his family allowances on alcohol.[19]

Nor did school census-takers, truancy officers, and classroom teachers find many cases of negligence among parents who were too poor to ensure their children's minimum level of education. As early as 1942, francophone elementary-school teachers attributed only 6 per cent of eight- to fourteen-year-old children's school departures to "negligence." Once compulsory education was in effect, census-takers put only 4 per cent of families who hadn't registered their children in any school into this category, a proportion that decreased over time.[20] In that category were parents who demonstrated lower norms than those of the State's new levels, such as those who maintained that the time of the grade-six solemn communions was the time for transition from school and work,[21] or those whose low level of education seemed to interfere with their children's education. This was the case for the parents of a twelve-year-old Montréal boy who did not attend school: "This father and mother are illiterate; they have no concept of the importance of education. Their judgment is far from brilliant," declared the court's agent.[22]

In a few cases in Montréal, the Compulsory School Attendance Act seems to have permitted judges and social workers to identify, as the legislators had hoped, irresponsible parents. In these cases, children were placed in the care of another family or in a reform school; most wanted to return home, sometimes going so far as to run away. These children paid dearly for their "right to education," as their confinement placed them in the very situations of fear and submission the reformist promoters of the juvenile courts had originally hoped to avoid.[23]

The Survival of Juvenile Labour: Market Insufficiencies and the Persistent Needs of Families

Among delinquent parents, rare were those who disagreed with the new legal norm of compulsory school attendance until fourteen years of age, and those who withdrew their children from school under the Compulsory School Attendance Act age did so with regret. However, officials were not inclined to ascribe their disobedience to poverty. Each year, officers attributed only 100 departures by children of school age to "destitution"; most often it was a case of lack of shoes or clothing.[24] Once the Compulsory School Attendance Act had been promulgated, the provincial census-takers found 294 boys and 257 girls of compulsory education age who were not registered in any school by reason of destitution. On the eve of the next return to school, the situation had barely improved, and during the course of the 1944–45 school year, destitution led 115 boys and 53 girls between the ages of five and eight to leave urban elementary schools altogether.

Agents entrusted with the task of applying the Family Allowances Act and the Compulsory School Attendance Act faced a considerable contingent of children who, though too young according to the new provisions, continued to leave school to go to work. In the summer of 1941, before the implementation of the Compulsory School Attendance Act, 2,930 boys and 3,643 girls aged thirteen and under had permanently left primary public school; of those children, at least two-thirds went to work, meaning fewer than 1 per cent of all the children aged seven to thirteen. Outside these permanent departures, we can calculate the number of registered children who were frequently absent: between September 1941 and March 1942, 10,500 boys and 7,963 girls in primary elementary schools had missed more than ten days of school for work, and 10 per cent of them had been absent for more than half the school year.[26] Thus, before the province followed the compulsory education regime, approximately 18,500 intermittent young workers were added to the 4,000 full-time workers, for a total of 22,500 children aged seven to thirteen having worked for at least ten days in the year 1941–42. This was one out of twenty children, a number calculated based on the province's total population of children in that age group.

In September 1943, the new school censuses discovered as many children under fourteen who were not registered for school because they were working, a total of 2,070 boys and 2,349 girls among the 491,394 children aged six to thirteen the school enumerators had counted in the province. The most common cause for not being registered was work, which just outranked sickness, followed far behind by a considerable number of unknown reasons and then the distance between home and school. In all, some 20,000 non-registered children were thus accounted for.[27] Furthermore, that year, approximately 4,400 boys and 2,400 girls missed over ten days because of work; of this group, one-seventh were absent for over forty days.[28] In all, more than 10,000 children of compulsory-school-attendance age would have missed school to work, either permanently or temporarily—that is, 2 per cent of the children in the age brackets indicated. The rare surveys of subsequent years showed that the phenomenon persisted: in the year 1948–49, at least 7,000 children aged fourteen and under still worked. Moreover, 6,741 permits to work at home were issued for students of compulsory education age, as well as 318 permits to work outside the home.[29] One of the indirect aims behind the law was to bring older children to attend school, but 40 per cent of fourteen-year-olds and 60 per cent of fifteen-year-olds were still not registered in school in the year 1943–44, the large majority of them holding jobs. The phenomenon of the "tumbling down at the end of grade six" continued so that well into 1950, half the province's children would still not reach grade seven, the Godbout government's designated minimum.[30]

Who were the children who slipped through the cracks of the new economic and social security regimes? Before compulsory education, the large majority of those under fourteen who left school did so to do unpaid work for their parents—that is, at least 54 per cent of boys and 59 per cent of girls. Most of the boys worked on the family farm, and most of the girls helped their mothers at home. Furthermore, an increased proportion of children of small commercial or industrial business owners worked for their parents.[31]

The officials operated on the principle that all parents benefited from the minimums they were promised.[32] However, the new Welfare State left some families without sufficient resources to be able to conform to the new law and did not protect them from the opprobrium now allotted to the values and the economic strategies they had inherited from another time. In 1945, many of these families were still facing a constrictive economic structure that forced them to go against their long-held hopes of providing their children with a good education: "I would rather see my child at a desk at school," explained a mother in Havre-Saint-Pierre who could not manage her house without the help of her fourteen-year-old son, as her husband was an invalid.[33] In all the twenty-five cases of illegal absences examined by a Montréal social worker, "the parents [wanted] their children to acquire a minimum of education but the difficult economic conditions in which they lived prevent[ed] this"; most expected their situation to improve again, and a large majority still hoped that their sons and daughters would attain at least the legal minimum of education.[34]

In the late 1940s, the increase in the cost of living added more pressure to certain families' incomes. In the words of the chief officer of the Montréal Catholic School Commission (MCSC) commenting on the 1951 census, "The continuous increase of the cost of living was able to force many parents to make their children of schooling age work in order to help parents make ends meet given a completely insufficient family budget."[35] If over the course of the 1950s the average income increased more rapidly than prices, the inflow of money remained insufficient in many families. Still, in 1954, by the admission of the chief inspector of the Québec Department of Labour (QDL), "there was nothing surprising about a father of a large family being obligated to put his children to work as soon as they reached the prescribed age."[36] In short, the general increase of mass consumption, to which family allowances contributed, created new pressures on family incomes. To those who were rejected from the "average standard of living," the models of consumption could have been part of the reason why they sent their children to work.[37]

In poor families, the number of children weighed heavily in the decision to pull children out of school before the prescribed age. In the new universal rights regime, where the family allowances were supposed to help larger families most of all, these were still the families in which it was most likely for children's attendance to be disrupted. Before the inauguration of compulsory education, the majority of children aged nine to thirteen who had left school belonged to families with over seven members.[38] Beginning in 1943, the requests for exemption from the Industrial and Commercial Establishments Act and the Compulsory School Attendance Act could often be explained by a single provider's trouble in feeding one large family.[39] The parents whose greater need for more of their children's help asked for these exemptions not only because tasks and needs had multiplied but also because they ran a higher risk of falling ill; repeated and short-interval pregnancies sometimes weakened the mother, and the parents, often older and tired, earned less money. These families were particularly short on clothing. Following interviews with wives of Montréal francophone labourers, Thérèse Roy wrote: "In families of [seven, eight, nine, and ten children] it is impossible to properly dress the children who, in reality, are lacking the most important clothing items, particularly in winter, especially in cases when the youngest do not go to school yet." Sometimes, so that the older children could be sent to college or to the convent, the younger children took their place working in the family. Inversely, sometimes the eldest were withdrawn from school early to earn an income that would permit the younger children to be educated, as a mother of twelve from Rouville County explained to the Superintendent of Public Instruction (SPI): "I am far from being resistant to education, but for the children currently in class to continue their education until grade ten we need the older kids' help."[40]

Over and above family size, adult labour-market fluctuations often obliged a child to work. Among the twenty-five families of children absent from school who were met by social worker Delphine Périard in 1951 in Montréal, ten family heads had precarious jobs. "I don't fill my weeks," a Saint-Sauveur father working for the municipality sewer collector explained to the SPI. Like many public-works labourers, he was employed only when the weather permitted.[41] The unemployment insurance payments lightened the financial burdens of many households: between 1946 and 1960, the benefits paid to Québec went from $19 million to $155 million. But such payments were still not enough to support a family, as in the case of a household with eight children whose father, a skilled worker, had been out of work for two months. The weekly unemployment insurance payments of $14 and the family allowances of $10 were used to purchase clothing and food; the family did not even have to include the cost of rent, as they lived with their mother-in-law. To the family allowance investigators who discovered that two of the children under sixteen were working illegally, the mother explained that she had not been able to make ends meet. Similarly, the provincial government's allowances for needy mothers often did not provide sufficient assistance.[42] In many instances heads of family were not eligible for unemployment insurance, and they were even more likely to withdraw a child from school. In 1942, elementary-school teachers mentioned that 238 students who had left school in the summer of 1941 had unemployed fathers. Some were able to count on their savings, but those only lasted so long. Thus, in 1955 a Drummondville family whose father had lost his job was able to subsist on savings for fourteen months, but once these had been exhausted, the parents had to ask their fifteen-year-old son to take on a job. A little later, they considered sending their fifteen-year-old daughter into the labour force. Given the differences between the sexes in remuneration for industrial and commercial work, the choice of making the son work first was logical. Other households with irregular incomes did not have the same capacity for economic resistance and turned immediately to a child's illegal labour: "I am very sad to say that I am forced by dire need to make [my child] work to bring food to the family," explained a mother to a social welfare court judge. "My husband has not worked in three weeks... [;] this week, we have no income." She explained that she had to pay the rent and the heating, that there was not a single grocer who would let her buy on credit, and that she had difficulty obtaining social assistance.[43]

Furthermore, even when they regained some stability, families accustomed to irregular income kept their children out of school as a safeguard in case of future hard times or to pay off previous debts—land or home purchases, or even hospital bills—that kept parents in precarious financial situations.[44] Finally, some families whose economic situation had long been difficult had taken up habits that even the youngest children did not want to give up: "Sometimes even if the child could continue his studies, he almost voluntarily shirked this choice, which would go against the family tradition established by the eldest children."[45]

More than the risk of losing income, reasons of parental illness, weakness, invalidity, and fatigue were behind requests for exemption from the Compulsory School Attendance Act addressed to the Department of Public Instruction (DPI). Parents also emphasized their greater age, or a history of having been overworked that contributed to the onset of illness, as did one woman who said she had "been ruined by doing others' laundry." Similarly, half the letters sent to the Department of Labour requesting a work permit, often in the instance of a young man's first job, mentioned the father's illness or invalidity. Sometimes the mayor or the parish priest added to the request, confirming that the child would only work until the father had returned to health. A mother's sickness would generally force the eldest daughter to take over the housework, but occasionally mothers kept a boy at home to chop wood and "run errands." Finally, younger children took over when their older siblings fell ill themselves.[46]

The death or departure of a parent could seriously compromise the family economy and cause the definite withdrawal of a child from school: "I have been a widow for 15 years," wrote a mother from Saint-Jean to the federal minister of labour, "and at present I have only one girl working. I am too ill to work myself now." Girls had to take charge of the house and the children, as was the case with one thirteen-year-old girl from Montréal whose mother had deserted home when the father returned from the front.[47] Many fathers who had lost their wives asked the SPI for permission to keep a girl at home to "fill the mother's role," like this father from Beaupré, a carter and municipal employee. Without her, he would have no one to make his lunch and dinner and answer the phone and receive his work offers. He explained to the superintendent that barring this arrangement, he would have to move in a boarding house. Another widower, a father of six school-aged children from Saint-Vallier, requested an exemption for over six weeks for his twelve-year-old girl, "who sees to the everyday tasks and keeps up the house," as he did not benefit from any aid from his relatives.[48]

Juvenile workers had often lost their father. This was the case for 20 per cent of the young labourers who appeared before the Montréal Social Welfare Court (MSWC) for non-attendance.[49] Most of these single-parent families spent their allowances on clothing, as the governmental publicity encouraged them to do through the medium of the fictive personality of the widow Leduc (see figure 10 in chapter 3). Meanwhile, in moments of crisis unforeseen by the official documents, there was no other way of paying the rent, and the allowances could not prevent some from getting into debt with the butcher and the grocer.[50]

In short, the new standards remained out of reach for a minority of households, for reasons that were mostly related to the structure of the labour market and which were worsened by accidents in family life. The State had surrounded families with more rigid norms, but it had not provided all of them with the means to reach these new standards, something many officials deplored already: "It is understood that the allowance helps; but it is far from enough to meet the needs of each child" the truancy officer from Saint-Gédéon-de-Frontenac reported in 1949. "It is not enough to convince people to send their children to school," a Saguenay inspector said regretfully. "We must also put them in a situation where they are able to follow through."[51]

The Development and Tolerance of Exceptions to Universal Rights: Sons of Self-Sufficient Farmers, Girls of Disadvantaged Homes, and Ghettos of Paid Juvenile Labour

After the right to a minimum of education had been instituted, the phenomenon of family work for children under fourteen years of age decreased considerably, as discussed in the previous chapter. The number of school-aged children who left school permanently for this reason was relatively low: we know that over the course of the 1945–46 school year, for example, 233 children in urban districts left elementary Catholic school illegally to work at home, and in rural districts, 514 children left school for the same reason.[52] However, there remained vestiges of this type of work, when legislators had announced its disappearance. How were they about to confront these irregularities?

Each year, the truancy officers would generally issue limited duration "permits for work at home." In 1948, for example, there were 6,741 of these permits. In fact, based on only the case in Montréal for the 1943–44 school year, the officers had direct access to these types of requests. This example came from higher ranks: when requests were addressed to him personally, the SPI himself authorized the extension of the absence permits in the majority of cases where parents needed their children by their sides.[53]

To understand the establishment of these legal exceptions, we must remember that most of the groups previously involved with the development of the law still considered child labour acceptable in family businesses, such as work conducted in the home or on the farm. This tolerance of those who stayed close to their parents can be explained, in turn, by the rigid structure of the labour market. Many truancy officers believed that, unable to offer an alternative solution to destitute families, they had no choice but to accommodate their demands.[54] Incomes were not sufficient to hire a salaried employee, and the labour pool to replace the children was limited, a lack that was accentuated during the war. Finally, the safety net of the Welfare State allowed youths to slip through another way: while working full time prevented them from enjoying the new protection for children, their absence from the paid labour market also prevented them from having access to the universal rights reserved for adults.[55] Instead of resolving this problem, the federal officers only supplied occasional case-by-case justifications.

Industrial or commercial businesses belonging to families did, however, benefit from such protection. Since its creation at the end of the nineteenth century, the Industrial and Commercial Establishments Act had always made an exception in favour of all "the family workshops where not a single worker from outside the family is employed, unless the workshops are classified as dangerous, insalubrious, or unsuitable..."[56] The Dominion Bureau of Statistics also demonstrated leniency by not enumerating individuals working without pay in a family business.[57] Once family allowances had been instituted, the truancy officers continued to find situations in which, without an alternative solution, they had to meet the demands of destitute families that wanted their children to work. Such was the case for a baker in Sainte-Cécile-de-Milton who wrote about his thirteen-year-old son: "He has been working in the bakery for me for nine months, since hiring a man to do it would cost me approximately $700 per year and I cannot afford that."[58] In circumstances such as these, and particularly "in cases of large families and poor families, taking away the allowance would do more harm than good."[59]

The new regime of universal rights curtailed the old exceptions in favour of farmers' sons by allowing them to work only during the hours and days they were not subject to compulsory school attendance; besides, there was no law regulating rural labour for fourteen- and fifteen-year-old children. In Québec, the head inspector for the Department of Labour avoided responding to criticisms regarding this tolerance by minimizing the nature of labour for children under fourteen: "The law does not include the agricultural industry and sometimes, during the harvest, children are asked neither to work in production nor in canning, but in the fields or in the gardens[;] children under 14 pick and pull stalks for approximately one or two hours per day, once or twice a week..."[60] The Compulsory School Attendance Act itself remained flexible with regard to children working on farms. It exempted all children under fourteen from attending school for a maximum period of six weeks (one-seventh of the school year) whose "services...are required for farm work or for urgent and necessary tasks at home or for the support of the child or his parents." If a longer period was needed, the SPI reserved the right to apply the law less strictly.[61] In addition to these exceptions in the law itself, there existed a greater laxness in the implementation of the regulations. In some rural districts, the number of demands for exception was in fact so great that the provincial inspectors asked the DPI to amend the law of compulsory schooling to exclude thirteen- and fourteen-year-old children from the country. Victor Doré refused and passed the problem on to the truancy officers, who, according to him, could judge the particular circumstances, keeping in mind the "conditions of location, age and season."[62] Other rural officers, who wished to take advantage of the law to reaffirm their authority by administrating punishments as examples, asked the superintendent for the means to prosecute or issue fines in the absence of a juvenile court outside Montréal and Québec: "If we do not take more rigorous measures with these people between now and the holiday," predicted the Sainte-Adélaïde-de-Pabos officer, "half of the children will stop attending school." "Do not prosecute," read the SPI's response to the officers, "but note it as an 'illegal absence.'" He then developed a "Special Warning," destined to restrain parents further, and which proved sometimes of a "salutary" nature.[63] The federal officials having to respect the tolerances of provincial administrations in the matter of education, their attitude regarding agricultural work only manifested itself in the case of the fourteen- and fifteen-year-olds. It did not seem much more severe. The family allowances regulations stated that boys aged fourteen and fifteen who were employed by their fathers for farm work would remain eligible for the program.

Farmers' children had always been more likely to leave school. The 1942 survey revealed that sons and daughters of farmers represented 50 per cent and 41 per cent, respectively, of the children under fourteen who had left school over the summer of 1941, while the farmers had come to represent only 20 per cent of the province's entire labour force.[64] Among these young labourers of 1941, 1,373 boys and 910 girls under fourteen were doing proper agricultural work, which corresponded to 50 per cent and 25 per cent, respectively, of that age's labour force. After September 1943, they continued to hold the records of school leaving. The school census-takers again found, outside of Montréal and Québec, 1,249 boys of compulsory school age working at home, most of them on farms. The following year, this number remained high, at 1,267.[65] Other than those who were permanently absent, thousands of boys from rural districts stayed away from school more than ten days each year. The number of students leaving after reaching the age of thirteen continued to be a problem despite hopes that it would diminish. An inspector continued to worry, in 1948, that

> few boys return to school after grade 7 [because of the] multiple tasks a boy of a dozen years can, and is often forced to, carry out on the farm for which the father alone would not be enough. This is why, as soon as his grade 7 is completed, he will often be found at the handlebars of the plough, when not at the factory, where the attraction of a salary would have already drawn him.[66]

A full ban on juvenile labour would have received a poor reception from farmers, since few welfare measures had been offered to them in the past. Before 1940, the living conditions of rural families had been the subject of the more generous myths, an ideal that did not only belong to the French-Canadian elite. In 1933, for example, the provincial Montpetit

Commission on social insurance had dismissed the proposals for family allowances, arguing that the rural families would not need them and allowances given to parents in cities would encourage the rural exodus.[67] Even after the war, there were still intellectuals who affirmed that, outside cities, families were shielded from all insecurity.[68]

As we have seen, Mackenzie King himself had hoped that the allowances would liberate rural parents from their needs for juvenile labour, and beginning in 1942, the federal Department of Labour's advisory body described the dangers of rural labour for children:

> Reports received from different provinces indicate that each year certain rural schools [especially in sugar-beet- and tobacco-growing regions] function in an almost disorganized state during the active seasons. The volume of a similar labour varies with the type of harvest, the value parents put on their children's education, and the generosity and skill they demonstrate in finding help elsewhere, as is also the case with local school authorities' foresight and influence. When the workload is not considerably high and the hours are short, the main objection to such work is in the fact that it hinders school attendance, which by nature develops the habit of irregular attendance, and holds the student back in his classes and encourages him to leave his books as early as possible.[69]

But after the programs had been implemented, the officials soon had to face the rural families whose economic situation was precarious to the point where a complete ban on juvenile labour could have caused, according to Victor Doré, "a serious prejudice against a child's family."[70] The family allowances surveys revealed the existence of pockets of extreme poverty in the country. Many parents used their allowances, not to fill the gaps in their towns with regard to social and medical services as the legislators had hoped, but rather to satisfy essential needs. A large proportion of families in the Nicolet and Gaspé-Nord Counties, for example, spent their allowances on food, and only 20 per cent of the rural families saved their allowances for medical or dental care, a comparable proportion to that of poor Montréal families.[71] In 1946, in 60 per cent of the families social worker Thérèse Légaré met with in the county of Gaspé-Nord, neither the mother nor the children had ever received medical care, and only 40 per cent of childbirths had been overseen by a doctor.[72]

Having been made aware of these situations, the governments were still not ready to ensure means for farmers to go without their children's labour. Deeply rooted family traditions still fed on the reality that a number of farmers could not earn a living without the help of sons, a problem aggravated by the considerable size of rural families. As Montréal sociologists Haythorne and Marsh observed in 1941, the use of child labour on farms, though not very productive, was often the only possible immediate solution for the economic tensions of the business. This solution brought with it a vicious circle that was difficult to break, as the maintenance costs for children came in direct competition with the cost of farm operation and technological improvements:

> To meet the expenses of rearing a large family, providing some members with education beyond primary school, establishing others on farm, is no small feat. If the farm is not exceptionally prosperous, these costs compete heavily with the technical demands of the farm itself, for equipment, maintenance, fertilizer and improvement.... And in "the application of the additional labour to the land" the possibilities of diminishing returns must be considered not merely as an economic matter, but in far-pervading social terms.[73]

In the absence of boys old enough to work, girls were often called upon. Poor farmers' daughters often had to leave home prematurely:

> Having reached a certain age, [they] must earn to help the family, or at least to no longer be dependent upon the family home. Many [of those interviewed in Montréal by the Jeunesse ouvrière catholique (JOC)] admitted that on an estate, boys are more valuable than girls and so have all the privileges; girls, however, have the pleasure of hearing far too often that they are a burden.[74]

Hiring a day labourer to replace a child seemed costly and unnecessary given the irregular nature of the work the farmers had their young sons do:

> "Three municipalities in my district, essentially market gardening centres, have almost no regular traffic," complained an urban district inspector in 1946. "The rarity of labour is used as an excuse to keep little boys and girls from 10 to 13 years old at the service of potatoes or green onions, as the children easily lose the taste for school and disorganize elementary school teachers' planning. Work permits are extorted or are quite simply gone without."[75]

As the resulting absences were short but frequent, it was difficult to control them:

> "This is how it goes," reported the Sainte-Élisabeth truancy officer: "One fine morning the parents need their children for work on the farm; the distance between home and the officer's house is of four or five miles. I don't need to tell you that they simply keep the child at home and send him back once the work is done. These kinds of absences generally last two or three days."[76]

The boys were often responsible for preparing and transporting firewood, harvesting potatoes, transporting water, looking after the animals, making maple sugar, or even helping their fathers: "You know," wrote a father from Portneuf, "that heavy hardwood chopping isn't a one-man job." Little disposed to face the restraints of the agricultural market, the Catholic Committee to the Public Instruction Council (CCPIC) set up, in the mid-1940s, special rural schools for older boys, whose schedules varied according to local labour needs.[77]

The farmers' situations became increasingly polarized over the course of the 1940s and 1950s, between commercial farms and their increasing reliance on mechanization (which constituted two-thirds of the establishments in 1961) and subsistence farms, "left behind by the technological revolution." The high number of the latter largely explains why the global rates of juvenile activity in the province were higher than in other provinces.[78] In the regions of recent settlement, both properties and yields were small, which required a mixed economy. For some less-affluent farmers, family allowances were enough to replace a secular dependence vis-à-vis forestry activity; the phenomenon was far from being widespread however, as 65 per cent of such marginal farms had another source of income in 1961.[79] When the land continued to constitute only a part of family income, fathers and older sons often left the care of the farm to the mothers and younger children during the winter, as one father from Saint-Rémi-Lac-aux-Sables described to the SPI:

> As soon as my bigger jobs are done I leave the rest to my little boy because me I have to go and seriously earn outside to support my family[;] on a little piece of gravel land the money isn't enough to support a big family of 19.... [My] son has to see to all the stable chores and care for the hen-house. In the winter we have a horse that needs to be taken out every day.[80]

Hiring a replacement would have monopolized all the money they earned outside the home: "I cannot hire a man," explained a railroad worker from Saint-Nazaire-d'Acton to the SPI. "It would swallow all my salary and my son would do it just as well."[81] Fathers attempted to gain additional income by working in the mines, in lumber camps, in factories on a seasonal basis, or even in skilled labour workshops. When the forestry camps were far from farms, which was increasingly the case after 1940, the fathers could bring their whole families with them:

> A large number of farmers... are only there part of the time[;] that is, they do not live only on the income from their plot of land, which is basically only for growing. Cutting down trees constitutes, in reality, their main source of income. For a period of 6 to 8 months, these people "pull down wood." The comfort offered by more and more forest exploitation companies in their forest camps encourages, in a general manner, the complete exodus of families into the woods: father, mother, and children... In the past, it was relatively easy to leave the children to board with family

or friends. These days, with the overpopulation of lodging in villages and practically everywhere, this is no longer done.[82]

For the more recently established settlers, preliminary work required all family members to share labour, as in the Chazel family in Abititi, whose mother wrote:

> My little boy [of 13] can't manage to do everything at school and make the train because we are badly off we carry water for the stable and the house and he has to chop the fire wood for 2 stoves you understand that this is very hard we have 7 horned animals to look after its just me and my husband is in the woods he can't stay to do that we aren't rich and we have to live and we want to build a stable of wood and a shed for our hay so it's for that reason that he really has to work if we want to be better settled so I would like to ask you if I could keep my son at home without losing his family alowance.[83]

It all depended on the age and gender of the children who were free. Sometimes the mother took care of farm work while a daughter replaced her in the house, as was the case for one family in Saint-Eugène-d'Argenteuil:

> "We need our eldest of 13," a mother pleaded to the superintendent, "being on new land and my husband works for the aluminum company in Alma so I am alone to do everything on the land with 10 children.... This fall we have 40 potato patches to harvest with a pick me and the children looking after the stable all winter I could not do without my little girl to babysit...."[84]

Sons and daughters of lumberjacks, miners, and fishermen must be added to the category of farmers' children. Among the dropouts who left school in the summer of 1941, 201 boys and 242 girls under fourteen years of age had a father belonging to one of these employment categories; some of them helped their father directly (68 boys and 20 girls) and many lived on a land. The sons and daughters of fishermen were obliged to miss school on a seasonal basis, to help their fathers in Trois-Ruisseau (Gaspé), to pack the cod in Port-Daniel, or to salt and smoke the fish on Îsle-Verte. On the coast of Labrador, the Protestant truancy officer noted that

> [a] ten-month school year is not feasible in four out of the eleven schools, where the population is served by some schools that move to nearby islands in April and May, and few students stay for all ten months. This seasonal migration is necessitated by the fishing season, which, on the Labrador coast, has priority over all else, despite the attraction of the family allowances.[85]

There were parents who took up the old argument that too much education would encourage their children to leave the country: "at 14 years old on a farm, one has already been able for a long time to milk the cows and care for the pigs and the chickens and many other little jobs and if he goes to school he can not do his jobs so when he leaves school he will rather go see girls and write than do all his jobs it is not with this law that we will make farmers."[86] The leniency demonstrated by the truancy officers towards these parents contrasts with the fate of city parents who expressed the same opinion and whose children ended up in juvenile court.[87] In general, however, farmers valued extended education, and the lack of confidence in the benefits of school came instead from the educational system's weaknesses, as one inspector from Saint-Félicien indicated in 1948:

> One fact accounting for a large part of this...which incites parents to withdraw their children from school too early, especially the boys: it is that the current grade-school organization does not allow for the students to become interested, beyond grade 6, or allow them to devote the necessary time to occupy them and make them work in the manner required for the education. Often these students are the elementary-school teacher's nightmare. They cause disturbance for the whole class. The parents who make real sacrifices to keep them in school realize that they are wasting their time and they simply withdraw them.[88]

For children over fourteen years of age, the school was neither free nor available everywhere, and the pursuit of studies was becoming even more difficult.

During the war, the number of available farm workers decreased, so the farmers were faced with a new dilemma. A Marieville father attempted to convince the superintendent of his plight:

> I have just asked you if I could keep the older ones at home to help me. I have a good amount of tomatoes, corn, beans, and I still have to pick the beans in a pod. My clover seeds to reap and the oats and the temperature is not always favourable we're not making any headway and you know as well as me that the tomatoes and the beans, the corn when they're ready to be harvested if we wait it's a huge loss...so I'm asking you for permission to keep my children on the busiest days to help me between now and when the frost comes for the tomatoes.[89]

"Labour is so rare that I'm afraid of losing my vegetables," said a farmer and gardener from Terrebonne County who was obliged to count on his thirteen-year-old son for help. In Saint-Anaclet, in Rimouski County, the truancy officer saw no other solution but to increase the number of permits of absence from school.[90] More generally, one section of the Union des cultivateurs catholiques (UCC) asked the government to refrain from applying the law so rigorously: "The council is opposed to the implementation of the Compulsory School Attendance Act, since in these times of rare labour, there are cases in which a young boy or a young girl is precious to parents in the case of the mother's or father's illness."[91] By forcing an increase in demand for farm products, the war added other pressures to the demand for juvenile labour. Seizing this opportunity, rural families increased their production by carrying out work that was not previously profitable without modifying their growing methods. The result, according to Gérald Fortin, was that "the mother as well as the children were obliged to spend more time doing farm work." In order to do this, women and children left their trade work, which augmented families' dependence on the consumer goods.[92]

Behind these exclusions was the fact that pressures to regulate child labour in farming families had been lesser than the pressures against labour in industrial and commercial establishments. In the 1940s and 1950s, most organizations that fought in favour of a broader control of juvenile labour still did not include farms in their discussions; in fact, the Montreal Youth Bureau had expressly excluded it.[93] For their part, the farming associations did not directly fight against juvenile labour; their situation was distinct from that of the city unions' in the production sector, as the children did not directly threaten adults jobs and most farmers were employers themselves.[94]

The tolerance of farm work did not represent the secondary feature of an adventure whose centre would be elsewhere: rather, it constituted an essential aspect of the formation of universal Welfare State in Québec and in Canada. Starting in the second half of the nineteenth century, governments had presented the colonization of virgin soil as a remedy for the weakness of the industrial economy. Taking away the control farming families had over their work force would have also meant the complete abandonment of the usual logic of the State's answer in times of economic crisis.

Next to farmers' sons, the daughters of poor families were the other large group for whom the universal laws of the 1940s aimed to guarantee an extended education. During the first few months of the implementation of compulsory education, in the case of Cap-de-la-Madeleine, the law affected girls more than boys, and a homogenization of experiences occurred.[95] We can see that the image of a little girl heading to school determinedly, published by the DNHW, indicated a similar change (see figure 12). However, the difference in attendance rates between boys and girls reappeared quickly enough and this image can be seen as an exception, as most official representations of active children in the 1940s and 1950s continued to feature boys as a rule.

The State's attempts to extend the new privileges of universal rights to girls who were helping their mothers at home were relatively weak. In

Figure 12. The Information Service for family allowances circulated the new and still rare image of an autonomous girl, active and educated.

Source: NAC, Official Publications, National Library of Canada negative NL15299, Canada, DNHW, *You and Your Family* (Ottawa: King's Printer, 1949), 9. (Reproduced with the permission of the Department of Public Works and Government Services Canada, 1997.)

the early 1940s, helping the mother constituted the largest work sector for the province's children. In the summer of 1941, elementary-school teachers in Québec had already indicated that 2,160 girls under the age of fourteen had left school to work without pay for their parents, representing 59.3 per cent of female workers in that age group. In 1943, despite the adoption of compulsory education, census-takers enumerated 1,717 girls under fourteen who were not registered at any school and who were working at home illegally; of these girls, 159 were Montréal Catholics. Parents who withdrew their girls from school before the age of fourteen had a tendency to keep them at home for several years, until they were able to find paid work and a younger sister was able to take over. Often, between family work and factory work, there was a period during which the young girl worked as a servant in another family.[96]

It is possible that at the time, compulsory education would have kept in school girls who wanted to do something else: in 1944, when the census focused only on the Catholic population outside of Montréal and Verdun, there were only 667 girls under fourteen to fit this category, which represented a decrease by 50 per cent for this territory. It is not surprising, given the fact that the Compulsory School Attendance Act authorized children of school age to leave school to help their parents at home. The parents who took advantage of the home work permits numbered at least 349 across Québec in 1943, and 549 in 1944 outside Montréal and Verdun, according to the school census.[97] Over and above those numbers, the agencies entrusted with the implementation of the law could not prevent thousands of girls from being absent from school at least ten days a year to work at home "illegally." Some parents were able to disguise domestic work as illness, their presence at home facilitating the evasion. As for the girls, illness was by far the most common reason for leaving, after work, while for boys, this cause was much less frequent. Most simply profited from the tolerance of authorities. In 1956, the head of truancy monitoring at the Montréal Catholic School Committee (MCSC) reported that a "number of mothers, ill or overworked and unable to afford the services of a maid, managed to keep, without permission, a boy or girl of compulsory school age at home, to help them in their domestic work."[98] In this respect, the case of a mother of ten in Chambly was the focus of press attention in 1951 about the inadequacy of social programs: her eldest daughter, aged twelve, worked as a "maid" for five dollars per week, which meant that the family lost its allowance. The second, aged ten, stayed at home to help her mother after the birth of the youngest child.[99]

Girls' work at home received even greater tolerance than boys' work on the farm. Federal officials did not even try to investigate if parents could have hired someone else to assist them, which was often their routine with regard to boys' work. It is therefore not surprising that the new laws had less impact for girls aged fourteen and fifteen than for boys of the same age. The girls continued to leave school by the thousands to help their mothers at home. And the work counted by census-takers maintained the same absolute importance in the 1940s and 1950s. According to the federal government's decennial census, 20 per cent of fourteen- and fifteen-year-old girls from the province of Québec had looked after their homes full time during the last week of May 1951. Their numbers alone equalled the number of all boys their age in the active population.

Girls' work as maids was not subject to the Industrial and Commercial Establishments Act, and the surveys on juvenile labour did not demonstrate any particular concern with girls who did this work (only the family allowances officials considered this occupation in the same category as all other jobs and included it as a reason to suspend benefits, as it was paid work). The number of girls who worked as maids is impossible to judge, as the 1942 survey did not enter these girls into any particular category and the federal censuses excluded them completely, except in 1951, when it was found that 7 per cent of fourteen- and fifteen-year-old girls carried out "services" in a home other than their own.

These legislative gaps regarding girls' education and welfare bear witness to the rarity of organized groups ready to defend girls' interests. To our knowledge, in the procedures leading to the adoption of the three laws studied, not a single group specifically referred to the situation of girls working with their mothers. The province's educational authorities concern regarding girls working at home, which underlay the movement to create home-economics schools, never reached a level where it could have launched, as in the case of agricultural work, a questioning of the refusal of compulsory education. Numerous reformists even considered domestic family work as the most desirable job: "The JOC does not fear teaching young workers that they should orient themselves towards jobs suiting their gender, their condition and their health, such as domestic work."[100] It is also possible that the women's groups campaigning in favour of the restriction of children's work were largely composed of members of the bourgeoisie who enjoyed domestic servants and that it was not in their interest to attack that sector. Finally, the weakness of the feminine membership within the central labour bodies might explain those organizations' low level of interest in educating girls: neither the auxiliary leagues of union members' wives nor the central Catholic bodies' committee on the female condition paid much attention to the issue at all.[101]

In the eyes of the school inspectors, the bishops, and, ultimately, the legislators, it was country boys' school attendance that carried the most serious consequences. While boys should have received more education, lamented the bishops, it was the girls who tended to study longer, since "in our countryside, we push girls towards the convent more often in the hope that they will teach for a few years at least later on, and thus earn an honorable living," a vicious cycle encouraged by the low salaries offered by school boards.[102] There was no hesitation to blame the women's dominant role as elementary-school teachers for boys' problems. "At the age of 12, and sometimes even at the age of 11, the little boy begins to take up the ways of a man and hopes, without being aware of it, to receive training suitable for a man." The bishops believed that the "the number of boys would ask that they be sent neither to Sisters nor to female elementary-school teachers," and the inspectors had recommended that "boys' schools" be opened for those over twelve years of age.

This conception of female roles explains the considerable underdevelopment of the educational system beyond girls' primary education. The Champlain School Board, for example, did not make elementary school free for girls until 1949.[103] These circumstances affected the other social laws: if there were no places for them to pursue their studies, why keep the fourteen- and fifteen-year-old girls from working?

Besides, in the minds of many parents, domestic work offered girls a relatively valuable initiation into their future roles as wives and mothers. "I have never been to school and I was able to marry anyway!" objected a mother to a social worker at a family social assistance office.[104] For the girls who rarely considered leaving school to help their mothers as a direct sign of autonomy, marriage would be the path to a certain independence, one that at once broke away from the obligations of being a young girl and created the possibility of having one's own family. The students thus adopted gendered views on their economic roles relatively early; in farmers' and labourers' homes, the reproduction of the social relationships between genders passed through this intermediary stage.[105]

The State's hesitation to regulate work at home was the expression of the officials' double reticence—reticence, on one hand, to see paid work as a possibility for married women, and reticence, on another, to accord a solid economic recognition to women's work at home. In the eyes of political leaders, the situation of adult women was not wholly distinct from that of children: their economic existence was dependent on that of the masculine heads of family, and, up to a certain point, this was true at the civic and political levels. When we recall that family allowances had constituted a means of encouraging mothers to return to the home after the war, it is not surprising to note that the laws' administrators conceived of women within the domestic sphere.[106] In the official publications of the DNHW, the father was the only provider, the cheques were made out to the mothers, and, when a task concerned the family's relationship with public powers, or when it called for management of large sums of money (e.g., filling in the application for allowances or planning long-term spending), the husband appeared in the illustrations (see figure 13).

The struggle over making cheques out to mothers had admittedly ended in an official recognition of women's economic contribution, but this admission remained only partial and on the condition of certain moral standards. Similarly, specific moral requirements applied to schoolgirls. The agents of the juvenile court did not evaluate motives for delinquency in the same way for the two sexes. Girls' sexuality received systematic attention, and proof of their virginity was an element of the court's records. For boys, the personnel in charge of implementing the Compulsory School Attendance Act were more interested in disobedience.[107]

Many groups in Québec society adhered to the idea of women being dependent upon their husbands' incomes. This notion was present in the economic elite's and business unions' credo of individual liberty, in the proposal for a family wage expressed by workers' unions and Catholic reformist circles, as well as in the struggle against married women's work

Figure 13. In the minds of federal officials, management of the daily consumption was up to mothers, and important budgetary decisions were made by fathers.

Source: NAC, Official Publications, National Library of Canada negative NL15299, Canada, DNHW, *You and Your Family* (Ottawa: King's Printer, 1949), 10. (Reproduced with the permission of the Department of Public Works and Government Services Canada, 1997.)

led by the clerical and conservative elite.[108] The heterogeneous character of the group who had asked that the cheques be sent to mothers explains the fragility of the progress achieved in the civic recognition of women. The more conservative saw it as a means to bypass the problem of men's morality in poorer classes: a Jesuit magazine had suggested that the mother become the beneficiary "to prevent an always possible misuse of funds," and the editor of *Assurances* magazine confirmed that a "good precaution to take would be to give the sum to the mother and not the father, so that the latter does not drink it away."[109] In the House of Commons, social-democrat MPs approached the problem likely to arise from the combination of excessive economic dependence and an unfavourable judicial context, citing women who struggled with husbands who overlooked them. According to them, family allowances would allow women's circumstances to be corrected without undue intervention: "It is hard for a woman to complain when her husband is not doing what he should with regard to his children, and an intervention in the home and family life in my opinion would offend, and could have a dangerous result. I would therefore like the money to be given to the mother."[110] The allowances could increase the mother's standing in families in various other ways: the East-Edmonton Liberal MP recalled that we should not forget that the mother was often the least well fed member in the family.[111]

As with the farmers' sons, girls who helped their mothers at home belonged to a sector in which there was a very low supply of labour, and during the 1940s, the shortage and the high cost of maids worsened the already long-standing circumstances. This hiring sector was the least popular, as the wages were low. In 1944, a survey of 100 maids in Montréal established that 67 per cent earned less than ten dollars a month and that they worked over twelve hours a day, while the JOC recommended a monthly wage of twelve. Most often, these positions were occupied by girls whose farming families could no longer support them, and the maids carried out the same tasks for well-off families that poor families had their own daughters do. In fact, during the war, a certain number of middle-class families sent their children to boarding schools to remedy the lack of maids.[112] For even less well-off families, the lack of inexpensive maids created additional pressure to withdraw girls from school. "Impossible to pay expensive maids, and hard to find as so many young girls work in war factories," complained a sick mother from Kénogami in 1943. "Maids are impossible to find and their wages are so high that I haven't the means to pay one," emphasized a mother of ten from Saint-Jean-Port-Joli who requested an exemption from the Compulsory School Attendance Act for her eldest daughter of thirteen. The shortage did not end with the war, judging by this report from Inspector Filteau, who described in his 1947–48 report that

> attendance at school continues to be excellent for the lower grades. Over the age of 14, however, school leavings multiply and reach a previously unforeseen number, which cannot be addressed over the course of the ending year. The lack of domestic help and the constant increase in the cost of living are the main reasons behind parents' forcing their children to leave school and stay home.[113]

In more distant regions, the problem was even more serious. A father from Saint-Jean-Baptiste-d'Ascot who wanted to keep his thirteen-year-old daughter at home to help her mother feed the household's twelve members had made his request made for him by a letter writer: "There can't be a servant because of the distance from town. He has published advertisements in newspapers to have a maid and no one has answered the ad and he needs someone to help his wife maintain the house, make the meals, etc."[114]

Mothers of large families were most in need of this kind of help, which goes a long way to explain why, in Québec, the proportion of fourteen- and fifteen-year-old girls busy with domestic tasks (20 per cent) was at least twice that in other provinces.[115] More than the new State norms, it seems that, the later decrease in family size may have helped to eradicate the last pockets of labour for girls under sixteen years of age.

During the war, the federal government allowed the fourteen-year-old girl norm to be contravened by encouraging mothers to take up industrial labour. Actually, across the entire country, the proportion of married women working outside the home went from 10 per cent in 1939 to 35 per cent in 1944. A journalist from *Le Devoir* estimated that "in Montréal alone, more than five thousand children of women working in the war factories are left alone or in the uncertain care of older brothers or sisters, grandparents, or even neighbours."[116] In 1942, the JOC deplored this fact:

> Little girls will stay at home to "babysit," while mothers work in war factories. It is surprising to learn the number of little girls of 14, 13, 12 and even 10 years of age are keeping house, making the meals, looking after children of all ages, even babies of only a few months old, and this to allow mummy to work and bring more home. It is one of the sad consequences of mothers working outside the home.[117]

The six daycares set up in the province by the federal government between 1943 and 1945 that received, on average, 115 to 120 children each did not really measure up. Some mothers found that their children were treated better in the daycares than anywhere else, while others feared sending their very young children to these centres. They preferred to keep them at home and entrust them to their older daughters, a decision reinforced by hygiene problems and accidents in private daycares, which media attention had helped to highlight. Only two of the Montréal public daycares received Catholic francophone children, and one was forced to close because of a lack of clientele.[118]

Besides, it is possible that compulsory education and the tightening of the labour laws indirectly influenced birth rates: in increasing the costs of child care, they may have contributed to a decrease in family size. It is difficult to know if, inversely, the allowances contributed to the baby boom in the years following the war, even more so because any such suggestion was, at the time, the subject of ethnic tensions. Concerned with awakening ethnic conflicts, federal officials made it a point of honour to minimize the impact of the payments on fertility rates. They insisted that the increase in the birth rate in the U.S., where this type of social law had not been adopted, was higher than that in Canada between 1939 and 1948 (28.2 per cent compared with 20.2 per cent).[119]

Girls, like their mothers, had to look after families, something the Welfare State did not yet take into consideration. They were called upon when their mothers' or older sisters' work at home was interrupted by illness. Among the eight workers under the age of fourteen appearing before the MSWC for non-attendance at school, four of them worked at home. In the first case, the mother was sick; in the second, the mother had left; in the third, the mother of nine needed her twelve-year-old daughter to help her; and, in the fourth, the mother was sick and the eldest sister worked outside the home. Girls' work at home could also liberate mothers who wished to work for payment to make up for their husband's insufficient work. A Montréal mother of seven, for example, began to work in 1948 when her husband fell ill. "I don't send [my thirteen-year-old daughter] to school, so she can look after the house and I can work and help my husband pay our debts," confided another Montréal mother in 1948 to the juvenile court's probation officer.[120] Finally, it was sometimes necessary to take care of relatives, as was the case for a Saint-Hyacinthe girl looking after her ninety-year-old grandfather, who needed special care. The Sainte-Séraphine officer recognized this phenomenon when he took the liberty of extending the meaning of the legal excuse of "illness" from the girl's state of health to that of her parents, which meant they could keep their daughter at home illegally without being disturbed.[121]

Thus, material considerations and family obligations combined to keep girls of schooling age at home. Parents also knew that family work had the advantage of unrivalled loyalty. "Servants don't want to work on farms…apart from that we couldn't find any who would want to do my daughter's work," wrote a father of ten from Girardville (Roberval) whose thirteen-year-old daughter looked after thirty dairy cows and 125 chickens and had ninety pounds of wool to spin while his wife went out into the fields.[122] In such cases, the specific harshness of the tasks was in extreme opposition to the image of protected family labour, which made many reformists and legislators tolerant. Banning domestic labour for girls under the age of fourteen and prohibiting it for girls aged fourteen and fifteen would have required the government to make a considerable investment into allowances allowing mothers to obtain domestic help, particularly in the situation of large families—a series of reforms the government was not willing to entertain.

The prime minister of Québec had hoped that the Compulsory School Attendance Act, by bringing children to attend school until at least grade seven, would increase these children's chances of continuing beyond the threshold and towards secondary education. With this ideal in mind, primary school could offer the general knowledge necessary for developing children's potential, and the higher studies could offer the specific knowledge necessary for allowing them to earn a living.[123] In this way, he had believed, the movement of specialized school beyond elementary school, begun in the 1910s, could finally provide the desired results. But Adélard Godbout had not been ready to embed these wishes into the law. The commissioners of the school municipality of Victoriaville, who asked what boys and girls between fourteen and fifteen years old should do, received the following answer from the secretary of the DPI: "I should first tell you that we hope most of these children will continue to attend school without being forced to. Secondly, we must consider that the proposed policy could always be modified if we find that social welfare demands it.[124] What was this "social welfare" that affected the limit after age fourteen?

At first glance, it seems that Québec businesses still had such a large need for juvenile labour that the government would not dare to ban it, as is demonstrated in the increase of the fourteen- and fifteen-year-old workforce in factories and businesses during the war, which happened under the complicit eye of Department of Labour officials. Beginning in 1940, the annual amount of age and education certificates issued by the Department of Labour increased considerably: approximately 2,000 in the 1930s, it reached a maximum of over 20,000 over the last three years of the war and diminished progressively to settle around 10,000 in 1950.[125] With no indication of change in the issuing of certificates or in business-inspection assiduity around 1941, these figures reveal an increase in industrial and commercial labour of fourteen- and fifteen-year-olds, which is far less known than that of women's work during the war. In Québec, where married women's work was the subject of a particularly strong ideological ban, it is possible that the pressures on juvenile labour were even stronger than elsewhere in North America.[126] Numerous were the employers who, to support their requests for work permits or exceptions to the law, mentioned this decrease in the number of available adult labourers. "We need employees very badly and we are prepared to employ this child providing our request meets your approval," wrote an administrator from textile company Belding-Corticelli to the Department of Labour in 1945 to request the exception of a thirteen-year-old boy.[127]

The increase in demand for labourers under the age of fourteen during the war is difficult to evaluate, as the employers and young employees had their own reasons for hiding their game. Take, for example, the report of QDL Inspector M. Rivest, who visited J.A.M. Côté Ltée of Saint-Hyacinthe in 1944: "There was great care taken to hide," he explained, "and the young girl from the office hid one or many timecards... [the] manager... told me that he had been informed by telephone, and that they were careful to hide any compromising evidence before my arrival."[128] It was the "disappearing act" unions had denounced for so long, which also explains why in 1942, the Ligue ouvrière catholique had been able to find fifty-five thirteen-year-olds working in the eight industries of a small town where it conducted a survey. The normal employees who had left for military training had been replaced by younger boys, who were subsequently replaced by their younger siblings: "We are noticing that the messengers' average age has decreased... since the war," commented the JOC. "Currently, the young messengers are 12, 13 and 14 years old.... There are even young girls of 15 and 16 years old filling these functions in some urban centres."[129]

In Montréal, the Rue Notre-Dame office of the province's Department of Labour, where the fourteen- and fifteen-year-olds came to fetch their permits, was up to its eyes in work. The increase in school population precipitated by the Compulsory School Attendance Act was largely compromised by the decrease in school population of those older than fourteen due to the "lure of wages." In 1945, for example, five classes were forced to close in one of the MCSC's inspection districts due to "the ease with which students with study certificates or who have reached the age of 14 are hired, the main reason for this decrease."[130] Worried by this "sudden increase," the provincial secretary wrote to the minister of labour: "The reason for the increase in the number of certificates issued during the 1942–43 school year is due to the fact that adult labour is rare and the massive production in war industries requires more employees, while new civil industries have sprung up in the province."[131] Once the war had ended, hiring school-aged children in factories and businesses decreased. After the demand for juvenile labour had cooled, the minister of labour invited his inspectors to adopt a more energetic attitude, asking them to carry out visits with the sole aim of tracking down illegal juvenile labour:

> The Minister...has expressed the desire to apply the prescriptions of the Industrial and Commercial Establishments Act more severely, regarding the admission age of messengers and delivery boys; you will want to give the necessary instructions to the two inspectors of the districts of Montréal and Québec to carry out the visits to the commercial establishments day and night, in the aim of monitoring the delivery boys' age...[132]

But there were still sectors of industrial or commercial employment in which the entrepreneurs' high demand for juvenile labour enjoyed the government's indulgence. In September 1945, for example, the Minister of Labour Antonio Barrette still believed that "banning fourteen- and fifteen-year-old children from cheaply filling particular positions such as delivery boys or messengers is equivalent to letting other provinces that share the same attitude become competitive."[133] Even the hiring of youths under fourteen was allowed to continue despite the State's move towards a less-compromising supervision: in 1945, the labour inspectors found twelve children aged thirteen in the 1,096 commercial establishments of Lévis and Québec; in 1952, following a Confédération des travailleurs catholique du Canada (CTCC) complaint, the inspectors visited the three Wabasso textile factories in Mauricie, where they ordered "the dismissal of all employees under 14, an order to which no one objected." Across the entire region, they established that 3 per cent of children working in factories or businesses were under the age of fourteen.[134] In March 1953, the Society for the Protection of Women and Children declared that

Québec's provincial law on children's work was "more honoured in violation than respect. Even recently, we have had to bring actions against the cases of 200 children, in which some were only ten years old and working in factories, particularly in canning factories, in the summer."[135]

Once these exceptional circumstances had dissipated, industrial and commercial work was confined to jobs that were beginning to be seen as traditionally children's jobs. In a general manner, the mechanization of businesses had increased the demand for educated workers but continued to create tasks that children could complete without any qualifications. Two-thirds of the fourteen- and fifteen-year-old workers known by the Department of Labour through the permit system had industrial jobs: the large majority of girls worked in the clothing industry (30 per cent); next on the list were the textiles and food trades, attracting 10 per cent of permit holders. As for the boys, numbers were more widely distributed among different types of industries.[136] Two jobs were typically identified with boys: grocery or pharmacy delivery boy and office or factory messenger. We know that in September 1941, Montréal's 494 "licensed" grocery stores employed 87 boys aged fourteen as delivery boys and 148 boys aged fifteen; these youths constituted one-third of the city's 749 delivery boys. The 1942 school survey enumerated 200 messengers under the age of fourteen, which constituted the largest majority of children in this age group who did not work for their parents and whose occupation was known to the statisticians. The survey also determined 823 boys aged fourteen and fifteen were messengers, representing half the children of that age who did not work for their parents and who held jobs known to the government.[137]

Generally prisoners to distinctive jobs, children thus constituted a labour pool available to employers depending on the situation. The irregular demand for juvenile labour is proof of these circumstances. The 1951 survey established that the annual period of activity for fourteen- and fifteen-year-old children was at least twice as short as that of their older counterparts and, the younger children were, the more possible it was to place them in a temporary job.[138] Furthermore, the children constituted cheap labour: the average wage for boys was one-quarter of the average man's, and the average wage for girls was a little over one-third of the average woman's. The CTCC's attitude on the increase of juvenile labour during the war demonstrates that children working in these particular sectors were not among its main cause for concern. In this increase, it saw a "new phenomenon due either to the poverty of the head of the family, the lure of income for the child, or parents' apathy or lack of authority."[139]

As low as wages were, those for fourteen- and fifteen-year-olds matched the amount of the family allowances, and "if the child earns more working," remarked Montréal Inspector Gosselin, "parents do not need to worry about losing the family allowance."[140] In 1941, a boy's monthly salary was sixteen dollars, a girl's was thirteen dollars, and the allowances were but eight dollars for children of that age. The Family Allowances Bureau could not assume that a child whose allowance had been withheld would cease working: among the some 10,000 children in Québec who lost their eligibility each year, only 700 re-established it.

In principle, the instability and low pay involved in juvenile labour were justified by the notion that children's contribution was complementary, as they were economically dependent on their families. In reality, however, employers made children work in regions where there were unemployed older men.[141] Juvenile labour contributed to the creation of another vicious cycle: hiring children perpetuated adult unemployment and parents without jobs asked their children to work to increase family income. Take, for instance, the case of Trois-Rivières: "There are at least 600 fathers without work," reported the inspector who visited the region at the request of the CTCC, "and…this is the main reason forcing young people under 16 to get work permits at The Wabasso Cotton factory…"[142] The gender division of the labour market favoured the replacement of women with younger boys. In 1952, female labour in the textile industry decreased because of the numerous marriages that took place after the war.[143]

Some employers were eager to show that they shared the protection and education values connected with the development of universal rights of children. In September 1945, out of the eighty-seven ads for boys under the age of sixteen in a randomly chosen issue of *La Presse,* nine alluded to the possibility of children's advancement and the learning of a skill, and four clearly indicated that the call was for "light work." But not all employers waited for the State's authorization to employ young people. Some business owners acted illegally, with full knowledge of the facts, and the Department of Labour officials, despite their renewed efforts to track down these employers, rarely succeeded in thwarting their plans.[144]

For these delinquent employers, the official tolerance of family work provided another pretext. When the director of Canadian International Paper wanted to hire children younger than sixteen to work alongside their fathers in lumber camps, where the law concerning dangerous establishments outlawed employing males under the age of eighteen, he had every opportunity to recall the customs of family labour and the exception attached to them: "In most cases the applicants we have in mind have worked with their fathers on fishing and farming work and are familiar with the bush work to a certain extent."[145] At Valleyfield Silk, under the pretext of encouraging "[our] establishment's excellent family spirit," young children were hired while older labourers were dismissed, which met the demands of adult employees who were "satisfied with the work conditions [and who wanted] to bring in their younger brothers or sisters."[146] Poor parents and children could sometimes count on the tacit collaboration of these delinquent employers. Madame Méthot, for example, was ten years old when she began working at the Raymond confectionery in south-central Montréal, a company that hired all the children after school and on Saturdays to hull strawberries. She knew that even though a certificate was required, some businesses would not ask for one.[147] In general, industrial and commercial establishments rarely required the services of children, but, at times, parents' insistence overpowered employers, which happened to the Grand-Mère Shoe Company: "The reason we are so interested in this child [under the age of fourteen]," explained the president, "is because we know his mother [a sickly widow] very well."[148] In these cases, the same entrepreneurs who maintained practices and wages that destabilized families had pushed some families to go against the public norms, which the same employers claimed to accept.

Not all family heads earned a sufficient enough income to ensure their families' subsistence, as the legislators' ideas had supposed. In 1942, the average Québec wage was not enough to allow the head of the household to meet the needs of a family with three children, an amount the federal Department of Labour set a $30 per week. In 1942, the price and wage stabilization policy instituted by Mackenzie King's government had helped to increase Québec wages to meet the lowest level of wages across all Canadian provinces, and the cost of living had increased by 16 per cent since the beginning of the war. By 1951, the situation had barely improved: while a family with three children under the age of fourteen needed $2,250 per year according to the Federation of Classical Colleges, 37 per cent of family heads did not even earn $2,000 per year.[149]

The same State that was not ready to accept a close examination of the question of wage levels finally authorized children under the age of fourteen to work in industrial and commercial establishments. In the same manner as employers, it cited the "needs of the family" to justify these exceptions to universal rights it had promised to guarantee. The SPI stated that he did not want the law to "disrupt family life." "It would be unacceptable," he wrote in the instructions accompanying the new education law, to charge families whose need for their children's help is valid and justifiable," but he reserved the right to take special measures, since officers had to submit these cases to him personally. In the files of the Department of Labour, we found four examples from Montréal in which the "need" justified the tolerance shown. Regardless, the Department of Labour came to tolerate part-time work for children up to thirteen years of age by referring to the poor children's need for money.[150]

After Victor Doré's departure from the Department of Public Instruction, it was the Family Allowances Bureau employees who took up the task of granting exceptions, as we have seen, and the head of school attendance, P.-A. Fournier, also showed that he could be quite flexible.[151] To excuse these tolerances, the DNHW propagandists also played on the idea of the educational and moral values of work: in that some tasks had an instructive value for fourteen- and fifteen-year-olds, and when work did not compromise children's school attendance, federal officials were prepared to continue paying the family allowances. The idea that children's education could be accomplished "on the job" had not disappeared altogether but had rather been translated into a language compatible with the rhetoric of children's universal rights—it had a limited reach. Minor tasks outside class time received the bureau's approval, which was also the case with summer jobs. Included among these tasks were newspaper delivery, lawn mowing, messenger work, boot polishing, work as a cadet in the forces, milk delivery, and the "little jobs" done in exchange for small bonuses. In reducing all images of juvenile labour to that of the middle-class child seeking to make "pocket money," and in moving away from the term "salary," officials were able to place juvenile labour outside the formal economy.[152] However, the same public administrations planned to consider these incomes as real "salaries" when it came to saving money from the state budget: from the moment children left school to work, the DNHW withdrew their eligibility for allowances, alleging that their incomes would be sufficient to cover their needs. If a child agreed to quit the job, the allowance would be re-established, offering a partial compensation for the loss of wages. Thus made victims of official fictions, children working in industrial or commercial establishments decreased their chances to become financially independent.

What the new universal rights regime accomplished for many of these parents was to put the official seal of illegality on old practices. An architecture of exceptions allowed many to elude discredit, but the new regime brought with it minute examinations of families by state employees, bringing attention to those who had previously been left alone. There were always families who were able to circumvent these rigorous inquiries, and they employed a number of means to do so, from exploiting legislative confusion to blackmailing the official responsible for applying the law and falsifying documents. Some parents refused to meet the enumerator, while others changed their children's ages for the annual school enumeration; others masked their children's work with the more acceptable excuse of illness, with their doctor's complicity (the proportion of those who did not attend school because of illness or the distance between home and school was relatively higher for children between the ages of ten and fourteen, which confirms this type of cheating): "Children are not shy to give teachers a forged note or an excuse that did not hold water."[153] In factories and stores, they could modify their age certificates, present the permit of their older brother or sister, or simply hide from the inspectors. Upon entering a munitions factory on Montréal's Rue Vitré during the war, Madame Mercier, who was thirteen years old at the time but "looked older," said that she was sixteen.[154] Regarding family allowances, some families avoided reporting their child's work. That they had little to fear—at the worst they would have to repay overpaid sums—was the QRO's employees most common and repeated complaint.[155]

In short, legislative policies reinforced the industrial and commercial labour market's tendencies far more than they opposed them. The number of absence permits and work permits increased, and by the end of the war, once an abundance of adult labour had returned, the government enforced its monitoring more rigorously. Powerlessly, school administrators observed the negative effects of this type of economic logic on public education, which could not possibly be reversed by any legislation. Even after the war, the district inspector for Trois-Rivières and Cap-de-la-Madeleine reported that "the schools' efforts are often hampered by the employers' rushed eagerness to take on fourteen- and even thirteen-year-old employees."[156] In these circumstances, Health and Welfare officials found themselves in the paradoxical situation of having to suspend family allowances for households who had the greatest need for the additional income. While the State reduced children's chances to enter the industrial and commercial work forces, it relegated those who were able to find jobs to work that, when it was not illegal, was more precarious, less well paid, and reserved for youths. As the Welfare State prepared to guarantee employees of industrial and commercial enterprises income-security programs, children were pushed away from these very sectors. As with the farmers' sons and daughters, who worked the land and helped their mothers at home, these children found themselves to be at once excluded from both the new economic rights reserved for adult labourers and the new rights reserved for dependent children.[157]

More generally, the juvenile labour phenomenon may have diminished during the 1940–55 period, but the decline was irregular and unevenly distributed. Hundreds of children under the age of fourteen still worked, some temporarily, and some regularly; they did so most often at home, on the farm, or in the family business, or as messengers or delivery boys in industrial and commercial establishments. For fourteen- and fifteen-year-olds, work was always easy to find and almost half of them did not attend school. In marginal economic regions, for large families and families who were not sufficiently protected against interruptions of income, the tradition of family labour continued, maintained by the persistent shortcomings of the economic structure and by the lack of social assistance. At the same time, new forces added new needs for families, forces such as the increase of opportunities to work in industries and businesses during wartime; the lack of domestic and day labourers in agricultural work in the 1940s; the increase in agricultural commodities; the increase in the number of mothers working outside the home during the global conflict; and, in the second half of the 1940s, the increase in the cost of living and new consumption incentives.

The Rigidity of the School Structure, Children's Persistent Needs, and the New Conceptions of Abnormal Childhood

Civil-service employees determined that a final group of children who were able neither to reach the new minimums nor to enjoy the tolerances and official exceptions were personally responsible for breaking the new laws. They were placed in the "refusal to attend" category, into which the province's enumerators had entered 7 per cent of the cases of urban boys who were not registered in any school in September 1943. That proportion decreased considerably for girls from all areas and for country boys, as though the "refusal" category represented the inverted image of the categories of work at home and on the farm.[158]

This category was made up of those who did not obey their parents and those who played hooky without an economic need that would have forced them to come to their families' aid. For example, an eleven-year-old boy told his machinist father, who had "explained to him that if he goes to school and acquires some education, he would have a brighter future," that he didn't care. Some delivery boys worked in secret and "frittered away a large part of the income they earned selling newspapers before giving it to their families." Occasionally, this evasion only revealed a superficial or temporary conflict, when, for instance the family implied the moment had come for a child to enter the work force, while the explicit messages it voiced in favour of extended schooling were proof of a different reasoning.[159]

Sometimes, however, parents who took the responsibilities the two new laws conferred upon them seriously did not succeed in having their children obey them. Parents had their own tactics to promote school attendance, from persuasion to promises of rewards, threats, and the last resort of corporal punishment.[160] To some parents with little authority, the modes of application of the Compulsory School Attendance Act had offered a new means: the threat of appearance in juvenile court or being placed in a reform school. Some even called on the court directly. In 20 per cent of the Montréal court appearances, it was the parents who had reported their own children.[161] The fear of a court appearance or a stay in an establishment for delinquents could make a difference; in certain extreme cases, the court also kept recalcitrant pupils in detention for a week, and these situations ended with children promising to return to school. The younger ones cried out of despair; the probation officer reported, for example, that a nine-year-old boy "cried incessantly and pleaded for a chance to go home, promising to attend school faithfully in the future." Some older children showed a more practical understanding of the situation: "I prefer going to class than being locked up," declared a thirteen-year-old child detained by the court.[162]

What were the circumstances in which children seemed to have their own reasons for wanting to leave school? School was far from having become as interesting as Victor Doré had predicted. To some, compulsory education prolonged an awkward situation that could have ended differently. Uncomfortable in their old clothes, poor children would have preferred to stay home rather than suffer their friends' criticisms: "He says he likes to go to school and have friends his own age but the lack of clothes and organization at home are the reason [for his absences]."[163] The hazards of school sociability added to the reasons youths disliked school. Children feared being beaten or being the laughing stock of the class because of their absences or poor results. Older children already treated as adults outside school also suffered, as their time at school represented too childish an experience.[164]

The situation was much the same for children whose studies progressed little. Before the implementation of the Compulsory School Attendance Act, many of them could have left school prematurely. After 1943, the officers were faced with a new problem. While auxiliary classes for slower students existed, compulsory education allowed for the detection of problems in children who would have otherwise left school. This precipitated plans to build other special schools with the intention of helping pupils with difficulties. But these cases were rare, and learning difficulties quickly became insurmountable in some students' minds, who found themselves trapped by the system. They developed a dislike for school: after a few absences, they were frightened of being scolded by the teacher or of not being able to follow the class. "I don't like school," declared a delinquent to a probation officer. "I'm often late and since the month of January, I miss a lot of school, I do badly in class and it discourages me."[165] If they were a little behind in school, they could become embarrassed to be bigger than the other students of their level. If they were temporarily excluded, shame could prevent their return. Numerous grade repetitions discouraged students in the end: "He detests studying," explained a mother to the SPI regarding her thirteen-year-old son, "because he has been in the same grade for too long."[166] Older children received absence permits from the officers easily; the local, provincial, and federal authorities were ready to tolerate exceptions because "the presence of certain children in schools caused serious problems for the elementary school teachers."[167] At the MCSC officers told that they would excuse those who had reached the age of fourteen during the course of the school year and who were "retarded"—that is, "special cases of backward children... children who have attained their ceiling, who are too big or too old for their grade, etc., borderline cases where it is more advisable that children be left at home or sent to work." The case files for school non-attendance demonstrate that exclusions of younger children were carried out under the same pretext. At his appearance before the MSWC, a thirteen-year-old child received authorization from the Montreal Protestant School Board to "leave school and seek employment" after having been unsuccessfully placed in a special class because of his low intelligence quotient (IQ). The child was said to be having a bad influence on his environment.[168] Some "retarded" children who appeared before juvenile court were placed in reform school "to learn a trade": "placement in the Sœurs Marie Réparatrice convent will help her," deemed the psychologist in the case of a twelve-year-old girl, "because it offers the advantage of providing [the accused] with companions, while providing her with the useful distraction of work."[169] In these cases, the administrators invested work with moral virtues that had been lost in the case of other children.

The law of compulsory education also produced its own centrifugal forces. Tensions between elementary-school teachers and students had not ended: "The child says she does not like going to school and likes her teacher even less, because she played favourites.... She does not want to return to school at all," read the note taken for the juvenile court appearance of a thirteen-year-old girl. One elementary-school teacher always punished the same student, another was always unfair; children were afraid of the corporal punishment some teachers carried out.[170] One Outaouais inspector aptly summarized this type of problem: "The teacher is the primary factor in assiduity and in the pursuit of school attendance.

A disorderly class, an intolerable teacher, insipid lessons, excruciating homework, an atmosphere of struggle, a certainty that they will learn nothing will unfailingly force older students to leave school. Our law, even applied severely, can do nothing to combat this."[171]

In situations where the students' interests were not enough to keep them in school, educational establishments could prove to be rather difficult. Oppositions could be violent when elementary-school teachers had the right to expel irritating students, and the threat was carried only rarely: in September 1944, for example, in the Catholic school municipalities excluding Montréal and Verdun, the number of expulsions reached 135 for boys and 74 for girls; during the 1945–46 school year, 134 boys and 15 girls were expelled from urban schools.[172]

When they left school, some children played, went to the movies, read magazines, or spent time with friends, activities they associated with increased freedom.[173] But a large number of them wanted to work. Many young boys valued work over education, such as the newspaper vendors of Québec City who had "a real aversion for anything that could remind them of the school environment."[174] In general, they said they didn't like school or didn't want to go, or they believed they had finished their studies (see table 1 in chapter 4). The haste to help one's father or to go with him to the factories came out in some court testimonies. Friends who were already in the work force had a significant influence in these cases. Children wanted to work to earn money, but the freedom and maturity associated with work were also attractive to them. The feeling of independence that came with work was invaluable.[175] Children could be given greater respect in their own families. A variation of this rush to take on a role in society appeared during the war, when children attested to a "genuine desire to participate in some real way in the war effort." Inversely, some children left school with the belief that the labour market would allow them to be exempted from military service once they had reached the age of conscription.[176] Officials from the Family Allowances Bureau also met a girl working in a factory who thought she should "do something useful," and that in order to do that she had "asked her mother's permission [to leave school]."[177] In the same way, the freedom of movement and time that came with work could be advantageous, and the children who wanted to return to school were rare: "These young people will hardly be disposed to submit again to the discipline of school life in order to complete their education."[178] Given the relatively limited possibilities for young girls to find paid work, it is not surprising that there were fewer of them who wanted to leave school. According to a survey carried out by the JOC, 28 per cent of young workers had left their studies because they were "sick of school," whereas the proportion of girls in this case was only 6 per cent (see table 1 in chapter 4).

Children for whom the State had been unsuccessful in its attempts to make school interesting came into a more limited labour market than before. They were far from the legal fiction in which the young paid workers ceased to be supported by their parents. They rarely found themselves in the situation of material and psychological independence they dreamt of when they left school. The lower wages and job instability could rapidly erase their initial contentment. In this way, young people from lower classes who committed an act of freedom by leaving school increased their chance of experiencing economic dependence in the future. The paradox was not new, but in condemning and marginalizing juvenile work, the Welfare State had made it more pronounced.[179]

In erecting laws for the right to minimum education and a minimum standard of living, officials from the Québec and Canadian governments had confirmed that they could modify market forces in the name of social principles. But their powerlessness to enter into the workings of the economy often jeopardized their commitment to new egalitarian principles, which left a large margin for entrepreneurs' manoeuvring.[180] The new economic and political regime still condemned a minority of parents to an insufficient income to support a family, and those parents found themselves forced to use family labour. In doing so, they had to withdraw their sons and daughters from the protective field of the Welfare State.[181] Children who considered school to be of little use did not benefit from the new rights. The attention paid to the wishes and aptitudes of the children was narrowly defined, and children were asked more to conform than to be interested. For those who criticized the norms or the mechanisms of their implementation, the network of elementary teaching created a variety of exits.[182]

The collection of exceptions examined in this chapter were not just a part of the laws' early stages, or an insignificant anomaly, but were a vital part of the new regime of rights. In fact, the legislators used them as a place of disposal for the individuals rejected by the regulated sectors. To families in need, they advised directing children towards work that was less visible, traditional, or tolerated,[183] as if maintaining these spare solutions would allow the public authorities to avoid considering the contradictions in their own messages. In short, the social laws contributed to a decrease in the number of juvenile workers, but those who worked regardless were condemned to an even greater marginality, that of the arbitrariness of the exceptions, of disgrace, of cheating, or of criminality. Young workers belonged to a world in which they did not always have legal status. The combined effect of prosperity and of more rigid public norms accentuated their marginalization and, in these circumstances, "to be poor... was to be doubly poor."[184]

6

The Transformation of the Political Culture of Families

Did the experiment of a new universal rights regime affect families' practices and political values? This chapter will focus on families' immediate relations with public institutions in order to identify the elements of a new political culture. It will also explore how this political culture was articulated to party politics and governmental activity in order to demonstrate how poor families affected the creation of social laws in the early 1960s.

From 1940 to 1960, the implementation of universal social programs contributed to the flustering of political identities. We will first examine its effects on the various social groups. We will then put this still portrait in motion and identify the new play of alliances and tensions surrounding the post-war political institutions. Finally, we will examine the relationships between the political culture and the implementation of the social policies as the 1960s approached.

The Maintenance and Dissipation of the War Consensus

A significantly large number of parents signed up for the family allowances program—which was optional, let us remember—and the Canadian Institute of Public Opinion also noted a phenomenal approval of the program: between 1943 and 1955, the acceptance rate among Canadians went from 49 per cent to 90 per cent, one of the most spectacular majorities ever seen in national and international questions since the surveying organization's inception in 1940. Ninety-six per cent of those interviewed expressed an unprecedented enthusiasm.[1] During the 1949 federal election, all parties attempted to take credit for the family allowances program. Similarly, on

Notes to chapter 6 start on p. 256.

the eve of the 1944 provincial elections, Adélard Godbout knew that his education reforms would be largely accepted. During the radio program during which he announced the date of the coming elections, he included compulsory education in the list of his government's significant achievements when five years earlier, he had kept his reform projects secret.[2]

However, after the war, education and welfare issues were less and less important in political debates, and parties only made incidental mention of them in their campaigns. It was not until the early 1960s that there was a new stage in the strengthening of the Welfare State. Historians generally attribute this fifteen-year silence to the rupture of wartime consensus and, further, to the population's disengagement regarding social policies.[3] Inversely, "the sudden onset of strong social pressures"is cited to help explain the return of the welfare issue to the forefront of Canadian politicians' and officials' attention in the early 1960s.[4] What was the true nature of these significant changes in opinion? What was their origin?

The population's support contributed to the fact that public authorities upheld most of their commitments towards universal social rights. State employees passed on parents' expectations and disappointments to governments. If they could become the spokespeople for parents who were satisfied with the programs or even represent those who were dissatisfied with the gaps between politicians' promises of universality and the realities of the actual means made available to households, it was in part because they themselves suffered from the same finicky constraints of administrative logic. "The educational profession," protested the eleven members of Matane's Association des institutrices rurales, for example, "does not consist of amassing statistics upon statistics."[5] From time to time, the elementary-school teachers' interests were the same as those of the parents. An elementary-school teacher from Deschambault wrote to the Superintendent of Public Instruction (SPI) that she did not believe a fine would be strong enough to force parents to obey compulsory education: "We, who live in the country, know that the fathers of families, particularly when they have children of school age, have such financial problems that it could be considered a crime to ask them to spend a single cent."[6]

The administration of universal laws led some of the employees to discover the extent of poverty. The figures on children became extremely precise, their scope unprecedented. They allowed portions of the population to emerge from the shadows, giving rise to more solid public debates than before. Similarly, by dint of meeting poor families, some probation officers came to recognize structural causes for school absenteeism, even when the casework method did not lend itself easily to larger political or social solutions.[7] The State had attempted to lead its own surveys to interpret the "needs" of families in the scientific and rational terms of the economic and political elite, but circulating more information via structures that were now more efficient could have unintended effects.

Some parents took advantage of the new opportunities to make contact with public administration, and the officials who participated in the creation of the universal social program struggled with an astounding number of requests. Even when these petitions were presented in a "language different from that of the experts [without necessarily referring to] their conceptions of public morality," their professional ethics often prevented officials from rejecting parents' complaints on sight. Elementary-school teachers, truancy officers, commissioners, inspectors, probation officers, and social workers wished to maintain the legitimacy of their expertise.[8] Meanwhile, employees of the State were interested in making sure that the policies that justified their jobs continued to be applied. On a broader level, these workers constituted an increasingly large portion of the total labour force, partly excluded from the capitalist logic, who would not criticize the Welfare State with the same ardour as the partisans of free enterprise.[9]

Other similar experiments brought middle-class families closer to poorer classes. In many ways, the policy of universality linked the two groups' respective fates, and it prevented programs from sinking into oblivion as the partial policies from preceding decades had done. For a State that had attempted to isolate workers' claims to higher wages, these new solidarities between parents of different classes were a marked reversal. Among wealthier families registering for the program were parents of large families whose salaries were substantial but whose number of children placed them in difficult situations, or families who were used to living in relative comfort but found themselves in a difficult financial situation after an accident. Many parents, in fact, had registered in case their families were affected by unemployment or illness. Parents who bridged the two worlds were even more likely to notice officials' evasion. This was the case for former elementary-school teachers, who, because of their knowledge of school authorities, had acquired a certain perceptiveness. They knew how to present their cases using the accounting language of the department's experts, such as this farmer's widow, who described the tasks her family had to carry out:

> I am a widow and mother of two children. The eldest, who will be 14 in November, finds himself forced, under the new law, to attend school every day of the year. This bothers me very much. Having a relatively large piece of land to farm, and being the only boy who can help me, his work

> saves me an awful lot of money. Otherwise I would never be able to manage to maintain the land, the buildings, pay the taxes or the church, etc. I receive only $20.00 a month and I have $5.00 extra because I am well enough to look after the home myself. So with this small sum, I could not pay a man for the year, or every time I would need one. I would have to give up many things. First of all my health, since it already leaves much to be desired, the payments, my two little children, since life is so expensive, and I would have debts I'm sure.... I am currently having even more trouble, and my little boy does man's work for me most times... I am not coming to ask you that he not attend the school year, as I do not want to neglect his education, but I still have a great need for his help.

She included the following schedule:

> I wanted to ask you that instead of six weeks during the year if you would allow me a time limit of four months or more. That would give me:

Ripe oats raking and collection	1 week
Cultivation of potatoes	1 week
Autumn labour	1 week
Taking out the firewood, which I ask him to do after the first snowfall, though it nearly kills me with worry as he's so young	4 weeks
Spring cutting	4 weeks
Seeding, rolling, repairing fences, fertilizing the soil	5 weeks

> This adds up to 17 weeks.[10]

A number of former elementary-school teachers also requested permission to teach their own children at home and they clearly explained the superiority of their own methods. Such was the case for an Abitibi mother who had a teaching certificate and all the necessary items to teach her children—a globe, books, a blackboard—while the region's teacher was not even certified.[11] Thus, many groups associated with the arrival of universal social laws continued to ensure their survival.

Like State agents, workers' associations acted as intermediaries. They had greeted the programs with optimism—*Le Monde ouvrier* had written that "the people... will appreciate [Prime Minister Godbout's compulsory education,] as it is essentially the low-wage earners, the labourers, who have suffered most because of the lack of education in Québec"—but they also criticized him vigorously. Throughout the entire decade following the war, unionists fought for the laws to be applied in a more realistic and equal manner.[12]

But the groups calling for teaching reform did not stop at calls for the governments to be accountable. Once compulsory education had been adopted, they started to direct the public's attention towards other requests. There was a call to return to the original free education plan Godbout's

Liberals had established as well as to extend provisions to higher levels, and from that point on, a fight began for free higher education[13] and compulsory education until the age of sixteen. These causes were supported not only by the three central labour bodies but also by the Alliance catholique des professeurs de Montréal (the Montréal Catholic teachers' association); the Fédération des commissions scolaires (FCS); and the team from the *Cité libre* magazine.[14] History repeated itself: in 1948, the Department of Public Instruction (DPI) ordered a survey on the causes for students' leaving school between grades seven and eight. Similarly, complaints about children's work concerned new topics. In 1954, the Confédération des travailleurs catholique de Canada (CTCC) called for a prohibition of all labour during school, and the Society for the protection of Women and Children campaigned to protect and maintain long summer holidays, as "employers have not understood that depriving children of their summer holidays in whole or in part to help a factory is not much better than depriving children of their education to increase cheap production."[15]

The campaign to index family allowances is an example of this kind of extension of the war consensus and its role in maintaining social policies. Many parents deplored insufficient family allowances. Thus, in 1948 in a poor neighbourhood in Montréal, 90 per cent of the women interviewed asserted that "it was possible, at one time, at the beginning of the family allowances, to see a real improvement and buy more milk, more fruit, and especially more vegetables. But at the current prices of these goods, mothers must content themselves with a very small quantity of each of them." The paradox of having the bonuses end when children reached sixteen years of age, regardless of whether they continued to attend school or not, while the State declared it was in favour of extending studies beyond the age of obligation was not lost either. "Without help," declared a mother from Bellechasse County, "we won't be able to send our 16-year-old daughter to the convent."[16]

In the later 1940s, two central labour bodies, the CTCC and the Fédération professionnelle des travailleurs du Québec (FPTQ), called for the allowances to be indexed. In 1951, the old champion of allowances, Father Léon Lebel, added his objections to theirs: "At the current price of a pint of milk—19 cents a pint—the $5.00 monthly allowance paid for children under six does not even pay for the pint of milk that the hygienist doctors advise as a minimum daily dose for children and adolescents to ensure their normal development…the allowances are but insignificant help for blue-collar families in big cities."[17] From July 1954 until May 1955, a number of unions, 327 school and municipal councils, and multiple associations organized a provincial campaign. At the same time, 2,835 citizens from different areas of the country signed a petition to this effect. Lionel Bertrand, Terrebonne MP in the House of Commons, had indicated as early as 1953 that he had "received hundreds of letters, calling for an increase in the base family allowances amount. I wasn't able to answer them all, there were so many."[18] The Co-operative Commonwealth Federation (CCF) and Progressive Conservative Party MPs asked that the allowances continue for sixteen- to eighteen-year-old children still in school, which was already the case for tax exemptions. The complaints concerning the extension of family allowances after sixteen years of age were taken up in the House by numerous MPs. On the heels of the feminists at the origin of the law, whose attention was focused as much on the mothers as on the children, a CCF MP also asked that the allowances be paid as soon as the mothers became pregnant, which would help the "little ones, as much as possible, to get through their first year."[19] Finally, some MPs decided to enter into direct contact with the program heads: "I receive so many letters from my voters asking me for help to extend their family allowances for their children who are still in school,"[20] wrote Antoine Fréchette, MP for Rivière-du-Loup-Témiscouata in 1959, to Lionel Lafrance, the director of family allowances in Québec.

Very early, family allowances officials had noticed inflation's depreciative effect and informed their superiors of it. The department's 1947–48 annual report took on a prudent tone regarding the part the allowances played in the family budget: "It is highly possible that the family allowances, destined to increase the standard of living, have mostly contributed to maintaining the current standard...." Three years later, this time in the annual report of the Québec Regional Office (QRO), the cautious tone had been replaced by the advocacy of parents: "Family allowances are not too much of a good thing.... We may safely assume that the [monies] are currently spent by the parents who, in the great majority, are in need of this 'extra' income."[21] The Nutrition Service of the Department of Health and Welfare resolved the problem by circulating even more vague advice. In 1951, the draft of a publicity text on the various ways of getting more for one's money had first promised that, for five dollars per year, "you can be sure that your child receives the foods that are needed most to improve the diets of Canadian children. 1. Milk: at least one pint daily. 2. Vitamin D:... That still leaves money for other foods...." This false optimism possibly explains why the final brochure, published in 1951, made no allusion to the purchasing power of the allowances. The social workers responsible for surveying family allowances also indicated the inadequacy of policies in which the rates remained stable during a period of inflation. Thus, Thérèse Roy recommended abolishing the decreasing rate from the fifth child on. "It is a little difficult to believe," she explained alluding to the type of argument Mackenzie King had used to justify the decreasing rate, "that the clothing of the first four children could still be worn by the time the thirteenth and fourteenth children were born."[23]

Mackenzie King had adopted the family allowances reluctantly, and in the years following the war, he had neither the intention of implementing the extended welfare program of his 1945 electoral program nor a plan to increase the allowances. In 1946, he wrote in his journal that the law "was as far as we should have thought of going in that class of expenditure until the end of another four of five years."[24] Reassured by the postwar economic revival, important pressure groups had withdrawn their support of the extension of social security policies, in particular the Canadian Medical Association and Canadian Manufacturers' Association. In the same way, eager to replace the wartime State management with the private management of a peacetime economy, Mackenzie King's most influential mandarins only followed from Keynes's propositions the techniques of fine tuning.[25] In the 1950s, they no longer called for public monies to be poured directly into the pockets of citizens: the government no longer feared a decrease in the demand for consumer goods, and seen in this way, the decision not to increase family allowances may have constituted a balancing technique. It was necessary to put the State's coffers back on a sound financial footing (the family allowances already took up 25 per cent of the social security budget), and from the point of view of the households of average means, the general increase in revenues and the progress of social services made the family allowances less necessary.[26] When international relations were cited, it was no longer to justify additional social spending that reinforced national solidarity, as was the case in 1944, but rather to favour a particular category of spending, "the cost of the current national defence program," over the social security budgets.[27]

Meanwhile, one of Keynes's main objectives, to curb unemployment and avoid poverty, was relegated to the back burner. Faced with testimonies about the insufficiency of the allowances for poor families, officials adopted a different rhetoric, which distinguished these families from what they saw as more legitimate groups of interlocutors. Officials were no longer dealing with a nation of universal parents but rather a nation of taxpayers. In 1957, the national assistant director of allowances expressed his reasons for not increasing social benefits: "In present times, I am convinced, and I am certain that all among you will be as well, that it would be desirable to increase these rates but we must never forget that these monies must come from the pocket of each Canadian and I am equally certain that public opinion would look poorly on any tax increase to this end."[28]

This reasoning was able to convince most citizens, who were seeing their income taxes increase and the funds coming from public transfers decrease.

The number of relatively comfortable households had multiplied. Family allowances had played a role in this increase, but for most well-off parents, the 1945 program had not had a significant effect on total income. Through the income tax, the federal government recovered part of the allowances from families earning over $1,200 per year and all the allowances from families earning over $3,000 pear year; it thus recovered $50 million of the $250 million it paid out each year.[29] In these circumstances, certain parents had chosen not to enroll in the program; others had shown themselves to be hostile towards policies that did not help them directly. The feeling was widespread according to one reporter from the monthly Jesuit publication *Relations*:

> Many of them are from the middle class...for [them], the family allowances are a favour offered with one hand and taken away with the other. The favour is accepted to keep from disrupting the administrative routine; it isn't talked about much, and if it is at all, it is discussed with a small air of ironic contempt, with a certain bitterness that comes with the feeling of material poverty in balancing the budget, when the most part of their income goes to train men who will be the glory of tomorrow's generation.[30]

The growth of the middle class contributed to the decrease in the number of those who would have had an immediate interest in the support of policies that would assist the poor. Politically speaking, according to many historians, the general enrichment would have made the voters less inclined to support left-wing parties posing a threat to Mackenzie King.[31] At the federal level, the CCF, which sought to ensure that many parental demands were heard, saw its popularity dissolve. The politicians' project to replace the workers solidarities with the more isolated identity of parents was thus gaining ground.

By addressing the taxpayers in this manner, officials could count on deeply rooted elements of the political culture. In the countryside in particular, many parents relied on their legitimate status as school taxpayers to call for changes in the educational system. The monthly school fees and taxes parents paid led some consider that they were the commissioners' and teachers' employers. This was the case for those parents who asked the head officer of the Protestant School Board of Greater Montreal (PSBGM) to punish students who did not attend school regularly so that their own children would not follow such a bad example. This attitude was less prevalent in municipal school policy, as commissioners had not been elected there since the early century's progressive reforms.

During the war, the government had been able to minimize the relationship between social programs and taxes: it was in the name of the national effort that the portion of public revenue from taxpayers had increased. But the alliances surrounding this new phenomenon had not yet been solidified. After 1946, the federal prime ministers were convinced that what Canadians wanted most was a decrease in taxes, more than the creation of social programs, while three years earlier, Mackenzie King had written in his journal that "a post-war program of reform was to be 'the main subject of appeal.'" Many reformist groups who continued to call for social laws henceforth also pushed for the decrease of sales tax and income tax.[32]

Though the federal government may not have been solely responsible for creating this taxpayer identity, it certainly contributed to defining and reinforcing it. In January 1947, while it still refused to increase allowances, it did respond to pressures from the middle class: it allowed families in this category to deduct an additional $100 from their taxable income for each child eligible for family allowances. Enrollment in the program increased following this decision. Policies such as these added to the general increase in incomes, to the climate of insecurity precipitated by the Cold War, and to the shift towards the suburbs, accentuating the individualism of the middle classes that characterized the 1950s. As more time passed since the years of the Depression, fewer families considered themselves to be susceptible to poverty to the extent that they might one day need the allowance.[33] The number of affluent parents grew, and the idea of associating allowances with poorer classes became more prevalent.

The governmental prescriptions concerning children's education also began to break down wartime solidarities. In fact, the government promised that the social programs would help increase access to a minimum of property on the condition that the canons of respectability were followed. Economic citizenship was conditional upon the adoption of individualist values, which moved away from former solidarities. By encouraging the transfer of citizens' aspirations outside industrial relations and beyond partisan politics towards the administrative sphere, officials had effectively consolidated the Welfare State.[34]

At the end of the war, the urgency of many questions faded—the increase in juvenile delinquency and the need for educated labourers did not loom with the same intensity—and the middle classes' reformist surge diminished. The regime of universal rights might have lent systematic character to the middle classes' "collective guilt," but this feeling was volatile and preserving the rights of the poor was subject to economic fluctuations.[35]

While increasing the status of the middle classes, the federal government involved itself in a campaign that denigrated citizens incapable of gaining access to the new universal norms. For example, in 1952, during the debates on indexation, Minister of National Health and Social Welfare Paul Martin took up the scornful rhetoric regarding the poor families his government had denounced during the debates on the establishment of the allowances. He declared, "I believe that it would be unfortunate to give our people the impression that there are no limits to what we can do in this area."[36] The head of family allowances in Québec was of the same opinion: "Certain families do not understand the role of the truancy officers...and attack them when family allowances are withdrawn by reason of non-attendance, while in reality the parents should rather take on the responsibility themselves for having taken their child out of school too early or for having neglected to make them finish their year."[37] Thus the ministers and high officials who had described poor parents as the nation's labourers and as universal parents could now present them as the eventual profiteers of the State's help.[38]

Similarly, Adélard Godbout had defined the notion of a minimum of education vaguely enough that his government could be tolerant and allow some poor children to slip through the nets of universal norms. It was these already fragile protections that Maurice Duplessis would now attempt to make disappear. In fact, at the provincial level, it was a change in government, the return of the Union nationale in 1944, that sanctioned and furthered the break in the consensus favouring the reforms. With his 1946 law to "improve education," Duplessis hoped to seduce owners, professors, and protestants, all while freeing himself of his predecessors' commitments to increase the maximum age of education. For Omer Côté, the provincial secretary during the initial phases of the 1946 project, new school-board subsidies would favour education more than any obligation policy, to the point where it would eventually lead to the abolishment of Godbout's law:

> "Attendance and assiduity will be ensured much more efficiently than by the Compulsory School Attendance Act! And we will probably be able, a few years after the policy has been implemented, to prove that the Compulsory School Attendance Act has no use and we may cancel the statutes. It is certain," he wrote to Duplessis, "that a policy bearing so broadly with our school problems will produce a stir of opinion that the Union nationale will be able to use to its advantage."[39]

For the provincial government as well as the federal government, this step outside universality came with a certain withdrawal of the State and with a strategic condemnation of poor parents. In 1949, Duplessis' administration made destitution an official excusable reason for missing school and, in his 1950 annual report, the new SPI abandoned the responsibility of improving school attendance. "A great majority of our young people leave school after grade seven," he wrote. "Enrollment in higher education is simply too low. It would be highly desirable for parents and teachers to study this question in greater depth and to seek practical means for keeping children in school at least until grade nine, if not until grade twelve."[40]

This was not, however, a real step backwards. This condemnation of the poor, as we saw previously in the chapter dealing with the implementation of laws, had never disappeared from official practices; in a regime of universality, parents who steered clear of school for economic reasons had to carry on their shoulders the weight of the responsibility for their children's being far from the norms. The temporary exemption labels placed them in vague categories which implied that they were ignorant and incapable. In this context of renewed suspicion, it is not surprising that parents contacting officials often insisted that they were not being negligent: "It is not a whim which guides me I assure you," stated a woman from Chicoutimi County, a mother of a thirteen-year-old girl and thirteen other children: "I would like for her to be educated." "We are too aware of the importance of education to neglect it," said the elder sister of a thirteen-year-old girl who had to leave school to help her sick mother.[41]

For the parents in whom the publicity of universal laws had succeeded in inculcating the idea of minimum standards but who remained incapable of attaining them, the universal laws could create a feeling of powerlessness. The McGill Social Science Research Project found women, in the southwest area of Montréal, who added the amount of their allowances to the whole of their family budgets set aside for the absolute necessities, while having the feeling that this new money should not have been spent in this way. "Apparently," the surveyors wrote, "this attitude arose from emphasis in family allowances publicity on the use of money for children specifically."[42] A similar problem may have plagued poor children: having absorbed the positive message related to school attendance they may have had similar frustrations upon their entry into the work force.

For many parents excluded from the new advantages connected with citizenship, the State's intervention appeared to be harassment by a greedy and illogical bureaucracy. When the Rivière-Bleue School Board reinstated monthly payments, a discouraged mother reported the incongruities of a situation in which the State's demands were contradictory: "They tell us to pay 0.50 per student each month on the family allowances cheques and if we don't pay by the 10 every month, our children will be kept out of class and we'll lose our cheques if students don't go to class...If this is the law, people are ready to pay by the 20 every month when they receive their cheques only if they have to."[43] Some parents avoided contact with the social workers out of fear of being chased out of their houses and seeing their children placed with other families, while others denounced the municipalities who continued to call for monthly remuneration despite the law, as well as school boards who turned children away due to a lack of space: "I don't see why a fine is imposed on those of us who don't send our children to school and I believe that a fine should be given to those schools who refuse to take them," declared a mother of two boys aged eight and eleven, who tried in vain to challenge the law through solicitors and the Valleyfield MP.[44]

Other parents did not understand why they were losing their family allowances eligibility. "My child completed grade eight," wrote the mother of a fourteen- or fifteen-year-old boy to the Dependants' Allowance Board (the federal agency in charge of soldiers' families) to justify his employment, "and he has not been able to pursue his studies because there were no secondary schools nearby and boarding was too expensive."[45] One anecdote told by a social worker entrusted by the Montréal "Cercle du Terroir" to study the effects of the allowances in the Gaspé-Nord region demonstrates to what degree this mistrust influenced the results of such surveys of social programs: "During our study, it got around that the investigator visiting families was from the allowances board and that she would "take away the allowances" from the families who were not using them for their children... This obviously influenced their answers."[46] Having to deal with the most negative aspects of social policies could lead to indifference according to British historian David Sutton: "The apparent apathy felt by working people for the benefits of citizenship derives from their experience of its bureaucratic forms... the working-class skepticism felt towards official society and the intrusion of its agents."[47] The reformists and the officials leaned more towards blaming the poor themselves for their lack of interest regarding political life. Thus, in 1950, Victor Doré's successor, Omer-Jules Desaulniers, explained that the State needed to intervene in matters of education because of parents' indifference.[48]

For the children who became acquainted with the State for the first time through the medium of a school that was irritating, disapproving, inescapable, and deaf to their requests, the Compulsory School Attendance Act provided more reasons to be distrustful. While the new law forced rebellious children to stay in school, it also deprived them of an old means of exerting pressure. Before compulsory education, parents and children could express disapproval by withdrawing the pupil from school; now they were forced to be subjected to the whims of elementary-school teachers who seemed unqualified: "I'm not the only one who doesn't want Mme Bélanger teaching anymore," explained a father from Témiscouata, "but if it weren't for the allowances, I promise you the school would be empty."[49]

When children who did not respect the Compulsory School Attendance Act had to face the school monitoring system, they used the little power available to them at their age. They lied, openly defied the officers, or refused to answer the judge. Childhood is a period of life during which traditions of organized opposition take root with difficulty. However, even temporary resistance could have a deep meaning for the development of their political culture.[50]

Gangs that presented a more organized resistance, a rare instance of collective manifestation and the possible site of a distinct culture, were quickly repressed by school principals, who feared that these more charismatic delinquents would have a devastating effect on the other children.[51] Many children had their parents' approval for non-attendance while others played truant on their own. Isolated at once by their parents and by public institutions, the latter could engage in a real "war on adults."

Caught between opposing forces, one supporting the era's wartime reforms and one moving away from a consensus it had helped to establish, the governments also seemed to have decided to postpone the confrontation by diverting the public's attention away from the elevated costs of social programs: "In the rush to plan a collectively oriented postwar society, had there been any time to build a supporting political constituency? Apparently not, if we are to judge by the ease with which the glittering prize of comprehensive health, housing and social security was withdrawn from public gaze."[52]

Traditional Means of Defending Parents' Rights and the New Struggles for Democracy

Some parents belonging to the specific economic sectors abandoned by the universal programs fought the problems connected with the new egalitarianism. Their voices took over administrative correspondence. Farmers were forced into a subsistence economy, and in their wake, some truancy officers from the country even accused the legislators of being unaware of the requirements of the rural economy. "I understand that in cities it is easier to make ends meet but on farms it is not the same thing," remarked a father from Saint-Camille whose son looked after the farm while he went to saw wood for a pulp and paper company. As did a Beauce farmer who wanted to withdraw his eldest daughter, aged twelve, from school, some even attempted to teach the SPI something: "You must know that a single man doesn't work on a farm by himself."[53] Many of those for whom compulsory education had brought difficulties continued to "vote with their feet"—that is, to sustain the same rural exodus the religious elite had attempted to curb when they had become open to the principle of compulsory education. Their departure would contribute to the decrease in the general rural electorate's negotiating power, which had been in decline since 1920.

In the same way, some mothers took offence to the idea that a daughter was being brought to school when it was impossible to find replacement for her at home. Some reminded the department of the costs they faced at home: "Send a work permit to the house for my 13-year-old daughter," wrote a sick mother from Chicoutimi, "or at least help me pay someone who can do my work." Parents of large families deplored the contradictions of the legislators who claimed to be pro-natalist: "Large families are strongly encouraged, but what will we become if our right to help ourselves with our children is taken away?"[54]

For those parents whose point of view was also influenced by their position as autonomous employers, the effect of laws regulating the status of children on the family economy weighed doubly, since the departure of one child for school did not only mean the loss of one income but also the loss of a worker. To their ears, the image of a collective of parents as individuals with rights resonated deeply. They also saw children's contributions to the general economy clearly enough to permit them to question the logic of politicians' macro-economic understanding of their lives. A farmer, for example, called into question the fate of Québec agriculture: "If... we leave the farm... those who are waiting for us to feed them will have to keep waiting."[55] Similarly, the settlers focused their complaints on the national importance of clearing. War-factory workers were proud of the patriotic importance of their work, and to work outside the home, they would need their children's help at home. An immigrant cited the years he had "given" to Canada in his denunciation of the court's unjust treatment his twelve-year-old son.[56]

The image of a society of parents owed a large part of its plausibility to forms of family economy, which had more in common with the pre-industrial world and the ideologies that had continued to propagate them, such as the Social Doctrine of the Catholic Church.[57] For these adults, "the attachment to the private sphere," in which a man is master of his own home, was particularly strong. It seemed to "counterbalance egalitarianism," and to offer a basis from which to "question the definition the State had of them."[58] It was Father Léon Lebel, who was also general chaplain of the Union des cultivateurs catholiques (UCC) from 1929 to 1934 and from 1937 to 1952, who most accurately expressed this perspective. In modern societies, he wrote in 1927, since the Welfare State affects rural families and laws forbid child labour and call for extended education, "the labourer has...been expropriated by reason of the general good from a part of his earnings. What has he received in return? Nothing."[59]

Criticism of the Compulsory School Attendance Act also came from urban parents whose children had to suffer through the law's most oppressive characteristics. Many of them promptly protested when a youth-court judge proposed a child be placed at the Mont Saint-Antoine reformatory or at the Boys' Farm Training School, invoking their parents' rights in the matter of their children's education. Generally, they did not accept these placements for their children because this punishment did not seem to match the nature and severity of the infraction.[60] Even the parents who had gone to court to reinforce their own authority had not imagined that in doing so they would have to abandon the fate of the child to the hands of the State. An offended probation officer reported as much:

> In contrast to many clients of the court who tend to expect guidance and accept control, Mr X has seen the court and it would seem other agencies as well, only as a means of extending his own power. He has not accepted[,] probably not understood[,] that his appeal to the court involves giving over a measure of control and much less even the necessity of co-operation.[61]

In the past, the Catholic Church had known how to channel and reinforce this kind of distrust of the State: when it came time to vote or adopt the platforms of the working-class and Catholic farmers' associations, many citizens had accepted to share Church worries about the State's increasing social prerogatives. In fact, the fear of compulsory education had been crucial in founding the central Catholic labour bodies at the end of the Great War. As for the UCC, it had long opposed compulsory education with the notion that economic encouragement for families was worth more than institutional reform: "Family allowances and an insurance plan could reduce the burden of the family budget," declared a farmer from Laterrière at a meeting of the association. "The family allowance could be paid to families with children attending school, which would ease the situations of larger families and would curb plans with socializing tendencies to make school free."[62] The UCC also feared that the farmers would only have to take on more debt to make the law applicable and to ensure that the rural school boards would not disappear. In the same spirit, the central Catholic labour body did not believe that compulsory education would succeed unless family salaries and allowances for large families were implemented concurrently. And the JOC had refused to look into the problem of compulsory education so long as the problem of the standard of living was not solved: "The main cause for our children's premature school departures is indeed parents' poverty. Let us improve the working-class family's standard of living, let us give them the vital salary they deserve, let us simply treat it with social justice, and we will surely see that the question of school attendance will sort itself out at once."[63]

During the post-war years, this type of discontent still acted as support for conservative campaigns against the State's universal programs. Thus, Duplessis' education policy played an important role in his resounding victory of 1948, following which he used spending in the education sphere as one of the main elements of his network of patronage: he "didn't fail to... tell the voters that they would have such and such a school... if they knew who to vote for."[64] To a certain degree, Duplessis recognized the importance of local rural politics in a way Godbout had not. He also adopted social measures for the benefit of farmers that were more immediately useful than the urban reformist officials' universal reforms. Again in 1962, the Union nationale won the vote of the poorest regions and counties.[65]

The family allowances have been understood as an update of such personalized political relations, to fit the requirements of mass urbanization: "At the Federal level and in an urban society,... the social allowances play the same role in the provincial elections as that held by distributing seeds and paving roads."[66] Conservative critics emphasized most insistently the contradiction between the general principle of respect of family autonomy claimed by the Liberals and the powers of investigation and propaganda held by the Department of National Health and Welfare (DNHW). For Québec economist François-Albert Angers, for example, there was no more reason to tell parents how to spend their allowances than to tell them how to spend their wages. Catholic propagandist of family allowances Léon Lebel also disapproved of this intrusion into households: "This constitutes a very real threat to family autonomy: an overzealous official could take it on himself to enter a home and make inquiries, requiring documents proving that the family allowances had been used exclusively... for the children."[67]

Families who criticized the erosion of parents' rights belonged to a disappearing world that politicians and reformists could neglect more and more. By claiming a monopoly on defending parent's rights and being careful to develop the school system at a slower pace, the Church and the Conservative politicians had contributed to the impoverishment of the reflections on the place of individuals' rights in relation to the Welfare State. The wartime leaders made criticism of State intervention even more difficult.

The main associations representing the working-class as well as the middle-class reformist groups rarely expressed public concern about the State's interference in family affairs. Their silence was also due to the fact that at the time, most members of these associations did not suffer the unlucky consequences of the decline in parents' rights. In 1951, university researchers invited 214 mothers, selected on the basis of their benefit amounts, to give their opinions on the family allowances regime and suggest improvements to researchers, who took great care to distinguish themselves from the government enumerators. None of the mothers complained about the program. However, among the 79 mothers with preschool-aged children and modest income in the southwest of Montréal who met in the spring of 1947, 11 per cent were against the allowances or were skeptical of them because they either disapproved of the government's interference or had little interest in the program. Generally, the small proportion of families suspected of misspending their allowances reassured the defenders of family integrity.[68] On two separate occasions, in 1947 and 1951, Father Lebel recognized that federal employees were not intrusive: "until now, the officials entrusted with the implementation of the law have known to respect the families' autonomy."[69]

For the State to envisage the management of the welfare of rural families as thoroughly as that of salaried urban families, it would be necessary, later, for rural producers' associations to present rural families in the terms of the paid-work market. For the time being, they had only begun to view the nature of labour relations within their businesses in terms connected with the formal economy: the UCC called for farmers to be able to deduct the wages paid to their sons from their taxes, and the circle of women farmers asked that wives be considered as collaborators in the agricultural business. The State had contributed to this change by conceiving social policies that favoured the majority of its citizens—wage earners and taxpayers. However, by sending testimonials of opposition based on the principle of family autonomy, the province's autonomous labourers kept alive a rich stream of criticism of the State's intrusion, at a time when the majority of citizens were ready to give up such an idea.

In the case of young girls' work at home, the political argument of economic contribution (the same one farmers' groups began to use in the case of their sons), was even more rare. The boys were considered future citizens or participants in the labour market, and the girls were not. Their mothers had just obtained the right to vote in provincial elections and, in the economic domain, they still had difficulty obtaining the recognition of their unpaid work, and sometimes even of their potential for paid work.

Criticisms of the universal laws were not all based on previous political traditions. The evolution of the public sphere itself brought new means of criticism to the political culture.[70] The change in political habits did not always go in the direction the legislators had hoped. To ensure dialogue between parents and public administration around the implementation of the new welfare laws, they had created specific institutions: the family allowances court and the associations of parents of schoolchildren. Only rarely did parents take advantage of these organizations. The allowances court was organized belatedly, without much publicity, and less than ten mothers brought their cases to be heard there.[71] The movement for parents' associations encouraged by school inspectors developed unevenly; they took on a certain scale during the 1940s only to decline later on. By supporting these associations, the DPI had wanted to put an end to the "misunderstanding between parents and schools" and to "the thoughtless criticisms" by parents.[72] But the Department had a fixed idea of the role parents should play in such associations: they had to attend several hours in class to be informed of school activities, in order to help teachers in their work.[73] The rare groups of parents that used these assemblies as a means to call for the modification of certain practices had slight success. It seems they were a predominantly middle-class group, with values similar to those of the elementary-school teachers.[74]

Some families, whose needs prevented them from conforming with the law, used the rhetoric of the universal economic citizenship to denounce the State's infringements on their rights as parents. A farmer from Montmorency County whose children could not get to school because they hadn't any shoes, wrote to the SPI: "The law has to plan for exceptions. I hope that parents can still take care of their own children. We're not in Germany, are we?"[75] One father from Roberval with four sons in college and three daughters in the convent, for whom he paid a total of $9.50 per month in school fees "aside from text books and clothes," declared, "I find it very strange Mr. Minister, and even a little pathetic, when I open the newspaper and read about family, family and family democracy and liberty...." The State did not guarantee the right to education that it had promised. "Since we are under the thumb of a compulsory law," one parent summed up, "it seems to me that we should have the right to demand the advantages of following it faithfully."[76] Without free books, classes, transportation, and school furnishings, they stated, the law would not be what it meant to be, "a compulsory education law, which should be free and not cost us a penny":[77]

> Being a father of 7 children who are old enough to go to School, I was eager to see how the famous compulsory education law worked, a law

which has long been praised on the radio as a godsend for the working class, since it would be free.

I am sorry to say since the class opened in Bury (Compton County), that after the first day, I can see it will cost me more this year than it did last year. And this is why: this year, the Rvd. Nuns required each child to have (11) notebooks, instead of (4) from last year.

Does the uniformity of books require so many notebooks? I would also like to say I don't think this qualifies as free. It is rather compulsory since for me I am required to pay more this year than last year.

Please tell me by return mail what exactly the law means by free schooling.[78]

There were incidences of the Bury example throughout the province: "We have accustomed the population to the idea so well with the radio and the newspapers," reported the missionary priest who was also the truancy officer in Baie-Trinity, "that if education is compulsory it is also free. We are therefore going to have some difficulty in asking them pay for books and school taxes."[79]

In the eyes of some protesters, the law's contradictions and gaps were the result of the difference in status between themselves and the political leaders. The wife of a sick farmer living in Montmorency County addressed the SPI as she would someone of a superior class, negotiating to reach her goals: "Do not forget, Monsieur," she wrote, "it is not only rich or 'higher' people who can have talent and intelligence, my children particularly my daughter, could be, if they had the chance, first in your 'high schools.'"[80] Josaphat Lapierre, the La Sarre truancy officer, collected similar criticisms, which he sent to the SPI in the following virulent terms:

It can be presumed that these same parents who make themselves guilty of negligence these days will make every possible sacrifice to get their children a good education as long as governments adopt a financial regime which will permit everyone to live normally in a civilized country, without worry of tomorrow; to know that tomorrow, they can eat, be clothed, have a roof over their head; if someone does not come and take away the means they have acquired with the sweat of their brow. When for 10 years we held a people in misery in a country of abundance, and then took away its sons in their prime, asking them to pay the tax of blood, and from all other sides, a collection of restrictions and obligations are imposed upon it, taking away almost all freedom to act and ability to govern itself according to its tastes and hopes, it is not in the least bit surprising that this treatment would result in angry reactions throughout the population.[81]

The right to a minimum of education established by the Compulsory School Attendance Act conferred a new legitimacy on rural municipality landowners, who had long been sending letters and petitions to school commissioners demanding schools, transportation, new classes, and better elementary-school teachers. The tensions between parents and commissioners had not begun in 1943, but the new law led powerless parents to seek out the support of provincial authorities. Taking advantage of the climate of trust created by Victor Doré, parents played the card of the SPI's norms against that of local incompetence.[82] Further, it is possible that the universal program had contributed to strengthening the identity of citizen, as suggested by a single case in Trois-Rivières. In 1945, when petitioners asked the Commission scolaire Saint-Louis-de-France (CSSLF) to build a village school that would go up to grade nine, they presented themselves as 88 of the village's 188 landowners; ten years later, at the neighbouring Commission scolaire de Cap-de-la-Madeleine, a resolution asking for the increase of family allowances by a group introduced as a "voter's union." The "newly formed" association, perhaps for this exact occasion, stated that the allowances had been "a precious help and [that they had] greatly contributed to the support and further education of the children, especially in larger families."[83]

On top of fortifying old demands, the universal rights regime also entailed new ways of carrying out policy-making. Citizens felt "closer to the governments," as the officials from the federal Department of Finance in their 1943 plea in favour of family allowances had predicted. There is not a more eloquent testimony to this phenomenon than the September 1948 episode in which the Family Allowances Bureau, forced to delay the mailing of 500,000 cheques in the Montréal region by two weeks, received nearly 10,000 calls and the post offices were overwhelmed with complaints.[84] Through those citizens who attempted new ways to approach the collection of provincial and federal institutions, the Welfare State contributed to the movement of expansion of the scale of political life. It was as if the new public institutions themselves helped to change the configuration of the parties and of the pressure groups in a way that would contribute in turn to the reinforcement of the Welfare State.

On the provincial level, the trade unions directed many social claims, and according to political analyst Gérard Bergeron, it was in matters of education that they showed themselves to be most insistent and most precise. Since the end of the Second World War, unions represented a larger part of the population; their numbers had in fact doubled.[85] During the post-war years, the CTCC structures democratized, and little by little the organization adopted a more collective approach to social problems. Behind the changes in the Catholic associations were more general changes within the Church: a minority current of lay people critical of the authorities' traditionalism, had successfully alerted the bishops to the low level of urban school attendance.[86]

As well as being opposed to the exceptions allowed by universal laws (which helped to perpetuate the inequalities, contrary to what had been predicted in the initial project), the unions called for a modification of the power relations within institutions of education. During the 1950s, the CTCC called for policies aiming to redistribute incomes. "It is necessary," declared the central labour body in 1954, "for a significant number of scholarships to be given to less-fortunate gifted students to allow them to pursue their higher education like their schoolmates from more well off families."[87] Through the medium of their unions, fathers who were not landowners asked to be represented in school boards. At the same time, neo-nationalists, intellectuals of the journal *cité libres,* and the FCS criticized the composition of the Council of Public Instruction and the Montréal Catholic School Commission (MCSC). Finally, Gérard Filion, editorial writer at *Le Devoir*, asked that the nature of the relationships between the commissioners and their voters be modified so that the former would be accountable to the latter.[88]

It does not seem that the new laws had a powerful enough impact on the women's movement for the democratization of the school system to become the object of their official debates. Renée Vautelet, author of a report on women and reconstruction for the Québec government, proposed a renewal of rural women's political activity with the development of social services, which would allow for an extension of their citizenship.[89]

School Boards and the Struggle against the Centralizing of Social Institutions

When Adélard Godbout allowed a rumour about the centralization of public-education structures to circulate, the school boards' fear of losing prerogatives led to the creation of a federation. To appeal more legitimately to the provincial government, the boards committed themselves to ensuring that universal political rights were guaranteed, and they rethought their own structures. The FCS asked that the school board elections be opened to non-landowners and that the Catholic Committee to the Public Instruction Council (CCPIC) be modified to give the country commissioners an independent voice. In the name of country parents, they reproached officials for being ignorant of the living conditions of the people they administered. "Whatever their [method]," proclaimed one of the FCS's first circulars, "whatever their preferences, these authorities, we believe, are not aware of all the difficulties of living in the country."[90] In contrast with the Church's recriminations, it saw the exodus from the country as a *fait accompli* for which the cities should compensate rural communities:

> The rural population constitutes our reservoir of building blocks of life, as Pie XII would say, supplying the Church, the State, and all other professions. This means that the rural environment is constantly being emptied of its human capital, constantly leaving for the benefit of the urban environment without receiving anything in return. This human capital does not leave with an empty mind. In fact it receives its education partly in the country, partly in the city. In both cases the rural dwellers pay for an education which benefits the city.[91]

From their predecessors, the defenders of the country maintained the idea that the rural communities would help prevent the depopulation of the country, but their projects to return to the land were replaced by plans to develop the regional economy. They were in agreement with a renewal of nationalist thinking, which permanently abandoned agriculturalism, the social project based primarily on farming.[92]

With his 1946 law, Maurice Duplessis had attempted to obtain the support of school boards which had been jeopardized by Adélard Godbout's centralizing ambitions. The new premier had assured them of his intention to maintain the boards' autonomy and avoid the "socialization of teaching," in the words of the provincial secretary. Thus, Duplessis did not attempt to alter significantly the province's educational structure: "all that was added was in the order of quantity," to use political analyst Gérard Bergeron's terms.[93] However, Duplessis' government used the new education fund to establish more political control over the boards' financial activities. The absorption of their debts came with more rigorous financial monitoring.[94] Furthermore, they were still given insufficient money, and in the form of a patronage that created insecurity. Assistance in constructing schools, opening higher grades, providing free books, and expanding the scope of activities in favour of a regime of universality depended on an MP's goodwill, and the development of the educational network took place in a extremely politicized climate. It was the rural school boards, in real need of the department's help, that suffered the most from this blackmail. Thus the "ghost of state control," to take up the virulent phrase of journalist and school commissioner Gérard Filion, would interfere with the schools, not through the Department of Public Instruction but rather through the members of the Union nationale.

Individually, the boards called for more and more money from the government by way of their MPs. Collectively, they continued to claim their autonomy: beginning in 1949, the FCS fought to make school construction subsidies uniform.[95] Meanwhile, Duplessis' practices undermined the credibility of his own system: he did not use all the education funds and he devoted one portion of it to ends other than those for which they were destined—to the construction of highways in particular. In fact, during the fifteen years following the adoption of the Compulsory School Attendance Act, a large portion of the burden of school expansion continued to be borne by the school boards. Between the years 1944–45 and 1952–53 their total contribution doubled, going from $29 million to $68 million.[96]

In this context, it was the school boards that took the initiative of changing school structures. They sought means of increasing their income: many raised their tax rates by more than 100 per cent, and in the 1950s, nearly 100 towns even took it upon themselves to levy a "school sales tax." Following the example of the MCSC, some created their own administrative reforms, availing themselves, for example, of the services of a permanent secretary.[97] More and more boards also chose to build central schools, which had a positive impact on attendance and the Protestants demonstrated a systematic approach to reach this aim. The spectacular increase in provincial subsidies for children's transportation, also distributed in an arbitrary fashion, is testament to the rise of central schools: in 1945, subsidies were up to $65,000, and fifteen years later they would reach $810,000.[98] The Fédération des secrétaires de municipalité and the FCS played an important role in managing and uniting these disparate efforts. These organizations became involved, for example, in board personnel training.

Other sectors of Québec society called for financing methods that would provide a way out of the impasse into which the fights between bishops, school boards, and the department had pushed education reform. Trade unions had long been asking for the State to finance all education. Beginning in 1949, the FCS took a step in this direction with its plea for the standardization of the sales-tax law, which still only provided 50 per cent of its potential yield. The FCS also called for special education taxes, a part in the management of the education fund, and expansion of the taxation zones. Those involved drew upon lessons learned in the 1943 experience. Arthur Tremblay, for example, added a precise cost evaluation to his proposal for increasing the compulsory school attendance age, and pressure groups proposed new sources of revenues that would make their program possible.[99]

For the institutions dedicated to childhood welfare, a comparable evolution occurred in the province, caused by the institution of the family allowances. Clerics, federal authorities, and social workers took on the project of establishing a national network of diocesan placing agencies to allow children in orphanages to benefit from the family allowances.[100] A recent history of the Montréal parish of Saint-Pierre-Apôtre sheds light on the nature of this phenomenon. Solving most education and urban welfare problems was still in the realm of the possible at the parish level until after the Great War, which had allowed the Church to retain a major role in society. Subsequently, the economic segregation of city neighbourhoods obliged the upper clergy to amalgamate its own structures of finance and care distribution.[101] In so doing, the Church, like the school boards, proceeded to a certain centralization of its own institutions, both to face its own material difficulties and to exert some control over the terms of its more numerous collaborations with public authorities. In the case of orphans, as in that of truancy monitoring, by helping to maintain central and hierarchic institutions, the Catholic Church had laid the groundwork for a centralized Welfare State while also delaying its advent.[102] This is what sociologist Jean-Charles Falardeau perceived in the early 1950s: "The parochial universe of the French-Canadian worker is becoming disenchanted. It is already impersonal and bureaucratic." It became easier for the State to replace impersonal structures with the complicity of overwhelmed clerics.[103] This phenomenon could also explain the Québécois' stronger degree of approval for the Welfare State in recent decades' compared with Canadians in other regions with equal incomes.[104]

Social Policy and the Constitution

The same reformist trend, open to State intervention, critical of bureaucratic centralization, and more sensitive to rural needs, had dominated the foundation of the Action libérale nationale (ALN) in the 1930s, a group of young Liberals disappointed with their leader's close-minded approach to social policies. They had helped Conservative leader Maurice Duplessis to win the 1936 provincial election. The premier had subsequently broken his alliance with the reformist Catholic elite to obtain the support of the Conservative Catholic hierarchy, with symbolic, anticommunist, or moralizing measures, such as the needy mothers' allowances.[105] Disappointed, some heads of the ALN had joined the Liberals, while others had chosen to try alone again for the 1939 poll, without much success, though the division played into the Liberals' hands.[106] In 1944, the latter had participated in the foundation of the Bloc populaire, a party that hoped to profit from the wave of opposition against conscription to bring to Québec City a nationalist team with more reformist character than Duplessis. The party's platform proposed ambitious social policies and a decentralized administrative structure that would favour local-level collaboration.[107]

During the electoral campaign that year, the Bloc populaire associated compulsory education with "educational conscription."[108] In doing so, it did more than scare voters off with the threat of federal centralization. By accusing Adélard Godbout of having effected impersonal centralized reforms, it hoped to attract part of the reformist vote that had brought Godbout into power. Duplessis' success in the 1944 election did not seem to have been to the result of an increase in unionist votes but rather of rerouted Bloc populaire votes.[109] After 1944, however, the Bloc's popularity melted away; Duplessis used the social institutions he controlled to consolidate his power and to bring back many nationalist elements to his party.

The failure of the boycott of family allowances—which was instigated by the Bloc populaire in the name of provincial autonomy, the preservation of the principle of paternal authority, and the interests of large families—illustrates the party's dilemmas. It surprised many organizers who had, in 1942, succeeded in leading a campaign against conscription at the federal level. The only CCF MP at the legislative assembly of the province, David Côté, was possibly correct when he observed that families "wanted allowances and not speeches on autonomy." For this statement he received the approval of workers' unions.[110]

Duplessis was at once more nationalist than Godbout and, regarding the province's economic development, less reformist as well. For sixteen years, education would be marked by a vicious cycle, as would many other sectors of Québec social life. Patronage maintained the rural county's fidelity for Maurice Duplessis, which in turn let down the Liberal government's hopes of re-election, thus contributing to the "myth of Duplessis' electoral invincibility."[111] During this time, the universal social rights regime helped reduce the nationalist elite's scorn of the State without any party's knowing how to take on this reformist nationalism themselves. In 1947, Father Lebel expressed in vain the wish that mothers and fathers of large families "create and lead public opinion which would force officials to provide an essentially family-oriented policy, paying particular attention to the needs of large families, the nation's benefactors."[112] Far from being the most discontent, large families, as previously discussed, were among those who felt the greatest relief when the family allowances were distributed.

Citizens increasingly directed their social-policy demands to the federal government. Léopold Richer addressed the issue in *Le Devoir* in 1944: "If the provincial authorities had followed the advice of our sociologists, our working classes would not now be turning toward the federal government to address their grievances and to solve their problems and they would not be ready to sacrifice provincial autonomy to obtain social security laws."[113] Twenty years later, historian Michel Brunet had a similar perspective: "When the federal government, influenced in no way by French Canada's agriculturalist and anti-State thinking, invaded the spheres where the provincial state had been refused entrance, and refused itself the right to intervene or intervened only timidly, the field was open to it, and it very easily gained the support of the French-Canadian electorate."[114]

At the provincial level, in the absence of an active Liberal opposition in the early 1950s, it was trade unions that ensured the conduct of social demands.[115] Without provincial initiatives, the centralization trend precipitated by the war fed itself. Duplessis, who had regained power, blocked access to the Québécois State to unions and reformists. They increasingly looked towards federal officials. We have seen that the central Catholic unions, which had opposed Mackenzie King during the 1942 referendum on conscription, approved the federal government's labour legislation. As for the Union des cultivateurs catholiques, it welcomed the federal family allowances enthusiastically. In Québec, as in all other Western Catholic regions, many Catholic associations kept their distance from the bishops' instruction, a position from which they had the option of being less autonomist.[116]

The federal government thus managed to transform a temporary centralization of authorities regarding prices and wages into one durable centralization of prerogatives regarding social policies. Similar to other Western cases, here "[t]he institutional legacy of first decisions taken in social legislation...cemented loyalties to particular ways of doing things."[117] Family allowances gave the Canadian prime minister additional leverage during the post-war meetings of the federal and provincial governments. In the summer of 1945, the prime minister was able to found his proposition to repatriate all the taxing power to Ottawa by citing the already high costs of the social welfare program. In fact, the allowances alone monopolized $200 million, a sum equivalent to 40 per cent of the pre-war federal budget. It was in vain that the Ontario premier, Conservative George Drew, had joined Duplessis in denouncing federal centralism. They would succeed in opposing the Federal proposals for other social programs, such as the improved old-age pensions and shared-cost health insurance, but with regards to family allowances, they had to accept it was a *fait accompli.*[118] Thus, the mandarins who, since the 1939 publication of the *Royal Commission on Dominion Provincial Relations* (the Rowell-Sirois Report), had advocated a conquering centralism, had been able to benefit from the war to strengthen the foundations of the federal welfare state.

Alvin Finkel considers that these constitutional adventures, which limited debates to a group of high officials and politicians, weakened the democratic process and with it, the opportunities for reform.[119] The history of family allowances and compulsory education seems to confirm his assertion. It was in the name of provincial power that Maurice Duplessis fought the federal government's social laws, and he only allowed the democratization of political life with deep reluctance. Having abandoned the sphere of material aid for families once his struggle against the federal allowances was lost, the provincial prime minister managed to create some confusion with regard to the program's origins. "The Union nationale was the first provincial government to adopt a family allowances law," he declared in September 1945, making a misleading allusion to the needy-mothers' allowances.[120] The tactic was successful judging from the federal ministers' reaction, such as the following from Paul Martin: "Certain provincial ministers had sought, during election times and at other moments, to give voters the impression that they were responsible for the family allowances, [that] a large part of the credit came from the provincial governments: in one case, they even took credit for the allowances."[121] For similar reasons, during the federal and provincial governments' meetings on reconstruction, Duplessis was ready to renew the post-war fiscal agreements: he did not want to be blamed for having forgotten the welfare measures promised during the war.[122]

Away from the higher-level political struggles, the union of constitutional and social politics encouraged a certain democratization of the public system. It seems that when the government faced reformists' demands, the constitutional quarrels often forcing it to protect its legitimacy with particular care, it showed a particular respect for parents' needs as it did for those of intermediary associations.

Armed with a Family Allowances Act with ambitious rules, the federal officials made sure that the social-policy seeds Adélard Godbout had sown during the war would germinate, even if Duplessis was attempting to set them aside. We have seen how the QRO became the centre for the inspiration and training of Québec's truancy officers. In some fields, the federal government's objectives even went beyond the compulsory education aspect pursued by Godbout's government. The Family Allowances Bureau approached the cases of absence due to poverty more methodically: it systematically called on the charitable agencies, and the final measure was to call the social workers from its "welfare" sector, who attempted to help the poor families.[123] The school boards considered the family allowances officials to be convenient allies because they were at once reformists and opposed to a larger provincial centralism. The numerous provincial school boards had resisted Godbout's "managerial" centralization, but they also imagined educational reforms. Behind this attitude, we can see the opinions of parents who did not believe that patronage could be useful to them as well as those who deplored that such patronage contributed to the maintenance of a low quality of teaching.[124]

Besides, at the heart of Duplessis' civil service, individuals continued in the shadows to give institutions a more democratic form. Officials began to adopt new minimum standards. For instance, DPI Secretary B.-O. Filteau wrote in 1952:

> We must remember…that grade 9 is currently the minimum required to apprentice various trades, and for acceptance to the secondary occupations of commerce, industry and civil service. Grade 9 is also required for Arts and Trade schools, to regional agricultural schools, to vocational schools and home economics schools. Further, the minimum age for admission for these various schools, where one can learn a trade, perhaps even one where one might find legal employment in a commercial or industrial establishment, is 16 years of age. There is therefore no reason, especially for boys, to leave school before the age of 16, with the exception of certain farmers' sons. We cannot watch thousands of children leave school every year at 14, and vegetate for two years to later join the class of the unskilled and unemployed.[125]

Given the stance of these civil servants, it is not surprising that Maurice Duplessis prevented the DPI from presenting a report to the Tremblay Commission.[126] The experiences of the orphanages and the child-placement agencies recounted in chapter 2 are comparable: over fifteen years, QRO employees worked towards the transformation Adélard Godbout's government had not had the opportunity to complete by 1944, with the collaboration of Catholic agencies.

It was only in 1956 that the province's Liberal Party also undertook to democratize its structure and to include an even firmer engagement in favour of social policies. It was helped in part by the arrival of a Conservative government in Ottawa in 1957 and by the Union nationale's abandonment of a certain measure of provincial autonomy. When the Conservative Party had attempted a similar reconciliation during the 1949 federal election and had attempted to draw the voters' attention to the non-nationalist elements of family allowances,[127] its efforts had been in vain: for the Liberal Saint-Laurent, the French-speaking Québécois were a captive audience—as the federal Conservative Party still held the handicap of an enthusiastic support of conscription in both world wars. In 1958, however, Duplessis decided for the first time to lend his electoral machine to the federal Conservatives. We can therefore suggest that it was the general consensus on social policies, above all nationalist criticism, that ensured Diefenbaker's party received the majority of votes.[128]

The Quiet Revolution, State Formation, Nationalism, and Family Values

In 1960, with the arrival of Jean Lesage's "équipe du tonnerre" in power, nationalism and statism entered into Québec hand in hand. Over a period of four years, the government proceeded to transfer most educational and charitable religious institutions from the Church to the State, thus relegating the clerics' power to the private sector. It abolished the orphanage system and secularized the placement of dependent children, increased the age of compulsory school attendance to fifteen years of age, instituted school allowances for children aged sixteen and seventeen, abolished school and textbooks fees until grade eleven, obliged all the boards to welcome students until grade eleven, and created the Department of Education; it also secularized most teaching structures and instituted a provincial program to supplement old-age pensions. In 1961, its "great education charter" proclaimed that "each child has a fundamental right to receive an appropriate education" whatever their background.[129] The Liberal Party's commitments on the social level appeared to be responses to the population's increased expectations, to which fifteen years of family allowances and compulsory education had contributed.

The Lesage government proceeded to institute a major reform of the State's role. When the Department of Education was created in 1964, Paul-Gérin-Lajoie declared: "[To] those who say that we are moving too quickly and that we want to do everything at once, I answer that it [is] this type of moment in a peoples' history when everything must be done at once, because all things are interdependent."[130] That most of the social security and education reforms did not come to pass after the large economic and policy reforms of the Lesage administration is proof of this phenomenon.[131] In some way, the increase in the State's role in the exploitation of natural resources helped to accomplish in Québec what the expansion of the Canadian State role in international relations had accomplish in Ottawa in the interwar period. Subsequently, federal–provincial diplomacy would contribute to this expansion. To explain this "revolution," historians usually conclude that the Liberal government could count on the presence of more experts in Québec society and on a larger budget. The change in political culture caused by the universal social laws of the 1940s had also contributed to the creation of a favourable climate.

In 1956, after a twelve-year eclipse in orphanage supervision, the provincial government attempted to bring back within its power a movement that it could no longer ignore. It reorganized the Department of Social Welfare and Youth and it began a process of closing institutions which it entrusted to social workers. The provincial directory cited the new "family needs" to explain the change of course.[132] However, these "needs" had not waited for a benevolent provincial government to be discovered: the suddenness and facility with which Jean Lesage completed the social welfare and education reforms were in large part due to the "hallway work" of federal officials and politicians since the end of the war, in collaboration with the mid-level Québec institutions.

In many ways, Lesage's education and assistance policies represented the appropriation and development by the new Québec interventionist State of federal initiatives, themselves built on old religious and local structures. For the Québec government, as with the governments of many other provinces, the 1960s would be the decade in which many Keynesian measures would be repatriated on the regional scale. It was around the federal government that the nationalist Québec elite had been in contact with the workings of a Welfare State for the first time, and it seems that this beginning within the federal State would influence the shape of the provincial institutions. Over a span of two decades, the federal government had indirectly prepared the coming of a provincial Welfare State by providing laws, structures, and expertise to support the Québec reformists who had supported Adélard Godbout's reforms during the war, and Mackenzie King's as well. Behind an apparent political impasse, an administrative adventure had occurred between 1944 and 1960, during which the federal government had contributed to enlarging the legitimacy of universal social policies to groups of Québec society that had previously been hostile towards State intervention, namely certain reformist groups, and large portions of the clergy and of the upper provincial civil service. Thus, these groups were able to amass a considerable amount of knowledge, consolidate their own structures, form associations, and work together. Their extensive participation in public affairs, supported or provoked by federal initiatives, allowed them to become interlocutors increasingly difficult for the Québec government to ignore.[133]

In their conquest of political and administrative power in social matters, Lesage's mandarins met two fewer obstacles on their path than the federal government. There were no constitutional limits barring their entry into education and assistance jurisdictions, and no institution strong enough to support and unite the various population sectors opposed to the State's increased role. The Liberal team would also benefit from its predecessors' campaigns, which had favoured provincial autonomy. At times, Duplessis' jealousies had been the only obstacle facing the "Ottawa Men's" centralizing project, and for the period studied here, the results of this opposition are significant. Duplessis had recovered the domain of direct provincial taxes after the war and instituted them in the 1950s; moreover, in 1951, when Louis Saint-Laurent implemented universal old-age pensions, he had agreed to support a constitutional amendment to this effect in exchange for a promise that, if the province wanted to create its own program, it would be free to do so.[134]

These constitutional reforms were not the only routes by which Duplessis' actions had set the stage for the Quiet Revolution. It is possible that the premier's obstinacy brought about a significant transformation of the State's role in nationalist thinking. Not all the traditional nationalist elements disappeared under Duplessis, but we must be careful to treat the emotional strength of nationalism as an unaltered phenomenon inherited from the past.[135] Duplessis' nation was based as much, if not more, on a notion of political autonomy with its own worth as on Catholic family traditions. In a certain way, Duplessis had multiplied the State's homage to the Church, as a way to mask a real loss of power on the Church's part, and the post-war bishops were not always so unhappy to "allow the State to carry the burden of the nation,"[136] a point finding evidence in the history of the orphanages and school boards. After Duplessis, Jean Lesage and his successors would be able to count on this first distance between nationalism and Catholic values in order to use the provincial State in the way Mackenzie King had used the federal State in 1940: with the aim of supporting—even creating—new national values.

Beginning in 1963, the federal government would enter another period of creating social programs for a multitude of new reasons. The combination of the economy's slowdown in the 1950s, the desire of Lester B. Pearson's Liberal government to counter the American domination of the country's culture and economy, and its worry about acting as a counterbalance against the province's demands, all called for new national social programs. In Québec, the social policies would soon be first on the list of efforts to construct a strong provincial government.[137] The two governments were about to enter into a competition to check "the sudden appearance of strong popular pressures" of the 1960s.[138]

"Neo-nationalism" would be bureaucratic and centralizing. The hopes of the FCS, the Bloc populaire, and certain other officials from the DPI would be dashed, which would have made for an increased autonomy for local institutions. The nature of the relations between the FCS and the QRO in the 1950s on one hand and the authors of the educational reforms of the Quiet Revolution on the other helps to explain the outcome. In 1953, informed about the hearings of the Royal Commission of Inquiry on Constitutional Problems, which Duplessis had created to study the question of provincial taxes, Paul-André Fournier, head of school attendance at the

QRO, believed that the moment had come to influence the teaching networks in Québec. He persuaded the FCS, with which he was deeply involved, to hire two lawyers, constitutional specialist Paul Gérin-Lajoie and Arthur Tremblay, to prepare the FCS's report. The preparatory meetings revealed the gaps between the reform promoters: those close to Fournier respected the autonomy of local institutions, and those surrounding Gérin-Lajoie advocated centralization. The diocesan associations of the school boards chose the first solution, and the FCS's report was valued so highly by the Royal Commission that its president retained the services of the main author, Arthur Tremblay, to write the final section of the commission's educational report, a document that took up the FCS's solution.[139]

The other expert Fournier chose, Paul Gérin-Lajoie, would become the main architect for the report of the Royal Commission of Inquiry on Education in the Province of Québec (the Parent Report), prepared between 1961 and 1963. This government took up his more technocratic and centralizing ideals. Wartime social and educational policies had helped this development in their contribution to the rise of the number of young technocrats who saw in the expansion of the existing centralized model an increase in their own numbers. Wartime policies had also helped increase the proportion of provincial francophone employers with whom the local progressive projects could be popular. The Liberal Party of the province had adopted these ideals only recently: granting statutory subsidies to the school boards and re-establishing their autonomy was still on the 1956 electoral program.[140] Furthermore, the next generation's administrators looked to France, where public instruction was organized around a central administration.[141] The centres of resistance to the centralization of school structures, which Duplessis had known to use for their political strength, still existed, and if they were responsible for the return of the Union nationale in 1966, they were not able to reverse the movement.

Support for this more centralized and technocratic version of the development of social policies also came from the original reformists, the very same group who had supported Adélard Godbout during the war. In making spending in the educational sector one of the main elements of his patronage network, Duplessis had weakened the legitimacy of the intermediary institutions considerably, and it is possible that he contributed to making them seem more suspect in the eyes of the young nationalists. In other words, the discretionary subsidies in education doubtlessly played a role in the increase of the rural voters' support in 1948, but in the middle term, the marriage between relatively autonomous local institutions and patronage may have proved fatal.[142]

In the same way, nationalist thinking on welfare had come to an impasse. Duplessis had opposed federal intervention and had not proposed provincial policies in exchange as Taschereau and Godbout had done before him. By rejecting the nationalist reform projects since his arrival in power, he had condemned himself to remain in the shackles of the old economic development solutions. Subsequently, autonomous reformists favouring his party were never able to convince him to counterattack with provincial social laws.[143] The authors of the Tremblay Report, when they called for Québec social policies that would respect intermediary agencies, used the failed experience of provincial allowances from 1943 to prove that it was possible.[144] The example was not promising when we view the provincial allowances' failure as being the result of, in large part, problems internal to Québec society and not simply a casualty of federal intervention, as the report's authors suggested.

In 1960, while political conditions had been reunited so that nationalist social policies could be set up, values, practices, and new institutions had won the majority of the province's voters, which were no longer all that different from other Canadians. There would soon be few institutions or programs founded on "the religious convictions of Québec's social and cultural traditions," family, parish, and autonomous work, which the authors of the Tremblay report recommended the province of Québec conserve in every future establishment of social programs.[145]

The provincial governments following Jean Lesage attempted to go beyond the simple catching-up proposed by Adélard Godbout twenty years earlier, by giving certain programs a nationalist orientation: in 1961, provincial family allowances for students over fourteen years of age were added to the federal allowances, and beginning in 1973, they provided generous help for larger families in particular.[146] But the hopes that the allowances would bring about a higher birth rate, as Maximilien Caron had predicted in 1945, had faded, and the aid for large families came more as a measure to struggle against poverty.[147]

Finally, the change in family values, which had been encouraged by the universal programs, reduced the specificity of Québec institutions. Jean Lesage himself undertook to realize a series of civil-law reforms in this homogenizing direction, which affected the status of married women, adoption, and the extent of fathers' authority. Similarly, the federal government was able to amend a law relative to divorce and adoption before a Catholic Church that would henceforth surrender its power in civil affairs to the State.[148] It is even possible that by recognizing domestic work and by conferring upon mothers an added degree of public existence, an economic basis to support their citizenship, the program of family allowances had laid the groundwork for the demands from the feminist movement in the 1960s. And it is also possible that the recognition of economic and cultural rights for children had prepared the politicization of young people, which helped to bring the Lesage government into power.

The nationalist thinking about the family was also changing. The nationalists' fights in the name of the French-Canadian family henceforth appeared to be less important, and the loss of the symbolic value of large families doubtlessly explains why, in 1949, the federal government was able to abolish the decreasing rate without much opposition.[149] In 1953, economist Esdras Minville justly emphasized that "the conflict between a political thought always connected with the idea of autonomy and a social thought ready to accept certain forms of integration…as social evolution will…tend to assimilate French Canada with the rest of the continent."[150]

In 1954, the Tremblay Report had warned the province's officials that without provincial social policies, the French-Canadian culture could disappear: the government would have to go back on three decades of inaction, a move without which the population would soon accept the idea of a Welfare State led from Ottawa. Without such remedial actions, 150 years of history and provincial progress would be jeopardized.[151] In so doing, the nationalist reformist authors of the report had pointed out a social and political phenomenon on which this work has attempted to shed light. However, they had exaggerated the responsibilities of the federal government. In two decades, the federal and provincial Liberals' universal programs had certainly contributed to making cultures uniform, but they were not the only ones responsible for it. In fact, the history of compulsory education and family allowances developed in a close and dynamic proximity with that of economic changes, the evolution of citizens' political values, and the transformation of social relations.

Notes

Introduction

1 P. Lévêque, "Histoire politique," in *Dictionnaire des sciences historiques,* ed. André Burguière (Paris: Presses Universitaires de France, 1987), 520–22; and Carl Berger, "Aspects of English-Canadian Historical Writing: 1900–1970," in *The Writing of Canadian History* (Toronto: Oxford University Press, 1986), 303–319. For general works on the history of social policies in Canada and Québec, see Dennis Guest, *Histoire de la sécurité sociale au Canada* (Montréal: Boréal, 1995); Serge Mongeau, *Évolution de l'assistance au Québec* (Montréal: Éditions du Jour, 1967); and Elizabeth Wallace, "The Origin of the Social Welfare State in Canada," *Canadian Journal of Economic and Political Science* 16 (1950): 383–93.

2 This image is from B.B. Gilbert, *British Social Policy, 1916–1939* (Ithaca: Cornell University Press, 1970). See also Frances Fox Piven and Richard A. Cloward, *Regulating the Poor: The Functions of Public Welfare* (New York: Vintage, 1971); and Barry Gewen, "The Intellectual Foundations of the Child Labour Reform Movement" (Ph.D. diss., Harvard University, 1972), 285.

3 Veronica Strong-Boag, "Wages for Housework: Mothers' Allowances and the Beginning of Social Security in Canada," *Journal of Canadian Studies/Revue d'études canadiennes* 14, no. 1 (1979): 24–34; Michiel Horn, "Leonard Marsh and the Coming of the Welfare State in Canada: A Review Article," *Histoire sociale/Social History* 9 (1976): 197–204; and Jane Lewis, "The English Movement for Family Allowances, 1917–1945," *Histoire sociale/Social History* 11, no. 22 (1978): 441–59.

4 On the history of education, see, for example, Ruby Heap, "L'Église, l'État, et l'enseignement primaire public catholique au Québec, 1897–1920" (Ph.D. diss., Université de Montréal, 1987); Wendy Johnston, "Keeping Children in School: The Response of the Montreal Roman Catholic School to the Depression of the 1930s," *Communications historiques/Historical Papers* (1985): 193–217; and J. Donald Wilson, "Some Observations on Recent Trends in Canadian Educational History," in *An Imperfect Past: Education and Society in Canadian History,* ed. J. Donald Wilson (Vancouver: Canadian History of Education Association/University of British Columbia Centre for the Study of Curriculum and Instruction, 1984), 7–29. On the history of social policy, see Brigitte Kitchen, "Wartime Social Reform: The Introduction of Family Allowances," *Canadian Journal of Social Work Education/Revue*

canadienne d'éducation en service social 7, no. 1 (1976): 29–54; and C. David Naylor, *Private Practice, Public Payment: Canadian Medicine and the Politics of Health Insurance, 1911–1966* (Montréal: McGill-Queen's University Press, 1986). On a more general level, see Richard M. Tittmuss, "Social Administration in a Changing Society," in *Essays on "The Welfare State,"* ed. Richard M. Tittmuss (1958; reprint, London: George Allen & Unwin, 1976).

5 On public instruction, see Chad Gaffield, "Schooling, the Economy, and Rural Society in Nineteenth-Century Ontario," in *Childhood and Family in Canadian History,* ed. Joy Parr (Toronto: McClelland & Stewart, 1982), 69–92; Ian Davey, "The Rhythm of Work and the Rhythm of School," in *Egerton Ryerson and His Times,* eds. Neil McDonald and Alf Chaiton (Toronto: Macmillan, 1978), 221–53; Susan E. Houston, "Social Reform and Education: The Issue of Compulsory Schooling, Toronto, 1851–1871," in *Egerton Ryerson,* eds. McDonald and Chaiton, 254–76; Michael Katz and Ian Davey, "Youth and Early Industrialization in a Canadian City," in *Turning Points: Historical and Sociological Essays on the Family,* eds. John Demos and S.S. Boocock (Chicago: University of Chicago Press, 1978), 81–119; and Jane Synge, "The Transition from School to Work: Growing Up Working Class in Early-Twentieth-Century Hamilton," in *Childhood and Adolescence in Canada,* ed. K. Ishwaran (Toronto: McGraw-Hill Ryerson, 1979), 249–69. On social policy, see Brigitte Kitchen, "The Family and Social Policy," in *The Family: Changing Trends in Canada,* ed. Maureen Baker (Toronto: McGraw-Hill Ryerson, 1984), 178–97; and Terry Copp, "Montreal's Municipal Government and the Crisis of the 1930s," in *The Usable Urban Past: Planning and Politics in the Modern Canadian City,* eds. A.F.J. Artibise and G.A. Stelter (Toronto: Macmillan, 1979), 112–29. On a more general level, see Jane Lewis, "Dealing with Dependency: State Practices and Social Realities, 1870–1945," in *Women's Welfare, Women's Rights,* ed. Jane Lewis (Sydney: Croom Helm, 1983), 17–37.

6 On child industrial labour in Montréal between 1897 and 1929, see Terry Copp, *Classe ouvrière et pauvreté: Les conditions de vie des travailleurs montréalais, 1897–1929* (Montréal: Boréal Express, 1978), 45–59; and Fernand Harvey, *Révolution industrielle et travailleurs: Une enquête sur les rapports entre le capital et le travail au Québec à la fin du XIXe siècle* (Montréal: Boréal Express, 1978), 270. On New England industries, see Tamara Hareven, "Family Time and Industrial Time: Family and Work in a Planned Corporation Town, 1900–1924," in *Family and Kin in Urban Communities, 1700–1930,* ed. Tamara Hareven (New York: Franklin Watts, 1977), 199. Rebecca Coulter proposes a review of this perspective based on the case of Edmonton in "The Working Young of Edmonton, 1921–1931," in *Childhood and Family,* ed. Parr, 143–59.

7 Leo Panitch, "The Role and Nature of the Canadian State, 1930–1980," in *The Canadian State: Political Economy and Political Power,* ed. Leo Panitch (Toronto: University of Toronto Press, 1977), 3–28; Frédéric Leseman, *Du pain et des services: La réforme de la santé et des services sociaux au Québec* (Montréal: Albert Saint-Martin, 1981); Yves Vaillancourt, *L'évolution des politiques sociales au Québec, 1940–1960* (Montréal: Presses de l'Université de Montréal, 1988); Alvin Finkel, "Origins of the Welfare State in Canada," in *The Canadian State,* ed. Panitch, 344–70; and James Struthers, *No Fault of Their Own: Unemployment and Canadian Welfare State, 1914–1941* (Toronto: University of Toronto Press, 1983). For more classical Marxist studies emphasizing the history of relations of production without focusing on the inherent complexities in the history of the State, see Thérèse Hamel, "L'obligation scolaire au Québec: lieu et enjeu de la lutte des classses"

(Ph.D. diss., Paris V René Descartes, 1981); Michel Pelletier and Yves Vaillancourt, *Les politiques sociales et les travailleurs* (Montréal: n.p., five mimeographed booklets published between 1974 and 1978); and David A. Wolfe, "The Rise and Demise of the Keynesian Era in Canada: Economic Policy, 1930–1982," in *Modern Canada, 1930–1980s,* eds. Michael Cross and Gregory Kealey (Toronto: McClelland & Stewart, 1984), 46–78.

8 Bram de Swaan, *In Care of the State* (Cambridge: Polity, 1988), 4. See also Alain Noël, "L'après-guerre au Canada: Politiques keynésiennes ou nouvelles formes de régulation?" (first version, GRETSE/AEP Symposium, Montréal, QC, 1987), 91–107; Allan Greer and Ian Radforth, eds., *Colonial Leviathan: State Formation in Mid-Nineteenth-Century Canada* (Toronto: University of Toronto Press, 1992); Bruce Curtis, *Building the Educational State: Canada West, 1836–1871* (London: Althouse Press, 1988); John Carrier and Ian Kendall, "Categories, Categorizations, and the Political Economy of Welfare," *Journal of Social Policy* 15, no. 3 (1986): 315–32; Philip Abrams, "Notes on the Difficulty of Studying the State," *Journal of Historical Sociology* 1, no. 1 (1988): 58–89; Philip Corrigan and Derek Sayer, "Introduction," in *The Great Arch: English State Formation as Cultural Revolution* (Oxford: Basil Blackwell, 1985), 1–15; Theda Skocpol, "Bringing the State Back In: Strategies of Analysis in Current Research," in *Bringing the State Back In,* eds. Peter B. Evans, Dietrich Rueschemeyer, and Theda Skocpol (Cambridge: Cambridge University Press, 1985), 3–43; and Ira Katznelson, "The State to the Rescue? Political Science and History Reconnect," *Social Research* 59, no. 4 (1992): 719–37.

9 Bettina Bradbury, ed., "Introduction," in *Canadian Family History: Selected Readings* (Toronto: Copp Clark Pitman, 1992), 1–12; Bettina Bradbury, *Familles ouvrières à Montréal: Âge, genre, et survie quotidienne pendant la phase d'industrialisation* (Montréal: Boréal, 1995); Chad Gaffield, "Demography, Social Structure, and the History of Schooling," in *Approaches to Educational History,* ed. David C. Jones et al. (Winnipeg: University of Manitoba Press, 1981), 71–89; Joy Parr, *Labouring Children: British Immigrant Apprentices to Canada, 1869–1924* (Montréal: McGill-Queens University Press, 1980); Tamara Hareven, "Introduction," in *Family and Kin,* ed. Hareven, 10; and Tamara Hareven, "The History of the Family and the Complexity of Social Change," *American Historical Review* 96 (1991): 95–124.

10 Emily N. Nett, "Canadian Families in Social-Historical Perspective," *Canadian Journal of Sociology* 6 (1981): 254–55; Martine Segalen, "La révolution industrielle: Du prolétaire au bourgeois," in *Histoire de la famille,* vol. 2, ed. André Burguière et al. (Paris: Armand Colin, 1986); and David Morgan, *Social Theory and the Family* (London: Routledge & Kegan Paul, 1975).

11 Cynthia Comacchio, "Beneath the Sentimental Veil: Families and Family History in Canada," *Labour/Le travail* 33 (1994): 279–302; "Family Strategies: An Historian Invention?" (round-table discussion at a meeting of the Social Science History Association, St. Louis, MO, 1986); Louise A. Tilly and Myriam Cohen, "Does the Family Have a History? A Review of Theory and Practice in Family History," *Social Science History* 6, no. 2 (1982): 162; and Morgan, *Social Theory and the Family,* 97.

12 Thelma McCormack, *Politics and the Injury of Gender: Feminism and the Making of the Welfare State* (Ottawa: Canadian Institute for the Advancement of Women, 1991); Jane Ursel, "The State and Maintenance of Patriarchy: A Case Study of Family, Labour, and Welfare Legislation in Canada," in *Family, Economy, and the State: The Social Reproduction Process under Capitalism,* eds. J. Dickinson and

B. Russell (Toronto: Garamond, 1986), 150–91; Carole Pateman, ed., *The Disorder of Women: Democracy, Feminism, and Political Theory* (Cambridge: Polity, 1989); Linda Gordon, "The New Feminist Scholarship on the Welfare State," in *Women, the State, and Welfare,* ed. Linda Gordon (Madison: University of Wisconsin Press, 1990); Gill Jones and Claire Wallace, *Youth, Family, and Citizenship* (Buckingham: Open University Press, 1992); and Stephen Humphries, *Hooligans or Rebels: An Oral History of Working-Class Childhood and Youth, 1889–1939* (Oxford: Basil Blackwell, 1981).

13 A. Wei Djao, "Social Welfare in Canada: Ideology and Reality," *Social Praxis* 6, nos. 1–2 (1978): 35–53; and Elwood Jones, "Dependency and Social Welfare," *Journal of Canadian Studies/Revue d'études canadiennes* 14, no. 1 (1979): 1–2.

14 Alison Prentice, *The School Promoters: Education and Social Class in Mid-Nineteenth-Century Upper Canada* (Toronto: McClelland & Stewart, 1977); Marcel Fournier, *Entre l'école et l'usine: La formation professionelle des jeunes travailleurs* (Montréal: Éditions coopératives Albert Saint-Martin, 1980); and Ursel, "The State and Maintenance of Patriarchy."

15 See, for example, P.T. Rooke and R.L. Schnell, *Discarding the Asylum: From Child Rescue to the Welfare State in Canada (1800–1950)* (Lanham: University Press of America, 1983).

16 This geography of theoretical positions is drawn from Sarah Eisenstein, *Give Us Bread but Give Us Roses: Working Women's Consciousness in the United States, 1890 to the First World War* (London: Routledge & Kegan Paul, 1983), 2–11. See also Eli Zaretsky, "The Place of the Family in the Origins of the Welfare State," in *Rethinking the Family: Some Feminist Questions,* eds. Barrie Thorne and Marilyn Yalom (New York: Longman, 1982), 188–92.

17 Tilly and Cohen, "Does the Family Have a History?" 164; and Arlene Skolnick, "Public Images, Private Realities: The American Family in Popular Culture and Social Science," in *Changing Images of the Family,* eds. Virginia Tufte and Barbara Myerhoff (New Haven: Yale University Press, 1979), 297–318. For an eloquent example of the implementation of this approach, see Richard L. Bushman, "Family Security in the Transition from Farm to City, 1750–1850," *Journal of Family History* 6 (1981): 238–56.

18 Marcel Gauchet and Gloria Swain, *La pratique de l'esprit humain: L'institution asilaire et la révolution démocratique* (Paris: Gallimard, 1980); Carole Pateman, *The Problem of Political Obligation: A Critical Analysis of Liberal Theory* (Cambridge: Polity Press, 1985); and Robert Pinker, *The Idea of Welfare* (London: Heinemann, 1979).

19 See, for example, Joy Parr, ed. "Introduction," in *Childhood and Family,* 15; Asa Briggs, "The Welfare State in Historical Perspective," in *The Collected Essays of Asa Briggs,* vol. 2 (1961; reprint, Urbana: University of Illinois Press, 1985), 177–211; and James Dickinson and Bob Russell, "The Structure of Reproduction in Capitalist Society," in *Family, Economy, and the State,* eds. Dickinson and Russell, 1–20.

20 NAC, Department of National Health and Welfare, RG 29; ANQQ, Department of Education, E 13, correspondence received (records subsequent to 1942 are filed in the CDSA); and ANQQ, Department of Labour, E 24, correspondence received.

21 AMCSC and ACSRVF, where the following collections are filed: ACSCM, ACSSLF, ACSC, and ACSSMCM.

22 Records used with the authorization of Youth Court Chief Justice Albert Gobeil and the assistance of criminologist Jean Trépanier of the Université de Montréal. The AMSWC are filed at the Centre de préarchivage judiciaire de Montréal.

23 AQRO (at the time of consultation in 1989, these archives shared the office of family allowances and old-age pension of Québec; we were able to consult them thanks to the federal Access to Information Act).

24 Tamara Hareven, "L'histoire et la famille aux États-Unis: Bilan et perspectives" (paper presented at the Congrès de l'Institut d'histoire de l'Amérique française, 1984).

25 See in particular James Struthers, *The Limits of Affluence: Welfare in Ontario, 1920–1970* (Toronto: University of Toronto Press, 1994).

26 P.-A. Linteau, "La nouvelle histoire au Québec vue de l'intérieur," *Liberté* no. 147 (1983): 44–45; René Durocher, "L'émergence de l'histoire du Québec contemporain," in *Continuité et rupture: Les sciences sociales au Québec,* ed. G.-H. Lévesque et al. (Montréal: Presses de l'Université de Montréal, 1984), 302–303.

Chapter 1

1 Québec, DPI, *Instructions concernant la loi de fréquentation scolaire obligatoire,* 1943, 2, 12; Québec, DPI, *ARSPI, 1944–1945,* 22; and Jean-Guy Genest, "Vie et œuvre d'Adélard Godbout, 1892–1956" (Ph.D. diss., Université Laval, 1987), 487.

2 William Lyon Mackenzie King, Canada, *Débats de la Chambre des communes,* 1944, 2 (our translation); Brooke Claxton, *Débats,* 1944, 5593; and Claire Langlois, "L'œuvre des petits vendeurs de journaux et sa clientèle" (M.A. diss., Université Laval, 1952), 109.

3 On the pressures of workers' groups at the beginning of the twentieth century, see Ruby Heap, "L'Église, l'État, et l'enseignement primaire public catholique au Québec, 1897–1920" (Ph.D. diss., Université de Montréal, 1987), 890–91. See also Thérèse Hamel, "L'obligation scolaire au Québec: Lieu et enjeu de la lutte des classes" (Ph.D. diss., Paris V René Descartes, 1981).

4 Pierre Trépanier, "Vie intellectuelle," in *Guide d'histoire du Québec du régime français à nos jours: Bibliographie commenté,* ed. Jacques Rouillard (Montréal: Méridien, 1992), 281; Bruno Théret, "Les dépenses d'enseignement et d'assistance en France au XIXe siècle: Une réévaluation de la rupture républicaine," *Annales ESC* 46, no. 6 (1991): 1335–38, 1364; and Bryan Young, "Positive Law, Positive State: Class Realignment and the Transformation of Lower Canada, 1815–1866," in *Colonial Leviathan: State Formation in Mid-Nineteenth-Century Canada,* eds. Alan Greer and Ian Radforth (Toronto: University of Toronto Press, 1992), 50–63.

5 ANQQ, Ministry of Education, E 13, C.r., 1942–294, box 2235, Gilbert-A. Latour, Board of Trade of Metropolitan Montreal, 4 June 1942; Heap, "L'Église, l'État, et l'enseignement," 132–55, 938; Victrice Lessard, "L'enseignement obligatoire dans la province de Québec de 1875 à 1943" (Ph.D. diss., University of Ottawa, 1962), 54–55, 232; Louis-Philippe Audet, *Histoire de l'enseignement au Québec,* vol. 2 (Montréal: Holt, Rinehart, & Winston, 1971), 253, 263; and Bernard Vigod, "'Qu'on ne craigne pas l'encombrement des compétences': Le gouvernement Taschereau et l'éducation, 1920–1929," *Revue d'histoire de l'Amérique française* 28, no. 2 (1974): 213. Thérèse Hamel posits that the petit-bourgeois were opposed to compulsory education because of their own needs for juvenile labour ("Obligation scolaire et travail des enfants au Québec: 1900–1950," *Revue d'histoire de l'Amérique française* 38, no. 1 [1984]: 58). For a discussion of the concept of "Fordism," see Michel Aglietta, *Régulation et crises du capitalisme: L'expérience des États-Unis* (Paris: Calmann-Lévy, 1982).

6 Jean Hamelin and Nicole Gagnon, *Histoire du catholicisme québécois: Le XXe siècle,* vol. 1, *1898–1940* (Montréal: Boréal Express, 1984), 241–52, 908–910. Louis-Alexandre Taschereau believed that education should be modernized first, to meet the need of industrial companies, before the system of social welfare. See Bernard Vigod, *Québec before Duplessis: The Political Career of Louis-Alexandre Taschereau* (Montréal: McGill-Queen's University Press, 1986), 71, 131. Antonin Dupont affirms that Taschereau's government did not see the need to educate the masses (*Les relations entre l'Église et l'État sous Louis-Alexandre Taschereau, 1920–1936* [Montréal: Guérin, 1973], 252).

7 Louis-Marie Tremblay, *Le syndicalisme québécois: Idéologies de la C.S.N. et de la F.T.Q., 1940–1970* (Montréal: Presses de l'Université de Montréal, 1972), 196.

8 Robert Rumilly, *Histoire de la province de Québec,* vol. 38, *La guerre de 1939–1945* (Montréal: Fides, 1968), 59.

9 "Fréquentation scolaire obligatoire?" *Le Monde ouvrier,* 20 March 1943, p. 1 (our translation). See also ANQQ, E 13, C.g., 1942–96, box 2218, "Mémoire de législation proposée soumis par le Comité législatif conjoint de Québec, organisation des employés de chemin de fer," 7 February 1940, 4.

10 ANQQ, E 13, C.r., 1942–199, box 2223, Montréal Day Nursery President Marie Papineau, 16 February 1942; and ANQQ, E 13, C.r., 1942–199, box 2223, Pétition des Services bénévoles féminins à Hector Perrier, 27 April 1944. See also André Laurendeau, cited in Michael D. Behiels, "The Bloc Populaire Canadien and the Origins of French-Canadian Neo-Nationalism, 1942–1948," *Canadian Historical Review* 63, no. 4 (1982): 508.

11 MCCPIC, 2 December 1942.

12 Thérèse Casgrain, *Une femme chez les hommes* (Montréal: Éditions de l'Homme, 1971), 124; NAC, Fonds Thérèse Casgrain, MG 32 C25, League of Women's Rights, press clippings, vol. 9; *Historique du Congrès Libéral de 1938 tenu à Québec les 10 et 11 juin,* 42; and Canada, Advisory Committee on Reconstruction, VI, *Post-War Problems of Women: Final Report of the Subcommittee* (Ottawa: King's Printer, 1944), 23.

13 Journalist from the *Standard* (Montréal), quoted in Valère Massicotte, "La délinquance juvénile et la guerre," *L'Œuvre des tracts,* April 1944, 11. Similarly, Montréal Youth Court Judge Robillard called for compulsory education to get children of school age off the streets and into grades eleven and twelve. Furthermore, beginning in 1939, a group of Catholic women had called for compulsory education in the pages of *Le Jour* based on an investigation showing that the majority of delinquents aged seven to fourteen did not attend school (Lessard, "L'enseignement obligatoire," 201–204). See also ANQQ, E 13, C.g., 1942–199, box 2223, H.S. Bishop to Godbout, 11 February 1941.

14 "Emploi des enfants et fréquentation scolaire au Canada: Comparaison avec la législation en Grande-Bretagne et aux États-Unis," *La Gazette du travail,* January 1942, 48–49; and Chad Gaffield and W. Gordon West, "Children's Rights in the Canadian Context," in *Children's Rights: Legal and Educational Issues,* ed. Heather Berkeley et al. (Toronto: Ontario Institute for Studies in Education Press, 1978), 3–14. See also Susan E. Houston, "The 'Waifs and Strays' of a Late-Victorian City: Juvenile Delinquents in Toronto," in *Childhood and Family in Canadian History,* ed. Joy Parr (Toronto: McClelland & Stewart, 1982), 129–42; and Leroy Ashby, "Partial Promises and Semi-Visible Youths: The Depression and World War II," in *American Childhood: A Research Guide and Historical Handbook,* eds. Joseph M. Hawes and N. Roy Hiner (Westport: Greenwood Press, 1985), 509.

15 Godbout's speech, cited in *Le Monde ouvrier,* 20 November 1943, p. 4; and the 1943 speech from the throne, reprinted in Genest, "Vie et œuvre," 487, 572.

16 Godbout was reacting to the announcement of a federal training program and was denouncing the dangers of the central government's interference in provincial affairs. In the same vein, he also favoured practical and realistic education; the teaching of advanced mathematics, science, and English; and the reform of classical colleges towards this goal (Genest "Vie et œuvre," 363, 368, 489, 555).

17 Wilfrid Bovey, member of the Legislative Council of the province, cited in "Le Conseil législatif adopte la loi de l'instruction obligatoire," *Le Monde ouvrier,* 22 May 1943, p. 1. See also ANQQ, E 13, C.r., 1942–199, box 2223, Women's Canadian Club President Margareth Hugessen, 20 March 1943. On the First World War, see Heap,"L'Église, l'État, et l'enseignement," 937–39.

18 Léon Lortie, "Le système scolaire," in *Essais sur le Québec contemporain,* ed. Jean-Charles Falardeau (Québec: Presses de l'Université Laval, 1953), 171–75; Esdras Minville, "Conditions de notre avenir," in *Essais sur le Québec contemporain,* ed. Falardeau, 236–37; and Mason Wade, *The French Canadian Outlook: A Brief Account of the Unknown North Americans* (1946; reprint, Toronto: McClelland & Stewart, 1964), 80–81.

19 During the 1930s, a minority of CTCC members already looked on compulsory education with a favourable eye in the wake of a larger movement of criticism of authorities' traditionalism, conducted by a Catholic minority consisting mostly of lay people. See the description of the organization's change of heart on the issue of compulsory education in 1942 in Hamel, "L'obligation scolaire au Québec," 314, 367. L'Action catholique also expressed a similar opinion on 23 July 1941 (Lessard, "L'enseignement obligatoire," 206). On the rush to endorse the policy as soon as the Public Instruction Council's authorization was given, see Jacques Rouillard, *Histoire du syndicalisme au Québec* (Montréal: Boréal, 1990), 254.

20 Catholic Church, Archdiocese of Québec, "Graves fautes des parents en matière de fréquentation scolaire" (clergy circular), 22 August 1941, in *Mandements des évêques de Québec,* vol. 16, *1940–1943,* 249–50 (our translation); and Jean Hamelin, *Histoire du catholicisme québécois: Le XXe siècle,* vol. 2, *De 1940 à nos jours* (Montréal: Boréal Express, 1984), 23–32. For a description of this trend, see P.-A. Linteau et al., *Histoire du Québec contemporain,* vol. 2, *Le Québec depuis 1930* (Montréal: Boréal, 1986), 112–13.

21 As told by District Inspector J.-E. Boily, *ARSPI, 1946–1947,* 98–99. See also Lessard, "L'enseignement obligatoire," 208–209; and Genest, "Vie et œuvre, " 492. La Fédération des chambres de commerce held a conference on the subject of public instruction in the fall of 1942 according to Vigod (*Québec before Duplessis,* 245–54). See also Linteau et al., *Histoire du Québec contemporain,* vol. 2, 274.

22 In addition to a group of "managerial" political values, historians of Liberal reformist movements also recognize the existence of a "progressive" trend, concerned with transforming public institutions not to help business but rather to increase the participation of social groups that were powerless until then. I borrow this typology from Alan Dawley, *Struggles for Justice: Social Responsibility and the Liberal State* (Cambridge: Harvard University Press, 1992), cited in Alan Brinkley, "The Progressive Impulse," *Times Literary Supplement,* 29 May 1992, p. 8.

23 Rumilly, *Histoire de la province de Québec,* vol. 38, 236–44; and Genest, "Vie et œuvre," 366–68.

24 The Committee consisted of, on one hand, all the province's bishops and, on the other, just as many lay people, selected by the cabinet. The large attendance of the

former, their exclusive privilege of having their positions renewed, and the latter's being members of the Catholic elite educated in classical colleges, account for why the committee was controlled by the episcopate. Legally, the cabinet could proceed without the committee's approval to adopt the compulsory education law, but since the end of the nineteenth century, its initiatives in education had been limited. The PCPIC was made up of as many members as there were lay people on the CCPIC (Audet, *Histoire de l'enseignement au Québec,* vol. 2, 339–43; and P.-A. Linteau et al., *Histoire du Québec contemporain,* vol. 1, *De la confédération à la crise* [Montréal: Boréal Express, 1979], 242.)

25 For a long time among nationalist lay people, there were divergent points of view on the meaning of compulsory education for Catholic instruction. A minority among them adopted an "ambivalent progressivism" (Yves Saint-Germain, cited in Linteau et al., *Histoire du Québec contemporain,* vol. 2, 109). See also Olivar Asselin in 1906, cited in Joseph Levitt, *Henri Bourassa and the Golden Calf: The Social Program of the Nationalists of Québec, 1900–1914* (Ottawa: University of Ottawa Press, 1992), 89.

26 Pie IX's address, cited in DPI, *Instructions,* 1943, 3 (our translation). Furthermore, in 1931, the Vatican had decreed education to be compulsory for its own citizens. See also Linteau et al., *Histoire du Québec contemporain,* vol. 1, 531; and ANQQ, E 13, C.r. 1939, 320, CCPIC Secretary B.-O. Filteau to PCPIC Secretary W. Percival, 31 May 1939. Percival recommended the implementation of compulsory education until fourteen years of age, reiterating the recommendation of the Hepburn Commission, which he himself had set up in 1937 to examine problems of protestant teaching in Québec.

27 Murdoch C. MacLean, "Alphabétisme et fréquentation scolaire," monograph no. 5 in *Recensement du Canada, 1931* (Ottawa: King's Printer, 1937), 54, 110; Hermas Lalande, s.j., *L'instruction obligatoire: Principes et conséquences* (Montréal: Imprimerie du messager, 1919), 125–34; General Inspector for Catholic Schools C.-J. Magnan, *Éclairons la route* (Québec: Librairie Garneau, 1922), 214, 223; Heap, "L'Église, l'État, et l'enseignement," 873, 929, 960–61; Jean Hulliger, *L'enseignement social des évêques catholiques* (Montréal: Fides, 1958), 99–100; and Marie-Paule Malouin and Micheline Dumont, "L'évolution des programmes d'études, 1850–1960," in *Les couventines: L'éducation des filles au Québec dans les congrégations religieuses enseignantes, 1840–1960,* eds. Micheline Dumont and Nadia Fahmy-Eid (Montréal: Boréal, 1986), 83–112.

28 Linteau et al., *Histoire du Québec contemporain,* vol. 2, 483–89; Jean-Pierre Kesteman, *Histoire du syndicalisme agricole au Québec, UCC-UPA, 1924–1984* (Montréal: Boréal Express, 1984), 72; Hamelin and Gagnon, *Histoire du catholicisme québécois,* vol. 1, 442; and Vigod, "'Qu'on ne craigne pas l'encombrement des compétences,'" 215–17, 229–31.

29 Catholic Church, Archdiocese of Québec, "Lettre pastorale collective sur le problème rural au regard de la doctrine sociale de l'Église," 30 November 1937, in *Mandements des évêques de Québec,* vol. 15, *1936–1939,* 255–95; Les fils du sol, Saint-Jean-de-Dieu, "L'école primaire et nos jeunes garçons," *La Terre de chez nous,* 19 December 1934, p. 3; ANQQ, E 13, C.g., 1939–1082, General Inspector for Primary Schools C.-J. Miller to Victor Doré, 20 March 1940; and Kesteman, *Histoire du syndicalisme agricole,* 174. On the "rural renaissance" and its educational aspects, see James Douglas Thwaites, "The Origins and the Development of the 'Fédération des commissions scolaires catholiques du Québec,' 1936–1963" (Ph.D. diss., Université Laval, 1975), 26–35; and Linteau et al., *Histoire du Québec contemporain,* vol. 2, 108.

30 Report of the Commission des finances et de la législation on a meeting held in Montréal on 23 November 1940, mentioned in MCCPIC, 11 December 1940, 13 (ANQQ, E 13, C.r., 1940–1390, box 2169).

31 *La Gazette,* 16 April 1941, cited by Lessard, "L'enseignement obligatoire," 205; and Robert Rumilly, *Histoire de la province de Québec,* vol. 39, *1914* (Montréal: Fides, 1969), 49.

32 Louise Charpentier, "Les programmes et les manuels d'histoire de la réforme scolaire de 1948" (M.A. diss., Université de Sherbrooke, 1983), 14–19; and *ARSPI, 1939–1940,* xvii. The episcopate's opinion was revealed by Riverain, a journalist from *Le Jour,* cited in Lessard, "L'enseignement obligatoire," 205–206.

33 Catholic Church, Archdiocese of Québec, "Graves fautes des parents en matière de fréquentation scolaire" (clergy circular), 22 August 1941, in *Mandements des évêques de Québec,* vol. 16, 249–50; Report of the Comité de régie du certificat d'études primaires, 15 September 1941, presented to the CCPIC (MCCPIC, 18 September 1941, 10–15); and Charpentier, "Les programmes et les manuels," 15–17. Already by the end of the 1930s, Cardinal Villeneuve had pronounced in favour of better coordination between different institutions and different grade levels (*ARSPI, 1939–1940,* xii). On the role of Cardinal Villeneuve, see Gérard Filion, *Les confidences d'un commissaire d'écoles* (Montréal: Éditions de l'Homme, 1960), 74.

34 MCCPIC, 10 December 1941, 32. The author of the questionnaire was Paul-Émile Beaudoin, a Jesuit. In selecting him, Perrier perhaps strove to reassure the clergy. See also Genest, "Vie et œuvre," 491; and Charpentier, "Les programmes et les manuels," 18.

35 Joseph Pagé, president of the subcommittee of educational inquiries, Report of the Alliance catholique des Professeurs de Montréal titled *Les réformes de l'enseignement primaire,* 1941, 29. See also ANQQ, E 13, 1939–1082, box 2128, Resolutions of the Conseil de la corporation scolaire de Beauharnois, 11 June 1941; and Genest, "Vie et œuvre," 491.

36 ANQQ, E 13, C.r., 1942–96, DPI, Office of the Superintendant, "Synthèse des mémoires adressés au surintendant de l'Instruction publique en réponse à la deuxième et à la troisième questions inscrites à l'agenda de l'enquête scolaire," 10, 13, 12.

37 ANQQ, E 13, 1942–1339, box 2266, DPI French Secretary B.-O. Filteau to Victor Doré, 25 September 1942; ANQQ, Provincial Secretariat, E 4, Écoles de réforme, 1921–1868, box 593, Maurice Brodeur, Service de recherches et de documentation du DPI, "Compulsory Education in the U.S. School Laws," 2 mimeographed volumes; and ANQQ, E 13, C.r., 1942–199, box 2223, Charles Bilodeau to Victor Doré, "Notes pour le surintendant à propos de fréquentation obligatoire aux États-Unis," 10 December 1942.

38 MCCPIC, 2 December 1942.

39 MCCPIC, 17 December 1942, 14–15. The PCPIC received the news favourably. After the 1939 failure, when it had asked the Catholics to study compulsory education, it had entrenched itself in a partial strategy by adopting the Protestant School Attendance Act in 1941. But the bill had not been submitted in time to the Assembly. MPCPIC, 29 November 1941 and 29 December 1941, *Educational Record* 58, no. 2 (1942): 120–21; and MPCPIC, 26 February 1943, *Educational Record,* 59, no. 3 (1943): 190.

40 Catholic Church, Archdiocese of Québec, "Fréquentation scolaire" (clergy circular), 26 August 1943 in *Mandements des évêques de Québec,* vol. 16, 604–605; MCCPIC, 6 November 1942, 24; MCCPIC, 2 December 1942, 21; and MCCPIC, 17 December 1942, 5.

41 ANQQ, E 13, C.r., 1942–199, box 2223, Victor Doré to legislative legal clerk Louis-Philippe Pigeon, 5 March 1943. A New Brunswick legal text annotated by Hector Perrier is attached to the letter. See also Genest, "Vie et œuvre," 495.

42 Loi concernant la gratuité de l'enseignement et des livres de classe dans certaines écoles publiques, *SQ,* 1944, 8 Geo. 6, c. 14. The Compulsory School Attendance Act had already instituted free obligatory instruction until the end of the school year in which the child was fourteen years of age. See the Loi concernant la fréquentation scolaire obligatoire, *SQ,* 1943, 7 Geo. 6, c. 21, art. 4; Québec, DPI, *Instructions concernant la fréquentation obligatoire et la gratuité des livres,* 1944, 12, 14–15; and Genest, "Vie et œuvre," 487. In 1912, T.-D. Bouchard succeeded in getting the assembly to adopt a resolution allowing school boards to abolish monthly payments (Heap, "L'Église, l'État, et l'enseignement," 879). The MCSC had not demanded more payments until grade eight inclusively since the 1910s (Wendy Johnston, "La Commission des écoles catholiques de Montréal face à la Crise des années 1930" [M.A. diss., Université de Montréal, 1984], table 5; fees had been temporarily re-established in the year 1940–41 to one dollar per semester until grade nine). See also MCSC, *Livres des délibérations,* resolution 16, 14 and 16 August 1940, and 14 and 15 July 1941.

43 Richard Jones, "Social Doctrine of the Roman Catholic Church," *Canadian Encyclopedia* (Edmonton: Hurtig Publishers, 1988); and Pierre Elliott Trudeau, "Québec on the Eve of the Asbestos Strike," in *French-Canadian Nationalism: An Anthology,* ed. Ramsay Cook (Toronto: Macmillan, 1969), 32–48.

44 Catholic Church, Archdiocese of Québec, "Lettre pastorale collective à l'occasion de l'anniversaire des encycliques *Rerum novarum* et *Quadragesimo anno* sur la restauration de l'ordre social," 11 March 1941, in *Mandements des évêques de Québec,* vol. 16, 165, 184. They had endorsed the principle of family allowances twenty years before, in that they encouraged large families. The ease with which the bishops rushed to designate a "cost of living increase," distributed to Québec City employees under the name of "family allowances," demonstrates their lukewarm support (Catholic Church, Archdiocese of Québec, "Salaires, allocations familiales, et économie" [clergy circular], 21 January 1942, in *Mandements des évêques de Québec,* vol. 16, 371–72). For a typical corporatist plea in favour of family allocations and based on the French experience, see Father Cloutier in *Semaines sociales* of 1927, mentioned by Sister Marie Agnès de Rome Gaudreau in *The Social Thought of French Canada as Reflected in the* Semaine Sociale (Washington, D.C.: Catholic University Press of America, 1946), 90–91.

45 Lalande, *L'instruction obligatoire,* 95.

46 Robert Rumilly, *La plus riche aumône: Histoire de la Société de Saint-Vincent-de-Paul au Canada* (Montréal: Éditions de l'Arbre, 1946), 218.

47 Esdras Minville, Appendix 5 in *Labour Legislation and Social Services in the Province of Québec: A Study Prepared for the Royal Commission on Dominion Provincial Relations* (Ottawa: King's Printer, 1939), 97–98.

48 Reverend Émile Cloutier, "Le salaire et la famille," in *Capital et Travail: Semaines sociales du Canada,* 3rd session (Ottawa: Bibliothèque de l'Action française, 1922), 150–74; Georges Pelletier, "Le budget familial," *La famille: Semaines sociales du Canada,* 4th session (Montréal: École sociale populaire, 1933), 19–39; Léon Lebel, *Les allocation familiales: Solution du problème des familles nombreuses,* nos. 159–60 (Montréal: École sociale populaire, 1927); Alfred Charpentier, "La question ouvrière," in *Programme de restauration sociale,* nos. 239–40 (Montréal: École sociale populaire, 1933), 19–39; Bibliothèque de l'Assemblée nationale, CTCC, *Mémoire de la*

C.T.C.C. à l'honorable conseil exécutif de la province de Québec, 20 December 1939; Hamel, "L'obligatoire scolaire au Québec," 266, 316; R. P. Archambault, s.j., "Pour restaurer la famille," *École sociale populaire* 371 (1944): 25–27; and Gérard Forcier, o.m.i., *Les allocations familiales: Savez-vous ce qu'elles sont?* (Ottawa: Centre social de l'Université d'Ottawa, 1944).

49 Lebel, *Les allocations familiales,* 40–41; and Léon Lebel, "Les allocations familiales au Canada," *Relations* 11, no. 122 (1951): 48.

50 Rouillard, *Histoire du syndicalisme au Québec,* 167–68.

51 *Débats,* 1944, 5564–68, 5592, 5598–5600, 5613; Léon Lebel, "Le problème de la famille nombreuse: Sa solution, les allocations familiales," *Le Devoir,* 1928, p. 25; Lebel, *Les allocations familiales,* 51; and *Family Allowances as a Means of Preventing Emigration: A Plea for the Family of the Worker So That It May Share the Prosperity of the Nation,* Montréal, 1928, cited in Mark E. Palmer, "The Origins and Implementation of Family Allowances in Canada" (M.A. diss., Queen's University, 1976), 23. Lebel's information on the lowered birth rate and immigration were from the *Annuaire du Canada.*

52 Catholic Church, Archdiocese of Québec, "Lettre pastorale collective à l'occasion de l'anniversaire des encycliques *Rerum novarum* et *Quadragesimo anno,*" in *Mandements,* 165.

53 Maximilien Caron, "Les familles nombreuses, la législation fiscale, et les allocations familiales," *École Sociale Populaire,* nos. 373–74 (1945): 42.

54 "Canadian Provisions for Aid for Dependents of Members of the Army and Air Force," *Social Security Bulletin,* November 1941, 19–24; and Renée Vautelet, *Mémoire sur l'orientation du travail féminin d'après-guerre,* prepared for the Conseil d'orientation économique (published under the auspices of the FNSJB, 1944), 8. Vautelet was a member of the Conseil.

55 Dominique Marshall, "Nationalisme et politiques sociales au Québec depuis 1867: Un siècle de rendez-vous manqués entre l'État, l'Église, et les familles," *British Journal of Canadian Studies* 9, no. 2 (1994): 301–347. At the beginning of the 1940s, the average number of children per family was larger in Québec than all other provinces: it went as high as 2.9, while the national average was 1.9 (Canada, Dominion Bureau of Statistics, *Recensement du Canada, 1941,* vol. 5, 178–237).

56 Robert Lévesque and Robert Mignier, *Camillien et les années vingt suivi de Camillien au Goulag, cartographie du Houdisme* (Montréal: Éditions des Brûlés, 1978), 84. Duplessis then belonged to the group that authored the program (Jean-Louis Roy, *Les programmes électoraux du Québec,* vol. 2, *1931–1966* [Montréal: Léméac, 1971], 246).

57 Loi concernant le paiement d'allocations familiales en vertu de conventions collectives de travail, *SQ,* 1943, 7 Geo. 6, c. 29. Godbout increased the level of the provincial needy-mothers' pensions and proposed the creation of family courts (Vigod, *Québec before Duplessis,* 183). On the history of "comités paritaires," see Rouillard, *Histoire du syndicalisme au Québec,* 170–75. In 1930, Gérard Tremblay had also become a member of the Commission sur les assurances sociales (Monpetit Commission).

58 Rumilly, *Histoire de la province de Québec,* vol. 39, 108; Catholic Church, Archdiocese of Québec, "À propos du suffrage féminin" (clergy circular), 1 March 1941, in *Mandements des évêques de Québec,* vol. 16, 86–87; and Thérèse Casgrain, *Woman in a Man's World* (Toronto: McClelland & Stewart, 1972), 71. Renée Vautelet supported her demands by pointing out that women had "emerged as voters" (*Mémoire sur l'orientation du travail féminin d'après-guerre,* 6); her report included "opin-

ions presented during two conference round tables held in Montréal...under the aegis of the FNSJB and of the Local Council of Women," these two organizations being the city's main feminist associations. See also Yves Vaillancourt, *L'évolution des politiques sociales au Québec, 1940–1960* (Montréal: Presses de l'Université de Montréal, 1989), 359.

59 ANQQ, Ministry of Labour, E 24, folder 123, item 190, Edgar Rochette, "Allocations familiales: 1941," 3. In 1933, the Montpetit Commission on social insurance had also rejected the idea of mandatory allowances in fear of offending businesses. Meanwhile, the commissioners looked favourably on a "regime of freedom" in which employers would establish their own programs (Commission sur les assurances sociales de Québec, *3e rapport,* 1933, 80, 90, 108–109). The economist and president of the commission, Édouard Montpetit, was himself in favour of family allowances, and had been inspired by the social thinking of American bishops (Édouard Montpetit, *Pour une doctrine* [Montréal: Librairie d'action canadienne-française, 1931], 120). In 1939, economist Esdras Minville, charged by the Royal Commission on Dominion–Provincial Relations (Rowell-Sirois), of the study of the province of Québec's social regime, had not retained the idea of family allowances (*La législation ouvrière dans la province de Québec,* 74). His reservations about free pensions and statism had been behind his silence on the issue, as well as his disapproval of federal intervention. For another call for family allowances as a means to reinforce the relations between employers and workers in matters of welfare, see A.-J. Pelletier, "La famille canadienne," a monograph of *Recensement du Canada, 1931,* 182. In February 1944, the Garneau Commission, whose mission was to research health insurance, was still in favour of allowances paid by employers (*La Presse,* 5 February 1944).

60 On the Superior Labour Council, which would later be abolished by Duplessis, see Rumilly, *Histoire de la province de Québec,* vol. 38, 10, 156; and Rouillard, *Histoire du syndicalisme au Québec,* 174. In the same vein, in 1941 the Québec government had established minimum wage; "to consider the forced acceptance of insufficient compensation," reads the preamble of the law, "is to not keep in mind the dignity of work and the needs of the worker and his family" (*SQ,* 1939–40, 4 Geo. 6, c. 39). On the Godbout government's closed attitude towards the unions, see Behiels, "The Bloc Populaire Canadien," 508.

61 Lebel, "Après deux ans d'allocations familiales," 228–30. On the difficulties of establishing Catholic employers' organizations at the beginning of the 1940s, see Hulliger, *L'enseignement social des évêques catholiques,* 267. The "Lettre pastorale collective à l'occasion de l'anniversaire des encycliques *Rerum novarum* and *Quadragesimo anno*" shows that the bishops still believed in their future (177). On the international unions and family allowances, and on the reservations on the part of some of the employers regarding another law inspired by corporatism, the Loi d'extension juridique des conventions collectives of 1934, see Rouillard, *Histoire du syndicalisme au Québec,* 171, 181; and Robert Rumilly, *Maurice Duplessis et son temps,* vol. 2 (Montréal: Fides, 1973), 636. Trudeau understood the lack of success of the Social Doctrine in this way as well ("Québec on the Eve of the Asbestos Strike," 39).

62 ANQQ, E 13, 1942–294, box 2235, Gilbert Latour for the Montréal Chamber of Commerce, report no. 90, 4 June 1942. In 1941, the bishops declared that the Catholic workers' adoption of corporatism pleased them more than the Catholic employers' attitude (Hulliger, *L'enseignement social des évêques catholiques,* 267).

63 On the history of the Professional Association of Industrialists, founded in 1943 to regroup the Catholic employers, see Jean-Louis Roy, *La marche des Québécois: Le temps des ruptures, 1945–1960* (Montréal: Léméac, 1973), 164–81.

64 "Le bill no. 45," *Relations* 3, no. 31 (1943): 80, 170. At best, the law would have helped 19 percent of the province's children; that is, 116,000 children whose fathers worked in businesses where committees existed.

65 John Macnicol, *The Movement for Family Allowances, 1918–1945: A Study in Social Policy Development* (London: Heineman, 1980), 11.

66 Rouillard, *Histoire du syndicalisme au Québec,* 171–81; and Rumilly, *Maurice Duplessis et son temps,* vol. 2, 636. The Fédération nationale du travail was against the 1943 provincial system for this reason, according to Genest ("Vie et œuvre," 509). J.-C. Falardeau, Maurice Tremblay, Maurice Lamontagne, and Roger Marier mention numerous unions in *Mémoire sur les allocations familiales,* prepared at the request of Québec's Superior Labour Council (n.p., 1944), 73–75. See also *ARQDL, 1944–1945,* 15. The CTCC had also feared that the family allowances would freeze minimum wage below "minimum living wage," though it did not reject the idea entirely. Charlotte Whitton, a social worker, conservative, and ex-director of the Canadian Welfare Council, also believed that the universal family allowances constituted the employers' abandonment of their salary responsibilities (Thelma McCormack, *Politics and the Hidden Injury of Gender: Feminism and the Making of the Welfare State* [Ottawa: Canadian Institute for the Advancement of Women, 1991], 22.)

67 Camille L'Heureux, "Les salaires dans le Québec," *Le Droit,* 12 February 1943, cited in JOC, *Mémoire sur l'orientation des jeunes travailleurs,* 1944, 25 (CDSA, 1944–629, box 112 314).

68 Frank Breul, "The Genesis of Family Allowances in Canada," *The Social Service Review* 28, no. 3 (1953): 264–80; Doug Owram, *The Government Generation: Canadian Intellectuals and the State, 1900–1945* (Toronto: University of Toronto Press, 1986), 312; J.L. Granatstein, *Canada's War: The Politics of the Mackenzie King Government, 1939–1945* (Toronto: Oxford University Press, 1975), 279; and JOC, *Mémoire sur l'orientation des jeunes travailleurs,* 25. Jane Lewis reports the same preponderance of salary stabilization objectives and production costs in relation to welfare objectives in England during the Second World War, on the eve of the adoption of family allowances ("The English Movement for Family Allowances, 1917–1945," *Histoire sociale/Social History* 11, no. 22 [1978]: 455–56). Rob Watts explains the advances of family allowances in Australia through the central government's responsibility for salary monitoring since the beginning of the twentieth century ("Family Allowances in Canada and Australia, 1940–1945: A Comparative Critical Case Study," *Journal of Social Policy* 16, no. 1 [1987]: 19–48).

69 Rouillard, Chapter 4, *Histoire du syndicalisme au Québec*. The policy was comparable with the one international unions were subject to in the United States since 1935.

70 *Débats,* 1944, 5944 (our translation).

71 *Débats,* 1944, 5534 (our translation). See also *Débats,* 1944, 5530, 5594–95; NAC, RG 29, 1934, acc. R233/100/13, Joseph Willard, *Family Allowances in Canada: A Background Paper,* 1967, 4–5; *Santé et bien-être social,* July 1948 (special issue on family allowances); Linteau et al., *Histoire du Québec contemporain,* vol. 2, 276; and Jean-Pierre Charland and Mario Désautels, *Système technique et bonheur domestique: Rémunération, consommation, et pauvreté au Québec, 1920–1960* (Québec: Institut québécois de recherche sur la culture, 1992), 60, 77.

72 *Débats,* 1944, 5619–20. See also *Débats,* 1944, 5595, 5559; *Débats,* 1946, 2790; Lacroix and Rabeau, cited in Alain Noël, "L'après-guerre au Canada: Politiques keynésiennes ou nouvelles formes de régulation?" (first version, GRETSE/AEP Symposium, Montréal, QC, 1987), 11; Raymond B. Blake, "Mackenzie King and the Genesis of Family Allowances in Canada, 1939–1944," in *Social Welfare Policy in Canada: Historical Readings,* eds. Raymond B. Blake and Jeff Keshen (Toronto: Copp Clark, 1995), 244–54; and Palmer, "Origins and Implementation," 87, 101.

73 Graham Towers to Deputy Finance Minister W.C. Clark, 13 June 1943, and attached memo entitled "The Case for Children's Allowances," cited in Blake, "Mackenzie King and the Genesis of Family Allowances," 254. Towers added that children were even more vulnerable than older people.

74 *Débats,* 1944, 5593, 5603. See also Lebel, *Le problème de la famille nombreuse,* 17. For a demonstration of this thesis in the world of labour relations, see Paul Craven, *"An Impartial Umpire": Industrial Relations and the Canadian State, 1900–1944* (Toronto: University of Toronto Press, 1980).

75 Montréal nationalist economist François-Albert Angers identified this reasoning with fascism. ("Les allocations familiales fédérales de 1944," *L'actualité économique* 21, no. 3 [1945]: 228–62).

76 *Débats,* 1944, 5930, 5926, 5882, 5942–43.

77 Bill Parenteau, "Settlement and the Frontier Forest Revisited: Class Politics and the Administration of the New Brunswick Labor Act, 1919–1929," in *Contested Countryside: Rural Workers and Modern Society in Atlantic Canada, 1800–1950,* ed. Daniel Samson (Fredericton: Acadiensis Press, 1994), 180–224.

78 Michael Horn, "Leonard Marsh and the Coming of the Welfare State in Canada: A Review Article," *Histoire sociale/Social History* 9 (1976): 197–204. Deputy Minister of Finance W.C. Clark presented the allowances to the cabinet as a means of preventing "other questions," such as housing or social assistance, from becoming too great after the war. The policies Marsh proposed would have cost, according to Clark, $900 million (John Porter, *The Vertical Mosaic: An Analysis of Social Class and Power in Canada* [Toronto: University of Toronto Press, 1965], 426–27). See also Owram, *The Government Generation,* 306, 307, 311, 314. Minister of Munitions and Supplies C.D. Howe did not share Clark's pessimism: he believed that the reconversion of war industries would occur without the State's energetic intervention (Dennis Guest, "World War II and the Welfare State in Canada," in *The Benevolent State: The Growth of Welfare in Canada,* eds. Allan Moscovitch and Jim Albert [Toronto: Garamond, 1987], 217).

79 Blake, "Mackenzie King and the Genesis of Family Allowances," 251.

80 *Débats,* 1944, 5726. See also Dennis Guest, *The Emergence of Social Security in Canada* (Vancouver: University of British Columbia Press, 1981), 110.

81 Leonard Marsh, *Report on Social Security for Canada* (1943; reprint, Toronto: University of Toronto Press, 1975), 88; and *Débats,* 1944, 5940–41.

82 Peter Baldwin, "The Welfare State for Historians: A Review Article," *Comparative Studies in Society and History* 34, no. 4 (1992): 706. According to Philip Resnick, in general, Canada's efforts were more arduous than those of many other Western countries due to its dependence on the United States and the fragility of Canadian federalism (*The Mask of Proteus: Canadian Reflections on the State* [Montréal: McGill-Queen's University Press, 1990], 208–211). On the promises of the Atlantic Charter, see my article "Reconstruction Politics, the Canadian Welfare State, and the Ambiguity of Children's Rights, 1940–1950," in *Uncertain Horizons: Canadians and Their World in 1945,* ed. Greg Donaghy (Ottawa: Canadian Committee on the History of the Second World War, 1996), 261–83.

83 Palmer, "Origins and Implementation," 261–69; Noël, "L'après-guerre au Canada"; Granatstein, *Canada's War,* 251, 282, 397, 406; Thomas L. Church, *Débats,* 1944, 5928; and *Débats,* 1944, 5543, 5741. Thirty Conservatives voted against the law. See *Débats,* 1944, 5542, 5899; and Frank Breul, "The Genesis of Family Allowances in Canada."

84 *Débats,* 1944, 5701. In 1929, the head of the CCF, James Woodsworth, had already asked that the allowances issue be studied by a special committee designated by the House. See *Débats,* 1944, 5750; and Dorothée H. Stepler, *Les allocations familiales au Canada,* no. 362 (Montréal: École sociale populaire, 1943), 19–23, first published by the Canadian Institute for International Affairs and Canadian Association for Adult Education; and Owram, *The Government Generation,* 310, 313. On the CCF, see *Débats,* 1944, 5543, 5732; on the Social Credit Party, see *Débats,* 1944, 5742.

85 Watts, "Family Allowances in Canada and Australia," 42.

86 Regarding the comparable impact of pro-natalism on post-war British public policy, see Denise Riley, "Some Peculiarities of Social Policy Concerning Women in Wartime and Postwar Britain," in *Behind the Lines: Gender and the Two World Wars,* ed. Margaret Randolph Higonnet et al. (New Haven: Yale University Press, 1987), 260–71.

87 *Santé et bien-être social Canada,* July 1948. Father Lebel had carried this idea even further: his contribution-type plan asked single employees to pay a significant portion of their wages.

88 *Débats,* 1944, 5740, 5564. See also *Débats,* 1944, 5928, 5633, 5704, 2790, 5695. During his training at the London School of Economics, Marsh had worked for Beveridge.

89 Pelletier, "La famille canadienne," 189–90. Stepler took up these results in the propaganda brochure *Les allocations familiales au Canada,* 26–27. Frederick Wright of the Bureau du Service municipal de Montréal, who wrote the preface for the 1928 translation of one of Father Lebel's opuscules, also relied upon the fertility arguments. See Léon Lebel, *The Problem of the Large Family in Canada: Its Solution, Family Allowances* (Montréal: Georges, 1928), 2. See also "Arguments or Citizens," *Liberty Magazine,* 14 April 1945; Brigitte Kitchen, "Wartime Social Reform: The Introduction of Family Allowances," *Canadian Journal of Social Work Education/Revue canadienne d'éducation en service social* 7, no. 1 (1981): 48; and W.R. Tracey, "Fécondité de la femme canadienne," in *Recensement du Canada, 1931,* vol. 11.

90 Vautelet, *Mémoire sur l'orientation du travail féminin d'après-guerre,* 7, 10.

91 Robert H. Bremner, *From the Depths: The Discovery of Poverty in the United States* (New York: New York University Press, 1964), 213. See also Falardeau et al., *Mémoire sur les allocations familiales,* 11, 34, 38, 39, 40; *Débats,* 1944, 5740, 5528, 5529, 5553, 5630, 5594–95; and Stepler, *Les allocations familiales au Canada,* 8–12.

92 *Débats,* 1944, 5604. See also Canada, DHNW, *Allocations familiales: Charte de l'enfance* (Ottawa: King's Printer, 1945–1946), 1; and ANQQ, E 13, C.r., 1942–96, box 2218, François Cloutier, Mémoire no. 17, p. 3.

93 *Débats,* 1944, 5602. See also Marsh, *Report on Social Security for Canada,* 93.

94 *Débats,* 1952, 1984.

95 Watts, "Family Allowances in Canada and Australia," 29. Cora S. Casselman recalled the demands of the Association canadienne des ouvrières du progrès social (*Débats,* 1944, 5554). See also Vautelet, *Mémoire sur l'orientation du travail féminin d'après-guerre.* Jane Lewis demonstrates how this recognition of mothers' contribution to

the economy was at the origin of the first calls for family allowances in Great Britain ("The English Movement for Family Allowances," 441–44).

96 Gail Cuthbert Brandt, "Pigeon-Holed and Forgotten: The Subcommittee on Post-War Problems of Women, 1943," *Histoire sociale/Social History* 25, no. 29 (1982): 239–59; and *Débats,* 1944, 5612.

97 Advisory Committee on Reconstruction, *Post-War Problems of Women,* 13. Renée Vautelet's nationalist pamphlet emphasized the return of the women who had left the countryside. See Vautelet, *Mémoire sur l'orientation du travail féminin d'après-guerre,* 14. See also Geneviève Auger and Raymonde Lamothe, *De la poêle à frire à la ligne de feu: La vie quotidienne des Québécoises pendant la guerre, 1939–1945* (Montréal: Boréal Express, 1981), 160; and Ruth Roach Pierson, *They're Still Women after All: The Second World War and Canadian Womanhood* (Toronto: McClelland & Stewart, 1986), 219.

98 In February 1944, following in the steps of the federal government, Godbout's government inaugurated its own labour-relations law obliging employers into collective negotiations, and he recognized the principle of the union monopoly (Rouillard, *Histoire du syndicalisme au Québec,* 250–51).

99 Robert Rumilly, *Maurice Duplessis et son temps,* vol. 1 (Montréal: Fides, 1973), 648–49. It appears that Leonard Marsh had participated in the Superior Labour Council committee's works (*RGMTQ, 1944–1945,* 14–15). See Falardeau et al., *Mémoire sur les allocations familiales,* 13–21, 23. On similar reasoning regarding the Bloc Populaire's nationalist reformist elite, see Behiels, "The Bloc Populaire Canadien," 507.

100 Letter from Godbout to Mackenzie King, 4 February 1944, cited in Palmer, "Origins and Implementation," 171; Mackenzie King's response remained vague. See also Falardeau et al., *Mémoire sur les allocations familiales,* 33–34, 62–64; and NAC, RG 29, vol. 1934, R233/100–2-9, proposals reported by *The Globe and Mail,* 2 August 1944. Father Lebel had also foreseen a joint program: to the federal and provincial governments, he added the municipalities, employers, bachelors, and married men without children. According to Genest, the creation of the Garneau Commission, entrusted with the preparation of a regime of universal health insurance, was part of this autonomist riposte ("Vie et œuvre," 509). See also *RGMTQ, 1944–1945,* 14; and Granatstein, *Canada's War,* 286.

101 In 1940, he had been forced to amend the Canadian Constitution to adopt unemployment insurance, something the Conservative leader would not let him forget. See Canada, *Débats,* 1944, 5731, 5863, 5960. At that time, a letter of approval from Godbout had been enough to solve the problem of the provincial government's prerogatives. Even the highly centralist report of the Rowell-Sirois Commission had declared that the area of children's welfare spending was under provincial jurisdiction (cited by Diefenbaker in the House: *Débats,* 1944, 5870). For controversies on the constitutionality of the policy and the provinces' administration, see *Débats,* 1944, 5539, 5543, 5547, 5549, 5551, 5563, 5690, 5963. Minister of Finance J.L. Isley also wanted an initial consultation with the provinces, according to Granatstein (*Canada's War,* 273). Falardeau et al. had not foreseen Mackenzie King's and Louis Saint-Laurent's arguments; rather, they relied on the precedent of non-constitutionality set by the New Deal policies R.B. Bennett had made in 1935 and London had declared *ultra vires* in 1937 (*Mémoire sur les allocations familiales,* 62–64). As for Leonard Marsh, he believed that the considerable sums being spent called for the responsibility of the federal government, even if certain programs could be administered by the provinces; his position echoed that of the

League for Social Reconstruction, founded by Toronto and Montréal socialist reformists in 1931 and of which Marsh was a member (Horn, "Leonard Marsh and the Coming of the Welfare State," 202).

102 *Débats,* 1944, 6053. See also *Débats,* 1944, 5734, 6053. Similarly, until 1933, the promoters of the old-age pensions had asked that the program be exclusively provincial (Vigod, *Québec before Duplessis,* 277).

103 Theda Skocpol affirms that in the United States the mobilizing force of the war did not create the same centralization, though it did in Great Britain. She believes this centralization to be a condition for the emergence of a national welfare state ("A Society without a 'State'?: Political Organization, Social Conflict, and Welfare Provision in the United States," *Journal of Public Policy* 7, no. 4 [1988]: 363).

104 Rumilly, Chapter 32, *Maurice Duplessis et son temps,* vol. 1. Duplessis wrote to Mackenzie King on 30 January 1945. In his February 1945 answer, Mackenzie King challenged Duplessis to prevent the payment of premiums.

105 *SQ,* 1945, 9 Geo. 6, c. 6; and "Agreement Likely on Bonus Scheme, Duplessis Believes Friendly Pact Possible with Federal Government," *Gazette* (Montréal), 17 February 1945. Independent MP René Chaloult suggested that Duplessis threaten Mackenzie King with the abolition of the 1942 taxation agreement for wartime emergency.

106 Rumilly, *Maurice Duplessis et son temps,* vol. 1, 62, 636; and Genest, "Vie et œuvre," 509. In 1943, while a member of the Opposition, Duplessis had approved Godbout's universal family allowances, but he soon began to consider the policy too weak to put the other federal projects in jeopardy. Furthermore, during his first mandate, Duplessis had curtailed the power of "comités paritaires" by modifying the Collective Labour Agreements Extension Act of 1934.

107 The CCF's provincial MP, David Côté, had called for a provincial supplement to the allowance of all mothers (*Gazette* [Montréal], 17 February 1945). See also Rumilly, *Maurice Duplessis et son temps,* vol. 1, 95; NAC, RG 36/18, Antonio Barrette, Lettre circulaire to the recipients of needy mothers' allowances, 20 September 1945, 8, 4–10; Québec, *Annuaire statistique, 1945–1946,* 183; and "Québec Backs Family Bonus: Bill Passes Assembly 51–34," *Gazette* (Montréal), 21 February 1945.

108 *Débats,* 1944, 5564–69, 5592, 5598–5600, 5613, 5619, 5633; *Débats,* 1947, 4451; and *Débats,* 1947, 1779. All the Québec members of the cabinet approved the program according to Granatstein (*Canada's War,* 280). Palmer hypothesizes that the popularity of family allowances with the federal cabinet ministers from the province played a determinant role in Mackenzie King's adoption of the program ("Origins and Implementation," 153).

109 *Débats,* 1944, 5563. At the head of the alarmists, Charlotte Whitton and C.E. Silcox published the most virulent of pleas in 1945, entitled *The Revenge of the Cradles*. See also Charlotte Whitton, "The Family Allowances Controversy in Canada," *The Social Service Review* 18, no. 4 (1944): 432. The same divergences long delayed Canadian family-planning laws, according to Angus McLaren and Arlene Tigar McLaren in *The Bedroom and the State: The Changing Practices and Politics of Contraception and Abortion in Canada, 1880–1980* (Toronto: McClelland & Stewart, 1986), 13.

110 *Débats,* 1944, 5594. The reduction was set at one dollar for the fifth child, two dollars for the sixth and seventh, and three dollars for subsequent children, with the premiums set at five, six, seven, or eight dollars depending on the child's age: under six, between six and nine, ten and fourteen, or thirteen and fifteen.

111 *Débats,* 1944, 5526; and *Débats,* 1944, 5974–75.

112 *Débats,* 1944, 5552.

113 F. Dorion, Independent MP from Charlevoix-Saguenay to the House, *Débats,* 22 July 1944, 5571; Micheline Carrier, "Les craintes de l'élite clérico-nationaliste face à la Loi des allocations familiales, 1944–1945: Essai d'interprétation d'une idéologie conservatrice" (M.A. diss, Université Laval), 26; and Lebel, "Après deux ans d'allocations familiales," 228. Charles Bilodeau, special DPI officer, made statements to this effect through the Association des ministères de l'éducation du Canada in a 5 October 1944 letter to Charles E. Philipps, secretary to the Canada and Newfoundland Education Association (CNEA). See CDSA, CNEA, Correspondance, Généralités, 1945–1235, box 112 375. In the same file, a 5 February 1945 letter from Brooke Claxton to L. Masson of the Wartime Information Board affirms that they did not want to step on the toes of other provinces. A 5 May 1945 circular from Curry, national director of family allowances, to all the regional directors officially states this policy. See AQRO, 8–0, vol. 1.

114 *SC,* 1944, 8 Geo. 6, c. 40, art. 4.

115 The clause linking allowances and school attendance was proposed for the first time in the House in 1944 by Thomas Reid, Liberal MP from British Columbia, one of the pioneer provinces in this type of legislation. See *Débats,* 1944, 5636–37. See also Veronica Strong-Boag, "Wages for Housework: Mothers' Allowances and the Beginning of Social Security in Canada," *Journal of Canadian Studies/Revue d'études canadiennes* 12, no. 1 (1979): 24–34.

116 The first rules included recognition of the provincial laws. See "Règlements sur les allocations familiales," P.C. 5093, *La Gazette du Canada* 79, no. 34 (25 August 1945): 3755. This recognition was included into the law itself by means of an amendment. See *SC,* 10 Geo. 6, c. 50. In 1944, Conservative MP Karl Homuth had attempted, without success, to draw the House's attention to the differences between the provinces' legislation on education. See *Débats,* 1944, 5874. The jurisdiction problems surfaced again with application of the clause on equivalent instruction. See AQRO, 8–0, vol. 1, T.F. Phillips to J.-E. Beauvais, 18 June 1946, and N.A. Mathieu, memo to Lionel Lafrance, 20 July 1946, citing an article by Father Voubier, s.j.

117 AQRO, 7–6, "Travail," vol. 1, P.A. Fournier, head of the "Travail juvénile" division, to QRO Director Lionel Lafrance, 12 February 1949.

118 *SC,* 8 Geo. 6, c. 40, art. 2, f; "Règlements sur les allocations familiales," art. 2, d; C.P. 6588, art. 1, d, *La Gazette du Canada* 79, no. 46 (6 November 1945); "The Family Allowances Regulations," art. 1, d, *The Canada Gazette,* Part 2, *Statutory Orders and Regulations* 82, no. 19 (13 October 1948); and AQRO, 7–3, vol. 1, Senez, "Éligibilité des garderies-pouponnières," 1 February 1952. For commentaries from an American social worker on the originality and the generosity of the Canadian program in this regard, see Edward E. Schwartz, "Some Observations on the Canadian Family Allowances Program," *Social Service Review* 20, no. 4 (1946): 462.

119 *RAMSNBES, 1945–1946,* 74; NAC, RG 29, 1286, 266-5-49, *Welfare Annual Report—Fiscal Year 1949–1950,* 5; NAC, RG 29, acc. 82–83/152/269–9-2, Untitled document, 1946, 3.

120 NAC, RG 29, acc. 82–83/152, 264–9-2, Canadian Council of Welfare, Memorandum on a meeting held at the Archbishop's Palace, Québec, QC, 16 November 1950; Geneva Report on children's placement in families, adopted by the Commission consultative des questions sociales de la Société des nations and cited in the Garneau Commission, *Premier rapport de la Commission d'assurance-maladie de Québec sur le problème des garderies et de la protection de l'enfance,* 1944, 7; and Ashby, "Partial Promises and Semi-Visible Youths," 495. Earlier, the wish to keep

families together had also inspired the country's aid programs for needy mothers. See Strong-Boag, "Wages for Housework," 32.

121 *Débats,* 1949, 1731–32. The CCF MP accused the Liberal government of political propaganda, which the Minister of National Health and Welfare denied.

122 Caron, "Les familles nombreuses," 44. See also Québec Independent MP Frédéric Dorion, *Débats,* 1944, 5571.

123 AQRO, 8–0, vol. 2, McKinnon to Lafrance, 26 October 1956. The QRO reported to its superiors that the DPI did not apply to the law. See *ARQRO, 1952–1953,* 10; and *ARQRO, 1953–1954,* 14–15. See also CDSA, 1944–879, box 112 346, letter from Filteau to a mother from Thetford-Mines, 8 February 1943, and another from Doré to Madame Labelle, 14 March 1945. When he abolished free education, he announced to the school boards that they could demand that parents pay their "monthly payment" to the schools by way of the federal government's family allowances. The DPI continued, meanwhile, to provide funding to help poor schools and indigent children—$92,076 in the year 1951–52, double the sum of $45,000 from the year 1938–39 (*ARSPI, 1939–1940,* xxxvii; and *ARSPI, 1951–1952,* 4).

124 Audet, *Histoire de l'enseignement au Québec,* vol. 2, 220; and James Iain Gow, *Histoire de l'administration publique québécoise, 1867–1978* (Montréal: Presses de l'Université de Montréal, 1986), 186.

125 ASJCF, Côté to Duplessis, 30 January 1945; Loi concernant les livres de classe et la rétribution mensuelle dans certains écoles publiques," *SQ,* 1949, 13 Geo. 6, c. 27; CDSA, 1945–1110, box 112 376, Commission d'enquête sur la répartition des impôts municipaux et scolaires, *Rapport sur les aspects financiers du problème scolaire,* 23 January 1946, 11. This commission had been entrusted by the minister of municipal affairs to evaluate the school tax exemptions, from which large companies benefited (Robert Rumilly, *Histoire de la province de Québec,* vol. 41, *La guerre de 1939–1945: Duplessis reprend les rennes* [Montréal: Fides, 1969], 210). In the year 1948–49, the DPI spent $168,406 on books for Catholics; in the year 1951–52, the amount increased to $221,587 and, in the year 1952–53 to $217,512. For the Protestants over the same two school years, the numbers were, respectively, $73,378 and $57,445 (*ARSPI, 1951–1952,* 4; and *ARSPI, 1952–1953,* 18). In the year 1959–60, the provincial contribution was raised again to 75 per cent. See *RSQ,* 8–9 Eliz. 2, c. 9, art. 23.

126 *SQ,* 1949, 13 Geo. 6, c. 27; and CDSA, 1944–430, box 112 228, superintendent to Saint-Octave (Matane) Secretary-Treasurer J.G. Martin, 4 April 1949.

127 *Rapport sur les aspects financiers,* 11–12; and "Family Bonuses Seen Tied to School Fee: Authorities Study Relationship to Bring about Easing of Situation," *Gazette* (Montréal), 26 June 1945.

128 For an exhaustive list of these groups, see my thesis Dominique Jean, "Familles québécoises et politiques sociales touchant les enfants, de 1940 à 1960: Obligation scolaire, allocations familiales, et travail juvénile," (Ph.D. diss., Université de Montréal, 1988), 24–25. See also the demands on Québec's social workers as presented to the Garneau Commission, *Le Soleil,* 26 February 1944; Advisory Committee on Reconstruction, *Post-War Problems of Women,* 23; Canon Harbour, 1942, in Sister Gaudreau, *The Social Thought of French Canada,* 161; and Vautelet, *Mémoire sur l'orientation du travail féminin d'après-guerre,* 11–12, 25, which emphasizes the specific problems of girls. See also "Une plaie sociale: Le travail des enfants," *La Patrie,* reprinted in *Le Monde ouvrier,* 20 February 1943, p. 3; and ANQQ, E 13, C.r., 1942–199, box 2223, Victoriaville school municipality to the SPI, 26 January

1943, and Alice Standon, Sociology Group, St. John the Evangelist, to A. Godbout, 4 February 1943.

129 ANQQ, E 24, 222, A-8, Tremblay to Doré, 30 October 1943. Tremblay, the deputy minister of labour, thought that compulsory attendance rendered the requirement of a certificate of education for children under 15 obsolete.

130 This was the 1937 Loi de la protection de la jeunesse, *RSQ,* 1961, c. 176, which authorized the government to ban work for all children of fourteen and fifteen years of age. See also *RGMTQ, 1919–1920,* 80.

131 ANQQ, E 24, 222, A-8, Macnamara to Tremblay, 3 February 1944, and Tremblay to Macnamara, 7 February 1944.

132 *RGMTQ, 1940–1941,* 97; ANQQ, E 24, 251, A-8, Tremblay to Camille L. de Montigny, 25 February 1946; *RAMTQ, 1953–1954,* 271; and ANQQ, E 24, 222, A-8, Tremblay to CNEA Secretary Phillips, 9 December 1943.

133 *RGMTQ, 1940–1941,* 97; *RGMTQ, 1941–1942,* 81, 90; *RGMTQ, 1945–1946,* 164; *RGMTQ, 1953–1954,* 270–71; *RGMTQ, 1959–1960,* 296; ANQQ, E 24, 209, A-8, Rochette to Renaud, 27 July 1942; and ANQQ, E 24, 312, A-8, Bernier to Barrette, 21 June 1954.

134 NAC, MG C25, League of Women's Rights, vol. 7, Minutes of the Assembly, 10 February 1943. The secretary paraphrases the response of Macnamara, head of the National Selective Service, in the League's letter denouncing child labour.

135 ANQQ, E 24, 235, A-8, circular of the National Selective Service, no. 278–1, 20 June 1944. The NSS was also guilty of laxism. See A. Roberge, superintendant of the maple producers, to the Department of Labour, 29 May 1943; the NSS had sent him girls under sixteen years of age "following a lack of female labour."

136 Brooke Claxton, *Débats*, 1944, 5932; and *Débats,* 1944, 5546.

137 The Provincial Employment Service had received the responsibility to create work permits for children of fourteen and fifteen years of age in 1945. See *ARQDL, 1952–1953,* 53.

138 *Débats,* 1944, 27 July 1944, cited in A. M. Willms, "Setting Up Family Allowances, 1944–1945" (M.A. diss., Carleton University, 1962), 14. Falardeau et al. shared this opinion (*Mémoire sur les allocations familiales,* 52).

139 ANQQ, E 24, 235, A-8, Maher to Bernier, 29 March 1945. In 1945 he created similar learning boards composed of employers and workers, and overseen by a new service of aid to learning, which was destined to set up and finance the free education centres. See Robert Rumilly, *Maurice Duplessis et son temps,* vol. 2, 45.

140 *RGMTQ, 1947–1948,* 171. See also Québec, Provincial Employment Agency, 252, E 4, Internal Board, Department of Labour General Superintendant Alfred Crowe to Superior Labour Council President Anatole Désy, 23 March 1945.

141 *RGMTQ, 1944–1945,* 132. See also ANQQ, E 24, 235, A-8, Bernier to Barrette, following a meeting with the Youth Bureau, 5 April 1945; *RGMTQ, 1944–1946*, 168–70, 211; *RGMTQ, 1950–1951,* 254; and *RGMTQ, 1951–1952,* 297. The new system was established in April 1946. See ANQQ, E 24, 251, A-8, "Résumé des décisions arrêtées à la réunion tenue le 25 mars à Montréal," 29 April 1946. In 1947, the department called on the Unemployment Insurance Commission to send him a monthly list of the children to whom it had issued a carnet. This directive, affirmed Deputy Minister Tremblay, "gives us, in my opinion, sufficient guarantees to monitor children from 14 to 16 years old" (ANQQ, E24, 263, A-8, Tremblay to Crowe, 29 March 1947).

142 Bibliothèque de la législature à Québec, "Étude sur la législation du travail de la province du Québec et des conventions internationales qui s'y rapportent," August

1948. Certain placement offices established the practice. See ANQQ, E 24, 222, A-8, Children's Labour, 1943–44, Deputy Minister of Labour Gérard Tremblay to L.-P. Pigeon, greffier, 26 November 1943, and Wilfrid Beaulac, director of the Bureau du service de l'inspection de Québec, to Tremblay, 29 November 1943.

143 Raymond Boudon and F. Bourricaud, "Consensus," in *Dictionnaire critique de la sociologie* (Paris: Presses Universitaires de France, 1985), 111–15. This article also provides the basis for the following discussion, on the nature of consensus.

144 Union organizations had maintained that the provincial candidates' eligibility, the possession of property worth less than $2,000, should be abolished, and they had campaigned to reduce the electoral census, set at $300. In 1895, the Conseil des métiers et du travail de Montréal had managed to achieve the abolition of the property requirement to vote; simply an income of $300 was required. The required amount would be lowered to $10 in 1912 and abolished in 1936 (Rouillard, *Histoire du syndicalisme au Québec,* 61).

145 Linteau et al., *Histoire du Québec contemporain,* vol. 2, 122–23.

146 Michael Shalev, "The Social Democratic Model and Beyond: Two 'Generations' of Comparative Research on the Welfare State," *Comparative Social Research* 6 (1983): 315–51 (special issue on the welfare state edited by Richard F. Tomasson).

147 Vigod compares the type of progress made in the domain of education by the Duplessis and the Taschereau governments in "'Qu'on ne craigne pas l'encombrement des compétences,'" 244. The former, he suggets, was less "optimistic."

148 Boudon and Bourricaud, "Consensus"; and Ashby, "Partial Promises and Semi-Visible Youth," 493.

Chapter 2

1 The title of this chapter is drawn from Bryan S. Turner, "Outline of a Theory of Citizenship," *Sociology* 24, no. 2 (1990): 194.

2 Québec, DPI, *Instructions concernant la loi de fréquentation scolaire obligatoire,* 1943, 3–4. For more on the Godbout government's vision of the State, see Bernard Vigod, "History According to the Boucher Report: Some Reflections on the State and Social Welfare in Quebec before the Quiet Revolution," in *The Benevolent State: The Growth of Welfare in Canada,* eds. Allan Moscovitch and Jim Albert (Toronto: Garamond, 1987), 182–83; and P.-A. Linteau et al., *Histoire du Québec contemporain,* vol. 2, *Le Québec depuis 1930* (Montréal: Boréal, 1986), 142. On Taschereau, see Bernard Vigod, "'Qu'on ne craigne pas l'encombrement des compétences': Le gouvernement Taschereau et l'éducation, 1920–1929," *Revue d'histoire de l'Amérique française* 28, no. 2 (1974): 223, 237. On the close relationship between the rise of bureaucracy and compulsory education in the United States, see Samuel Bowles and Herbert Gintis, *Schooling in Capitalist America: Education Reform and the Contradictions of Economic Life* (New York: Basic Books, 1976), 44.

3 For a deeper look at the nature of this relationship, see my article "The Language of Children's Rights, the Formation of the Welfare State, and the Democratic Experience of Poor Families, Québec, 1940–1955," *Canadian Historical Review* 78, no. 3 (1997): 409–441 (special issue on childhood). These letters constitute the main sources for the history of families found in the fourth and fifth chapters. Officials kept the parents' complaints for the first few years; they organized them by subject with the intent of systematically answering them (CDSA, 1943–1200, box 112 317, parts 1–6, "Exemptions de fréquentation scolaire"). This correspondence between parents and the SPI is less and less abundant with the passing years. The

series ends, abruptly, in 1950. Perhaps the inspectors ceased to advise the parents to write to the superintendent when the law's implementation was relaxed. From then on, many demands of this kind could be addressed to the Family Allowances Bureau, as letters to the superintendent requesting exemption (also deposited in this archive) demonstrate. Or perhaps the department ceased keeping the letters once a certain jurisprudence had been established. Lastly, it is possible that the continuation of these files was not sent to the CDSA. We have studied in detail the first part, 150 letters dated from July 1943 to September 1943; a portion of the fifth part, 50 letters dated from September 1945 to February 1949; and the last 50 letters, dated from September 1949 to December 1949. I have numbered these files to abbreviate references.

4 Bruce Curtis, *Building the Educational State: Canada West, 1836–1871* (London: Althouse Press, 1988), 372, 376.

5 E.P. Hennock, "Central/Local Government Relations in England: An Outline, 1800–1950," *Urban History Yearbook,* 1982, 38–49.

6 At the request of the provincial inspector and the truancy officers, the school inspectors had to provide "a list of all children living in the municipality and required to attend school according to the annual census." As there was no compulsory education at the time, it is surprising to see the expression "required to attend school" used (Québec, *Code scolaire de la province de Québec,* 1940, "Loi de l'instruction publique," art. 285, 290). See also Québec, DPI, Statistical Research Service, *Recensement scolaire, septembre 1943,* 1944, xi–xii.

7 C.-J. Magnan, *Éclairons la route* (Québec: Librairie Garneau, 1922), xvi, 46–48; and Ruby Heap, "L'Église, l'État, et l'enseignement primaire public catholique au Québec, 1897–1920" (Ph.D. diss., Université de Montréal, 1987), 958, 963–67.

8 Victrice Lessard, "L'enseignement obligatoire dans la province de Québec de 1875 à 1943" (Ph.D. diss., University of Ottawa, 1962), 96–100, 110–19, 146, 202, 211; and Louis-Philippe Audet, *Histoire de l'enseignement au Québec,* vol. 2 (Montréal: Holt, Rinehart & Winston, 1971), 252–54.

9 Québec, DPI, PCPIC, *Protestant Education in the Province of Quebec: Report of the Quebec Protestant Education Survey,* 1938, 48–49.

10 ANQQ, Ministry of Education, E 13, C.r., 1939–1082, box 2128, circular 1082–39, 28 August 1939; and ANQQ, E 13, C.r., 1939–1082, C.-J. Miller and B.-O. Filteau to Victor Doré, 20 March 1940. A later letter from Filteau, secretary since 1937, makes it appear that he was already converted to compulsory education (CDSA, 1942–1339, Filteau to Hector Perrier, 25 September 1942).

11 ANQQ, E 13, C.r., 1940–988, box 2163, Perrier to Doré, 19 July 1940, and Doré to Perrier, 5 August 1940.

12 DPI, *Instructions,* 1943.

13 ASJCF, box 234–1, item 2, Paul-Émile Beaudoin, curriculum vitae. His move to the DPI later earned him several credits from the Institut pédagogique Saint-Georges at the Université de Montréal (ASJCF, box 234–1, item 2, Institute Director Brother Luc, 14 April 1947). Similar to his work at the department, he carried out a study for the MCSC (ASJCF, box 234–1, "MCSC, traitement de principaux et professeurs, 1893–1950," manuscript, 196 pp.). He left the department in 1947 and went on to study education at Fordham and Columbia, where he completed his doctorate examinations without ever obtaining a diploma. He then became dean of the Faculty of Education at Addis-Abeba from 1950 until 1956. From 1959 to 1963, he returned to assist the head of training for the country's leaders. In the meantime, he participated in setting up the Faculty of Education at the University of Sudbury. Beau-

doin also researched the history of education; see, among others, ASJCF, box 234–5, item 8; box 126–1, item 1, and box 126–1, item 2. He died in 1985.

14 ASJCF, H-37, Perrier to Jesuit Superior Papillon, 4 August 1941, 24 July 1941, and the superior's response, 29 July 1941.

15 DPI, Statistical Research Service, *Census 1943,* vi.

16 Two operations of this kind took place, one in 1939 and one in 1942. See AMCSC, Information Service, Statistics, School Census, Generalities, 1920–1969: Statistician J.-F. Vincent to Trefflé Boulanger, 18 June 1947; circular from MCSC General President A.-F. Larose to the priests, 21 September 1938; and Vincent to Doré, 20 October 1938.

17 ACSSMCM, 1656, 1—34/07, *Census scolaire, 1924–1963.* It is difficult to know if the municipality is an exception; but we know that the CSSMCM was the only one of five commissions in the Vieilles-Forges region to keep track of the surveys before 1943.

18 ASJCF, box 234–5, item 7, DPI, "L'éducation est un placement," mimeographed document prepared by P.-É. Beaudoin, undated; CDSA, 1943–44, box 112 302, Beaudoin manuscript, 22 March 1944.

19 J.-B. Gagnon, cited in Québec, DPI, *ARSPI, 1946–1947,* 244. Having noted a dissonance between the priests' and board's count of students not attending school, the members of the CSSMCM asked the inspector to make the necessary corrections (MCSCM, 17 October 1944).

20 DPI, Statistical Research Service, *Census 1943,* vi.

21 DPI, Statistical Research Service, *Census 1943,* vii.

22 ANQQ, E 13, C.r., 1942–199, box 2223, Canadian Press, Doré to Guy Gagnon, 16 December 1943; and DPI, Statistical Research Service, *Census 1943,* xi.

23 DPI, *Census 1943,* vii; and ANQQ, E 13, C.r., 1942–96, box 2218, Beaudoin to Bilodeau, 6 October 1944.

24 Raymond E. Callahan, *Education and the Cult of Efficiency: A Study of the Forces That Have Shaped the Administration of the Public Schools* (Chicago: University of Chicago Press, 1962), 178; and Philip Corrigan and Derek Sayer, *The Great Arch: English State Formation as Cultural Revolution* (Oxford: Basil Blackwell, 1985), 134.

25 Québec, DPI, Statistical Research Service, *Rapports de juin 1945: Organisations scolaire et aperçus pédagogiques,* 1945, 5 (a copy of this publication is deposited in the Bibliothèque administrative du gouvernement du Québec). The compilations were carried out only for the urban districts between 1943 and 1944, but the following year, all the districts appeared in the report (CDSA, 1946–1137, box 112 305, *Rapports de juin 1946: Résumé des régions;* DPI, Statistical Research Service, *Census 1943,* viii, 183; and DPI, *L'Éducation est un placement,* 25–29).

26 DPI, *Instructions,* 1943, 6, 8, 10. See also AMCSC: general circular, March 1943, 4; Direction des études, general circular, *Écoles primaires, élémentaires, et complémentaires, 1943–1944;* and Students, Absence Monitoring, and Annual Reports, 1941–1962.

27 DPI, Statistical Research Service, *Census 1944,* 1945, vi.

28 The inquiry compilations took the form of ten manuscripts booklets (ASJCF, 126–11). On the history of the inquiry, see MCCPIC, 30 September 1942, p. 65; CCPIC, *Enquête scolaire,* 31 January 1942, 80 pp.; and ANQQ, E 13, C.g., Census, 1942–96, Beaudoin to Doré, 22 September 1942, Doré to Beaudoin, 25 September 1942, and Beaudoin to Doré, 26 September 1942. The Comité d'interprétation des statistiques scolaires met 28 times according to the *ARSPI, 1943–1944,* 6. Upon its clo-

sure in 1950, the DPI's Statistical Research Service transferred all the Québec school-survey notebooks to the Quebec Bureau of Statistics (CDSA, Department of Education, Statistical Research Service, R.-P. Beaulieu, Montréal, 1946–1137, box 112 405, SPI Omer-Jules Desaulniers to J.-F. Boivin at the Statistical Research Service). Eleven years later, the notebooks were destroyed (CDSA, C.g., Comité d'interprétation des statistiques de l'enquête scolaire, 1944–213, box 112 336, SPI to Superintendent of Public Works Alphonse Baillargeon, 30 March 1963).

29 From the year 1914–15 to the year 1929–30, the *Statistiques de l'éducation* had come from the provincial secretary. Subsequently, the Department of Municipal Affairs had taken up the job, then the Department of Industry, Trade, and Commerce in the year 1935–36. The *Statistiques de l'éducation* independent publication folded after the collection of 1944–45 statistics, which were not published until 1951. The bureau then added a typed summary of twelve pages of statistics from the years 1945–46, 1946–47, and 1947–48, of which one copy is deposited at the Bibliothèque nationale à Montréal (annexe Aegedius-Fauteux). Until the year 1949–50, they were added to the *ARSPI*. See CDSA, 1946–136, box 112 405, Statistical Research Service Associate Director G. Lemonde to J.- Minister of Industry, Trade, and Commerce P. Beaulieu, 24 July 1947.

30 CDSA, 1946–1136, box 112 405: unsigned letter to the minister, 16 November 1951; Deputy Minister of Industry, Trade, and Commerce Louis Coderre to Filteau, 25 September 1945; and Lemonde to Coderre, 19 January 1946. See also ANQQ, E 13, C.r., 1942–96, box 2218, Director of Provincial Statistics Samuel Gascon to Filteau, 12 December 1944. The department even attempted to rent the machines used by the federal government during the 1931 census (ANQQ, E 13, C.r., 1942–199, box 2223, Perrier to A. Cudmore of the Federal Statistics Bureau, 15 December 1943).

31 DPI, Statistical Research Service, *Census 1944,* xix.

32 DPI, *L'éducation est un placement.* To accomplish this goal, he hoped to increase the DPI's budget from $1.8 million to $2.8 million.

33 Québec, DPI, "Notes explicatives," *Journal d'appel* (a copy is deposed in the CDSA, 1943–1944, box 112 302); MCSCM, 7 March 1944; and CDSA, 1943–1080, box 112 317, Jarry to Doré, 17 October 1943, and Doré to Jarry, 19 October 1943. Doré asked Léopold Fortin from the École du meuble to poll the manufacturers on their reserve of scales, as he wanted to order between 5,000 and 10,000 of them (ANQQ, E 13, C.r., 1942–199, box 2223, 11 December 1943). See also DPI, *Rapports de juin 1945*, 5: 2,010 boys and 3,197 girls surveyed weighed 20 per cent or more than the average; 3,315 boys and 5,935 girls weighed 10 per cent or less than the average—though the total number of students measured is not known. In 1945, the compilation of these results ceased (CDSA, 1946–1137, box 112 305, *Rapports de juin 1946: Résumé des régions*).

34 DPI, *Census 1944,* vi. See also Doré to Omer Côté, 1 July 1945, in the introduction to the work, p. i.

35 ASJCF, 126–1, Côté to Maurice Duplessis, 30 January 1945.

36 CDSA, 1946–1137, box 112 305: Boivin to Desaulniers, 20 February 1947; Boivin to Filteau, 20 February 1947; and Desaulniers to Boivin, 1 March 1947. The provincial secretary suspended the printing of the 1945 school census due to the cost of publication. According to correspondence, a typed version of the census exists, but we were unable to locate it (CDSA, 1946–1136, box 112 405: Desaulniers to Boivin, 31 May 1950; Boivin to Desaulniers, 13 June 1950; Desaulniers to Boivin, 3 November 1950; Desaulniers to Boivin, 25 November 1950; Provincial Auditor J. Dolbec to Doré, 30 October 30 1946).

37 Jean-Guy Genest, "Vie et œuvre d'Adélard Godbout, 1892–1956" (Ph.D. diss., Université Laval, 1987), 572. His source is *Le Devoir,* 21 July 1944.

38 School inspector A. Breton had been calling for compulsory education for years. See ANQQ, E 13, C.r., 1942–199, Breton's letter to Doré, 30 October 1943. See also ACSSLF, PVCSSLF, 10 October 1943. On inspection as a means of education, see Corrigan and Sayer, *The Great Arch,* 136.

39 PVCSC, school inspector's report, 15 April 1955. Others did not fulfill their information mission, as certain elementary-school teachers were not kept up to date on the terms of the law, a fact pointed out by the Saint-Eustache truancy officer (CDSA, 1946–789, box 112 398, June 1944).

40 CDSA, 1946–789, box 112 398, Superintendent of school inspectors' circular no. 1062–43, August 1943.

41 *ARSPI, 1943–1944,* xxi ff.; and *ARSPI, 1946–1947,* 7ff. See also Albini Lafortune, "À propos d'un article de *Relations,*" MCCIP, 6 February 1946, 15–18. In 1944, the provincial government incited the school boards to change the minimum wage from $400 to $600 per year and paid the authorized municipalities up to 56 per cent of the wages, a reform Godbout had talked about since the beginning of his time in the assembly in 1929 (Genest, "Vie et œuvre," 488, 548). With the 1946 law ensuring the progress of education, Duplessis established a minimum salary of $600 for teachers at the same time as withdrawing the rural teachers' rights to arbitration (James Douglas Thwaites, "The Origins and the Development of the 'Fédération des commissions scolaires catholiques du Québec,' 1936–1963" [Ph.D. diss., Université Laval, 1975], 183).

42 *ARSPI, 1943–1944,* xiv; and DPI, *Instructions,* 1943, 7–9.

43 On the lack of elementary-school teachers and what the government did to curb the problem, see MCCIP, 6 February 1946, 15ff. On teachers without degrees, see *ARSPI, 1946–1947,* 8, 9 (in 1946, 7 per cent of elementary school teachers did not hold an official teaching certificate). For a critique of the working conditions of elementary-school teachers in the Québec countryside, see George Haythorne and Leonard Marsh, *Land and Labour: A Social Survey of Agricultural and Farm Labour market in Central Canada* (Montréal: McGill-Queen's University Press, 1941), 82.

44 *ARSPI, 1943–1944,* 78; *ARSPI, 1943–1944,* 59; *ARSPI, 1946–1947,* 141, 210. See also CDSA, 1946–789; box 112 398: Officer C.-A. Langlois, undated; Sainte-Jeanne-d'Arc, 12 July 1944; Sainte-Herménégilde, 6 July 1944. An unidentified report in the same file states: "This state of things exists in almost every school municipality, particularly in colonized countries" (Monitor's report, 28 June 1944). On the subject of stamps, see CDSA, 1946–789, box 112 398, Officer Gilles Descôteaux, undated. On the administration's harassment of the elementary-school teachers, see Michael Katz, *Class, Bureaucracy, and Schools: The Illusion of Educational Change in America* (New York: Praeger, 1977), 131.

45 DPI, Statisitical Research Service, *Rapports de juin 1945,* 5; CDSA, 1943–1944, box 112 302, Association des institutrices de Matane to Doré, 29 June 1944; and ANQQ, E 13, C.r., 1942–199, box 2223, Breton to Doré, 11 February 1944.

46 ANQQ, E 13, C.r., 1942–96, box 2218, DPI, *Enquête scolaire 1942,* 13.

47 ASJCF, 126–10; and ASJCF, 234–5, "Instituteurs des écoles primaires atteints par l'enquête scolaire, 1941–1942," 5. The publication date of the survey results is not indicated.

48 On the elementary-school teachers of Saint-Jérôme (Saguenay), see *Rapport de la Commission de coordination et d'examens,* mentioned in *ARSPI, 1946–1947,* 101.

On the Eastern Townships, see *ARSPI, 1947–1948,* 109. On Westmount, see *ARSPI, 1946–1947,* 250. See also MCCIP, 15 December 1943, 9. Certain elementary-school teachers had already made the course more interesting and practical by insisting more on direct observation and achievement (Urban District Inspector Gagnon, in *ARSPI, 1945–1946,* 166).

49 Cited in *ARSPI, 1943–1944,* 8.

50 PVCSCM, school inspectors' report, 28 May 1948 and 15 January 1949. From 1945 to 1946, the new program was implemented in the first three years of elementary school and in all the English Catholic schools (*ARSPI, 1947–1948,* 11). Aiming to increase children's interest, the school libraries program begun in 1942 was important. Between 1942 and 1945, 2,308 libraries with 221,923 books were set up in 413 municipalities (*ARSPI, 1944–1945,* 180; G. Filteau, cited in *ARSPI, 1949–1950,* 175; and Gaspésie District Inspector Hubert, cited in *ARSPI, 1949–1950,* 106).

51 ANQQ, E 13, C.r., 1942–199, box 2223, Filteau to Breton, 16 February 1944; CDSA, 1943–44, box 112 302, Doré to Association des institutrices de Matane, 12 July 1944, and Doré to the Matane member of provincial parliament, Onésime Gagnon, 13 July 1944.

52 ASJCF, 123–1, Côté to Duplessis, 30 January 1945.

53 Michael D. Behiels, *Prelude to Quebec's Quiet Revolution: Liberalism versus Neo-Nationalism, 1945–1960* (Montréal: McGill-Queen's University Press, 1985), 159, 237; Vigod, "'Qu'on ne craigne pas l'encombrement des compétences,'" 215–17, 231, 237; and Jean Hamelin and Nicole Gagnon, *Histoire du catholicisme québécois: Le XXe siècle,* vol. 1, *1898–1940* (Montréal: Boréal Express, 1984), 442.

54 "Quebec Women Able to Vote on Education," *Montreal Star,* 14 March 1942. The first woman to insist upon this measure, Essel Dickson, was elected in Longueuil. The first female PSBGM commissioner was appointed in 1945. On the process of "public construction" progressing hand-in-hand with the extension of suffrage, see Corrigan and Sayer, *The Great Arch,* 145.

55 AQRO, 8–1, vol. 1, P.-A. Fournier to Lionel Lafrance, 20 January 1943.

56 Thwaites, "Origins and Development," 37–50.

57 *Le Nouvelliste,* 9 October 1953. The school boards' association protested against the creation of school boards by riding (PVCSCM, 18 April 1944). In 1954, the FCS defended the boards' principle of autonomy in its report to the Tremblay Commission (Behiels, *Prelude to Quebec's Quiet Revolution,* 159).

58 Leroy Ashby, "Partial Promises and Semi-Visible Youths: The Depression and World War II," in *American Childhood: A Research Guide and Historical Handbook,* eds. Joseph M. Hawes and N. Roy Hiner (Westport: Greenwood Press, 1985), 499–500.

59 Perrier's first parliamentary speech, in 1941, described the critical situation faced by most of the boards (Robert Rumilly, *Histoire de la province de Québec,* vol. 39, *1914* [Montréal: Fides, 1969], 49; *ARSPI, 1943–1944,* xvii). On the education budget, see the Liberal Party's 1944 program, cited in Jean-Louis Roy, *Les programmes électoraux du Québec,* vol. 2, *1931–1966* (Montréal: Léméac, 1971), 320.

60 Québec, DPI's presentation to the Tremblay Commission, Appendices P-1 and D-2, July 1954.

61 DPI, *Instructions,* 1943.

62 "Except in certain municipalities, there is as yet no machinery for putting the provision in force," wrote Montréal suffragette and advocate Elizabeth Monk to Catherine Lyle Cleverdon on 16 August 1945 (NAC, Catherine Lyle Cleverdon folder, MG 30, file 1942–49, McWilliams to Murray).

63 DPI, Statistical Research Service, *Census 1943,* v; DPI, Statistical Research Service, *Census 1944,* 70. That year (1944–45), the compilations were completed only for the Catholic population.

64 The overlap of parishes of different languages had complicated the enumeration. See AMCSC, Information Service, Statistics, School Census, Generalities, 1920–1969, Vincent to Boulanger, 18 June 1947; AMCSC, circular from Marc Jarry to priests, September 1943; AMCSC, Head of studies, general circular, *Écoles primaries, élémentaire et complémentaires, 1943–1944;* and DPI, Statistical Research Service, *Rapports de juin 1945,* 4.

65 For this reason, the department agreed to exempt the board during the two following years. See ANQQ, E 13, C.r., 1942–96, box 2218, G.-E. Marquis to Doré, 5 October 1944, and annual report to the MCSC Treasurer, 1943–1944, 39. See also CDSA, 1943–1080, box 112 317, letters on the subject between Jarry and Doré; and AMCSC, Information Service, Statistics, School Census, Generalities, 1920–1969, Jarry to Doré, 28 June 1945.

66 School inspector's report, PVCSSMCM, 18 December 1951. In Montréal in 1943, the enumerators attributed more than one-quarter (28.3 per cent) of the non-attendance cases to unknown causes. The per centage for the city of Québec was lower than one-half (14 per cent), but that of the entire province was higher (33.4 per cent). The superintendent concluded that the numbers could be attributed to a lack of rigour on the officers' part (*ARSPI, 1943–1944,* xi; DPI, Statistical Research Service, *Census 1943,* 183).

67 CDSA, 1943–1080, box 112 317, MCSC resolution, 19 November 1943. Verdun appointed two truant officers; the nurse in Saint-Viateur in Outremont received a new mandate; Lachine appointed one truant officer (CDSA, 1943–1080, box 112 317, Grégoire Bélanger to Doré, 15 May 1944; and *ARPBSCCM,* 1943–1944 to 1954–1955).

68 *SQ,* 1943, 7 Geo. 6, Loi concernant la fréquentation scolaire obligatoire, art. 290r; and DPI, *Instructions,* 1943, 5, 9–11. In the five school municipalities of the Cap-de-la-Madeleine region whose records we consulted, the commissioners added an annual premium that varied between $25 and $120 to the secretary-treasurer's salary. See also ANQQ, E 13, C.r., 1942–199, letters to the superintendent mentioning the nomination of officers.

69 ACSCM, School Boards, Correspondence, Convocations, Resolutions, 1926–1968, 1–36/05/1, box 1660, "Tableau comparatif des commissions scolaires de cités et de villes au 30 juin 1944" and "Tableau comparatif des commissions scolaires de cités et de villes au 30 juin 1950," compiled by Antonio Beaudoin, secretary general of the Association des secrétaires de municipalité. The first reported the state of affairs in fifteen cities and towns and the second in nineteen cities and towns. The cities of Québec, Trois-Rivières, and Montréal are absent.

70 On Saint-Léon-de-Westmount, Sainte-Madeleine-d'Outremont, and Saint-Sacrement-de-Lachine, see CDSA, 1943–1080, box 112 317, Bélanger to Doré, 15 May 1944. In Protestant schools, from 1945 to 1946, most boards fulfilled their duties in full, but some did so less strictly (*ARSPI, 1946–1947,* 251). The rural board of Champlain included officer duties with the secretary-treasurer duties every year, during the entire period. The position paid twenty-five dollars per year to start, rising later to eight dollars per month. See minutes from the Conseil des commissaries. See also ANQQ, E 13, C.r., 1942–199, Val-Brillant Inspector Odilon Chabot to Doré, 14 February 1944; and AQRO, 8–0, vol. 2, MacKinnon to Lafrance, 26 October 1956. According to P.-A. Fournier's study, based on a sample of 624 Catholic

boards, 72.1 per cent of the officers were secretary-treasurers (AQRO, 8–0, vol. 1, Fournier to Lafrance, 21 March 1950).

71 *ARSPI, 1943–1944,* 2, 8; and CDSA, 1946–789, box 112 398, secretary-treasurer of Saint-Ulric, 26 July 1944. Some truancy officers, such as E. Lemieux of Gatineau, complained about their salaries in relation to the onerousness of their duties. See CDSA 1946–789, box 112 398, Gatineau to the department, 27 June 1944; and Inspector M. Duval, cited in *ARSPI, 1944–1945,* 104.

72 ANQQ, E 13, C.r., 1942–199, box 222, Doré to L.-P. Pigeon, 5 March 1943. The average salary was $90.67 a year, with most earning $75 and some even less than the obligatory minimum (AQRO, 8–0, vol. 1, Fournier to Lafrance, 21 March 1950). But there were worse situations elsewhere, according to Fournier: in at least one other province, only the urban boards had officers.

73 DPI, *Instructions,* 1943, 10; and AQRO 8–0, vol. 1, Fournier to Lafrance, 21 March 1950.

74 *ARSPI, 1945–1946,* 192; *ARSPI, 1946–1947,* 307; *ARSPI, 1947–1948,* 98; *ARSPI, 1948–1949,* 17; and CDSA, 1946–789, box 112 398, *Rapport annuel du contrôleur de Compton.* Social workers entrusted with the application of the Compulsory School Attendance Act in Montréal also had access to the files of the Bureau central des œuvres. See, for example, AMSWC, case no. 46–608.

75 AQRO, 8–2, Annual Report, School Attendance Unit, MacKinnon to Lafrance, 2 April 1958; and ACSCM, Association des secrétaires de municipalité de la province de Québec, 1–10/02.1, comparative city and town school-board tables from 30 June 1950. (The original text is in English.) In the 1950s, 75 per cent of officers had annual reports sent to the department, as required by the *Instructions* (AQRO, 8–0, vol. 2, MacKinnon to Lafrance, 26 October 1956). For cases of deterioration, see *ARSPI, 1944–1945,* 201; *ARSPI, 1945–1946,* 39; *ARSPI, 1946–1947,* 251, 362; *ARSPI, 1947–1948,* 167; and PVCSSLF, 1946.

76 AQRO, 42–14, p. 8, Fournier, 14 April 1950; AQRO, 42–25, PSBGM Head of Truancy Officers B. H. Brown to Fournier, 23 June 1950; CDSA, 1943–1080, box 112 317, Doré to Bélanger, 28 December 1944; and AMCSC, Absence Monitoring, Généralités, 1924–1960, Gravel to Doré, 27 October 1930.

77 Hepburn Commission Report, p. 48. In English in the text.

78 ANQQ, Ministry of Labour, E 24, 22, A-8, letter to minister of labour, 30 April 1943.

79 CDSA, 1946–789, box 112 398, undated report. On the officer who knew neither how to read nor how to write and whose daughter wrote his correspondence for him, see CDSA, 1943–1200, box 112 317, Saint-Martyr (Wolfe) Secretary-Treasurer R. Laroche to the department, 2 October 1950. On the monitor who did not send his own children to school, see CDSA, 1943–1200, box 112 317, case no. 6–37, Superintendent to Québec School Inspector A. Roberge, 9 May 1950. The province's truancy officers had completed their eighth year, on average, according to AQRO, 8–0, vol. 1, Fournier to Lafrance, 21 March 1950.

80 On women officers, see CDSA 1946–789, box 112 398: Bourlamaque (Abitibi) Officer Madame J.-L. Cotnoir, who was also the school-board nurse, 22 June 1944; Pointe-Leber (Saguenay), 29 June 1944; Thetford-Mines, 26 June 1944; Compton (Mégantic), 1943–1944; and Saint-Luc Officer Madame Thibault, who resigned in a letter to the department, citing too many difficulties involved, 30 June 1944. In Cadillac, the chief of police was designated officer (CDSA, 1943–1200, box 112 317, part 5, secretary-treasurer to Doré, 4 December 1947). In Anticosti, the priest filled the function beginning in 1946, averaging a subsidy of fifty dollars (CDSA, 1943–1200, box 112 317, part 6, letter to superintendent, 17 September 1948).

81 J.-A. Dupuis, cited in *ARSPI, 1944–1945,* 26–24; and CDSA, 1943–1062, letter to Doré, 30 October 1943. The local influences reducing the role of the officer were not a phenomenon limited to Québec; see Ontario, *Report of Provincial School Attendance Monitor, 1928,* p. 51, cited in Canada, Ministry of Labour, *The Employment of Children and Young Persons in Canada* (Ottawa: King's Printer, 1930), 100.

82 AQRO, 8–0, vol. 1, Fournier to Lafrance, 29 May 1950.

83 Eugène Lamarre, cited in *ARSPI, 1943–1944,* 75.

84 *RSQ, 1941*, 5 Geo. VI, c. 59, art. 258.

85 ANQQ, E 13, C.r., 1943–199, model letter to secretary-treasurers; and CDSA, 1944–430, box 112 338, request form, 2 March 1944. The total payments for all levels had increased to $950,000 from 1938 to 1939 and to $1,092,658 from 1942 to 1943 (*ARSPI, 1939–1940,* xxxvii; *ARSPI, 1943–1944,* lxiii). From 1944 to 1945, payments did not exceed $515,000, a decrease by one-half (Québec, Ministère de l'Industrie et du Commerce, Bureau des Statistiques, *Statistiques de l'Enseignement, 1944–1945* [King's Printer, 1951], 350).

86 PVCSSMCM, 1943; ANQQ, E 13, C.r., 1942–199, Philippe Bouchard to Doré, 22 September 1943, and Wilfrid Rousseau to Doré, 22 October 1943; CDSA, 1943–1200, box 112 317, Bienville parent M.N. to the department, 14 September 1943, and answer, dated 21 December 1946; and CDSA, 1943–1200, box 112 317, part 5, Lafrance to Bilodeau, 17 December 1946.

87 In the whole province, the boards' total revenues coming from monthly payments for all grades went beyond those of the period previous to the year 1944–45, which allows us to suppose that many boards re-established the contributions despite the disapproval of the superintendent and of the director of family allowances regarding this practice (Audet, *Histoire de l'enseignement au Québec,* vol. 2, 368; and CDSA, 1943–1200, case no. 6–42, Madame B., 10 November 1949).

88 PVCSSMCM, resolutions from 3 July 1952; and PVCSNDV, 1949–1950, 2 October 1952. All the Protestant boards in one of the six districts of Protestant inspection for which we have information followed the new law (M. Brady, cited in *ARSPI, 1944–1945,* 201). In 1948, the MCSC put more than 1 million textbooks into circulation and disinfected them in September (*Le Devoir,* 28 September 1948). In 1954, the urban school municipality members of the Association des secrétaires de municipalities no longer offered free books, with the exception of Valleyfield, which paid $11,175 annually. Some boards paid for the poor, according the old school code's rules, an amount between $1,000 and $3,000 (ACSCM, 1—10/02.1, box 2136, Beaudoin, 9 June 1954).

89 PVCSCM, 18 July 1944, 5 September 1944, 7 September 1948, 7 September 1954; and MCCPIC, 23 February 1949. Beginning in 1949, the FCS asked that the cost of books be automatically shared: 50 per cent by the department, 25 per cent by the school boards, and 25 per cent by the parents so that they would take care of the books (ACSCM, 1–36/05–1, box 1660). In 1954, the FCS supported the principle of one textbook only. For a summary of the resolutions of the diocesan associations, brought to the FCS's attention, see ACSM, 1—10/03.2, 5 October 1954.

90 *SQ,* 1949, 13 Geo. VI, c. 27, Loi concernant les livres de classe et la rétribution mensuelle dans certaines écoles publiques; Commission on the allocation of municipal and school taxes (De La Bruère Fortier, President), *Report on the financial aspects of the school problem,* 23 January 1946, 11; CDSA, 1945–1110, box 112 376, Commission d'enquête sur la répartition des impôts municipaux et scolaires. In the year 1948–49, the department spent $168,406 for the Catholic schools; in the year

1951–52, the department's contributions towards free textbooks increased to $221,587 (*ARSPI, 1951–1952,* 4). In the year 1952–53, the amount reached $217,512. On the Protestant side during these two school years, the figures were $73,378 and $57,445, respectively (*ARSPI, 1952–1953,* 18). In the year 1959–60, the provincial contribution was increased to 75 per cent (*RSQ, 1964,* 8–9 Eliz. 2, c. 9, art. 23; and MCCPIC, 3 December 1952, 87).

91 In about ten cases, the superintendent first asked the officers to carry an investigation; he then had clothes purchased at the Syndicat du Québec, according to the models and sizes specified by the officers (CDSA, 1943–1200, box 112 317, and 1944–879, box 112 346). In another case, the provincial secretary authorized money to be sent to one father of a large family (ANQQ, E 13, C.r., 1942–199, G.B. of Saint-Jean-de-Brebeuf [Roberval] to Perrier, 21 September 1943, and answer, dated 15 October 1943).

92 The board advised the superintendent to deal with the regional officers who were managing distribution while, "as a result of a special arrangement the board has made with manufacturers, production of children's clothing is now being carried out under a special directive" (CDSA, 1944–789, box 112 346, Doré to Donald Gordon, 14 January 1944; ANQQ, E 13, C.r., 1942–199, C.-E. Jodoin to Doré, 16 December 1943, and answer dated 21 December 1943; and ANQQ, E 13, C.r., 1942–199, Mrs. Verne H. Dallamore, of the Consumer Branch of the Wartime Prices and Trade Board, to Doré, 25 January 1944). Original text in English.

93 Regarding the more general issue of the lack of clear distinction between volunteer charitable sectors and public institutions, see Chad Gaffield, "Demography, Social Structure, and the History of Schooling," in *Approaches to Educational History,* no. 5 in *Monographs in Education,* ed. Jones et al. (Winnipeg: University of Manitoba Press, 1981), 109.

94 DPI, *Instructions,* 1943, 12; Wendy Johnston, "Keeping Children in School: The Response of the Montreal Roman Catholic School to the Depression of the 1930s," *Communications historique/Historical Papers,* 1985, 193–217.

95 CDSA, 1944–430, box 112 338, 16 November 1949.

96 ANQQ, E 13, C.r., 1942–199, box 2223, letter to Doré, 30 June 1943.

97 "Fréquentation scolaire obligatoire," *Relations* 3, no. 25 (1943): 1. Terry Copp also states that if compulsory education had been adopted during the early decades of the twentieth century, the policy would have only increased school overpopulation, as the school system's method of taxation was deficient (*Classe ouvrière et pauvreté: Les conditions de vie des travailleurs montréalais, 1897–1929* [Montréal: Boréal Express, 1978], 75).

98 DPI, Statistical Research Service, *Census 1944,* xix. For a summary of the causes and extent of the "school explosion," see Québec, *Rapport de la Commission royale d'enquête sur l'enseignement dans la province de Québec,* vol. 1, 1963, 63–66; Behiels, *Prelude to Quebec's Quiet Revolution,* 153; *ARSPI, 1945–1946,* xii, 199, 231; *1946–1947,* 179; *1950–1951,* xiii; and PVCSCM, 14 January 1954.

99 DPI, *L'éducation est un placement,* 39.

100 CDSA, 1946–789, box 112 398, Bridgeville (Gaspé) officer's report, 3 July 1944; *ARSPI, 1946–1947,* 98; *ARSPI, 1948–1949,* 194–95; ANQQ, E 13, C.r., 1942–199, Curé Deslandes of Gaspé Nord to Doré, 13 September 1943; ANQQ, E 13, C.r., 1942–199, Sainte-Adélaïde-de-Pabos Secretary-Treasurer Jean Cyr to Doré, 16 October 1943; and ACSCM, 1–36/05–1, box 1660, CSCM's report to the Tremblay Commission, December 1953.

101 *ARSPI, 1946–1947,* 345.

102 Gérard Filion, *Les confidences d'un commissaire d'écoles* (Montréal: Éditions de l'Homme, 1960), 19, 67; CDSA, 1943–1200, box 112 317, Sainte-Perpétue (L'Islet) officer to Doré, 11 September 1943; *ARSPI, 1945–1946,* 192; PVCSCM, 6 February 1954; PVCSSMCM, 4 December 1953; PVCSCM, 3 July 1944, 5 December 1944, 5 June 1945, 27 August 1945, 7 June 1949, 7 August 1951; and PVCSC, 29 June 1948.

103 The amount raised from $325,000 to $340,000. Between 1943 and 1944, the DPI's construction budget went up to $85,000. For Catholic schools it was $133,103 between 1948 and 1949 and $208,818 between 1952 and 1953. In the years 1953–54 and 1954–55, the annual reports show amounts of over $15,000,000, an increase certainly due to different accounting methods of which we are not aware (*ARSPI, 1939–1940,* xxxvii; *ARSPI, 1943–1944,* lxiii, lxiv, xvi; *ARSPI, 1951–1952,* 4; *ARSPI, 1952–1953,* 18; *ARSPI, 1954–1955,* 6).

104 DPI, *L'éducation est un placement,* 34, 38.

105 Québec, DPI's report to the Tremblay Commission, Appendices P-1 and D-2, July 1954; *Rapport Parent,* vol. 5, p. 55, 56; Linteau et al., *Histoire du Québec contemporain,* vol. 2, 316; and Jean-Louis Roy, *La marche des Québécois: Le temps des ruptures (1945–1960)* (Montréal: Léméac, 1973), 248. On the quality of the buildings, see Filion, *Les confidences,* 42, 116–17.

106 AMSWC, file no. 44–7852, principal of S. F. Kneeland School to Brown, May 1945, and Brown to Nicholson, 16 May 1945; AMSWC, case no. 46–698, Brown, 14 November 1945. See also AMSWC, case no. 48–3623. Quotes already in English.

107 AMSWC, case no. 47–1547. Original in English.

108 AMSWC, case no. 48–388; AMSWC, case nos. 45–9612, 46–254, 47–769, 48–468.

109 The *ARPSBGM* tracks these policies beginning in the year 1948–49. The head officer was a social worker. In 1954, he hired five social workers (AQRO, 7–6, vol. 2, Lafrance, July 1954). On the MCSC, see Stéphane Valiquette, "Dix ans de service social à l'école," *Relations* 11, no. 123 (1951): 133–34; and Delphine Périard, "Fréquentation scolaire en regard du milieu familial et des parents" (M.A. thesis, Université de Montréal, 1952), 5–6.

110 *ARPBSCCM, 1945–1947,* 11; AMSWC, case nos. 48–362 and 47–1547.

111 AMCSC, Students, Absence Monitoring, Annual Reports, Special Inspector Ernest Couillard's report, 1943–1944; and AMCSC, Students, School Attendance, Compulsory Education, 1914–1962, Jarry to Doré, 30 June 1945. The reports of an employee of the Family Allowances Bureau, between 1955 and 1956, indicate that 810 Catholic children appeared at the Montréal court for non-attendance (AQRO, 8–0, vol. 2, MacKinnon to Lafrance, 26 October 1956). It seems that none of these cases was pointed out to the Dominion Bureau of Statistics, which counted between five and ninety-seven court appearances per year (Canada, Bureau fédéral de la Statistique, *Rapports annuels sur la statistique de la criminalité* [Ottawa: King's Printer]. Regarding the overpopulation of institutions, see CDSA, 1943–1080, Vincent to Labarre, 28 November 1946; and AMSWC, case nos. 1946–0721 and 1947–29.

112 *RGMTQ, 1947–1948,* 178; *RGMTQ, 1948–1949,* 186–87; *RGMTQ, 1949–1950,* 195; *RGMTQ, 1950–1951,* 196; *RGMTQ, 1951–1952,* 240; *RGMTQ, 1952–1953,* 220; *RGMTQ, 1953–1954,* 216; *RGMTQ, 1954–1955,* 187; *RGMTQ, 1955–1956,* 207.

113 *RSQ, 1941,* 5 Geo. VI, c. 175, art. 30. See also a number of sanction cases in ANQQ, E 24, 209, 235, and 251, A-8.

114 Filteau for Doré to Tremblay, 25 November 1943. After verification, however, Inspector Beaulac did not find any permits issued without birth certificates having been inspected (ANQQ, E 24, 222, A-8, Beaulac to Tremblay, 29 November 1943; Bernier

to Tremblay, 1 December 1943). The overlap of Public Instruction and Labour jurisdictions complicated the labour inspectors' work: children who reached fourteen years of age during the school year could receive a "certificate of age and studies" from the Department of Labour, while the DPI forced them to continue to attend school; the SPI encouraged the inspectors from the Department of Labour to change this practice. A number of exchanges on this topic can be found in ANQQ, E 24, 222, A-8, and 235, A-8.

115 Beaulac to Tremblay, 28 April 1952; Beaulac to Tremblay, 11 June 1952; ANQQ E 24, 309 and 310, A-8; "Pas de travail industriel pour les moins de 16 ans," *La Patrie,* 5 March 1953, p. 9.

116 NAC, RG 29, acc. 82–83/152, 264–1-6, Curry to Lafrance, 11 May 1946.

117 The head of the QRO was a major; the director of the Information Service was a publicist from the Royal Bank, whose skills had previously been called upon by the army to improve public relations with its soldiers. On the importance of the military model and personnel in the establishment of civil service, see Corrigan and Sayer, *The Great Arch,* 152, and Max Weber, "Bureaucracy," in *From Max Weber: Essays in Sociology,* eds. H.H. Gerth and C. Wright (1948; reprint, London: Routledge & Kegan Paul, 1977), 196–244. See also NAC, RG 29, Education and Nutrition Cooperation with F.A. re: Inserts, 109, 180–26–15, Canada, DHNW, *Économisez les vivres,* 1946; NAC, RG 29, 111–181–1-15, "Information Service Division," F.W. Rowse to Harvey W. Adams, 21 June 1954; AQRO, 8–0, vol. 1, Fournier to Lafrance, 1 August 1949; *ARDHNW, 1951–1952,* 120; and *ARQRO, 1952–1953,* 10.

118 Theda Skocpol, *States and Social Revolutions: A Comparative Analysis of France, Russia, and China* (Cambridge: Cambridge University Press, 1979).

119 Regarding a request for the Department of Labour's inspectors to act as social workers, see Renée Vautelet, *Mémoire sur l'orientation du travail feminin d'après-guerre* (published under the auspices of the FNSJB, 1944), 25.

120 Doug Owram, *The Government Generation: Canadian Intellectuals and the State, 1900–1945* (Toronto: University of Toronto Press, 1986); Franz-Xaver Kaufmann, "The Churches and the Emergent Welfare State in Germany" (paper presented at the International Conference on the Sociology of Religion, London, England, 1983); and Michel Brunet, "Trois dominantes de la pensée canadienne-française: L'agriculturisme, l'anti-étatisme, et le messianisme," in *La présence anglaise et les Canadiens: Études sur l'histoire de la pensée des deux Canadas* (Montréal: Beauchemin, 1964). On the lack of educated French Canadians, see Behiels, *Prelude to Quebec's Quiet Revolution,* 200. On federal recruitment favouring Anglophones, see J.L. Granatstein, *The Ottawa Men: The Civil Service Mandarins, 1935–1957* (Toronto: University of Toronto Press, 1982).

121 AQRO, 42–8, vol. 1, Lucille Avard, "Aux allocations familiales: Un bureau qui compte plus de 700,000 clients," *La Presse,* 25 January 1960; and AQRO, 42–25, Fournier to Lafrance, 18 February 1952. In 1948, the DHNW's monthly publication issued photos describing the path a request took to the final step of a cheque being written.

122 Raymond B. Blake, "Mackenzie King and the Genesis of Family Allowances in Canada, 1939–1944," in *Social Welfare Policy in Canada: Historical Readings,* eds. Raymond B. Blake and Jeff Keshen (Toronto: Copp Clark, 1995), 252, paraphrasing the report prepared in January 1944 by the Department of Finance.

123 Mark E. Palmer, "The Origins and Implementation of Family Allowances in Canada" (M.A. diss., Queen's University, 1976), 230; AQRO, Surveys and Studies, 40–20, vol. 1, *Ten Family Surveys;* and Canada, DHNW, Information Services, *You and Your Family* (Ottawa: King's Printer, 1949), 4.

124 Rob Watts, "Family Allowances in Canada and Australia, 1940–1945: A Comparative Critical Case Study," *Journal of Social Policy* 16, no. 1 (1987): 19–48; and Innes de Neufville, "Production de connaissances et processus de planification," *Revue internationale d'action communautaire* 19, no. 55 (1988): 187–93.

125 *ARDHNW, 1951–1951,* 92.

126 AQRO, 40–13, vol. 1, G.W. Gilchrist to Lafrance, 29 April 1948; *ARDHNW, 1945–1946,* 90; *ARDHNW, 1946–1947,* 94; *ARDHNW, 1947–1948,* 130; *ARDHNW, 1948–1949,* 92; *ARDHNW, 1949–1950,* 94; National Film, Television and Sound Archives (hereafter, NAC/NFTSA), DHNW folder, col. acc. 1984–0121, no. 62020, *Peppo et le Chèque des allocations familiales* (NFB, 1946), film clip, 76 tables, 35 mm, silent with French subtitles or with sound recording; NAC/NFTSA, DHNW folder, col. acc. 1982–0121, no. 62077, *Parlons des allocations familiales* (NFB, 1949), film clip, 35 mm, silent with French subtitles or with sound recording. On other department films, see DNHW, Information Services Division, *À voir! Films et projections fixes du ministère de la Santé nationale et du Bien-être social,* undated, 20 pp. I would like to thank Carole Séguin at the audiovisual archives of the NAC, who found these documents.

127 NAC, RG 29, vol. 1283, *ARSWSQRO, 1950–1951,* 5; *ARSWSQRO, 1949–1950,* 18. This average is drawn from a survey of the welfare services activities carried out over one month (NAC, RG 29, vol. 1933, R233–100/52, *Welfare Statistical Report: Definitions and Comments, Revised,* June 1950).

128 A.M. Willms, "Setting Up Family Allowances, 1944–1945" (M.A. diss., Carleton University, 1962), 31; and Edward E. Schwartz, "Some Observations on the Canadian Family Allowances Program," *The Social Service Review* 20, no. 4 (1946): 456.

129 *ARQRO, 1945–1946,* 3; *ARQRO, 1949–1950,* 2; *ARDHNW, 1945–1946,* 84; *ARDHNW, 1946–1947,* 75; *ARDHNW, 1947–1948,* table 51; *ARDHNW, 1948–1949,* 118; and AQRO, 8–0, vol. 1, J.-A. Blais to the regional directors, 23 March 1946. The conflicts between the provinces and the central government regarding birth-rate statistics had remained the same since 1921 according to John Herd Thompson and Allen Seager (*Canada, 1922–1939: Decades of Discord* [Toronto: McClelland & Stewart, 1985], 5).

130 *ARDHNW, 1949–1950,* 95; *ARSWSQRO, 1951–1952,* 13; and NAC, RG 29, acc. 82–83/52, box 25, 3435-2-1, Paul Martin to Minister of Agriculture James J. Gardiner, 11 June 1947, part 1.

131 AQRO, 42–45, Fournier to Lafrance, 18 February 1952.

132 CDSA, 1945–1235, box 112 375, "CNEA—General Correspondence," C. Bilodeau to CNEA Secretary Charles E. Phillipps, 5 October 1944; *ARDHNW, 1945–1946,* 86; *ARQRO, 1945–1946,* 10; *ARQRO, 1948–1949,* 3; *ARQRO, 1952–1953,* 10; AQRO, 8–0, vol. 1, Lafrance to Curry, 25 October 1946, and Blais to Lafrance, 8 May 1950; AQRO, 8–0, vol. 2, Lafrance to Curry, 14 August 1952, and MacKinnon to Lafrance, 26 October 1956; AQRO, 8–0, vol. 1, Lafrance to Curry, 15 March 1948; and AQRO, 8–1, vol. 1, J.-M. Caron, 22 June 1954.

133 This expression is MacKinnon's (AQRO, 8–0, vol. 1, 26 October 1956, p. 3). See also NAC, RG 29, acc. 82–83/152, box 3, 264–1-6, Curry's memorandum to the minister, 30 October 1945; AQRO, 8–0, vol. 1, Lafrance to the officers, February 1949; AQRO, 8–0, vol. 1, Fournier to Lafrance, 28 February 1949; AQRO, 8–0, vol. 1, Blais to Curry, 25 April 1950; and AQRO, 42–25, Fournier's talk, 6 and 7 June 1951.

134 See also the agreements made with Superintendent Labarre, mentioned in Labarre's correspondence with Curry on 15 March 1948 (AQRO, 8–0, vol. 1). Hector Perrier remained with the CCPIC during the entire period. The legal advisor for allowances, Philippe Miller, also appeared to be in favour of the allowances.

135 AQRO, 8–0, vol. 1, MacKinnon reporting the secretary's proposals to N.-R. Boutin (both QRO employees), 12 May 1945. See also CDSA, 1943–1200, box 112 317, part 5: Doré to a parent from Île-aux-Oies, 1 September 1945; Doré to a teacher from Saint-Tite, 28 August 1945, case no. 1; and Doré to Madame L. from Gros-Morne, 19 September 1945.

136 CDSA, 1943–1080, box 112 317: Labarre to Vincent, 4 December 1946; and Labarre to Madame A. Gagné from Montréal, 7 November 1946.

137 AQRO, 42–14, Fournier, 12 April 1950, p. 3 (original in English).

138 In 1953, 106 of the 624 truancy officers' annual reports sampled by Fournier mentioned the threat of suspending the allowances as an effective means of implementing the Compulsory School Attendance Act (AQRO, 8–0, vol. 1, Fournier, 21 March 1953). The maximum of tolerated allowable absences was ten days per month, and in 1949 it was decreased to eight days (AQRO, 8–0, vol. 1: Fournier to Lafrance, 20 November 1948, and Caron to staff, 18 January 1949).

139 In 1948, 250 of the 1,800 truancy officers were in contact with the bureau. See AQRO, 8–0, vol. 1, Lafrance to Curry, 25 October 1946; AQRO, 8–0, vol. 1, Lafrance to Curry, 15 March 1948; AQRO, 8–0, vol. 1, MacKinnon to Faguy, 27 May 1952; *ARQRO, 1945–1946,* 10; *ARQRO, 1949–1950,* 4; *ARQRO, 1951–1952,* 8; *ARQRO, 1952–1953,* 10–11; *ARQRO, 1953–1954,* 10; AQRO, 7–6, vol. 1, Curry to Faguy, 30 August 1946; and *ARPBSCCM, 1955–1956,* 34–35.

140 AQRO, 8–0, vol. 1, Lafrance's circulars to municipal secretary-treasurers, 20 November 1946 and February 1949; AQRO, 8–0, vol. 1, Lafrance to Curry, 15 March 1948; and CDSA, 1943–1200, box 112 317, part 6, Lafrance's circulars to the officers, 1950. When the bureau asked the school boards to respond beginning in the year 1950–51, 1,951 of the 1,967 boards did so. In the following years, the number fell from 1,263 to 1,153 (*ARQRO, 1951–1952,* 11; and *ARQRO, 1953–1954,* 10).

141 The original quotes are in English. AQRO, 8–0, vol. 1, Lafrance to Curry, 15 March 1948. Between 1946 and 1948, Fournier met approximately 200 officers personally. In 1946, Fournier's predecessor had visited 16 officers, most of them in cities. From 1951 to 1952, Fournier met 238 officers and gave seven conferences in the different school boards' diocesan meetings (*ARQRO, 1951–1952,* 7, 8, 11). For more on the conferences, see the frequent invitations in AQRO, 42–25. From 1952 to 1953, Fournier visited 264 school boards (AQRO, 8–0, vol. 2, MacKinnon to Lafrance, 26 October 1956; and *ARQRO, 1952–1953,* 11). Fournier was also responsible for the FCS's magazine (AQRO, 42–25, Fournier to Tremblay, 1 March 1950). On the truancy officers' education, see AQRO, 8–0, vol. 1, Fournier to Lafrance, 28 February 1950; and AQRO, 42–14, Fournier, 12 April 1950. See also AQRO, 8–0, vol. 1, Lafrance to the SPI, 11 January 1950.

142 AQRO, 42–14, Fournier, "Notes Prepared with a View to the Annual Report on School Attendance and Juvenile Work," 12 April 1950.

143 In 1950, Fournier took over the position of secretary for the Association diocésaine de Québec de la Fédération, which included approximately 300 school boards. The same year, Lafrance was named president of the urban division of the FCS. The book the FCS prepared on the laws and school regulations also contained a chapter on the regulations attached to the allowances. AQRO, 42–25, Fournier to Lafrance, 17 June 1950, and Provincial Association of Protestant School Boards Secretary-Treasurer A. Whitehead to Lafrance, 12 June 1950; AQRO, 8–0, vol. 1, Fournier to Lafrance, 16 September 1950; AQRO, 8–0, vol. 2, MacKinnon to Lafrance, 26 October 1956; AQRO, 42–14, Fournier, 3 April 1951; *ARQRO, 1949–1950,* 4; *ARQRO, 1952–1953,* 11; and *ARQRO, 1953–1954,* 14.

144 AQRO, 42–25, Florimond Ducharme to Lafrance, 10 October 1950.
145 AQRO, 8–0, vol. 2, Lafrance to Curry, 26 October 1956, pp. 2–3.
146 AQRO, 8–0, vol. 1, Fournier to Lafrance, 30 September 1949; AQRO, 8–0, vol. 2, Senez to Caron, 8 July 1954; and AQRO, 8–0, vol. 1, Caron, 22 June 1954. Doré had attempted to create a monitoring system in private schools, but in 1954, none of the officers seemed to worry about it (ANQQ, E 13, C.r., 1942–199, box 2223, Doré to Désilets, 11 August 1943; and CDSA, 1943–44, box 112 302, Doré's circular to private schools, 13 August 1943).
147 NAC, RG 29, 111–181–1-15, "Information Service Division," F.W. Rowse to Harvey W. Adams, 21 June 1954; AQRO, 8–0, vol. 1, Fournier to Lafrance, 1 August 1949; *ARDHNW, 1951–1952,* 120; and *ARQRO, 1952–1953,* 10.
148 AQRO, 7–5, vol. 1, Lafrance to Curry, 19 December 1951.
149 Schwartz, "Some Observations," 469; NAC, RG 29, 1 283, 266–5-49, *Welfare Annual Report: Fiscal Year 1949–1950,* 13; Heyda Denault, "L'insertion du service social dans le milieu canadien-français," *Service social* 10, no. 3 (1961) and 11, no. 1 (1962); and Lionel Groulx, "Le service social au Canada français: Ses énoncés et son rôle," *Revue '83/Review '83,* 148, 150.
150 Willms, "Setting Up Family Allowances," 31.
151 Canada, *Débats de la Chambre des communes,* 1944, 5560–61; 1951, 592.
152 Callahan, *Education and the Cult of Efficiency,* 117. See also Corrigan and Sayer, *The Great Arch,* 134.
153 Corrigan and Sayer, *The Great Arch,* 123.

Chapter 3

1 Michel Aglietta, *Régulation et crises du capitalisme: L'expérience des États-Unis* (Paris: Calmann-Lévy, 1982); "Legitimacy" and "Power," in *The Fontana Dictionary of Modern Thought,* 2nd ed., eds. Allan Bullock, Oliver Stallybrass, and Stephen Trombley (London: Fontana, 1988); André Turmel, "Folie, épidémie, et institution: Contrôle et régulation sociale de l'enfance," *Recherches sociographiques* 34, no. 1 (1993): 111–27; and Hannah Arendt, "What Is Authority?" in *Between Past and Future: Six Exercises in Political Thought* (New York: Viking Press, 1961), 118–19.
2 Raymond Boudon and François Bourricaud, "Égalitarisme," in *Dictionnaire critique de la sociologie* (Paris: Presses Universitaires de France, 1985), 217.
3 Cited in J.L. Granatstein et al., *Twentieth-Century Canada,* 2nd ed. (Toronto: McGraw-Hill Ryerson), 343 (original in English). He used the same words in preparing the passage for the Governor General's 1944 throne speech, which announced the allowances (Raymond B. Blake, "Mackenzie King and the Genesis of Family Allowances in Canada, 1939–1944," in *Social Welfare Policy in Canada: Historical Readings,* eds. Raymond B. Blake and Jeff Keshen [Toronto: Copp Clark, 1995], 253). Mackenzie King included a passage from his own work *Industry and Humanity,* published in 1918.
4 "Children's Allowance," memorandum prepared for Minister of Finance J.L. Ilsley, 12 January 1944, cited in Blake, "Mackenzie King and the Genesis of Family Allowances," 252. (Original in English.)
5 "La protection de l'enfance," *Le Soleil,* 23 February 1944.
6 Cynthia R. Comacchio, *"Nations Are Built of Babies": Saving Ontario Mothers and Children, 1900–1940* (Montréal: McGill-Queen's University Press, 1993).
7 "L'école de réforme, formule nécessaire.... La pédiatrie et son rôle dans Québec," *La Presse,* 11 March 1944. This excerpt is taken from a testimony to audiences of

the Garneau Commission on health insurance in Québec. In contrast, Comacchio's work (*Nations Are Built of Babies*) brings to light many moments over the course of the previous decades when doctors denied such a link between sickness and poverty even when it was uncovered in their own studies.

8 Dennis Guest, *The Emergence of Social Security in Canada* (Vancouver: University of British Columbia Press, 1981), 129–31.

9 Canada, *Débats de la Chambre des communes,* 1944, 11. For the same phenomenon in England, see Rob Watts, "Family Allowances in Canada and Australia, 1940–1945: A Comparative Critical Case Study," *Journal of Social Policy* 16, no. 1 (1987): 44.

10 Roger Lesgards, "Trompeuses sirènes au cœur froid," *Le Monde diplomatique,* January 1994, 32; and Boudon and Bourricaud, "Égalitarisme," 215–17.

11 Robert Rumilly, *Maurice Duplessis et son temps,* vol. 2 (Montréal: Fides, 1973), 499, 236; and Elwood Jones, "Dependency and Social Welfare," *Journal of Canadian Studies/Revue d'études canadiennes* 14, no. 1 (1979): 2.

12 Canada, Advisory Committee on Reconstruction, VI, *Post-War Problems of Women: Final Report of the Subcommittee* (Ottawa: King's Printer, 1944), 10–11. The committee meanwhile put full employment and the end of the shortage before this recommendation, which situated it more resolutely among the promoters of universal economic rights.

13 Lawyer from the Montréal Juvenile Court, cited in Valère Massicotte, "La délinquance juvenile et la guerre," *L'Œuvre des tracts,* April 1944, 10; and "Déclaration sur les droits de l'enfant: Signée par les représentants des Églises catholique, anglicane, russe orthodoxe, presbytérienne, unie, baptiste et de l'armée du salut," *La Presse,* 11 March 1943.

14 NAC, RG 29, vol. 1934, R233/100–6/25, DHNW Minister George Davidson, "Maintenance as an Eligibility Factor: Dr. Davidson's Remark at Supervisors' conference with Introductory Discussion," Ottawa, ON, March 1948.

15 *Débats,* 1944, 5336.

16 J.L. Granatstein, *Canada's War: The Politics of the Mackenzie King Government, 1939–1945* (Toronto: Oxford University Press, 1975), 273, 282; "Importance pour la jeunesse de continuer sa formation scolaire et technique," *La Gazette du travail,* October 1940, 1051; "Emploi des enfants et fréquentation scolaire au Canada: Comparaison avec la législation en Grande-Bretagne et aux États-Unis," *La Gazette du travail,* January 1942, 48; ANQQ, Ministry of Labour, E 24, 222, A-8, Macnamara to Tremblay, 5 July 1943, 1 July 1943, 3 February 1944; *Débats,* 1944, 5558, 5948; and *Débats,* 1946, 2788.

17 *Débats,* 1944, 2960.

18 *Débats,* 1946, 4592.

19 *Débats,* 1944, 2788. From 1953 on, new rules permitted the payments to go directly to parents on the recommendation of the Department of Mines and Resources and the Department of Economic Development (*ARDHNW, 1952–1953,* 89; "Règlements sur les allocations familiales," P.C. 5093, *La Gazette du Canada* 79, no. 34 (25 August 1945): 3757–58; Andrew Webster, "The Political Economy of Indian Relief, 1900–1956" [M.A. diss., Carleton University, 1993]; and *ARDHNW, 1949–1950,* 150).

20 Louis Saint-Laurent, *Débats,* 1944, 5896; and Paul Martin, *Débats,* 1949, 2565.

21 Compton Liberal Deputy Blanchette, *Débats,* 1944, 5568; and Dorothée H. Stepler, *Les allocations familiales au Canada,* no. 362 (Montréal: École sociale populaire, 1943), 23.

22 "Graves fautes des parents en matière de fréquentation scolaire" (clergy circular), 22 August 1941, in *Mandements des évêques de Québec,* vol. 16, *1940–1943,* 249–50.

23 J.-P. Poulin, "À qui la faute? À l'école?" *Le Devoir,* 18 July 1942. Poulin was also a member of the Comité d'action familiale and secretary general of the Comité permanent des familles.

24 Leroy Ashby, "Partial Promises and Semi-Visible Youths: The Depression and World War II," in *American Childhood: A Research Guide and Historical Handbook,* eds. Joseph M. Hawes and N. Roy Hiner (Westport: Greenwood Press, 1985), 489.

25 Marcel Gauchet and Gloria Swain, *La pratique de l'esprit humain: L'institution asilaire et la révolution démocratique* (Paris: Gallimard, 1980), 18; and Lesgards, "Trompeuses sirènes au cœur froid."

26 Ashby, "Partial Promises and Semi-Visible Youths," 505; and Testimony of Brother Gaudin from the Mont-Saint-Antoine reform school at the Garneau Commission on health insurance in Québec ("L'école de réforme," *La Presse*).

27 ANQQ, Ministry of Education, E 13, C.r., 1942–96, box 2218, Regional Inspector Paul Hubert, report no. 30; and ANQQ, E 13, 1942–294, box 2235, Sagabec School Board Secretary-Treasurer J.-A. Ross, 28 March 1942.

28 Québec, DPI, *Instructions concernant la loi de fréquentation scolaire obligatoire,* 1943, 7; and Louise Charpentier, "Les programmes et les manuels d'histoire de la réforme scolaire de 1948" (M.A. diss., Université de Sherbrooke, 1983), 31. Already this "discourse of pleasure" was present in the Ontarian reformists' vocabulary in the nineteenth century. See Bruce Curtis, *Building the Educational State: Canada West, 1836–1871* (London: Althouse Press, 1988), 378–79.

29 CDSA, 1944–629, box 112 341, *Mémoire de la J.O.C. sur l'orientation des jeunes travailleurs* (report presented on the occasion of the Semaine de la propagande, 12 September 1944), 2–3; MCCCIP, 20 December 1944; MCCCIP, 26 September 1945; *ARSPI, 1944–1945,* xxii; *ARSPI, 1945–1946,* 56; and *ARSPI, 1946–1947,* 211–12, 235.

30 Tamara Hareven, "An Ambiguous Alliance: Some Aspects of American Influences on Canadian Social Welfare," *Histoire sociale/Social History* 3 (April 1969): 93. See also my "The Construction of Children as an Object of International Relations: The Declaration of Children's Rights and the Child Welfare Committee of the League of Nations, 1900–1924," *The International Journal of Children's Rights* 7, 2 (1999), 103–47.

31 "Home Thoughts: Germaine Greer on the Folly of 'Children's Rights,'" *The Independent Magazine,* 20 January 1990, 16; Gill Jones and Claire Wallace, *Youth, Family, and Citizenship* (Buckingham: Open University Press, 1992), chapters 1 and 7; and Richard Lindley, *Autonomy (Issues in Political Theory)* (London: Macmillan Education, 1986), 117–39.

32 Gauchet and Swain, *La pratique de l'esprit humain,* 16–18.

33 Jerome Kagan, "The Moral Function of the School," *Daedalus* 110 (Summer 1981): 151–65; and Hamilton Cravens, "Child-Saving in the Age of Professionalism, 1915–1930," in *American Childhood,* eds. Hawes and Hiner, 416–88.

34 Comacchio, *"Nations Are Built of Babies,"* 126–32.

35 Gauchet and Swain, *La pratique de l'esprit humain,* 23–24; and Comacchio, *"Nations Are Built of Babies,"* final chapter.

36 AMSWC, case nos. 47–1647, 47–89, 47–769.

37 ANQQ, E 24, 222, A-28, circular sent to provincial labour ministers, 26 December 1943.

38 Harold Benenson, Family and Modern Society, sociology course, McGill University, fall 1987.

39 Robert Pinker, *The Idea of Welfare* (London: Heinemann, 1979), 11; and Ashby, "Partial Promises and Semi-Visible Youth," 496, 498.

40 Hector Perrier, cited in *Le Devoir,* April 1941. See also the *Rapport de la Commission de coordination et d'examens,* adopted by the CCPIC, 17 December 1942, cited in Victor Doré, in *L'Enseignement primaire,* February 1943, 445.

41 *ARSPI, 1939–1940,* cited in Robert Rumilly, *Histoire de la province de Québec,* vol. 39, *1914* (Montréal: Fides, 1969), 47.

42 *SQ,* 1943, 7 Geo. 6, Loi concernant la fréquentation scolaire obligatoire, art. 290r; and DIP, *Instructions,* 1943, 9–11.

43 *Débats,* 1945, 3683. On the Council, see *Débats,* 1944, 5600. The Council itself played a pioneering role in this field: in 1933, the Division of Child Welfare of the Department of Health, founded in 1919, had its doctors' and social workers' educational activities taken over by the family services sector of the Council (Hareven, "An Ambiguous Alliance," 91–92). When Charlotte Whitton left the Council's direction in 1941, it ceased to oppose the allowances.

44 *Débats,* 1946, 2787–88.

45 J.-C. Falardeau et al., *Mémoire sur les allocations familiales,* report prepared at the request of Québec's Superior Labour Council, 1944, 58; Thérèse Roy, "Influence économique et sociale des allocations familiales" (M.A. diss., Université de Montréal, 1949), 59; ANQQ, E 13, C.r., 1942–96, box 2218, Froment; Alliance catholique des professeurs de Montréal, *Rapport de l'enquête de l'Alliance catholique des Professeurs de Montréal: Les réformes de l'enseignement primaire,* report prepared by Joseph Pagé, president of the subcommittee of pedagogical surveys, 1941, 28; and ANQQ, E 13, C.r., 1942–96, box 2218, *Mémoire de l'École des Hautes Études Commerciales,* report prepared by Esdras Minville for Doré, 25 March 1942.

46 *Débats,* 1944, 5600.

47 Thérèse Hamel, "L'obligation scolaire au Québec: Lieu et enjeu de la lutte des classes" (Ph.D. diss., Paris V René Descartes, 1981), 314, 377, 399; Les fils du sol, Saint-Jean de Dieu, "L'école primaire et nos jeunes garçons," *La Terre de chez nous,* 19 December 1943, 3; ANQQ, E 13, C.g., 1939–1082, General Inspector of Primary Schools C.-J. Miller and B.-O. Filteau to Doré, 20 March 1940; Jean-Pierre Kesteman, *Histoire du syndicalisme agricole au Québec, UCC-UPA, 1924–1984* (Montréal: Boréal Express, 1984), 174; *Débats,* 1944, 5558, 5600; *Débats,* 1946, 2787–88; and *Débats,* 1950, 4030–31. The Advisory Committee on Reconstruction shared the belief that family allowances were used poorly for reasons of ignorance rather than incompetence. It also believed in the necessity of supervising parents lacking willpower or those who might be incompetent (*Post-War Problems of Women,* 30).

48 Canada, DHNW, *You and Your Family* (Ottawa: King's Printer, 1949), 21–22.

49 Interview with P.-A. Fournier, Sillery, QC, September 1988.

50 NAC, RG 29, 1934, R233/100/13, Research Division, 1946, 7. See also Canada, DHNW, *Allocations familiales: Charte de l'enfance* (Ottawa: King's Printer, 1945–1946), 9; AQRO, 40–15, "What They Are Saying about Family Allowances," *This Week,* CBC broadcast, 5 October 1946, 7; and NAC/NFTSA, DHNW folder, acc. 1984–0121, no. 62020, *Peppo et le Chèque des allocations familiales* (NFB, 1946), film clip, 76 tables, 35 mm, silent with French subtitles or with sound recording. On other countries, Jane Lewis, *The Politics of Motherhood: Child and Maternal Welfare in England, 1900–1939* (Montréal: McGill-Queen's University Press, 1980); J. S. Hurt, *Elementary Schooling and the Working Classes, 1860–1918* (London: Routledge & Kegan Paul, 1979), 114; and Cravens, "Child-Saving," 438.

51 DHNW, *You and Your Family,* 26 (original text in English).

52 Harrison, cited in Jones and Wallace, *Youth, Family, and Citizenship,* 22.

53 The great change in welfare financing was also at the root of the different tones of the two images: assured of the revenues of income tax, the State was freed from having to use representations of children as victims. Before this time, private charity associations, which had the task of collecting donations, had used these images of victimhood to attract possible donors.

54 AQRO, 40–13, vol. 1, rough draft of booklet on family allowances, April 1948. The *You and Your Family* brochure reproduced this text almost exactly, with the exception of the phrase "very remote," which was changed to "rather fantastic" (original text in English).

55 DNHW, *You and Your Family,* 4, 21; *Débats,* 1944, 5231, 5233, 5593, 5698, 5740; and *Débats,* 1947, 4462.

56 Canada, DHNW, *En parlant des allocations familiales* (Ottawa: King's Printer, 1950). The brochure, a French translation of *Speaking of Family Allowances,* constituted an abridged version of a freeze-frame produced in collaboration with the NFB: NAC/NFTSA, DHNW folder, acc. 1982–0121, no. 62077, *Parlons des allocations familiales* (NFB, 1949), film clip, 35 mm, silent with French subtitles or with sound recording.

57 Arlene Skolnick, *Embattled Paradise: The American Family in an Age of Uncertainty* (New York: Basic Books, 1991), 66–67.

58 NAC, RG 29, vol. 1283, *ARSWSQRO, 1954–1955* (original in English). The regional allowances bureaus also aimed to act as information agencies on available social services (National Head of Welfare Services R.H. Parkinson, "Ten Years of Family Allowances," *Canadian Welfare* 21, no. 4 [1955]: 195–200).

59 Boudon and Bourricaud, "Égalitarisme," 218.

60 Boudon and Bourricaud, "Égalitarisme," 217–18.

61 ANQQ, E 13, C.r., 1942–199, box 2223, Bilodeau to Doré, notes for the superintendent on compulsory attendance in the United States, 10 December 1942.

62 Boudon and Bourricaud, "Égalitarisme," 217–18.

63 *ARSPI, 1943–1944,* xiii.

64 *SQ,* 8 Geo. 6, art. 5; and DNHW, *You and Your Family,* 11.

65 "What The Are Saying about Family Allowances?"; *Débats,* 1944, 5555; and Falardeau et al., *Mémoire sur les allocations familiales,* 39–40.

66 A.M. Willms, "Setting Up Family Allowances, 1944–1945" (M.A. diss., Carleton University, 1962), 31; Edward E. Schwartz, "Some Observations on the Canadian Family Allowances Program," *The Social Service Review* 20, no. 4 (1946): 456; and AMSWC, case no. 1946–254. Investigators occasionally offered advice by preparing budgets for families (AMSWC, case no. 47–1967).

67 AQRO, 8–0, vol. 1, Rolland MacKinnon, reporting the secretary's remarks to N.-R. Boutin (both were employees at the QRO), 12 May 1945.

68 DPI, *Instructions,* 1943, 12. This analysis of the ideological meaning of the categories is drawn from Curtis, *Building the Educational State,* 374; and ASJCF, 126–2, P.-É. Beaudoin, *1941–1942 School Survey: Study on the age of admission to the first normal degree of primary education in the province of Québec, Preliminary report,* 29 April 1944, 4.

69 CDSA, 1946–789, box 112 398, Omer Bédard, *Annual Report, 1943–1944.*

70 AMSWC, cases nos. 45–9913, 46–1830, 46–1806, 47–493, 47–1647, 46–1830, 45–8486, 46–9802, 48–156, 46–902, 41–371, 48–362, 46–254, 46–1654, 47–307, 47–630, 47–754, 48–55, 47–224.

71 ANQQ, E 13, C.r., 1942–199, Assistant Attorney-General Léopold Désilets, 11 August 1943; and Marcel Blouin, "La Cour du bien-être social, son historique, ses rouages, son rôle," *La Presse,* 24 June 1956.

72 AMCSC, Students, School Attendance, Compulsory Education, 1914–1962, Doré to Marc Jarry, 5 May 1944, and Jarry to Doré, 17 April 1944; and AMCSC, Students, Absence Monitoring, and Annual Reports, 1924–1969, Dupire to Émile Girardin, 21 February 1956.

73 AMSWC, case no. 1946–296, Judge Nicholson to Brown, 3 May 1946 (original text in English).

74 DPI, *Instructions,* 1943, 3; Speech made in 1943 in the legislative assembly; and Robert Rumilly, *Histoire de la province de Québec,* vol. 41, *La guerre de 1939–1945: Duplessis reprend les rennes* (Montréal: Fides, 1969), 76.

75 Jones and Wallace, *Youth, Family, and Citizenship.*

76 Monseigneur L.-A. Paquet in 1909, cited in Ruby Heap, "L'Église, l'État, et l'enseignement primaire public catholique au Québec, 1897–1920" (Ph.D. diss., Université de Montréal, 1987), 871.

77 Father Hermas Lalande, SJ, *L'instruction obligatoire: Principes et conséquences* (Montréal: Imprimerie du messager, 1919), 6, 25. According to Monseigneur Paquet, Canada's most popular theologian and a specialist in education, this theory was in accordance with the Cardinal's opinion and the philosophical teaching of the seminaries and colleges. See also Michel Brunet, "Trois dominantes de la pensée canadienne-française: L'agriculturisme, l'anti-étatisme, et le messianisme," in *La présence anglaise et les Canadiens: Études sur l'histoire de la pensée des deux Canadas* (Montréal: Beauchemin, 1964), 157.

78 Speech by Pie XI, cited in DPI, *Instructions,* 1943, 3.

79 Carole Pateman, "Feminist Critiques of the Public/Private Dichotomy," in *The Disorder of Women: Democracy, Feminism, and Political Theory,* ed. Carole Pateman (Cambridge: Polity, 1989), 118–40; and Pinker, *The Idea of Welfare,* 11–12.

80 *Débats,* 1944, 5546.

81 This report called for the abolition of this exemption once the family allowances were in place (Advisory Committee on Reconstruction, *Post-War Problems of Women,* 30–31).

82 "Le Conseil législative adopte la loi de l'instruction obligatoire," *Le Monde ouvrier,* 22 May 1943, p. 1.

83 Edmond Turcottte, "L'attitude du Dr. Albiny Paquette," *Le Canada,* 1 May 1943, p. 4.

84 Leonard Marsh, *Report on Social Security for Canada* (1943; reprint, Toronto: University of Toronto Press, 1975), 199. Constitutional imperatives already obliged Mackenzie King to count on parents' freedom to register for the family allowances programs so that the law would not be contested.

85 Falardeau et al., *Mémoire sur les allocations familiales,* 23–24.

86 Peel Conservative Deputy Gordon Graydon, *Débats,* 1944, 5538; and *Débats,* 1944, 5540, 5903, 5932.

Chapter 4

1 The correspondence connected with the spread of information at the outset of compulsory education is held at the CDSA, box 112 317. See also ANQQ, Ministry of Education, E 13, 1942–199, box 2223, Mégantic School Inspector A. Breton to Victor Doré, 25 September 1943, and District Inspector Didier Savard to C.-J. Miller,

4 March 1944; *ARSPI, 1943–1944,* xiii, 8, 39, 75; *ARSPI, 1950–1951,* 19; and Gérard Filion, *Les confidences d'un commissaire d'écoles* (Montréal: Éditions de l'Homme, 1960), 76. On the publicity surrounding the beginning of family allowances, see Mark E. Palmer, "The Origins and Implementation of Family Allowances in Canada" (M.A. diss., Queen's University, 1976), 231; NAC/NFTSA, acc. 1973–0162CAVA/AVCA: 1973–0162, no. 1973–0162, *Prince Edward Islanders Register for Family Allowances* (Canadian Army Film and Photo Unit, 1945), 16 mm; NAC/NFTSA, acc. 1980–0175, no. 23429, *PEI Family Allowance Registration* (Fox Movietone News, 1945), 35 mm, black and white, English subtitles; NAC/NFTSA, acc. 1980–0197, no. 21867, *Family Allowances Plan Starts in Canada* (Twentieth Century Fox Film Corporation, 1945), 35 mm, English subtitles; and AQRO, 40–13, vol. 1, individual letter to mothers, 8 September 1950. The family allowances kiosks in Trois-Rivières, Sherbrooke, and Québec in 1950 were visited by 125,000 people (*ARQRO, 1950,* 6). Between 1947 and 1949, thirty rural daily papers published a weekly column of questions and answers on allowances, the combined print run being 500,000 copies (*ARQRO, 1947,* 2; and AQRO, 3–4, Lafrance to Curry, 11 April 1949).

2 ANQQ, E 13, C.r., 1942–199, box 2223, Doré to Guy Gagnon of the Canadian Press and *Le Soleil,* 16 December 1943; DPI legal advisor Ph.-A. Miller, *Administration et législation du système scolaire de la province de Québec,* 1954, cited in Louis-Philippe Audet, *Histoire de l'enseignement au Québec,* vol. 2 (Montréal: Holt, Rinehart, & Winston, 1971), 256, 276; AQRO, 8–0, vol. 2, Bernard Dupire to C.-O. Bilodeau, 27 April 1956; *ARPSBGM, 1952–1953,* 29; and Walter Pilling Percival, *Across the Years: A Century of Education in the Province of Quebec* (Montréal: Gazette Printing, 1946), 194.

3 *ARSPI, 1943–1944,* xiii.

4 *ARSPI, 1943–1944,* 205 (see also pp. 125, 59, 104); ANQQ, E 13, C.r., 1942–199, box 2223, J.-D. Ducharme to Doré, 30 October 1943, Rose and Blanche Lapierre to Doré, 26 June 1944, and F. Royer to Doré, 20 November 1943.

5 AQRO, 8–0, vol. 1, Curry to Lafrance, 6 July 1948; ACSCM, 1656, 1—34/07; Québec, DPI, Statistical Research Service, *Recensement scolaire, septembre 1943,* 1944, 2, 3, 77, 79, 141, 143; Québec, DPI, Statistical Research Service, *Recensement scolaire, septembre 1944,* 1945, 2, 3, 78; and John Porter, *The Vertical Mosaic: An Analysis of Social Class and Power in Canada* (Toronto: University of Toronto Press, 1965), 175.

6 *ARSPI, 1948–1949,* 62. He had already made the same statement in his 1944–45 statement (*ARSPI, 1944–1945,* 7).

7 *ARSPI, 1943–1944,* 125; *ARSPI, 1944–1945,* 201; *ARSPI, 1945–1946,* 227; *ARSPI, 1948–1949,* 254; and Percival, *Across the Years,* 194. In the year 1943–44, 3,696 boys and 2,695 girls in the province's urban districts had been absent for more than ten days for "abnormal" reasons; the following year, their numbers decreased to 3,056 and 1,650, respectively (Québec, DPI, Statistical Research Service, *Rapports de juin 1945;* Québec, DPI, Statistical Research Service, *Organisations scolaire et aperçus pédagogiques,* 1945, 7; and Québec, DPI, Statistical Research Service, *Rapports de juin 1946*).

8 Dominique Jean, "Familles québécoises et politiques sociales touchant les enfants, de 1940 à 1960: Obligation scolaire, allocations familiales, et travail juvénile," (Ph.D. diss., Université de Montréal, 1988), figure 5; CDSA, 1946–789, box 112 398, Mégantic Truancy Officer Madame A. Breton, *Rapport Annuel, 1943–1944; ARSPI, 1943–1944,* 23; *ARPBSCCM, 1948–1949,* 6; DPI, *Rapports de juin 1945,* 6–8; and DPI, *Rapports de juin 1946.*

9 *RACA de Saint-Fortunat,* 8 August 1944; *RACA de Saint-Clément* (Rivière-du-Loup County), 7 July 1944; *RACA de Mégantic* (Compton County), 1944, 2; and *RACA de Thetford-Mines,* 26 June 1946 (all in CDSA, 46–789, box 112 398).

10 *ARSPI, 1945–1946,* 231; and *ARSWSQRO, 1954–1955,* 6.

11 Everett Hughes, *French Canada in Transition* (Chicago: University of Chicago Press, 1943), 108–109; and Chad Gaffield, "Demography, Social Structure, and the History of Schooling," in *Approaches to Educational History,* no. 5 in *Monographs in Education,* ed. Jones et al. (Winnipeg: University of Manitoba Press, 1981), 95.

12 CDSA, 1943–1200, box 112 317, parts 1–6, "Exemptions de fréquentation scolaire," one of ten similar cases. This correspondence between parents and the SPI is less and less abundant with the passing years. The series ends, abruptly, in 1950. I have studied in detail the first part, 150 letters dated from July 1943 to September 1943; a portion of the fifth part, 50 letters dated from September 1945 to February 1949; and the last 50 letters, dated from September 1949 to December 1949. I have numbered these files to abbreviate references. See also ANQQ, E 13, 1942–199, box 2223, M.E. of Portage-Griffon, Gaspé, to Godbout, 1 October 1943; and CDSA, 1943–1080, box 112 317, Madame F., 8 November 1947. On the threat of sanctions, see Philip Corrigan and Derek Sayer, *The Great Arch: English State Formation as Cultural Revolution* (Oxford: Basil Blackwell, 1985), 114ff.

13 *ARSPI, 1945–1946,* 227.

14 DPI, *Rapports de juin 1945,* 6–8; DPI, *Rapports de juin 1946;* and Jean, "Familles québécoises et politiques sociales," figure 4.

15 Cited in *RAMSNBES, 1954–1955,* 118; the province is not named.

16 Jean, "Familles québécoises et politiques sociales," table 8. The tables on the household incomes to which the following pages refer are based on the following surveys: R. Blishen, J. Cawley, and J.E. Pears, "Family Allowances in Montreal: A Study of Their Uses and Meaning in a Selected Group of Wage-Earning Families" (M.A. diss., McGill University, 1948); NAC, RG 29, R233/100–63–2, Maurice Tremblay, Albert Faucher, and J.-C. Falardeau, *Family Allowances in Québec City: Report of a Study in the Faculty of Social Sciences of Laval University,* translation of the DHNW document, 1951; Thérèse Légaré, "Conditions économiques et sociales des familles de Gaspé-Nord, Québec" (Faculté des sciences sociales, Université Laval, 1947); NAC, RG29, R233/105–13/5, M.A. Macnaughton and G. Laflèche, *Preliminary Report on Distribution and Use of Family Allowances Payments in Nicolet County, Québec, 1947–1948,* prepared for the Economic Division, Marketing Service, Department of Agriculture (Ottawa: King's Printer, 1948); Thérèse Roy, "Influence économique et sociale des allocations familiales" (M.A. diss., Université de Montréal, 1949); Derek Griffin, *Family Budgets of Wage-Earners in Four Maritimes Communities, 1947* (Halifax: Dalhousie University, Institute of Public Affairs, 1952); and M.A. Macnaughton and J.M. Mann, *Distribution and Use of Family Allowances Payments in Three Areas of the Prairie Provinces,* publication 815, technical bulletin 69, supplement to M.A. Macnaughton and M.E. Andal, *Changes in Farm Family Living in Three Areas of the Prairie Provinces, from 1943 to 1947,* prepared for the Economic Division, Marketing Service, Departments of Agriculture and National Health and Welfare in co-operation with the Universities of Alberta and Saskatchewan (Ottawa: King's Printer, 1949). Many of the figures also appear in my article "Family Allowances and Family Autonomy: Québec, 1945–1955," in *Canadian Family History: Selected Readings,* ed. Bettina Bradbury (Toronto: Copp Clark, 1992), 401–437.

17 AQRO, Surveys and Studies, 40–20, vol. 1, *Ten Family Surveys,* April 1947, case no. 1, and August 1947, case nos. 2, 4, 5–10.

18 AQRO, 42–25, Senez, "Les allocations familiales en relation avec la fréquentation scolaire" (talk given at the Congrès annuel de l'Association des commissions scolaires, 25 November 1956); *RAMSNBES, 1950–1951,* 84; *RAMSNBES, 1953–1954,* 112; Mae Flemming, "Family Allowances in Canada: Interim Report on Effects," *Canadian Welfare* 22, no. 6 (1946): 11; R.H. Parkinson, "Ten Years of Family Allowances," *Canadian Welfare* 31, no. 4 (1955): 195–200; and Bernice Madison, "Canadian Family Allowances and Their Major Social Implications," *Journal of Marriage and the Family* 26, no. 2 (1964): 138.

19 AQRO, 8–0, vol. 1, 31 August 1949 annex to a letter from Fournier to Lafrance, 21 March 1950. In Montréal as well, attendance increased "greatly" following the efforts of the Regional Office of Family Allowance, according to AMCSC, 4. Students, 6. Compulsory Education, 1914–1962, MCSC General Director Eugène Simard to Curry, 6 November 1947, p. 4, and *ARPBSCCM, 1949–1959,* 11.

20 *ARQRO, 1952–1953,* 9.

21 Jean, "Familles québécoises et politiques sociales," table 4, based on the federal department's annual reports.

22 DPI, *Recensement 1943,* 3, 77, 79, 141, 143; DPI, *Recensement 1944,* 3; DPI, *Rapports de juin 1945,* 6–8; and DPI, *Rapports de juin 1946.*

23 ASJCF, 126–11, DPI, *Enquête scolaire, 1941–1942,* iii–20, iii–21 (figures for students across the province registered in school from 1940 to 1941 but unregistered from 1941 to 1942 and students attending French classes are used in Jean, "Familles québécoises et politiques sociales," table 9).

24 ASJCF, 126–11, DPI, *Enquête scolaire, 1941–1942,* ii–18, iii–19, iii–24 (figures for students across the province registered in school from 1940 to 1941 but unregistered from 1941 to 1942 and students attending French classes); and Canada, Dominion Bureau of Statistics, *Recensement du Canada (RC), 1921,* vol. 4, table 4; *RC, 1931,* vol. 7, table 40; *RC, 1941,* vol. 7, tables 4 and 5; *RC, 1951,* vol. 4, tables 3 and 11; and *RC, 1961,* vol. 3.2, bulletin 3.2–8. These figures are reproduced in Jean, "Familles québécoises et politiques sociales," tables 6 and 10 and are taken up in "The Decline of Child Labour in Quebec, 1940–1960: Conflict between Poor Families and the State," in *Historical Perspectives on Law and Society in Canada,* eds. Tina Loo and Lorna McLean (Mississauga, ON: Copp Clark, 1994), 254–88.

25 This type of generalization was often the result of a hasty interpretation of significant statistical correlations, such as those Murdoch C. MacLean had traced in 1931 between parents' illiteracy and children's absence from school (*Alphabétisme et fréquentation scolaire,* monograph no. 5 in Dominion Bureau of Statistics, *Recensement du Canada, 1931* [Ottawa: King's Printer, 1937], 23–25).

26 Gérald Fortin, "Socio-Cultural Changes in an Agricultural Parish," in *French-Canadian Society,* vol. 2, eds. Marcel Rioux and Yves Martin (Toronto: McClelland & Stewart, 1963), 105.

27 Of the 1,150 wage-earning fathers interviewed in 1959, 79 per cent wished they had had more education themselves (Marc-Adélard Tremblay, Gérald Fortin, and Marc Laplante, *Les comportements économiques de la famille salariée du Québec* [Québec: Presses de l'Université Laval, 1964], 223). See also CDSA, 1943–1200, box 112 317, Madame G., 13 August 1943, Madame L. Pellegrin, September 1943, Madame O., 16 August 1943; and ANQQ, E 13, 1942–294, J.A. Ross, report no. 82. For an earlier example of this type of attitude in southwest Montréal, see Denyse Baillargeon, *Ménagères au temps de la crise* (Montréal: Remue-Ménage, 1993), 103.

28 JOC, "Le problème des jeunes qui ne fréquentent plus l'école," *École sociale populaire* 351 (April 1942): 30. The memory of the 1930s influenced parents' values in many other ways; while some carried forward unfulfilled hopes, others perpetuated habits acquired during the years of misery. See CDSA, 1946–789, box 112 398, M.L. de Saint-Lasarre to Doré, 4 July 1944; and P.-A. Linteau et al., *Histoire du Québec contemporain,* vol. 2, *Le Québec depuis 1930* (Montréal: Boréal, 1986), 93.

29 Delphine Périard, "Fréquentation scolaire en regard du milieu familial et des parents" (report, Université de Montréal, 1952), 39–40; CDSA, 1946–789, box 112 398, *RACA de Saint-Léon-le-Grand, 1943–1944;* CDSA 1943–1200, box 112 317, case nos. 35, 37, 64, 107, 128, 136, 138, 5–5, 5–4, 6–2, 6–11, 6–17, 6–46; CDSA, 44–879, box 112 346, N. Veilleux to Doré, 27 July 1944; Tremblay, Fortin, and Laplante, *Les comportements économiques,* 221; *ARSPI, 1946–1947,* 100; PVC-SCM, 4 December 1944; and ANQQ, E 13, C.r., 1942–199, box 2223, J.-D. Ducharme to Doré, 30 October 1943.

30 1943, 7 Geo. 6, art. 290b: 30 April 1943, ANQQ, E24, 209, A-8; 25 July 1951, ANQQ, E24, Provincial Supplement Agency, 306, E3, miscellaneous. The permit was issued in the case of summer work (ANQQ, Ministry of Labour, E 24, 222, J.L. Brissette of the Saint-Jérôme Inspection Service, 11 November 1943). See also ANQQ, E 24, 222, A. Otis of Drummondville to the minister, 10 February 1944; AMSWC, 47–1507; AQRO, 7–6, vol. 1, Fournier to Lafrance, 25 February 1949, Curry to Lafrance, 11 May 1946 (which studied family allowances admissibility in this situation); and ANQQ, E 24, 235, J.-O. Ricard, 29 July 1944.

31 Bernier to Rochette, 31 March 1943; Maher to Garneau, 7 July 1944; Beaulac to Maher, 16 August 1944; Inspector A. Rivest to Bernier, 26 October 1944; Beaulac to Tremblay, 4 May 1945; and Tremblay to Beaulac, 31 October 1945 (in ANQQ, E 24, 209, 235, 251, A-8).

32 Canada, *Débats de la Chambre des communes,* 1944, 5560–61. For a similar argument put forward by the Family Endowment Society in England in the 1920s, see Jane Lewis, "The English Movement for Family Allowances, 1917–1945" *Histoire sociale/Social History* 11, no. 22 (1978): 447.

33 Deputy Minister of Labour Tremblay to Beaulac, 27 April 1945. In 1897, it appeared to Deputy Minister Louis Guyon that the limit, in the eyes of employers, was approximately twelve years of age: "All the exhortations we would make to parents to encourage them to keep their children in school," he still remarked in 1921, "will never have as much effect as the loss of wages the child brings home on the family budget" (*RGMTQ, 1920–1921,* 86). In 1921, the QDL was still torn between the desire to educate children and an awareness of their economic role in many families (Terry Copp, *Classe ouvrière et pauvreté: Les conditions de vie des travailleurs montréalais, 1897–1929* [Montréal: Boréal Express, 1978], 86). In 1933, the Montpetit Commission's second report on social insurance in Québec had concluded that it was "very difficult to earn a living" at fourteen years old; the commission proposed increasing the age at which boys could leave industrial school to sixteen (Commission sur les assurances sociales de Québec, *2e rapport,* 18).

34 ANQQ, E 24, 193, A-8, W.L. Bogie to Hector Perrier, 26 June 1941.

35 Letter to Mr. Minister, March 1945. In the margin, a handwritten note ("two inspections, Québec-Montréal. Visited.") indicates the minister's reaction (ANQQ, E 24, 222, A-8, Tremblay to Phillips, 9 December 1943, and Tremblay to Filteau, 14 April 1944).

36 ANQQ, E 24, 235, A-8, Bernier to Barrette, 5 April 1945.

37 "Emploi des enfants et fréquentation scolaire au Canada: Comparaison avec la législation en Grande-Bretagne et aux États-Unis," *La Gazette du travail,* January

1942, 48; the article refers to British and American studies that established the same correlation. On the researchers at the McGill Social Science Research Project, see Marlene Shore, *The Science of Social Redemption: McGill, the Chicago School, and the Origins of Social Research in Canada* (Toronto: University of Toronto Press, 1987), 206–209; and MacLean, *Alphabétisme et fréquentation scolaire,* 73. In 1937, a study on arts and trades schools had compared the earnings of two groups: 215 young people who had left school at eighteen years of age with technical training and 584 young people who had left school at fourteen years of age. It demonstrated that the first group's earnings exceeded the second's and that the gap increased with age to reach 200 per cent at twenty-four years of age (ASJCF, box 234–5, item 7, DPI, "L'éducation est un placement," mimeographed document prepared by P.-É. Beaudoin, undated).

38 ANQQ, E 24, 222, A-8, circular to the provincial labour ministers, 26 December 1943.

39 Shore, *The Science of Social Redemption,* 229; and Rob Watts, "Family Allowances in Canada and Australia, 1940–1945: A Comparative Critical Case Study," *Journal of Social Policy* 16, no. 1 (1987): 29. In the year 1937–38, the Dominion Bureau of Statistics led investigations on incomes and moving expenses, on which results reformists could now base their claim. See, for example, Dorothée H. Stepler, *Les allocations familiales au Canada,* no. 362 (Montréal: École sociale populaire, 1943), 23; Stepler used these statistics to reveal that 43 per cent of heads of household did not earn enough to feed their families sufficiently. Watts demonstrates that in Australia, these figures were available early thanks to the existence of a central authority that set the country's wages. On the same effect of the Depression in England, see Lewis, "The English Movement for Family Allowances," 454–55.

40 Canada, DNHW, *Allocations familiales: Charte de l'enfance* (Ottawa: King's Printer, 1945–1946), 2–3. The brochure was created for those who had to provide information about the allowances.

41 ANQQ, E 24, 209, A-8, Bernier to Barrette, 31 March 1943.

42 Guyon to Maher, 30 July 1942; Beaulac to a citizen of Nazareth, 29 April 1943; J.-O. Ricard, 29 July 1944; J.-L. Blanchard to Tremblay, 10 October 1946; Paul Brien to Beaulac, 2 August 1949, and Beaulac's response, 8 August 1949; Jules Biron to Barrette, 2 August 1950, and Barrette's response, 9 August 1950 (in ANQQ, E 24, 209, 222, 235, A-8). The first breach discovered in this inflexible policy was formed in 1951 because of, likely, the replacement of the assistant deputy; the new agent accepted that a widow who had been recently hospitalized placed her fourteen-year-old daughter with the Grand-Mère Shoe Company (Donat Quimper to P. Parent, head of hiring at the Grand-Mère Shoe Company, 30 March 1951). Another favour of this kind was awarded to a citizen in the Laviolette County, 7 July 1954 (ANQQ, E 24, 302, 312, A-8).

43 ANQQ, E 24, 209, 235, 251, A-8, Bernier to Rochette, 31 March 1943.

44 ANQQ, E 24, 193, A-8, Bernier to Maher, 22 September 1941, and Maher to Bernier, 24 September 1941.

45 ANQQ, E 24, 222, A-8, Bernier to Tremblay, 1 December 1943.

46 ANQQ, E 24, 312, A-8, Tremblay to Beaulac, 30 August 1954. For a comparable argument put forward by the federal minister of labour, see "Emploi des enfants et fréquentation scolaire au Canada," 58.

47 Described in J.L. Granatstein et al., *Twentieth-Century Canada,* 2nd ed. (Toronto: McGraw-Hill Ryerson), 342.

48 Léon Lebel, *Les allocation familiales: Solution du problème des familles nombreuses,* nos. 159–60 (Montréal: École sociale populaire, 1927), 43. See also J.-A.

Beaudoin, "L'hygiène à la campagne," *Semaines sociales du Canada*, 8th session, 152–72.

49 Jeunesse agricole catholique and Jeunesse ouvrière catholique, cited in Émilia Lacroix, "Le service domestique et la désertion des campagnes," *Le Devoir,* 5 November 1941, p. 2; and JOC, *Mémoire sur l'orientation professionnelle,* 1944, 5. Maximilien Caron had proposed a list of advantages the family allowances would bring to the country: "Farmers need a cash income to pay for certain foods, doctors' services, and, in particular, to ensure the instruction and establishment of their sons and daughters" ("Les familles nombreuses, la législation fiscale, et les allocations familiales," *La semaine nationale de la famille, École Sociale Populaire* no. 373–74 [February/March 1945]: 40). See also François-Albert Angers, cited in Michel Brunet, "Trois dominantes de la pensée canadienne-française: L'agriculturisme, l'anti-étatisme, et le messianisme," in *La présence anglaise et les Canadiens: Études sur l'histoire de la pensée des deux Canadas* (Montréal: Beauchemin, 1964), 139.

50 Stepler, *Les allocations familiales au Canada,* 26–27. Stepler also insisted that rural families raised relatively more children. Harry M. Cassidy, *Public Health and Welfare Reorganization: The Postwar Problem in the Canadian Provinces* (Toronto: Ryerson Press, 1945), 379n. 21.

51 Canada, *Débats,* 1944, 5543.

52 In *La Terre de chez nous*, 1 August 1945. See also Roger De Bellefeuille, "Les allocations familiales et la jeunesse agricole," *Revue Desjardins* 11, no. 6 (1945): 102.

53 Canada, *Débats,* 1949, 180.

54 Jeanne Grisé-Allard, "Les allocations familiales: Un chèque bien employé," *Relations* 7, no. 92 (1948): 240.

55 Edward E. Schwartz, "Some Observations on the Canadian Family Allowances Program," *The Social Service Review* 20, no. 4 (1946); Légaré, "Conditions économiques et sociales," 52, 74; and Nora Fox, "Family Allowances in Northern Ontario," *The Social Worker* 15, no. 3 (1947): 26, 35.

56 Horace Miner, *St-Denis: A French-Canadian Paris* (Chicago: University of Chicago Press, 1963), 258–60, 267–69. In Nicolet as well, Macnaughton and Laflèche found that the family allowances had freed families from their juvenile-labour needs (*Preliminary Report,* 10). However, the connections between mechanization and the need for labour were more complex according to George Haythorne and Leonard Marsh, *Land and Labour: A Social Survey of Agricultural and Farm Labour Market in Central Canada* (Montréal: McGill-Queen's University Press, 1941), 234.

57 For the children living in the country and on farms, see Canada, Dominion Bureau of Statistics, *Recensement du Canada (RC), 1941,* vol. 1, table 21; *RC, 1951,* vol. 1, table 21; and Jean, "Familles québécoises et politiques sociales," table 6, which also appears in Jean, "Le recul du travail des enfants."

58 Canada, *Débats,* 1948, 5485.

59 The precise payments were five, six, seven, or eight dollars per child depending on age (Statistics Canada, *Sécurité sociale: Programmes nationaux [Une revue pour la période 1946 à 1975]* [Ottawa: 1976], 246, 248, 530, 535). The sum of all the "transfers to households...paid by public administrations" represented far more—11.75 per cent of incomes in 1946, a considerable contribution when one recalls that it was 1.1 per cent in 1926, 5.5 per cent in 1936, and 3.4 per cent in 1941 (Jean-Pierre Charland, with the participation of Mario Désautels, *Système technique et bonheur domestique: Rémunération, consommation et pauvreté au Québec, 1920–1960,* no. 28 in "Documents de recherche" collection [Québec: Institut québé-

cois de recherche sur la culture, 1992], 71, 117–20). See also Jean, "Familles québécoises et politiques sociales," table 5.

60 Agnes Tennant, "Family Allowances Story," *The Social Worker* 15, no. 3 (1947): 27–28.

61 *ARSWSQRO, 1949–1950,* 13–14; and Québec, *Premier rapport de la Commission d'assurance-maladie de Québec sur le problème des garderies et de la protection de l'enfance,* 1944, 8.

62 Québec, *Rapport de la commission d'enquête sur les problèmes constitutionnels* (Tremblay Report), vol. 3, table 1 (Québec: Eugène Doucet Imprimeur, 1956), 81.

63 Griffin, *Family Budgets of Wage-Earners,* 81, examines this phenomenon in detail.

64 Blishen, Cawley, and Pearson, "Family Allowances in Montreal," 107.

65 *RAMSNBES, 1950–1951,* 81. At the time of the writing of the report, the distribution had not been completed in Manitoba, Saskatchewan, or New Brunswick. In Québec only, the QRO received 195,000 requests (AQRO, 40–13, vol. 1, 23 April 1950). In Cap-de-la-Madeleine, the health officer attempted to obtain 2,000 copies for his female patients (AQRO, 40–13, vol. 1, Jacques Gauthier, 28 April 1950). His request was rejected due to a lack of available copies (AQRO, 40–13, vol. 1, Lafrance to Curry, 25 January 1951).

66 *RAMSNBES, 1948–1949; RAMSNBES, 1952–1953,* 111; and Légaré, "Conditions économiques et sociales," 74. In 1947, the NFB produced *Mother and Child,* an hour-long colour film to communicate the information contained in the book in collaboration with the DNHW. It was "presented across Canada, as well as in social committees, Catholic action committees, circles of young boys or girls, etc." (NAC, RG 29, vol. 1683, Child and Maternal Health Division, 190–3-1, Albert J. Sarrazin, "Actualités canadiennes," Service international de la Société Radio-Canada, 9 January 1949, and Judith Jasmin, producer of the Société Radio-Canada to Mademoiselle Alberte Senécal, 19 January 1949).

67 *ARQRO, 1945–1946,* 4. It is interesting to note that, in the same way, the Dominion Bureau of Statistics was preparing to make housework more visible; in 1951, it began to compile tables on citizens "busy with their own housework or with the maintenance of their own home or their own children, who had helped, in the same way, other members of the household or who would have done it if not for a passing illness" (Canada, Dominion Bureau of Statistics, "Introduction," *Recensement du Canada, 1951,* vol. 4 [Ottawa: Queen's Printer], 1953), xi.

68 Blishen, Cawley, and Pearson, "Family Allowances in Montreal," 54–55, 96–105. Furthermore, mothers had more power over the allowances paid in their names than over the fathers' tax deductions, which richer families had received since the 1910s.

69 Tremblay et al., 1951, 23.

70 Canada, *Débats,* 1944, 5910. Minutes from the meeting of the archbishops and the bishops of the province of Québec, 25 September 1945, cited in Jean Hamelin, *Histoire du catholicisme québécois: Le XXe siècle,* vol. 2, *De 1940 à nos jours* (Montréal: Boréal Express, 1984), 40; Micheline Carrier, "Les craintes de l'élite clérico-nationaliste face à la Loi des allocations familiales, 1944–1945," M.A. paper, Université Laval, 1976), 18 (copy in René Durocher's possession).

71 J.-C. Falardeau et al. *Mémoire sur les allocations familiales,* prepared at the request of Québec's Superior Labour Council, 1944, 56–57.

72 Duplessis had just abolished the council (Renée Vautelet, *Mémoire sur l'orientation du travail féminin d'après-guerre,* prepared for the Conseil d'orientation économique [published under the auspices of the FNSJB, 1944], 4, 15, 26). Vautelet

did not propose family allowances, however, as the previous allowances for soldiers' dependants, at rates not adapted for larger families, made her doubt the potential of such a policy.

73 NAC, Thérèse Casgrain Folder, MG32-C25, vol. 7, League of Women's Rights, Assembly minutes, *Rapport annuel de la secrétaire, 1945–1946*.

74 Thérèse Casgrain, *Une femme chez les hommes* (Montréal: Éditions de l'Homme, 1971), 170–74; Susan Mann Trofimenkoff, "Thérèse Casgrain and the CCF in Québec," in *Beyond the Vote: Canadian Women and Politics,* eds. Linda Kealey and Joan Sangster (Toronto: University of Toronto Press, 1989), 144.

75 *ARQRO, 1945–1946,* 2; NAC, RG 29, 1283, R266/5/45; Collectif Clio, *L'histoire des femmes au Québec depuis quatre siècles* (Montréal: Quinze, 1982), 373–76; and Simone Monet-Chartrand, *Ma vie comme rivière,* vol. 2, *1939–1949* (Montréal: Remue-Ménage, 1982), 256–58.

76 On the situation in the United States, see Winnifred Wandersee, *Women's Work and Family Values, 1920–1940* (Cambridge: Harvard University Press, 1981), 55. On Canadian middle-class family values in the post-war period, see the sociological monograph *Crestwood Heights: A Study of the Culture of Suburban Life* (1956; reprint, New York: John Wiley & Sons, 1967).

77 Lemelin, in *Essais sur le Québec contemporain,* ed. Jean-Charles Falardeau (Québec: Presses de l'Université Laval, 1953), 64ff.; Miner, in *Essais,* ed. Falardeau; and *Ten Family Surveys*. For global statistics on appliance purchases, see Charland, *Système technique et bonheur domestique*.

78 Canada, *Débats,* 1944, 5546.

79 Canada, DHNW, *You and Your Family* (Ottawa: King's Printer, 1949), 10, 19, 27.

80 Horace Miner, "A New Epoch in Rural Québec," *American Journal of Sociology* 56, no. 1 (1950): 9.

81 ANQQ, E 13, C.r., 2223, Chabot to Doré, 14 February 1943; Québec, DPI, *Instructions concernant la loi de fréquentation scolaire obligatoire,* 1943, 6, 8; and Tremblay et al., 24–25.

82 Created by the federal government in order to study young people's problems, the Canadian Youth Commission organized conferences across the country. The conference in Québec, held in February 1945, attracted numerous groups of young people. In total, it received 800 papers. Furthermore, it asked the Canadian Institute of Public Opinion to conduct a national poll. In Québec, fifty-eight young people between the ages of seventeen and twenty-six were interviewed: seventeen were still in school, twenty-six were employed, eight worked while still in school, two were soldiers, and five had no remunerative work. Most were sons or daughters of office workers and labourers (Canadian Youth Commission, *Youth and Jobs in Canada* [Toronto: Ryerson Press, 1945], 2, 34). See also ASJCF, 126-1, 2, Canadian Youth Commission, Comité provincial du Québec, *Rapport sur l'éducation,* 9 April 1945.

83 Canadian Youth Commission, *Youth and Jobs in Canada,* 38. Fifty-eight per cent of respondents [in Québec] believed that a good job awaited them upon leaving high school or a vocational school compared with the 22 per cent who believed the job would not be a good one; the former demonstrated more optimism than the youth in the rest of Canada, for whom the proportions were, respectively, 49 per cent and 37 per cent.

84 *RAMTQ, 1949–1950,* 249; *RGMTQ, 1949–1950,* 249; and *RGMTQ, 1954–1955,* 240.

85 PVCSCM, 27 August 1945; and ACSCM, 1—06/02.1, box 2135, J. Caron, 2 August 1945, R. Rocheleau, 22 August 1945, and R. Duguay, 22 August 1945, all to Messieurs Commissioners.

86 JOC, "Le problème des jeunes qui ne fréquentent plus l'école," 1–32, esp. 12. The survey was conducted in over forty-five urban centres. It is possible that the survey highlighted the attitudes of a specific portion of the youth population—those who endorsed the JOC and already demonstrated a certain will to educate themselves further, or at least to conform to a group's standards. In this way, many may have been members of a "respectable" working class, which could explain in part why their opinions contradicted the results of oral surveys conducted by Stephen Humphries on growing up in the English working class from 1889 to 1939, in which the children did not regret having left school early (*Hooligans or Rebels: An Oral History of Working-Class Childhood and Youth, 1889–1939* [Oxford: Basil Blackwell, 1981], 55).

87 Grisé-Allard, "Les allocations familiales, " 240. Grisé-Allard was the editor-in-chief of the women's pages of the *Bulletin*, and she also hosted *Le Courrier de Jeanne* on the radio.

88 Girls left the country at thirteen, fourteen, and fifteen years of age to work as maids in Montréal (where 90 per cent of the maids came from the country), generally "with the aim of helping their families or dressing themselves. In the first case, they stayed faithful to their jobs; soon, the needs of the city forced them to spend their money, and nothing was sent home." According to journalist Émilia Lacroix, this material detachment from home could lead to a psychological detachment: "During the first six months that these young girls lived in the city, they ordinarily want to return to the country; afterwards, it is impossible to make them leave" ("Le service domestique," p. 2). Twenty-eight out of the one hundred girls interviewed for the article were under the age of sixteen.

89 Fortin, "Socio-cultural Changes," 104.

90 This paragraph is based on AMSWC, case nos. 46–92, 46–375, 46–606, 46–902, 46–1634, 46–1830, 47–1652, 48–468, 48–653, and on ANQQ, E 24, 309, A-8, letter from Terrebonne MP J.-L. Blanchard to Antonio Barrette.

91 PVCSCM, 1 February 1944, 1 May 1945, 2 March 1948, 15 March 1949, 16 October 1951; ANQQ, E 13, C.r., 1942–199, box 2223, Madame Napoléon Rousseau to the superintendent, 6 December 1943; CDSA 1943–1200, box 112 317, case nos. 143, 5–8, 5–39, 6–10, 6–17, 6–22, 6–36; CDSA, 1943–1080, box 112 317, Madame L. to the superintendent, 18 April 1949; CDSA, 1943–2519, box 112 325, M. L. to the superintendent, 24 August 1945; CDSA 1943–1200, box 112 317, case nos. 71, 5–16, 6–48, 6–6, 6–37, 6–50; AQRO, 8–3, Lafrance to Director of Protestant Education Percival, 26 January 1950, and his response, 13 February 1950; and AMSWC, case nos. 48–1814 and 47–224.

92 AMSWC, case nos. 48–653, 47–661, 47–179; ANQQ, E 13, 1942–199, box 2223, Montmagny MP, February 1942; and CDSA, 43–2519, box 112 325, Monsieur and Madame Sherbrook to the superintendent, 25 August 1944.

93 AMSWC, case nos. 44–7593, 44–7954, 44–8512, 46–378, 47–251, 47–371, 48–338, 47–1505, 48–388, 48–2047.

Chapter 5

1 Murdoch C. MacLean, *Alphabétisme et fréquentation scolaire,* monograph no. 5 in Dominion Bureau of Statistics, *Recensement du Canada, 1931* (Ottawa: King's Printer, 1937), 110.

2 Philip Abrams, "Notes on the Difficulty of Studying the State," *Journal of Historical Sociology* 1, no. 1 (1988): 77.

3 Interview with P.-A. Fournier, Sillery, QC, September 1988. The statistical data upon which this chapter is founded are drawn from my article "Family Allowances and Family Autonomy: Québec, 1945–1955," in *Canadian Family History: Selected Readings,* ed. Bettina Bradbury (Toronto: Copp Clark, 1992), 401–437. The complete list of surveys is indicated in note 16 of the preceding chapter, and the complete data on parents' hopes by different enumerators are available in table 15 of my thesis (Dominique Jean, "Familles québécoises et politiques sociales touchant les enfants, de 1940 à 1960: Obligation scolaire, allocations familiales, et travail juvénile" [Ph.D. diss., Université de Montréal, 1988]). These surveys are more revealing of the parents' ideas regarding the effects of the program rather than its simple effects, a separate topic also worth further study. DHNW employees themselves knew that the designation of a particular spending category was often the result of subjective elements. This circumstance is all the more probable considering the allowances began at a time when spending power was decreasing. The precision of mothers' memory added to the problem, since the surveys asked them for information on a period that varied between six and twelve months, and only 25 per cent of the families kept records of income and spending (NAC, RG 29, R233/100/13, memorandum to Willard, undated; and NAC, RG 29, R233/100–63–2, Maurice Tremblay, Albert Faucher, and J.-C. Falardeau, *Family Allowances in Québec City: Report of a Study in the Faculty of Social Sciences of Laval University,* translation, DHNW Quebec, 1951, p. 17).

4 NAC, RG 29, Annual Reports, FA Division, 1283, *ARSWSQRO, 1950–1951,* 14; R. Blishen, J. Cawley, and J.E. Pearson, "Family Allowances in Montreal: A Study of Their Uses and Meaning in a Selected Group of Wage Earning Families" (M.A. diss., McGill University, 1948), 74, 75, 92, 93; AMSWC, case no. 48–2026; and AQRO, 42–8, vol. 1, Lafrance to Curry, 19 November 1949.

5 Blishen, Cawley, and Pearson, "Family Allowances in Montreal," 77–78.

6 Thérèse Roy, "Influence économique et sociale des allocations familiales" (M.A. diss., Université de Montréal, 1949), 46.

7 Blishen, Cawley, and Pearson, "Family Allowances in Montreal," 92.

8 Roy, "Influence économique et sociale," 46.

9 AMSWC, case no. 48–653.

10 Canada, *Débats de la Chambre des communes,* 1944, 5620.

11 Tremblay, Faucher, and Falardeau, *Family Allowances,* 17; and Paul Johnson, *Saving and Spending: The Working-Class Economy in Britain, 1870–1939* (Oxford: Oxford University Press, 1985), 220–21.

12 Blishen, Cawley, and Pears, "Family Allowances in Montreal," 93; Roy, "Influence économique et sociale," 47; and Tremblay, Faucher, and Falardeau, *Family Allowances,* 45.

13 Tremblay, Faucher, and Falardeau, *Family Allowances,* 17; and Viviana Zelizer, *Pricing the Priceless Child: The Changing Social Value of Children* (New York: Basic Books, 1985), 131–35. John Modell demonstrates that most nineteenth-century parents lost the benefits of these policies at one time or another, as they had difficulty making their payments ("Changing Risk and Changing Adaptations: American Families in the Nineteenth and Twentieth Century," in *Kins and Communities,* eds. Allan J. Lichtman and John Chalindor [Washington, DC: Smithsonian Institute Press, 1979], 121–22).

14 NAC, RG 29, acc. 82–83/152, 260–8-1, letters to the Montreal Board of Trade, the Trust Companies' Association of Ontario, and a firm of Toronto, 1945. See also Stuart Ewen, cited in Denyse Baillargeon, *Ménagères au temps de la crise* (Montréal: Remue-Ménage, 1993).

15 NAC, RG 29, 1934, R233/100/13, correspondence between Willard and Sheldon, 1949. Furthermore, the QRO sent placards on family allowances to more than 500 of the province's bank managers (AQRO, 40–13, vol. 1, circular to bank managers from Lafrance, February 1950).

16 JOC, "Le problème des jeunes qui ne fréquentent plus l'école," *École sociale populaire* 351 (April 1942): 1–32; and Delphine Périard, "Fréquentation scolaire en regard du milieu familial et des parents" (report, Université de Montréal, 1952), 14.

17 NAC, RG 29, vol. 1283, *ARQRO* and *ARSWSQRO,* all years; and *RAMSNBES,* all years.

18 NAC, RG 29, vol. 1283, *ARSWSQRO, 1951–1952,* 85. Until 1952, there were a total of ninety-nine cases in the province of Québec (*ARQRO, 1952,* appendix 3).

19 CDSA, 1943–1200, box 112 317, case no. 5–37; AMSWC, case nos. 48–380, 48–468, 48–2076, 44–2854; CDSA, 1943–1080, box 112 317, E.L.'s denunciation from Montréal to the DPI, 1 September 1945; CDSA 1943–1200, box 112 317, case nos. 21, 29, 37, 43, 55, 60, 62, 68, 105, 137, 142, 5–42, 6–47; CDSA, 1946–789, box 112 346, *RACA de Ville de Mégantic,* 1944, 3; *ARSPI, 1945–1946,* 73–74; and *ARSPI, 1947–1948,* 94.

20 ASJCF, 126–11, Québec, DPI, *Enquête scolaire, 1941–1942: Élèves de toute la province inscrits à l'école en 1940–1941 mais non-inscrits en 1941–1942, Élèves fréquentant les classes françaises,* 16; Québec, DPI, *Recensement scolaire, septembre 1943,* 77, 79, 141, 143; Québec, DPI, *Recensement scolaire, septembre 1944,* 3; Québec, DPI, *Rapports de juin 1945,* 6–8; Québec, DPI, *Rapports de juin 1946;* CDSA, 1946–1137; AQRO, 8–0, vol. 1, Fournier to Lafrance, 21 March 1950; AQRO, 8–2, MacKinnon to Lafrance, 13 September 1957; AMCSC, MCSC, *Report of the Director of Studies, 1942–1943,* 47; and AMCSC, Students, Absence Monitoring, Generalities, 1924–1960, L.-P. Lussier, *Truancy Officers' Report,* 13 July 1944, 2.

21 CDSA, 1943–1200, box 112 317, case nos. 5–37; AMSWC, case nos. 48–380, 48–468, 48–2076, 44–2854; CDSA, 1943–1080, box 112 317, E. L. to the DPI, 1 September 1945; CDSA, 1943–1200, box 112 317, case nos. 24, 29, 37, 43, 55, 60, 62, 68, 105, 137, 142, 5–42, 6–47; CDSA, 1946–789, box 112 346, *RACA de Ville de Mégantic,* 1944, 3; *ARSPI, 1945–1946,* 73–74; and *ARSPI, 1947–1948,* 94.

22 AMSWC, case no. 1947–762. The two parents were born in Montréal.

23 AMSWC, case nos. 44–7593, 47–50, 45–8512, 46–92; Philippe Meyer, *L'enfant et la raison d'État,* "Points" collection (Paris: Éditions du Seuil, 1977), 184; Neil Sutherland, *Children in English-Canadian Society: Framing the Twentieth-Century Consensus* (Toronto: University of Toronto Press, 1976), 149–50; Jeffrey S. Leon, "New and Old Themes in Canadian Juvenile Justice: The Origins of Delinquency Legislation and the Prospects for Recognition of Children's Rights," in *Children's Rights: Legal and Educational Issues,* ed. Heather Berkeley et al. (Toronto: Ontario Institute for Studies in Education Press, 1978), 37.

24 Before compulsory education, the January 1942 general survey had attributed absences of more than ten days since the beginning of classes to poverty in the case of 1,126 boys and 957 girls; 385 of them had missed more than 60 days. During the preceding year, 16 boys and 20 girls under the age of fourteen had left school for the same reason. School children of all ages from all primary schools were included in these statistics with the exception of the last numbers, which referred only to French schools (Department of Education, *School Survey, 1942, Classes Held in English Catholic Schools,* p. c-59, p. c-75; *School Survey, 1942, Pupils Enrolled in Protestant Schools,* p. p-59; ASJCF, 126–11, DPI, *Enquête scolaire, 1941–1942:*

Élèves fréquentant les classes françaises, 63; and ASJCF, 126–11, DPI, *Enquête scolaire, 1941–1942: Élèves de toute la province, inscrits à l'école en 1940–1941, mais non inscrits en 1941–1942,* iii–16).

25 DPI, *Recensement 1943,* 3, 77, 79, 141, 143; and DPI, *Recensement 1944,* 3. These 1944 statistics refer to all Catholic schools except those in Montréal and Verdun.

26 Elementary-school teachers in 1942 did not report the departure of unregistered children who had attended school the previous year; otherwise, the numbers from 1942 would have been greater (ASJCF, 126–11, DPI, *Enquête scolaire, 1941–1942: Élèves de toute la province, inscrits à l'école en 1940–1941, mais non inscrits en 1941–1942;* and ASJCF, 126–11, DPI, *Enquête scolaire, 1941–1942: Élèves fréquentant les classes françaises,* iii–16).

27 DPI, *Recensement 1943,* 2–3, 76–78, 140–45. The following year, the number decreased slightly: 2,328 children did not attend school because they were employed; work was only the seventh most common cause for non-registration, and it is conceivable that parents hid behind legal reasons (DPI, *Recensement 1944,* 2–3).

28 This calculation was based on figures from the year 1944–45, the first available figures on attendance. During that year, 8,876 boys and 5,774 girls were absent from primary public schools for over ten days, but that number includes absences for all "abnormal" reasons—that is, work, destitution, refusal to attend, and "negligence." To isolate the children who worked, we have supposed that the relative importance of the absences' causes would remain the same as in 1942.

29 Statistics compiled in 1950 by P.-A. Fournier of the Family Allowances offices in Quebec City, who had access to 624 annual reports of truancy officers kept at the DPI (AQRO, 8–0, vol. 1, Fournier to Lafrance, 21 March 1950). As the figure included children having reached fourteen years of age during the school year, it cannot be directly compared with the preceding statistics, which exclude fourteen-year-old children.

30 *ARSPI, 1949–1950,* 217; DPI, *Recensement 1943,* 2–3, 76–78, 140–45; and DPI, *Recensement 1944,* 2–3.

31 The DPI's 1942 survey required elementary-school teachers to indicate the profession of the father for each child leaving school in 1942 as well as the tasks that the very young workers who should have been attending school were carrying out. The occupational sectors of one-third of the boys and over half of the girls are unknown, but the 1942 results remain unique, as the federal censuses had ceased to be interested in labour performed by those under the age of fourteen since 1931. The figures are presented in tables 9 and 10 in Jean, "Familles québécoises et politiques sociales."

32 François-Albert Angers, "Les allocations familiales fédérales de 1944," *L'Actualité économique* 21, no. 3 (1945): 234; and Theda Skocpol, "A Society without a 'State'?: Political Organization, Social Conflict, and Welfare Provision in the United States," *Journal of Public Policy* 7, no. 4 (1988): 369.

33 CDSA, 1943–1200, box 112 317, case nos. 47, 66, 113, 140; and CDSA, 1943–1080, box 112 317, Madame C., 10 July 1948.

34 Périard, "Fréquentation scolaire," 31, 52.

35 AQRO, 8–0, vol. 2, B. Dupire to C. Biodeau, 27 April 1956; P.-A. Linteau et al., *Histoire du Québec contemporain,* vol. 2, *Le Québec depuis 1930* (Montréal: Boréal, 1986), 295; and A. Asimakopoulos, "Price Indexes," in *Historical Statistics of Canada,* eds. M. C. Urquhart and A. H. Buckley (Toronto: Macmillan, 1965), 304.

36 Périard, "Fréquentation scolaire," table 1; and ANQQ, Ministry of Labour, E 24, 312, A-8, Bernier to Barrette, 21 June 1954. See also Camille L'Heureux, "Les salaires dans le Québec," *Le Droit,* 12 February 1943.

37 Winnifred Wandersee, *Women's Work and Family Values, 1920–1940* (Cambridge: Harvard University Press, 1981), 55; and John Modell, "Pattern of Consumption, Acculturation, and Family-Income Strategies in Late-Nineteenth-Century America," in *Family and Population in Nineteenth-Century America,* eds. Tamara K. Hareven and Maris Vinovkis (Princeton: Princeton University Press, 1978), 206–224.

38 Émilia Lacroix, "Le service domestique et la désertion des campagnes," *Le Devoir,* 5 November 1941, p. 2; J.-P. Poulin, "À qui la faute? À l'école?" *Le Devoir,* 18 July 1942; and Québec, DPI, *Enquête de 1942.*

39 Approximately one-third of the 235 requests for exemption made to the SPI over six weeks cited the family's large size; 16 of the 30 requests for exemption of children under fourteen made to the QDL cited the family's large size; and 4 of the 31 cases heard at the youth court saw children mention the family's large size as a determining reason for non-attendance in favour of employment. See CDSA, 1943–1200, case nos. 141, 5–28, 6–13, 6–31; ASJCF, 126–11, DPI, *Enquête scolaire, 1941–1942: Élèves de toute la province, inscrits à l'école en 1940–1941, mais non inscrits en 1941–1942, Élèves fréquentant les classes françaises,* iii-22; ANQQ, E 24, 278, Madame O. Labbé to O'Connel Maher, 28 August 1947; ANQQ, E 24, 302, Jules Biron to Barrette, 2 August 1950; J.-L. Brissette to the Inspection Service, Montréal Division, 11 November 1943; and ANQQ, E 24, 180, A-8, letter from the Granby chaplain priest, 8 July 1940.

40 Roy, "Influence économique et sociale," 44; and CDSA, 1943–1200, box 112 317, case nos. 66, 5–4.

41 Périard, "Fréquentation scolaire," table 5; and CDSA, 1943–1200, box 112 317, case no. 71.

42 Linteau et al., *Histoire du Québec contemporain,* vol. 2, 295; AQRO, 40–20, vol. 1, *Ten Family Surveys,* April 1947, no. 7.

43 CDSA, 1943–1200, case nos. 11, 25; ASJCF, 126–11, DPI, *Enquête scolaire, 1941–1942: Élèves de toute la province, inscrits à l'école en 1940–1941, mais non inscrits en 1941–1942, Élèves fréquentant les classes françaises,* iii–21; ANQQ, E 24, A-8, Bernard Pinard to Quimper, 16 June 1955; and AMSWC, case no. 44–7659.

44 CDSA, 1943–1200, case no. 6–17; ANQQ, E 24, 222, A-8, M. O. from Drummondville to the minister of labour, 10 February 1944; Katharine Dupré Lumpkin and Dorothy Wolfe Douglas, *Child Workers in America* (New York: International Publishers, 1937), 162; and Elizabeth Magee, "Impact of the War on Child Labor," *Annals of the American Academy of Political and Social Science* 236 (November 1944), reproduced in *Children and Youth in America: A Documentary History,* vol. 3, *1933–1937,* ed. Robert H. Bremner (Cambridge: Harvard University Press, 1974), parts 1–4, 360.

45 CDSA, 1943–1200, case nos. 29, 43, 55, 76, 77, 5–33; and Périard, "Fréquentation scolaire," 43.

46 CDSA, 1942–1200; Périard, "Fréquentation scolaire," tables 1 and 6, 27; CDSA, 1943–1200, case nos. 16, 11, 6–35; on age, see CDSA, 1943–1200, case nos. 111, 5–32, 5–45; on overworking, see CDSA, 1943–1200, case no. 116; ANQQ, E 24, 278, A-8, J.-O. Ricard to the ministry, and enclosures, 29 July 1947; AMSWC, case no. 46–1830; ANQQ, E 24, 209, A-8, 47–179.b, 30 April 1943; and ANQQ, E 24, 222, A-8, June 1943.

47 ANQQ, E 24, 164, A-8, 18 November 1940; and AMSWC, case no. 1947–233.

48 CDSA, 1943–1200, case nos. 14, 41, 129. Two per cent of girls and boys between nine and fourteen years of age who left elementary school from 1940 to 1942 were orphaned from their father (ASJCF, 126–11, DPI, *Enquête scolaire, 1941–1942:*

Élèves de toute la province, inscrits à l'école en 1940–1941, mais non inscrits en 1941–1942, Élèves fréquentant les classes françaises, iii–20, iii–21).

49 CDSA, 1943–1200, case nos. 26, 139, 151, 5–32, 6–9; and Périard, "Fréquentation scolaire," table 1.

50 CDSA, 1943–1200, box 112 317.

51 AQRO, 6–0, vol. 1,1948–49 annual letter, attached to a letter from Fournier to Lafrance, 21 March 1950; and *ARSPI, 1946–1947,* 99–100.

52 DPI, *Rapports de juin 1946.*

53 AQRO, 8–0, vol. 1, Fournier to Lafrance, 21 March 1950; and AMCSC, Students, Absence Monitoring, Generalities, 1924–1960, L.-P. Lussier, *Truancy Officers' Report,* 13 July 1944. See also CDSA, 1943–1200: the files end in 1948; we cannot know how Doré's successors used this discretionary power. Similar rules existed in the United States (Dupré Lumpkin and Wolfe Douglas, *Child Workers in America,* 82–104).

54 AMSWC, case no. 47–223. See also case no. 47–1505.

55 Gill Jones and Claire Wallace, *Youth, Family, and Citizenship* (Buckingham: Open University Press, 1992), 21.

56 Québec, *RSQ,* Commercial and Industrial Establishment Act, 1925, 16 Geo. 5, c. 182, art. 3, al. 2; and Québec, *RSQ,* 1941, 5 Geo. 6, c. 175, art. 3, al. 2, and art. 8, al. 1.

57 In 1941, when first asked to include the question, the enumerators had found that, in the province of Quebec, thousands of Québécois children aged fourteen and fifteen were working in commercial or industrial businesses belonging to parents, and the figures corresponded well enough with those of the 1942 school survey (Canada, Dominion Bureau of Statistics, *Recensement du Canada, 1941,* vol. 7, table 3).

58 CDSA, 1943–1200, case no. 46.

59 AMSWC, case no. 47–223, Officer from Saint-Gédéon-de-Frontenac. See also case no. 47–1505.

60 ANQQ, E 24, 310, A-8, press release to the province's newspapers, 5 March 1953.

61 Québec, *SQ,* 1943, 7 Geo. 6, Loi concernant la fréquentation scolaire obligatoire, art. 90d; and Québec, DPI, *Instructions concernant la loi de fréquentation scolaire obligatoire,* 1943, 12. Québec manifested the same tolerance as the other Canadian provinces, with the exception of British Colombia ("Emploi des enfants et fréquentation scolaire au Canada," *La Gazette du travail,* January 1942, 55).

62 ANQQ, Ministry of Education, E 13, C.r., 1942–199, box 2223, Doré to F. Royer, 7 December 1943, and Doré to Charles-A. Parent, 18 October 1943; and ANQQ, E 13, C.r., 1942–199, C.-J. Miller to Didier Savard, 7 March 1944. Katherine I. McLaren observes the same lack of sanctions for country children in Nova Scotia ("The Proper Education for All Classes: Compulsory Schooling and Reform in Nova Scotia, 1890–1930" [M.A. diss., Dalhousie University, 1984], 20).

63 CDSA, 1946–789, box 112 398, Wilfrid Ross to Doré, 27 June 1943; CDSA, 1943–2300, box 112 325, Doré to J.-M. Pérusse, 10 March 1944, Doré to A. Beauregard, 12 April 1944, and Doré to Secretary-Treasurer of Bois-Franc, 16 January 1944; ANQQ, E 13, C.r., 1942–199, Doré to: Charles A. Parent, 18 October 1943, Jean Cyr, 16 October 1943, F. Bouchard, 16 November 1943, and J.-A. Leblanc, 7 December 1943; CDSA, 1943–1200, box 112 317, L. Landry to the superintendent, 23 December 1950; ANQQ E 13 C.R., 1942–199, Doré to Savard, March 1944, and Doré to J.-A. Rochefort, March 1944; CDSA, 1946–789, box 112 398, Annual Report of Compton (Mégantic) Officer, 1944; and AQRO, 8–0, vol. 1, Fournier to Lafrance, 21 March 1950.

64 For the global structure of the Québec labour force, see Linteau et al., *Histoire du Québec contemporain,* vol. 2, 63–75 and 283–84; and Jean Hamelin, ed., *Histoire du Québec* (Montréal: Éditions France-Amérique, 1976), 457–58.

65 DPI, *Rapports de juin 1945,* 6–8; and DPI, *Rapports de juin 1946.*

66 Cited in *ARSPI, 1947–1948,* 127.

67 Report cited by Dorothée H. Stepler, "Les allocations familiales au Canada," *École sociale populaire* 362 (1943): 9; Susan Mann Trofimenkoff, *The Dream of Nation: A Social and Intellectual History of Quebec* (Toronto: Gage, 1983), 254; Sister Marie Agnes de Rome Gaudreau, *The Social Thought of French Canada as Reflected in the Semaine Sociale* (Washington, DC: Catholic University Press of America, 1946), 114; James Struthers, *No Fault of Their Own: Unemployment and Canadian Welfare State, 1914–1941* (Toronto: University of Toronto Press, 1983), 9; and W.R. Tracey, *Fécondité de la femme canadienne,* monograph in Dominion Bureau of Statistics, *Recensement du Canada, 1931* (Ottawa: King's Printer, 1937), 180.

68 Father Gonzalve Poulin, *Problèmes de la famille canadienne-française* (Québec: Centre de culture populaire de l'Université Laval, 1952), 34.

69 "Emploi des enfants et fréquentation scolaire au Canada," *La Gazette du travail,* January 1942, 59. On the Ontario regional director's hesitations relative to the status of farmers' sons work, see NAC, RG 29, acc. 82–83/152, 264–1-6, letters from Stehelin to Curry, 18 January 1946, and Curry to Stehelin, 21 January 1946.

70 Québec, DPI, *Instructions,* 1943, 12; Loi concernant la fréquentation scolaire obligatoire, art. 290d.

71 Jean, "Familles québécoises et politiques sociales," table 8, taken up in Jean, "Family Allowances and Family Autonomy."

72 Thérèse Légaré, "Conditions économiques et sociales des familles de Gaspé-Nord, Québec" (Faculté des sciences sociales, Université Laval, 1947), 83.

73 George Haythorne and Leonard Marsh, *Land and Labour: A Social Survey of Agricultural and Farm Labour Market in Central Canada* (Montréal: McGill-Queen's University Press, 1941), 211–12, 234.

74 Lacroix, "Le service domestique"; 28 per cent of them had begun to work at the age of sixteen.

75 *ARSPI, 1945–1946,* 166; and Superintendent of Maple Producers A. Roberge, 29 May 1943.

76 CDSA, 1946–789, box 112 398, undated annual report.

77 CDSA, 1943–1200, MCCCIP, 28 February 1945.

78 *Recensement du Canada, 1941,* vol. 7, table 3, 12–25; and *Recensement du Canada, 1951,* vol. 4, table 3, 3–1, 3–15.

79 Edward E. Schwartz, "Some Observations on the Canadian Family Allowances Program," *The Social Service Review* 20, no. 4 (1946): 471; AQRO, 42–8, vol. 1, "What Is Family Allowance Record?" *Gazette* (Montréal), 4 August 1949; and Linteau et al., *Histoire du Québec contemporain,* vol. 2, 242.

80 CDSA, 1943–1200, case no. 35.

81 CDSA, 1943–1200, case no. 77.

82 *ARSPI, 1946–1947,* 99–100; and *ARSPI, 1947–1948,* 213–14.

83 CDSA, 1943–1200, case nos. 5–24, 5–47. The spelling idiosyncrasies of the original letter have been lost in translation, here and in some of the following quotations.

84 CDSA, 1943–1200, case no. 62.

85 *ARSPI, 1945–1946,* 229; CDSA, 1943–1200, case nos. 43, 75, 148; Haythorne and Marsh, *Land and Labour,* 81–83; and ANQQ, E 24, 222, A-8, Élie Bisson of the Association des pêcheurs de grande rivière to the Department of Labour, 1 June 1943. Bisson also asked to hire men over the age of sixty-eight.

86 ANQQ, E 13, 1942–199, box 2223, M.P. from Montmagny County, February 1942.

87 AMSWC, case nos. 43–5930, 44–7854, 47–224, 48–361, 48–2045; and CDSA, 1943–1200, box 112 317, case no. 30.

88 Cited in *ARSPI, 1947–1948,* 95–96. See also *ARSPI, 1943–1944,* 59 and *ARSPI, 1945–1946,* 55.

89 CDSA, 1943–1200, case no. 72.

90 CDSA, 1943–1200, case nos. 3, 36; and CDSA, 1946–789, box 112 398, Saint-Anaclet Officer, 24 July 1944.

91 CDSA, 1944–1015, box 112 348, extract from a resolution adopted in the Congrès diocésain of the Saint-Jean chapter of the UCC of Québec, 27 August 1944.

92 Gérald Fortin, "Socio-Cultural Changes in an Agricultural Parish," in *French-Canadian Society,* vol. 2, eds. Marcel Rioux and Yves Martin (Toronto: McClelland & Stewart, 1963), 97.

93 ANQQ, E 24, 235, A-8, Katherine H. Gallery of the Barrette Youth Bureau, 2 December 1944.

94 Thérèse Hamel, "L'obligation scolaire au Québec: Lieu et enjeu de la lutte des classes" (Ph.D. diss., Paris V René Descartes, 1981), 399; and AQRO, 7–6, vol. 1, Monitoring eligibility, 17 February 1953.

95 Jean, "Familles québécoises et politiques sociales," figure 4. I explore this idea in further detail in my article "The Language of Children's Rights, the Formation of the Welfare State, and the Democratic Experience of Poor Families in Québec, 1940–1955," *Canadian Historical Review* 78, no. 3 (1977): 427–29.

96 For examples from the 1910s and 1920s, see Baillargeon, *Ménagères au temps de la crise,* 53–54, 56.

97 DPI, *Recensement 1943,* 3, 77, 79, 141, 143; DPI, *Recensement 1944,* 3; AMCSC, Students, Absence Monitoring, Generalities, 1924–1960, Service de la statistique de la MCSC, *Recensement 1943;* DPI, *Rapports de juin 1945,* 7; and DPI, *Rapports de juin 1946.*

98 AQRO, 8–0, vol. 2, B. Dupire to C. Bilodeau, 27 April 1956; ASJCF, 126–11, DPI, *Enquête scolaire, 1941–1942: Élèves de toute la province, inscrits à l'école en 1940–1941, mais non inscrits en 1941–1942, Élèves fréquentant les classes françaises,* iii–16, iii–18, iii–19.

99 AQRO, 42–8, vol. 1, Dollard Morin, "Une famille de dix enfants sans allocations familiales," *Le Petit Journal,* 15 March 1953, p. 85, with two photos of the family.

100 Letter from Joseph Charbonneau, archbishop of Montréal, to R.P. Villeneuve, o.m.i., chaplain general of the JOC, 27 October 1941, published in *Le Devoir,* 31 October 1941, on the occasion of the Semaine du service domestique. Renée Vautelet even proposed a plan complete with "post-war domestic training" (*Mémoire sur l'orientation du travail féminin d'après-guerre,* prepared for the Conseil d'orientation économique [published under the auspices of the FNSJB, 1944], 17–22).

101 In April 1945, E. Turner Bone, president of the local Council of Women of Montréal, wrote to Maurice Duplessis to call for the return to domestic service of women employed in factories (NAC, MG 32, C25, vol. 7, minutes of the League of Women's Rights). For their part, the women's subcommittee on reconstruction called for more domestic assistants to help women accomplish their volunteer work (Canada, Advisory Committee on Reconstruction, VI, *Post-War Problems of Women: Final Report of the Subcommittee* [Ottawa: King's Printer, 1944], 11). See also Sylvie Murray, "Quand les ménagères se font militantes: La Ligue auxiliaire de l'Association internationale des machinistes, 1905–1980," *Labour/Le travail* 29 (Spring 1992): 157–86; and Lucie Piché, "Entre l'accès à l'égalité et la préservation des

modèles: Ambivalence du discours et des revendications du Comité féminin de la CTCC-CSN, 1952–1966," *Labour/Le travail* 29 (Spring 1992): 187–210.

102 ANQQ, E 13, C.r., 1942–96, box 2218, Irénée Jolin, report no. 36, 14 April 1942; Catholic Church, Archdiocese of Québec, "Lettre pastorale collective sur le problème rural au regard de la doctrine sociale de l'Église," 30 November 1937, in *Mandements des évêques de Québec,* vol. 15, *1936–1939,* 272.

103 PVCCC, School inspector's report, 14 January 1955 and 14 April 1955; Micheline Dumont and Johanne Daigle, "Les couventines," in *Les couventines: L'éducation des filles au Québec dans les congrégations religieuses enseignantes, 1840–1960,* eds. Micheline Dumont and Nadia Fahmy-Eid (Montréal: Boréal, 1986), 190–249; Marie-Paule Malouin and Micheline Dumont, "L'évolution des programmes d'études (1850–1960)," in *Les couventines,* eds. Dumont and Fahmy-Eid, 83–112; and *ARSPI, 1947–1948,* 127.

104 Remarks reported by Jeanne Langlois to the Garneau Commission hearing, cited in "Sort pitoyable des enfants nécessiteux," *La Presse,* 5 February 1944.

105 Périard, "Fréquentation scolaire," 39–40; Marc-Adélard Tremblay, Gérald Fortin, et Marc Laplante, *Les comportements économiques de la famille salariée du Québec* (Québec: Presses de l'Université Laval, 1964), 228–29; Diana Gittins, *The Family in Question: Changing Households and Family Ideologies* (London: Macmillan, 1985), 111; and John Modell, *Into One's Own: From Youth to Adulthood in the United States, 1920–1975* (Los Angeles: University of California Press, 1989), 230.

106 Philip Corrigan and Derek Sayer, *The Great Arch: English State Formation as Cultural Revolution* (Oxford: Basil Blackwell, 1985), 133; and Jones and Wallace, *Youth, Family, and Citizenship,* 20–21.

107 Vautelet also drew this parallel between premature work and doubtful morality (*Mémoire sur l'orientation du travail feminine d'après-guerre,* 13, 22, 23). In boys' records, there are only a few mentions of homosexual practices or of prostitution (AMSWC, case no. 48–1945).

108 Jacques Rouillard, *Les syndicats nationaux au Québec de 1900 à 1930* (Québec: Presses de l'Université Laval, 1979); Semaines sociales de l'École sociale populaire, *La Famille* (Montréal: École sociale populaire, 1923), 136–37; "Le travail féminin et la guerre," *École sociale populaire* 342 (1942); and Valère Massicotte, "La délinquance juvénile et la guerre," *L'Œuvre des tracts,* April 1944. According to some education officers, children's poor school attendance was due to mothers' jobs outside the home (CDSA, 1946–789, box 112 398, Annual Report of Verdun truancy officers, 27 June 1944).

109 "Le bill no. 45," *Relations* 3, no. 31 (1943): 170; and Gérard Parizeau, "Fait d'actualité: Les allocations familiales," *Assurances* 12, no. 2 (1944): 86.

110 Dorise Nielsen and James Coldwell, *Débats,* 1944, 5546, 5601.

111 Casselman, *Débats,* 1946, 2789; and *Débats,* 1944, 5558.

112 Lacroix, "Pour faire du service domestique," citing a survey carried out by the JOC; and ANQQ, E 13, C.r., 1942–199, box 2223, Doré to Guy Gagnon, 16 December 1943.

113 Cited in *ARSPI, 1947–1948,* 198.

114 CDSA, 1943–1200, case nos. 9, 48.

115 *Recensement du Canada, 1941,* vol. 7, table 3, 12–25; and *Recensement du Canada, 1951,* vol. 4, table 3, 3–1 to 3–15.

116 Geneviève Auger and Raymonde Lamothe, *De la poêle à frire à la ligne de feu: La vie quotidienne des Québécoises pendant la guerre, 1939–1945* (Montréal: Boréal Express, 1981), 160; and Jacqueline Sirois, *Le Devoir,* 1 June 1942, according to the figures of a survey led by the *Gazette* (Montréal).

117 JOC, "Le problème des jeunes qui ne fréquentent plus l'école," 5ff.

118 Émilia Lacroix, "Existe-t-il un problème domestique?" *Le Devoir,* 3 November 1941; Ruth Roach Pierson, *They're Still Women after All: The Second World War and Canadian Womanhood* (Toronto: McClelland & Stewart, 1986), 50–60; Collectif Clio, *L'histoire des femmes au Québec depuis quatre siècles* (Montréal: Quinze, 1982), 372–73; AMSWC, case no. 44–8019; and Robert Rumilly, *Histoire de la province de Québec,* vol. 41, *La guerre de 1939–1945: Duplessis reprend les rennes* (Montréal: Fides, 1969), 13. These scandals were behind the creation of the Garneau Commission.

119 It is possible, however, that only the particularities of Québec's demographic transition are responsible for the low Canadian average (Angus McLaren and Arlene Tigar McLaren, *The Bedroom and the State: The Changing Practices and Politics of Contraception and Abortion in Canada, 1880–1980* [Toronto: McClelland & Stewart, 1986], 16ff; and *RAMSNBES, 1947–1948,* 101, 176).

120 AMSWC, case nos. 88–8019, 46–490, 47–223, 47–1505, 48–1976, 48–2026.

121 CDSA, 1943–1200, case nos. 71, 153, 123; YCW, "Le problème des jeunes qui ne fréquentent plus l'école," 4; and AQRO, 8–0, vol. 1, Annual Report of truancy officers, 22 September 1949, attached to the letter from Fournier to Lafrance, 20 March 1950.

122 CDSA, 1943–1200, case no. 117.

123 Louise Charpentier, "Les programmes et les manuels d'histoire de la réforme scolaire de 1948" (M.A. diss., Université de Sherbrooke, 1983), 28–41.

124 ANQQ, E 13, 1942–199, box 2223, Victoriaville school municipality to the SPI, 26 January 1943, and the department secretary to the municipality, 29 January 1943.

125 Jean, "Familles québécoises et politiques sociales," table 2.

126 U.S. Children's Bureau, *Wartime Employment of Boys and Girls under 18,* Pub. no. 289, Washington, D.C., 1943, 45, cited in Bremner, ed., *Children and Youth in America,* parts 1–4, 358–59; Magee, "Impact of the War on Child Labor," 360–62; "Emploi des enfants et fréquentation scolaire au Canada," 57; and "Une plaie sociale, le travail des enfants," *Saturday Night,* reproduced in *Le Monde ouvrier,* 20 February 1943, 3.

127 ANQQ, E 24 C.-F. Duclos to Bernier, 4 April 1945; Bernier refused in a letter dated 5 April 1944.

128 ANQQ, E 24 A. Rivest to Bernier, 26 October 1944.

129 CDSA, 1944–629, box 112 314, JOC, *Mémoire sur l'orientation des jeunes travailleurs,* 1944, 4–5; and Madeleine Maille, general propagandist for the JOC, "La semaine des jeunes: Problème des jeunes qui ne vont plus à la classe, Statistiques, Causes," *Le Devoir,* 10 December 1942, p. 4.

130 ANQQ, E 13, 42–199, Filteau, 15 October 1943; and *ARSPI, 1945–1946,* 160.

131 ANQQ, E 24, 209, A-8, Hector Perrier to Rochette, 25 March 1943, and Bernier to Rochette, draft of response to Perrier, 31 March 1943.

132 ANQQ, E 24, 235, A-8, J. O'Connel Maher to Head Inspector Clovis Bernier, 29 March 1945.

133 ANQQ, E 24, 251-A-8, Barrette to Brossard, 10 September 1945.

134 ANQQ, E 24, 310, A-8, Beaulac to Tremblay, 11 June 1952; ANQQ, E 24, 222, A-8, Beaulac to Tremblay, 9 December 1943; and "Pas de travail industriel pour les moins de 16 ans," *La Patrie,* 5 March 1953, p. 9.

135 George H. Corbett, Secretary, cited in "Pas de travail industriel pour les moins de 16 ans."

136 The statistics refer to years following 1951, when the QDL's annual reports began to present the labour sectors of fourteen- and fifteen-year-old permit holders (Jean, "Familles québécoises et politiques sociales," table 12).

137 ANQQ, E 24, 2222, A-8, Tremblay to Macnamara, 7 February 1944; ANQQ, E 24, 193, A-8, Survey of Montréal licensed grocery stores, 22 September 1941; and Jean, "Familles québécoises et politiques sociales," table 10. As for the girls, the paid-work stratification by age was less marked.

138 AMSWC, case no. 46–902; and ANQQ, E 24, 310, C.-H. Robitaille to the Department of Labour, 14 April 1953.

139 CTCC executive committee's report on compulsory school attendance, in the 1942 minutes, cited by Hamel, "L'obligation scolaire au Québec," 317. On wage levels, see Jean, "Familles québécoises et politiques sociales," table 11.

140 Cited in AMCSC, Generalities, 1924–1965, Assistant Director of the MCSC School Services Émile Girardin, undated.

141 ANQQ, E 24, 263, Octave Guénette to Barrette, 5 November 1946; and ANQQ, E 24, 309, Jean Marchand to Barrette, 21 January 1952.

142 ANQQ, E 24, 309, Beaulac to Tremblay, 5 February 1952.

143 ANQQ, E 24, 309, J.-M. Bureau to Tremblay, 4 February 1952, and Beaulac to Tremblay, 5 February 1952.

144 ANQQ, E 24, 312, Beaulac to Barrette, 22 March 1955.

145 ANQQ, E 24, 193, C.K. King to the minister of labour, 24 November 1942.

146 ANQQ, E 24, 180, Guyon to Bernier, 4 October 1941.

147 Bertheline Méthot, guide Écomusée de la Maison du Fier-Monde, Montréal, QC, 12 April 1987.

148 ANQQ, E 24, P. Parent to the minister of labour, 26 March 1951, and Quimper to Parent, 30 March 1951 (Quimper approved the request for a permit).

149 Hamelin, ed., *Histoire du Québec,* 457–58; YCW, "Le problème des jeunes qui ne fréquentent plus l'école," 11; and Report presented by the Federation of Classical Colleges to the Tremblay Commission, cited in John Porter, *The Vertical Mosaic: An Analysis of Social Class and Power in Canada* (Toronto: University of Toronto Press, 1965), 193.

150 DPI, *Instructions,* 1943, 12; ANQQ, E- 24, Guyon to Maher, 28 October 1943. See also ANQQ, E 24, 222, Bernier to Tremblay, 1 December 1943; ANQQ, E 24, 235, A-8, Bernier to Tremblay, 28 April 1945; ANQQ, E 24, 235, A-8, Bernier to Maher, 21 January 1944; ANQQ, E 24, 310, A-8, Beaulac to Quimper, 14 April 1953, and Quimper to Beaulac, 15 April 1953; and Clairė Langlois, "L'œuvre des petits vendeurs de journaux et sa clientèle" (M.A. diss., Université Laval, 1952), 89–95.

151 Interview with P.-A. Fournier, Sillery, QC, September 1988.

152 AQRO, 7–6, vol. 1: Fournier to Lafrance, "Interprétation des directives," 12 February 1949; Fournier, "Directives," April 1948; Head of "Education" Sector N.-A. Mathieu, "Extraits du livre d'instructions concernant la fréquentation scolaire obligatoire pour régie interne de la section 'Éducation,'" undated; P.-T. Légaré, "Notes sur le travail juvénile," 14 March 1949; J.-A.-M. Caron, "Directives et procédures spéciales à l'unité 'École,'" 1 March 1951. See also Canada, DHNW, *You and Your Family* (Ottawa: King's Printer, 1949), 24–25; Viviana Zelizer, "Special Money: Allowances in the Domestic Economy, 1870–1930" (paper presented at the Social Science History Association Conference, St. Louis, MO, 1986); and Zelizer, *Pricing the Priceless Child,* 73–112.

153 AMCSC, Computing Department, Statistics, School Census, Generalities, 1920–1969, J.-F. Vincent to T. Boulanger, 18 June 1947; CDSA, 1946–789, box 112 398, Madame

A. Breton, *Annual Report, 1943–1944*; and CDSA, 1946–789, box 112 398, Compton Officer's *Annual Report, 1943–1944*.

154 CDSA, 1946–789, box 112 398, unidentified officer from Moulin-Bélanger, *Annual Report, 1943–1944,* 27 June 1944, and Verdun truancy officers' *Annual Report, 1943–1944,* 27 June 1944; CDSA, 1943–1200, case no. 5–14; CDSA, 1943–1200, Lionel Lafrance to Bilodeau, 13 March 1947; *ARSPI, 1943–1944,* 40, 77; DPI, *Recensement 1943,* 3, 77, 79, 141, 143; DPI, *Recensement 1944,* 3; DPI, *Enquête scolaire, 1941–1942: Élèves fréquentant les classes françaises,* iii–16, iii–18, iii–19; Interview with Madame Georgette Mercier, Montréal, QC, 13 November 1986; JOC, *Mémoire sur l'orientation des jeunes travailleurs,* 5; and Denise Lemieux and Lucie Mercier, *Les femmes au tournant du siècle, 1880–1940: Âges de la vie, maternité, et quotidien* (Québec: Institut québécois de recherche sur la culture, 1989), 96.

155 *ARSPI, 1949–1950;* PVCSSLF, 1948; and NAC, RG 29, acc. 82–83/152, 3425-1-3, part 1, MacKinnon, 3 September 1958.

156 *ARSPI, 1947–1948,* 191.

157 Wallace and Jones, *Youth, Family, and Citizenship,* 20–21.

158 That year, there were 409 boys and 202 girls of compulsory school age. The partial statistics of the following year are largely comparable. The 1942 survey had indicated a wider use of the category (DPI, *Recensement 1943,* 3, 77, 79, 141, 143; DPI, *Recensement 1944,* 3; DPI, *Enquête scolaire, 1941–1942: Élèves de toute la province, inscrits à l'école en 1940–1941, mais non inscrits en 1941–1942,* 16).

159 AMSWC, nos. 48–156, 43–6209, 45–9665, 46–1634, 47–79, 47–630, 47–769, 48–56; Marcel Fournier, *Entre l'école et l'usine: La formation professionnelle des jeunes travailleurs* (Montréal: Éditions coopératives Albert Saint-Martin, 1980); and Paul Willis, *Learning to Labor: How Working-Class Kids Get Working-Class Jobs* (New York: Columbia University Press, 1981), 72–75.

160 *ARSPI, 1949–1950,* 209.

161 AMSWC, case nos. 46–489, 46–902, 47–1749, 48–1770, 48–335, 43–398; and CDSA, 1946–789, Verdun officer's *Annual Report, 1943–1944*.

162 AMSWC, case nos. 48–388, 48–55, 48–1770, 48–1814, 48–2099, 47–1800, 47–29, 46–488, 6–500, 46–729, 44–9802.

163 AMSWC, case nos. 48–362, 48–380.

164 AMSWC, case nos. 47–1800, 46–1653; AMSWC, case nos. 48–293, 47–754, 45–9655, 44–8176, 46–769; AMSWC, case no. 48–862; AMSWC, case nos. 46–729, 47–89, 9913, 44–8176; AMSWC, case nos. 48–1771, 44–7978; and AMSWC, case no. 46–378.

165 AMSWC, case nos. 48–156, 48–660; and AMSWC, case nos. 47–262, 47–479, 44–7659, 44–8019, 44–7854.

166 CDSA, 1943–1200, case no. 5–8; AMSWC, 48–115, where a young girl was turned away from school twice due to the extremely dirty condition of her hair; and CDSA, 1943–1200, case no. 6–2. The surveys, censuses, and reports contain masses of statistical informal on the grade reached by age and region.

167 CDSA, 1946–789, box 112 398, Verdun truancy officer's request to Doré, 27 June 1944. On the development of teaching "mental defectives," see *ARSPI, 1944–1945,* 227; "Loi concernant l'établissement de classes spéciales pour l'institution de certains enfants," dated from 1929 according to Louis-Philippe Audet, *Histoire de l'enseignement au Québec,* vol. 2 (Montréal: Holt, Rinehart, & Winston, 1971), 217. A.-H. Tremblay, a school inspector cited in *ARSPI, 1949–1950,* 217, deplored the little attention given to challenged children in the country. On the several thousand children "doubling their classes each year due to physical defaults," see DNHW Director of Hygienic Education Jules Gilbert to the Garneau Commission, "Nouvelles

suggestions faites à la Commission d'assurance-malade," *Le Soleil,* 29 February 1944.

168 AMSWC, probation officer's report, 8 April 1947, case no. 1946–902; and CDSA, 1943–108, box 112 317, Dupire to Filteau, 2 March 1948, and Doré to Dupire, 9 March 1948.

169 AMSWC, case nos. 47–1862, 44–793, 47–1652.

170 AMSWC, case nos. 47–262, 47–479, 44–7659, 44–8019, 44–7854; AMSWC, case nos. 48–380, 48–293, 47–1800, 46–368; and AMSWC, case nos. 47–179, 47–754.

171 *ARSPI, 1943–1944,* 8.

172 DPI, *Recensement 1943,* 3, 77, 79, 141, 143; DPI, *Recensement 1944,* 3; DPI, *Rapports de juin 1945,* 6, 8; DPI, *Rapports de juin 1946;* and AQRO, 8–0, vol. 1, Fournier to Lafrance, 21 March 1950.

173 AMSWC, case nos. 47–640, 46–92.

174 The children who appeared before the MSWC (see AMSWC, case nos. 47–72, 46–368, 47–81, 47–262) expressed their ardent desire to work without having to justify themselves. See also ANQQ, E 24, 310, A-8, E. B. (fifteen years and eight months old) to Quimper, April 1953; AMSWC, case no. 46–368; and Claire Langlois, "L'œuvre des petits vendeurs de journaux et sa clientèle," 89.

175 AMSWC, case no. 47–72; Langlois, "L'œuvre des petits vendeurs de journaux et sa clientèle," 16, 87, 52–60; ANQQ, E 24, 310, A-8, Beaulac to Quimper, 14 April 1953; Paul Thompson, "The War with Adults," *Oral History* 3, no. 2 (1975); and Samuel Bowles and Herbert Gintis, *Schooling in Capitalist America: Education Reform and the Contradictions of Economic Life* (New York: Basic Books, 1976), 41–42.

176 Langlois, "L'œuvre des petits vendeurs de journaux et sa clientèle," 30–37; AMSWC, case no. 47–81; ANQQ, E 24, 222, A-8, Latullippe, from Hull, to Rochette, 21 February 1944; Archives de la Société historique de la région de Terrebonne, "Témoignages II," undated study, 87; Interview with P.-A. Fournier, Sillery, QC, September 1988; and Magee, "Impact of the War on Child Labor," 360.

177 AQRO, 7–6, vol. 1, Fournier to Faguy, 23 January 1947.

178 ANQQ, E 24, 222, A-8, CNEA, 6 December 1943; Stephen Humphries, *Hooligans or Rebels: An Oral History of Working-Class Childhood and Youth, 1889–1939* (Oxford: Basil Blackwell, 1981), 55, 58.

179 Liesel Urtnowski, "Children and the Labour Market," in *Children and the State,* ed. James Albert (Proceedings of a conference held at the School of Social Work, Carleton University, Ottawa, ON, 16–18 April 1978), 112; and Willis, *Learning to Labor,* 120.

180 It is this reflex, habitual to the designers of social policies in a liberal state, that sociologists Michel Pelletier and Yves Vaillancourt called the "disconnecting effect" (*Les politiques sociales et les travailleur,* journal 5, *Les fonctions de la sécurité sociale: L'idéologie* [Montréal, 1978]).

181 Jane Ursel, "The State and Maintenance of Patriarchy: A Case Study of Family, Labour, and Welfare Legislation in Canada," in *Family, Economy, and the State: The Social Reproduction Process under Capitalism,* eds. J. Dickinson and B. Russell (Toronto: Garamond, 1986), 150–91; and Leroy Ashby, "Partial Promises and Semi-Visible Youths: The Depression and World War II," in *American Childhood: A Research Guide and Historical Handbook,* eds. Joseph M. Hawes and N. Roy Hiner (Westport: Greenwood Press, 1985), 516.

182 Bowles and Gintis, *Schooling in Capitalist America,* 41–42; and Bruce Curtis, *Building the Educational State: Canada West, 1836–1871* (London: Althouse Press, 1988), 387.

183 ANQQ, E 24, 222, A-8: Tremblay to Madame L. of Kénogami, to the Government of Québec, June 1943; Beaulac to H. Potvin, 29 April 1943; Tremblay to Potvin, 5 May 1943; and Tremblay to Beaulac 29 May 1943.

184 Charles E. Strickland and Andrew M. Ambrose, "The Baby Boom, Prosperity, and the Changing Worlds of Children, 1945–1963," in *American Childhood,* eds. Hawes and Hiner, 552.

Chapter 6

1 In Nicolet County, only one family out of the sixty-six eligible in a sample chosen by the federal enumerators did not register in the program. See M.A. Macnaughton and G. Laflèche, *Preliminary Report on Distribution and Use of Family Allowances Payments in Nicolet County, Québec, 1947–1948,* prepared for the Economic Division, Marketing Service, Department of Agriculture (Ottawa: King's Printer, 1946), 4; and Canadian Institute of Public Opinion, "Gallup Poll of Canada: 90 p.c. in Canada in Favour of Family Allowances," *Toronto Star,* 12 March 1955. Still in 1971, married women in Québec saw generous family allowances as the most interesting of the six measures proposed to them by demographers for lightening family responsibilities (Jacques Henripin and Évelyne Lapierre-Adamcyk, *La revanche des berceaux: Qu'en pensent les Québécoises?* "Démographie canadienne" collection [Montréal: Presses de l'Université de Montréal, 1974], iii). See also Rob Watts, "Family Allowances in Canada and Australia, 1940–1945: A Comparative Critical Case Study," *Journal of Social Policy* 16, no. 1 (1987): 44.

2 Cited in Robert Rumilly, *Histoire de la province de Québec,* vol. 41, *La guerre de 1939–1945: Duplessis reprend les rennes* (Montréal: Fides, 1969), 97; and AQRO, 42–8, vol. 1, "P.C., C.C.F. Exchange Accusations on Support of Family Allowances," *Gazette* (Montréal), 26 April 1949, p. 10.

3 Dennis Guest, *The Emergence of Social Security in Canada* (Vancouver: University of British Columbia Press, 1981), 217–18.

4 Reg Whitaker, "Images of the State in Canada," in *The Canadian State: Political Economy and Political Power,* ed. Leo Panitch (Toronto: University of Toronto Press, 1977), 58.

5 CDSA, 1943–44, box 112 302, Victor Doré to the Association des institutrices de Matane, 12 July 1944, and Doré to Matane County MLA Onésime Gagnon, 13 July 1944.

6 CDSA, 1943–1200, box 112 317, Marie L. Germain to the SPI, 15 August, 1943.

7 W.I. Trattner, *From Poor Law to Welfare State: A History of Social Welfare in America* (New York: Macmillan, 1979), 153; Leroy Ashby, "Partial Promises and Semi-Visible Youths: The Depression and World War II," in *American Childhood: A Research Guide and Historical Handbook,* eds. Joseph M. Hawes and N. Ray Hiner (Westport: Greenwood Press, 1985), 490.

8 William Greider, *Who Will Tell the People: The Betrayal of American Democracy* (New York: Macmillan, 1979), 153; and Ashby, "Partial Promises and Semi-Visible Youths," 490.

9 On officers sensitive to parents' demands, see AQRO, 8–0, vol. 1, P.-A. Fournier to L. Lafrance, 29 May 1950.

10 CDSA, 1943–1200, case no. 67.

11 AQRO, 40–20, vol. 1, *Ten Family Surveys,* 1948. In the year 1948–49, the truancy officers recorded 760 exemptions from the Compulsory School Attendance Act

across the province for equivalent education at home (AQRO, 8–0, vol. 1, Fournier to Lafrance, 21 March 1950).

12 *Le Monde ouvrier,* 15 May 1943, p. 1. On the meeting of the UCC and the Cercles de fermières in 1956, see Thérèse Hamel, "L'obligation scolaire au Québec: Lieu et enjeu de la lutte des classes" (Ph.D. diss., Paris V René Descartes, 1981), 375.

13 On the CTCC in 1950, see Hamel, "L'obligation scolaire au Québec," 323–24. Between 1950 and 1960, the CTCC's demands became more and more extensive. On the CTCC's report to the Tremblay Commission, see Jean-Louis Roy, *La marche des Québécois: Le temps des ruptures (1945–1960)* (Montréal: Leméac, 1973), 123–27; and Louis-Marie Tremblay, *Le syndicalisme québécois: Idéologies de la C.S.N. et de la F.T.Q., 1940–1970* (Montréal: Presses de l'Université de Montréal, 1972), 87–88. On the Liberals' 1945 program, see Jean-Louis Roy, *Les programmes électoraux du Québec,* vol. 2, *1931–1966* (Montréal: Leméac, 1971), 369. On the Fédération des unions industrielles du Québec, see Tremblay, *Le syndicalisme québécois,* 204–205. On the Gésu conference on free education, see Michael D. Behiels, *Prelude to Quebec's Quiet Revolution: Liberalism versus Neo-Nationalism, 1945–1960* (Montréal: McGill-Queen's University Press, 1958), 258. As early as 1946 among some school inspectors, the watchword was the promotion of the superior course (*ARSPI, 1945–1946,* 56; *ARSPI, 1944–1945,* xi, 7; *ARSPI, 1949–1950,* xiv). As early as 1952, Catholic Department Secretary B.-O. Filteau considered grade nine to be indispensable (*ARSPI, 1951–1952,* 7), a position taken up by his successor, Joseph Pagé (*ARSPI, 1954–1955,* xii), and held by the head of protestant schools in 1946 (*ARSPI, 1945–1946,* 227).

14 Behiels, *Prelude to Quebec's Quiet Revolution,* 152–53. The Tremblay Commission did not accept the request. See Hamel, "L'obligation scolaire au Québec," 266–67, 325–26. On the Fédération des unions industrielles du Québec, the CTCC, and the FTQ, see Tremblay, *Le syndicalisme québécois,* 87, 204–205, 207. In 1945, the Canadian Youth Commission called for compulsory education until age seventeen (*Youth and Jobs in Canada* [Toronto: Ryerson Press, 1945], 39). According to Charles Bilodeau, special officer for the DPI, educators generally favoured the extension of compulsory education until sixteen years of age, or grade nine (AQRO, 8–2, *Annual Report: School Attendance Unit, 1957–1958,* 3–4). See also the FCS, which wanted to generalize grades nine and ten in the country ("Le congrès des commissions scolaires: Chez nous l'éducation appartient d'abord aux parents," *Le Nouvelliste,* 9 October, 1953, p. 1). The FCS called for compulsory education to be extended to sixteen years of age in cities, and in the country when rural schools were adequately organized (ACSCM, 1–36/05, box 1660, FCS, résolution de la plénière, Congrès de Chicoutimi, 9 October 1954). On the increase of the compulsory school age to fifteen, see the "Études sur la législation du travail dans la province de Québec et des conventions internationales qui s'y rapportent," probably prepared by the Superior Labour Council, August 1948, 8. See also Thérèse Casgrain, "Le service social est une pitié dans Québec," *La Presse,* 8 February 1944.

15 CDSA, 1943–1080, box 112 317, circular to principals from Trefflé Boulanger, 4 June 1948, no. 22 1947–48.

16 Thérèse Roy, "Influence économique et sociale des allocations familiales" (M.A. diss., Université de Montréal, 1949), 53; and CDSA 1943–1200, box 112 317, case nos. 5–27, 5–38, 6–33, 6–36.

17 *La Terre de chez nous,* 15 August 1945, p. 1; Canada, *Débats de la Chambre des communes,* 1952, 1984; and Léon Lebel, "Notre système d'allocations familiales," *Relations* 11, no. 124 (1951): 93. The heads of the CCF and the Conservative Party

had called for indexation since the debates on the bill in 1944 (*Débats,* 1944, 5932–33). In 1956, the Liberal Party of Québec included a provincial school allowance of $150 per year in its program upon the request of the Federation of Classical Colleges and the FCS (Roy, *Les programmes électoraux du Québec,* vol. 2, 369; and AQRO, 8–0, vol. 1, J.-F. Vincent to Lafrance, 6 December 1946). According to the head of education at the Family Allowances Bureau, most educators favoured extending family allowances until eighteen years of age so that students could continue their studies (*Annual Report: School Attendance Unit, 1957–1958,* 3–4).

18 On the FCS's request, see FCS, résolution plénière; and NAC, RG 29, 1933, R233–100–1-6, Davidson to Willard, 1955. See also Knowles, Lockhard, and Jackman, in *Débats,* 1948, 5483, 5488, and 5890–91, respectively; Poulin, in *Débats,* 1949, 2nd session, 180; Poulin, *Débats,* 1951, 1st session, 2266–67; Poulin, Argue, and Brown, in *Débats,* 1951, 2nd session, 148–49, 220, 776; Dubé, Poulin, and Argue, in *Débats,* 1952, 1983, 3138, 1775–77; Bertrand and Argue, in *Débats,* 1953, 2959, 1182–1204; and Argue, Girard, and Dupuis, in *Débats,* 1954, 1354, 328, 352. In 1953, Argue even presented a project that attempted to index allocations to the cost of living. The discussion on this subject was delayed.

19 *Débats,* 1946, 4592, 2789; *Débats,* 1944, 5573, 5923, 5932–33; *Débats,* 1949, 2544; *Débats,* 1952, 1780; and Strum, in *Débats,* 1946, 2788–89.

20 AQRO, 40–10, vol. 2, 15 October 1959. Fréchette made other allusions to the allowances for needy mothers, extended in certain cases after children had reached age sixteen.

21 *RAMSNBES, 1947–1948,* 96; *RAMSNBES, 1946–1947,* 76; and *ARQRO, 1950–1951,* 12.

22 NAC, RG 29, 109, 180–26–15.

23 Thérèse Roy, 44. See also Delphine Périard, "Fréquentation scolaire en regard du milieu familial et des parents" (report, Université de Montréal, 1952), 55. Périard suggested providing families with a real minimum of security.

24 Journal, 6 May 1946, cited in Alvin Finkel, "Paradise Postponed: A Re-examination of the Green Book Proposals of 1945," *Journal of the Canadian Historical Association/Revue de la Société historique du Canada,* new series, vol. 4 (1993): 128.

25 Finkel, "Paradise Postponed"; Guest, *The Emergence of Social Security in Canada,* 217–18. These considerations are drawn from John Macnicol, who analyzes the same problem in Great Britain in *The Movement for Family Allowances, 1918–1945: A Study in Social Policy Development* (London: Heinemann, 1980).

26 Willard, 1968, p. 66, cited in Robert T. Kurdle and Theodore R. Marmor, "The Development of Welfare States in North America," in *The Development of Welfare States in Europe and America,* eds. P. Flora and R. Heidenheimer (London: Transaction Books, 1981), 98.

27 J.-A. Blais, "La collaboration du gouvernement fédéral dans la sécurité sociale du pays," 23 April 1954, cited in NAC, RG 29, acc. 82–83/152, 264–9-2, "Minutes of the Meeting of Child-Placing Agencies with the Staff of the Québec Regional Office, held at the Regional Office."

28 Blais, "La collaboration."

29 Jean-Pierre Charland, with the participation of Mario Désautels, *Système technique et bonheur domestique: Rémunération, consommation, et pauvreté au Québec, 1920–1960,* no. 28 in "Documents de recherche" collection (Québec: Institut québécois de recherche sur la culture, 1992), 71; *Débats,* 1944, 5934. The deduction was of $28 for each dependant, excluding the spouse, to a maximum of $108 per tax-

payer (Canada, *SC,* 1944, 9 Geo. 6, c. 23, art. 9; Canada, DNHW, Information Division, *Family Allowances and Income Tax* [Ottawa: King's Printer, 1946]).

30 *Ten Family Surveys;* AMSWC, case nos. 44–769, 47–769, 47–1 790, 44–8 176; and Jeanne Grisé-Allard, "Les allocations familiales: Un chèque bien employé," *Relations* 7, no. 92 (1948). See also René Chaloult, "La famille et l'État," in *Le foyer: Base de la société, Semaines sociales du Canada,* no. 27 (Montréal: Institut social populaire, 1950), 242.

31 Charland, *Système technique et bonheur domestique;* Raymond Boudon and François Bourricaud, "Égalitarisme," in *Dictionnaire critique de la sociologie* (Paris: Presses Universitaires de France, 1985), 216; and Peter S. McInnis, "Planning Prosperity: Canadians Debate Postwar Reconstruction," in *Uncertain Horizons: Canadians and Their World in 1945,* ed. Greg Donaghy (Ottawa: Canadian Committee for the History of the Second World War, 1996), 231–60.

32 J.L. Granatstein, citing the journal of January 1943 in *Canada's War: The Politics of the Mackenzie King Government, 1939–1945* (Toronto: Oxford University Press, 1975), 3; and Finkel, "Paradise Postponed." It concerned, in part, one sector of the workers' movement.

33 *SC,* 1945, 10 Geo. 6, c. 55; Arlene Skolnick, *Embattled Paradise: The American Family in an Age of Uncertainty* (New York: Basic Books, 1991), 68; and *Ten Family Surveys.*

34 Reg Whitaker, *The Government Party,* cited in John English, "The Second Time Around: The Political Scientists Reading History," in *Contemporary Approaches to Canadian History,* ed. Carl Berger (Toronto: Copp Clark Pitman, 1987), 249; and Philip Corrigan and Derek Sayer, *The Great Arch: English State Formation as Cultural Revolution* (Oxford: Basil Blackwell, 1985), 116ff.

35 Cynthia R. Comacchio, *"Nations Are Built of Babies": Saving Ontario Mothers and Children, 1900–1940* (Montréal: McGill-Queen's University Press, 1993), 8–9.

36 *Débats,* 1952, 1783. See also *Débats,* 1948, 5488; and *Débats,* 1954, 1371, 1378. Newspaper articles denouncing families misusing their allowances seem to have been numerous (cited in *Débats,* 1947, 3411, and *Débats,* 1948, 5483).

37 AQRO, 8–0, vol. 1, Lafrance to Monseigneur L.-O. Garant, 15 October 1951. See also AQRO, 8–0, vol. 1, Saint-Gédéon-de-Frontenac officer's *Annual Report, 1948–1949,* attached to Fournier to Lafrance, 21 March 1951. Maurice Tremblay's social-science research team took up these prejudices when they accused parents of negligence. As researchers felt that school was not very expensive, they deemed parents' economic justifications for removing their children from school prematurely unrealistic. See NAC, RG 29, R233/100–63–2, Maurice Tremblay, Albert Faucher, and J.-C. Falardeau, *Family Allowances in Québec City: Report of a Study in the Faculty of Social Sciences of Laval University,* translation of the DHNW document, 1951.

38 A. Wei Djao, "Social Welfare in Canada: Ideology and Reality," *Social Praxis* 6, nos. 1–2 (1978): 48. See AQRO, 42–8 for newspaper articles that depict some federal Liberals as taking the side of clients by saying there had been no abuse.

39 ASJCF, 126–6, 6, Omer Côté to Maurice Duplessis, 30 January 1945.

40 *ARSPI, 1949–1950,* ix, xiv.

41 CDSA, 1943–1200, box 112 317, case no. 61.

42 R. Blishen, J. Cawley, and J.E. Pearson, "Family Allowances in Montreal: A Study of Their Uses and Meaning in a Selected Group of Wage Earning Families" (M.A. diss., McGill University, 1948), 70.

43 CDSA, 1943–1200, case no. 6–42, Madame B., 10 November 1949. The SPI as well as the head of family allowances reproved this practice.

44 AMSWC, case no. 46–1872; CDSA, 1943–1200, box 112 317, case nos. 84, 6–42; CDSA, 1942–199, 2223, Wilfrid Rousseau of Saint-Gédéon Station to Doré, 22 October 1943; and ANQQ, E 13, C.r., 1942–199, 2223, Madame A. Tessier to Doré, 28 September 1943. Frances Fox Piven and Richard A. Cloward show how the fear of renouncing normal rights kept many parents from taking advantage of social measures (*Regulating the Poor: The Functions of Public Welfare* [New York: Vintage Books, 1971], 160–75).

45 Case cited as an example of a typical problem in applying the rules (AQRO, 7–6, vol. 1, Fournier, in a letter to Faguy, 23 January 1947).

46 Thérèse Légaré, "Conditions économiques et sociales des familles de Gaspé-Nord, Québec" (Faculté des sciences sociales, Université Laval, 1947), 9, 132.

47 David Sutton, "Liberalism, State Collectivism, and the Social Relations of Citizenship," in *Crises in the British State, 1880–1930,* eds. Mary Langan and Bill Schwartz (London: Hutchinson Centre for Contemporary Cultural Studies, 1985), 65.

48 André Laurendeau, cited in Michael D. Behiels, "The Bloc Populaire Canadien and the Origins of French-Canadian Neo-Nationalism, 1942–1948," *Canadian Historical Review* 63, no. 4 (1982); Adélard Godbout, cited in Jean-Guy Genest, "Vie et œuvre d'Adélard Godbout, 1892–1956" (Ph.D. diss., Université Laval, 1987), 489; and CDSA, 1943–1200, Omer-Jules Desaulniers to Lafrance, 1 November 1944.

49 CDSA 1943–1200, box 112 317, case no. 6–45; AQRO, 8–0, vol. 1, *RACA de Minerve* (Labelle), 1948–1949, annex of letter from Fournier to Lafrance, 21 March 1950; and CDSA, 1943–1200, box 112 317, case no. 6–2.

50 Paul Thompson, "The War with Adults," *Oral History* 3, no. 2 (1975), 37; and Stephen Humphries, *Hooligans or Rebels: An Oral History of Working-Class Childhood and Youth, 1889–1939* (Oxford: Basil Blackwell, 1981), 21–23. More recent interviews with Californian working-class parents reveal that, having spent their time in school with a fear of being inadequate, they were even more strict regarding their children than adults of higher classes, and they demanded more conformity (Lilian Rubin, *Worlds of Pain: Life in the Working-Class Family* [New York: Basic Books, 1976], 126–28).

51 AMSWC, case nos. 47–1800, 46–1653; AMSWC, case nos. 48–293, 47–754, 45–9655, 44–8176, 46–769; AMSWC, case no. 48–862; AMSWC, case nos. 46–729, 47–89, 9913, 44–8176; and AMSWC, case nos. 48–1771, 44–7978.

52 Guest, *The Emergence of Social Security in Canada,* 217–18; and Piven and Cloward, *Regulating the Poor,* 348.

53 CDSA, 1943–1200, box 112 317, case nos. 30, 94; and ANQQ, E 13, C.r., 1942–199, 2223, Amédée Poirier, February 1945, and Adélard Tremblay to the SPI.

54 CDSA, 1943–1200, box 112 317, case nos. 9, 5–22, Charles A. Parent, secretary-treasurer and officer for Saint-Gabriel-de-Gaspé, stated two other requests from servants [ANQQ, E 13, C.r., 1942–199, 2223, 20 September 1943]; and CDSA, 1943–1200, box 112 317, case no. 10.

55 CDSA, 1943–1200, box 112 317, case no. 30. On the importance of the manner in which individuals' work experiences determined their views of justice, see Alice Kessler Harris, "Gender Ideology in Historical Reconstruction: A Case Study from the 1930s," *Gender and History* 1, no. 1 (1990): 36.

56 CDSA, 1943–1200, box 112 317, case nos. 124, 140; CDSA, 1943–1200, box 112 317, case no. 94; and AMSWC, case no. 1946–96.

57 Sister Marie Agnes de Rome Gaudreau, *The Social Thought of French Canada as Reflected in the Semaine Sociale* (Washington, DC: Catholic University Press of America, 1946), 38, 68.

58 Boudon and Bourricaud, "Égalitarisme"; and Elizabeth Wilson, *Women and the Welfare State* (London: Tavistock, 1977), 41.

59 Léon Lebel, *Les allocations familiales: Solution du problème des familles nombreuses* (Montréal: École sociale populaire, 1927), 29–30. See also the critiques of compulsory education as they relate to the working-class families studied by Behiels ("The Bloc Populaire Canadien," 509).

60 AMSWC, case nos. 46–375, 46–902, 46–903, 46–1721, 47–29, 47–89, 48–115, 48–1813, 47–181; and AMSWC, case nos. 44–6726, 44–9361, 46–92, 48–850, 46–99, 44–7973, 44–7852, 44–8176, 47–1250, 48–260, 45–9612.

61 AMSWC, case nos. 46–92, 45–9655; Rubin, *Worlds of Pain,* 85–86; and Philippe Meyer, *L'enfant et la raison d'État,* "Points" collection (Paris: Éditions du Seuil, 1977), 59.

62 Latterière farmer Alfred Bouchard to the diocesan congress of the Roberval UCC, 1943, cited in Hamel, "L'obligation scolaire au Québec," 380–99; Jacques Rouillard, *Histoire du syndicalisme au Québec* (Montréal: Boréal, 1990), 139; and Jean-Pierre Kesteman, *Histoire du syndicalisme agricole au Québec, UCC-UPA, 1924–1984* (Montréal: Boréal Express, 1984), 174.

63 Hamel, "L'obligation scolaire au Québec," 266–316; JOC, "Le problème des jeunes qui ne fréquentent plus l'école," *École sociale populaire* 351 (April 1942): 30.

64 Genest, "Vie et œuvre," 637.

65 P.-A. Linteau et al., *Histoire du Québec contemporain,* vol. 2, *Le Québec depuis 1930* (Montréal: Boréal, 1986), 143.

66 Jean Hamelin and André Garon, "La vie politique au Québec de 1956 à 1966," in *Quatre élections provinciales au Québec, 1956–1966,* ed. Vincent Lemieux (Québec: Presses de l'Université Laval, 1969), 8, 18–19.

67 François-Albert Angers, "Les allocations familiales fédérales de 1944," *L'Actualité économique* 21, no. 3 (1945): 250; Léon Lebel, "Les allocations familiales au Canada," *Relations* 11, no. 122 (February 1951): 50–51; Léon Lebel, "Après deux ans d'allocations familiales," *Relations* 7, no. 80 (August 1947): 228; Charlotte Whitton, cited in A.M. Willms, "Setting Up Family Allowances, 1944–1945" (M.A. diss., Carleton University, 1962); and editorial in *Le Devoir,* 11 August 1944.

68 Tremblay, Faucher, and Falardeau, *Family Allowances;* and Blishen, Cawley, and Pearson, "Family Allowances in Montreal," 96–105. The same absence of criticisms is present in the 1948 study led by Macnaughton and Laflèche on the farms of 115 families in Nicolet County. This information on families' attitudes in Quebec matched those of a larger survey conducted in Alberta and in Saskatchewan with 416 rural families: out of the 6 families opposed to the system, only 3 explained that they wanted to take care of their children by themselves (M.A. Macnaughton and J.M. Mann, *Distribution and Use of Family Allowances Payments in Three Areas of the Prairie Provinces,* publication 815, technical bulletin 69, supplement to M.A. Macnaughton and M.E. Andal, *Changes in Farm Family Living in Three Areas of the Prairie Provinces, from 1943 to 1947,* prepared for the Economic Division, Marketing Service, Departments of Agriculture and National Health and Welfare in cooperation with the Universities of Alberta and Saskatchewan [Ottawa: King's Printer, 1949]).

69 Lebel, "Après deux ans d'allocations familiales," 230; and Lebel, "Les allocations familiales au Canada," 47–50.

70 "[A]fter several generations of welfare state development, all groups concerned have developed more sophisticated expectations, more alternative strategies..." (Flora and Heidenheimer, eds., *The Development of Welfare States,* 32).

71 NAC, RG 29, acc. 82–83/152, box 25, 3430–2-3, part 1.

72 M.J.-V. Gagnon, cited in *ARSPI, 1948–1949,* 83. See also Filteau to Perrier, 25 September 1942, which mentioned the idea that parents' associations presented at the Congress of the CNEA (ANQQ, E 13, C.r., 1942–1339, box 2266).

73 The JOC had called for the creation of such associations based on the models of the West and Ontario ("Le problème des jeunes qui ne fréquentent plus l'école," 31); PVCCC, 1 December 1946, 29 June 1948, 3 May 1950; PVCSSMCM, 1954; and PVCSSLF, 1946, 1948. In the year 1947–48, there were attempts to get parental associations underway in all districts. See *ARSPI, 1947-1948,* 14, 72; *ARSPI, 1946–1947,* 81, 87, 298; and *ARSPI, 1949–1950,* 106–108, 209.

74 This is the impression given the article "L'éducation familiale constitue un rampart," *La Presse,* 15 March 1944. See also PVCSCM, 1 March 1949, 2 October 1951; and *ARSPI, 1943–1944,* xxxiv.

75 CDSA, 1943–1200, box 112 317, case no. 71; La Sarre Secretary-Treasurer Josaphat Lapierre, who claimed to pass on parents' opinions, made the same comparison with Nazism and added Communism as well (CDSA, 1946, 789, box 112 398, letter to Doré, 4 July 1944). In the same file, see also the opinion of a secretary-treasurer whose riding is not known, 12 July 1944.

76 ANQQ, E 13, C.r., 1942–199, 222, Gagnon Boulanger to Perrier, 21 September 1943; CDSA, 1943–1200, box 112 317, case nos. 124, 6–43.

77 CDSA, 1942–199, 2223, Wilfrid Rousseau of Saint-Gédéon-Station to Doré, 22 October 1943. See also Madame Bélanger of Saint-Josaphat to the SPI, 18 September 1950; she deplored the reinstallation of the monthly payment (CDSA, 1943–1080). Finally, the QRO looked into the admissibility of parents who refused to make the monthly payment (AQRO, 8–0, vol. 1, Fournier to Lafrance, 30 September 1949). In 1950, this became a valid excuse.

78 ANQQ, E 13, C.r., 1942–199, 2223, J.-L. Richard to the board, 8 September 1943.

79 ANQQ, E 13, C.r., 1942–199, 2223, A. Poulin, 7 January 1944.

80 CDSA, 1943–1200, box 112 317, case no. 71.

81 CDSA, 1946–789, box 112 398, *DIP Annual Report, 1943–1944,* 4 July 1944.

82 PVCSCM, 17 October 1944; PVCSSLF, 1945; CDSA, 1943–1200, box 112 317, case nos. 71, 92, 5–11, 5–19, 5–23; and ASJCF, 126–1, 2, Canadian Youth Commission, Comité provincial du Québec, *Rapport sur l'éducation,* 9 April 1945, 2; and Gérard Filion, *Les confidences d'un commissaire d'écoles* (Montréal: Éditions de l'Homme, 1960), 26. Bruce Curtis believes that these momentarily liberating steps could have ended in further alienation (*Building the Educational State: Canada West, 1836–1871* [London: Althouse Press, 1988], 67).

83 PVCSCM, 12 April 1955. They added: "Given that, since the institution of the family allowances, the cost of living has doubled, and following that the family allowances provide families with only one-half of the products or services they originally provided them with when the allowances were first instituted; Given that there are enough products and services in the country to provide families with at least as much as in 1945, and given that finance should not be an obstacle to realities." They asked that the rates be doubled. The resolution was forwarded to the DNHW as well as to the county's MP (PVCSCM, 17 October 1944). See also PVCSSLF, 1945.

84 AQRO, 42–8, vol. 1, "Patience, Mothers, Cheque on Way," *Montreal Star,* 21 September 1949.

85 Gérard Bergeron, *Le Canada français après deux siècles de patience* (Paris: Éditions du Seuil, 1967), 31. On the CTCC in 1950 and the FPTQ, see Tremblay, *Le syndicalisme québécois,* 87, 196. On the Trades and Labour Congress of Canada after 1943, the Fédération des bâtiments, and the UCC, see Hamel, "L'obligation scolaire au Québec," 266–67, 321–22, 367.

86 Tremblay, *Le syndicalisme québécois,* 86; Jean Hamelin, *Histoire du catholicisme québécois: Le XX*e *siècle,* vol. 2, *De 1940 à nos jours* (Montréal: Boréal Express, 1984), 28–32. For a description of this trend, see Linteau et al., *Histoire du Québec contemporain,* vol. 2, 112–13.

87 Tremblay, *Le syndicalisme québécois,* 88. The JOC had been calling for such grants since 1942 ("Le problème des jeunes qui ne fréquentent plus l'école"). The demands were taken up in the Canadian Youth Commission's *Youth and Jobs in Canada,* 35.

88 Cited in Behiels, *Prelude to Quebec's Quiet Revolution,* 157. For more on the FPTQ in 1954, the Fédération des travailleurs du Québec (FTQ), and the CTCC in 1958, see Tremblay, *Le syndicalisme québécois,* 197, 207–208. Roy cites an FTQ and CTCC report submitted to the SPI in 1958 (*La marche des Québécois,* 251).

89 Renée Vautelet, *Mémoire sur l'orientation du travail féminine d'après-guerre,* prepared for the Conseil d'orientation économique (published under the auspices of the FNSJB, 1944), 17.

90 James Douglas Thwaites, "The Origins and the Development of the 'Fédération des commissions scolaires catholiques du Québec,' 1936–1963" (Ph.D. diss., Université Laval, 1975), 55, 198–99, 211, 216; Behiels, *Prelude to Quebec's Quiet Revolution,* 153–54; and Napoléon Veilleux, secretary-treasurer of the Association des commissions scolaires catholiques de la province de Québec, Diocèse de Québec, 5 November 1947.

91 CDSA, E 13, C.r., 1944–789, box 112 346, FCS, *Mémoire sur la question scolaire en campagne,* 16 August 1955, 9.

92 On ideas comparable among Catholic reformists in 1938, see Jean Hamelin and Nicole Gagnon, *Histoire du catholicisme québécois: Le XX*e *siècle,* vol. 1, *1898–1940* (Montréal: Boréal Express, 1984), 442.

93 Bergeron, *Le Canada français,* 173.

94 CDSA, 1944–789, box 112 346, Resolution of the Association des commissions catholiques de la province de Québec, which ensured that the law did not hinder the boards' autonomy, forwarded to the department by Secretary-Treasurer Veilleux, 5 November 1947; Behiels, *Prelude to Quebec's Quiet Revolution,* 156; and Filion, *Les confidences d'un commissaire d'écoles,* 50–64. In 1951, the FCS called for an increase in subsidies for higher levels of primary teaching (ACSCM, 1–36/05–1, box 1660).

95 The Tremblay Commission adopted the FCS's demand according to Behiels (*Prelude to Quebec's Quiet Revolution,* 159). See also *ARSPI, 1946–1947,* 106, 178–79; and CDSA, 1944–430, box 112 338, SPI to J. Coutu, 6 July 1950. The FCS also asked that the subsidies for elementary-school teachers' wages be increased by 75 per cent (ACSCM, 1–36/05–1, box 1660).

96 Behiels, *Prelude to Quebec's Quiet Revolution,* 157; Program of the 1952 Liberal Party, cited in Roy, *Les programmes électoraux du Québec,* vol. 2, 355. In the Champlain School Board, for example, the taxation rate went from 65¢ in 1948 to $1.25 in 1950; in Saint-Louis-de-France, from 70¢ to $1.50 between 1943 and 1948; in

Sainte-Marthe-du-Cap-de-la-Madeleine, 60¢ in 1943 to $1.40 in 1954; in Notre-Dame-de-la-Visitation, from 65¢ in 1946 to 90¢ in 1950. See also PVCSCM, 18 November 1951, where the commissioners accepted the school sales tax discussed below. We know that in 1954, the following municipalities also took advantage of it: Chicoutimi, Saint-Jérôme, and Saint-Hyacinthe (ACSCM, 1—10/02–1, Antonio Beaudoin, "Tableau comparatif de quelques commissions scolaires de cités et villes au 30 juin 1954," 5 June 1954). In the 1950s, the rural school boards came to carry 40 per cent of the debt against the 5 per cent of the year 1944–45; the government relied more and more exclusively on the educational fund, the contributions of the hydroelectric commission remaining stable (Thwaites, "Origins and Development," 55, 202, 204). For the compounded statistics, see Louis-Philippe Audet, *Histoire de l'enseignement au Québec,* vol. 2 (Montréal: Holt, Rinehart, & Winston, 1971), 356.

97 PVCSSMCM, 18 December 1947; PVCSCM, 27 August 1945; and FCS president's speech at the conference, reprinted in *Le Nouvelliste,* 8 October 1953, p. 1.

98 In the year 1954–55, the boards reserved $2.3 million for school bus service, divided equally between the Catholic and Protestant sectors. On patronage, see the congress of the FCS for October 1952, where a commissioner complained that he had to make special demands to his own MP to obtain a grant for transport while other commissions obtained the grant without solicitation (ACSCM, 1–36/05–1, box 1660, Rapport des comités, p. 3). For statistics, see DPI, *Mémoire du Département de l'instruction publique à la Commission Tremblay* (Tremblay Report), Québec, July 1954, appendice N-1; Québec, *Rapport de la Commission royale d'enquête sur l'enseignement dans la province de Québec,* vol. 5, 58; *Rapport de la Commission d'enquête sur le transport scolaire,* March 1968, Éditeur officiel, 25–27.

99 Thwaites, "Origins and Development," 203, 210; and Behiels, *Prelude to Quebec's Quiet Revolution,* 156, 158–59.

100 I describe this episode in "Nationalisme et politiques sociales au Québec depuis 1867: Un siècle de rendez-vous manqués entre l'État, l'Église, et les familles," *British Journal of Canadian Studies* 9, no. 2 (1994): 301–47.

101 Not only because of the new scale of city life, but also because the Church was losing its contact with believers (Lucia Ferretti, *Entre voisins. La société paroissiale en milieu urbain: Saint-Pierre-Apôtre de Montréal, 1848–1930* [Montréal: Boréal, 1992], the last two chapters in particular).

102 Richard F. Kenn, "On Secularization Patterns and the Westward Extension of the Welfare State, 1883–1983," in *Comparative Social Research,* vol. 6 (volume on the Welfare State), ed. R.P. Tomasson (London: Jai Press, 1983). According to the promoter of this type of interpretation, social-policy historian German Rimlinger, Catholic societies could have then adhered more easily to the principles of the Welfare State than those who had entered into it with less at stake and with less motivation (Peter Baldwin, "The Welfare State for Historians: A Review Article," *Comparative Studies in Society and History* 34, no. 4 [1992]: 706).

103 Jean Charles Falarteau, "The Changing Social Structure," in his *Essais sur le Québec contemporain* (Québec: Presses de l'Université Laval, 1952), 114.

104 The difference is small, but constant (Kenneth G. Banting, *The Welfare State and Canadian Federalism* [Montréal: McGill-Queen's University Press, 1987], chapters 3 and 8).

105 B.L. Vigod, "History According to the Boucher Report: Some Reflections on the State and Social Welfare in Quebec before the Quiet Revolution," in *The Benevolent State: The Growth of Welfare in Canada,* eds. Allan Moscovitch and Jim Albert

(Toronto: Garamond, 1987), 182; Hamelin and Gagnon, *Histoire du catholicisme québécois,* 447–48; and Gisèle Turgeon, "Appréciation de la Loi de l'assistance aux mères nécessiteuses, à la lumière des statistiques de la Sauvegarde de l'enfance" (M.A. diss., Université Laval, 1954), 117.

106 Rumilly, *Maurice Duplessis et son temps,* vol. 1, 648–49. It is possible that by launching early elections in 1939, Duplessis had attempted to minimize the impact of the discontent the electors had demonstrated regarding his disengagement, by focusing the election on nationalist problems (Vigod, "History According to the Boucher Report," 182).

107 Behiels, "The Bloc Populaire Canadian," 507.

108 Genest, "Vie et œuvre," 573. See also Duplessis' speech given in Saint-Flavien: "Conscription is now everywhere all the time.... Everything is conscripted in the province of Québec, our young people for the army, our women in the factories, and even our children in the school" [our translation] (cited in Rumilly, *Maurice Duplessis et son temps,* vol. 1, 697).

109 In 1939 Godbout had obtained 54.2 per cent of the vote, and in 1944 40 per cent. By virtue of the strong rural and Francophone representation, a decrease of 14 per cent was enough to bring the number of seats from seventy to thirty-seven, which cost him the majority. With 38.2 per cent of the vote, less than in 1939, the Union nationale could count on forty-eight seats (Linteau et al., *Histoire du Québec contemporain,* vol. 2, 141).

110 On Côté, see Rumilly, *Maurice Duplessis et son temps,* vol. 1, 44–45. See also Simone Monet-Chartrand, *Ma vie comme rivière,* vol. 2, *1939–1949* (Montréal: Remue-Ménage, 1982), 256–58; Defence plea of Ovila Bergeron, deputy of the federal wing of the Bloc populaire and MP for Stanstead County, in the House of Commons (*Gazette* [Montréal], 17 February 1945); and AQRO, 42–8, vol. 1, Jean-Paul Robillard, "Chronique," *Le Petit Journal,* 12 February 1948. In February 1945, the head of the Bloc, André Laurendeau, had blamed the provincial government for not having taken the initiative to institute the allowances (cited in Banting, *The Welfare State and Canadian Federalism,* 141).

111 Gérard Bergeron, "Introduction," in *L'État du Québec en devenir,* eds. Gérard Bergeron and Réjean Pelletier (Montréal: Boréal, 1980), 36.

112 "L'inexplicable taux décroissant," *La Terre de chez nous,* 23 June 1945, pp. 7–8; and Lebel, "Après deux ans d'allocations familiales," 230. See also Father Bouvier, "Les allocations familiales à Ottawa," *Relations,* August 1944, 202.

113 Cited in Robert Rumilly, *Histoire de la province de Québec,* vol. 41, *La guerre de 1939–1945: Duplessis reprend les rennes* (Montréal: Fides, 1969), 45.

114 Michel Brunet, "Trois dominantes de la pensée canadienne-française: L'agriculturisme, l'anti-étatisme, et le messianisme," in *La présence anglaise et les Canadiens: Études sur l'histoire de la pensée des deux Canadas* (Montréal: Beauchemin, 1964), 144; Québec, Commission royale d'enquête sur les problèmes constitutionnels, *Rapport,* vol. 3, 1954, 129–30.

115 Bergeron, "Introduction," 31.

116 Hubert Jedin and John Dolan, eds., *History of the Church,* vol. 9, *The Church in the Industrial Age* (New York: Crossroad, 1989), 215. In Québec, such trust in the leadership of lay Catholics was granted relatively late, according to Hamelin and Gagnon (*Histoire du catholicisme québécois,* 401).

117 Baldwin, "The Welfare State for Historians," 703; Robert Bothwell and John English, *Canada Since 1945: Power, Politics, and Provincialism,* 2nd ed. (Toronto: University of Toronto Press, 1989), 94.

118 Canada, *Conférence fédérale-provinciale du rétablissement,* August 1945, 30, 53; Doug Owram, *The Government Generation: Canadian Intellectuals and the State, 1900–1945* (Toronto: University of Toronto Press, 1986), 319; Rumilly, *Histoire de la province de Québec,* vol. 41, 24–25; and Granatstein, *Canada's War,* 278–79. In 1944, the old-age pensions cost $31.5 million (*Débats,* 1944, 5702). From April 1945 to March 1946, the family allowances represented 16 per cent of the federal government's civil expenses (Canada, Dominion Bureau of Statistics, *The Canada Year Book, 1947* [Ottawa: King's Printer, 1948], 956–57; and Guest, *The Emergence of Social Security in Canada,* 217).
119 Finkel, "Paradise Postponed."
120 *La Terre de chez nous,* 12 September 1945, pp. 5, 20.
121 *Débats,* 1949, 2546.
122 Finkel, "Paradise Postponed."
123 *AQRO, 1951–1952,* 8–11; NAC, RG 29, acc. 82–83/152, box 8, 265–3-3, "Policy Directives Resulting from Conference of Welfare Supervisors," 23–25 March 1948; AQRO, 3–4, Lafrance to Fleming, 11 May 1950; AQRO, 8–0, vol. 1, Fournier, 14 April 1947; AQRO, 8–0, vol. 1, Lafrance to the SPI, 30 September 1949, and the response, 17 October 1949; AQRO, 8–0, vol. 1, Fournier to his employees, 25 October 1949; AQRO, 8–0, vol. 1, Lafrance to the SPI, 28 October 1949; AQRO, 8–0, vol. 1, Fournier to Lafrance, 16 November 1949; AQRO, 8–0, vol. 1, Hendershot, 13 December 1950; AQRO, 8–1, vol. 1, Senez to Lafrance, "Non fréquentation scolaire attributable à un problème dans une famille," 25 April 1952; and AQRO, 42–14, Fournier, 12 April 1950, p. 7. It is difficult to know how much these good intentions actually materialized. On one occasion, the officers were proud to accomplish this aspect of their work. But Assistant Regional Director Faguy was discouraged by the little power, in practice, the office had in those cases where there were no social agencies nearby. The allowances employees had to take up the problem and transfer it to an agency. But the constitution did not permit them to do any social work (NAC, RG 29, acc. 82–83/152, box 2, 260–1-1, "Notes on Supervision Visit to the QRO," 17–19 June 1951, 2).
124 CDSA, 1943–1200, box 112 317, case nos. 7, 6–2, 6–37, 6–50.
125 Cited in *ARSPI, 1951–1952,* 7.
126 Thwaites, "Origins and Development," 234.
127 "Drew et les allocations familiales—Drew en faveur des familles nombreuses," advertisement published in an unidentified newspaper, found in the AQRO. The advertisement recalls that Drew was the first to promise the abolition of the decreasing rate, before the Liberal Party itself made it an electoral promise.
128 Murray Beck, *Pendulum of Power: Canada's Federal Elections* (Toronto: Prentice-Hall Canada, 1968), 365; and Vigod, "History According to the Boucher Report," 183. Québec had been the key to the 1945 Liberal victory. Mackenzie King had won 53 seats with 50.8 per cent of the votes. In total, he had obtained 127 out of 245 seats (Granatstein, *Canada's War*).
129 Linteau et al., *Histoire du Québec contemporain,* vol. 2, 483, 599.
130 Cited in Bergeron, *Le Canada français,* 178; Vigod, "History According to the Boucher Report," 183; and Theda Skocpol, "A Society without a 'State'?: Political Organization, Social Conflict, and Welfare Provision in the United States," *Journal of Public Policy* 7, no. 4 (1988): 363.
131 Hamelin and Garon, "La vie politique au Québec," 23.
132 *Annuaire statistique du Québec (ASQ), 1956–1957,* 140; *ASQ, 1958,* 163–64; *ASQ, 1959,* 160–67; *ASQ, 1961,* 184, 192–93; *ASQ, 1962,* 110; and *RSQ, 1959,* 7–8 Eliz.

2, c. 27. The texts of the young Quiet Revolution took up the same rhetoric. For a comparable critique of the rhetoric used by the Lesage government, see Vigod, "History According to the Boucher Report."

133 For a reflection on such indirect national centralization movements through the intermediary of the local professionalization associations, see E.P. Hennock, "Central/Local Government Relations in England: An Outline, 1800–1950," *Urban History Yearbook*, 1982, 38–49. For more on the multiple federal social programs in the expansion of social work in francophone Québec, see Heyda Denault, "L'insertion du service social dans le milieu canadien-français," *Service social* 10, no. 3 (1961), and 11, no. 1 (1962).

134 Banting, *The Welfare State and Canadian Federalism*, 141.

135 In 1962, sociologist Fernand Dumont critiqued for this reason the analyses of French-Canadian values conducted by the historians of the École de Montréal. Of Michel Brunet, Dumont said that "in constantly focusing on 1760, the author seems to prevent himself from considering the specific importance of the subsequent history; this period only appears, in the end, as the product of fatality" ("L'étude systématique de la société canadienne-française," in *Situation de la recherche sur le Canada français*, eds. Fernand Dumont and Yves Martin [Québec: Presses de l'Université Laval, 162], 281).

136 Hamelin and Gagnon, *Histoire du catholicisme québécois*, 449.

137 On Jean-Jacques Bertrand's and Robert Bourassa's declarations on the role of social policies in cultural transformations during constitutional negotiations in the 1970s, see Banting, *The Welfare State and Canadian Federalism*, 142; and Philip Resnick, *The Mask of Proteus: Canadian Reflections on the State* (Montréal: McGill-Queen's University Press, 1990), 208–211.

138 Reg Whitaker, "Images of the State in Canada," 58.

139 Interview with P.-A. Fournier, Sillery, QC, September 1988. Fournier created his own publishing house to print the text, the Maison Champlain, which also published a collection of laws on education. See also Paul Gérin-Lajoie, interviewed by Thwaites in "Origins Development," 205–207. On other episodes of the shift towards the province in the construction of welfare state initiatives, where the Church and the federal State played a large role before the provincial State took over and reoriented the existing structures, see Linteau et al., *Histoire du Québec contemporain*, vol. 2, 581; and Frédéric Leseman, *Du pain et des services: La réforme de la santé et des services sociaux au Québec* (Montréal: Albert Saint-Martin, 1981).

140 Roy, *Les programmes électoraux du Québec*, vol. 2, 347, 355, 368. See also Filion, *Les confidences d'un commissaire*, 50–64.

141 Roger Magnuson, *A Brief History of Quebec Education: From New France to the Parti Québécois* (Montréal: Harvest House, 1980), 115.

142 Ronald Rudin suggests that the "agencies and boards outside the politicians' control" are still a distinct characteristic of the province's political culture and that they owe their existence to the elites' anti-statism tradition ("Revisionism and the Search for a Normal Society: A Critique of Recent Quebec Historical Writing," *Canadian Historical Review* 73, no. 1 (1992): 52–53). Rudin's reflection is based on an article by Ralph Heintzman ("The Political Culture of Quebec, 1840–1960," *Canadian Journal of Political Science* 16, no. 1 [1983]: 3–59).

143 Bernard Vigod, "Conclusion," *Quebec before Duplessis: The Political Career of Louis-Alexandre Taschereau* (Montréal: McGill-Queen's University Press, 1986); Hamelin and Gagnon, *Histoire du catholicisme québécois*, 451; Banting, *The Welfare State and Canadian Federalism*, 137; *La Terre de chez nous*, 12 September 1945, pp. 5, 20; and *Débats*, 1949, 2546.

144 DPI, Tremblay Report, vol. 3, 126.

145 Resnick, *The Mask of Proteus,* 218, citing the abridged version of the Tremblay Report, 50, 70.

146 Linteau et al., *Histoire du Québec contemporain,* vol. 2, 583.

147 Banting, *The Welfare State and Canadian Federalism,* 143–44.

148 Renée B. Dandurand, *Le mariage en question: Essai socio-historique* (Québec: Institut québécois de recherche sur la culture, 1988).

149 *Débats,* 1949, 2542, 2548; *SC,* 1949, 13 Geo. 6. Consequently, the Family Allowances Bureau had spent $3.5 million in adjustments for Québec, 55 per cent of the country's total adjustments, while the province made up only 32 per cent of the eligible children (*RAMSNBES, 1949–1950,* 126–35).

150 Cited in Falardeau, *Essais sur le Québec contemporain*, 1953, 235.

151 DPI, Tremblay Report, vol. 3, 129–30. Twenty-four of the forty-five reports submitted to the Tremblay Commission concerning welfare pointed out the link between welfare measures and culture (Tremblay Report, vol. 3, chapter 4, p. 68).

Index

Page numbers in italics refer to illustrations.

Books in the Studies in Childhood and Family in Canada Series Published by Wilfrid Laurier University Press

Making Do: Women, Family, and Home in Montreal during the Great Depression by Denyse Baillargeon, translated by Yvonne Klein • 1999 / xii + 232 / ISBN: 0-88920-326-1 / ISBN-13: 978-0-88920-326-6

Children in English-Canadian Society: Framing the Twentieth-Century Consensus by Neil Sutherland with a new foreword by Cynthia Comacchio • 2000 / xxiv + 336 pp. / illus. / ISBN: 0-88920-351-2 / ISBN-13: 978-0-88920-351-8

Love Strong as Death: Lucy Peel's Canadian Journal, 1833–1836 edited by J.I. Little • 2001 / x + 229 pp. / illus. / ISBN: 0-88920-389-X / ISBN-13: 978-0-88920-389-1

The Challenge of Children's Rights for Canada by Katherine Covell and R. Brian Howe • 2001 / x + 244 pp. / ISBN: 0-88920-380-6 / ISBN-13: 978-0-88920-380-8

NFB Kids: Portrayals of Children by the National Film Board of Canada, 1939–1989 by Brian J. Low • 2002 / 288 pp. / illus. / ISBN: 0-88920-386-5 / ISBN-13: 978-0-88920-386-0

Something to Cry About: An Argument against Corporal Punishment of Children in Canada by Susan M. Turner • 2002 / xix + 317 pp. / ISBN: 0-88920-382-2 / ISBN-13: 978-0-88920-382-2

Freedom to Play: We Made Our Own Fun edited by Norah L. Lewis • 2002 / xiv + 210 pp. / ISBN: 0-88920-406-3 / ISBN-13: 978-0-88920-406-5

The Dominion of Youth: Adolescence and the Making of Modern Canada, 1920–1950 by Cynthia Comacchio • 2006 / x + 302 / illus. / ISBN: 0-88920-488-8 / ISBN-13: 978-0-88920-488-1

Evangelical Balance Sheet: Character, Family, and Business in Mid-Victorian Nova Scotia by B. Anne Wood • 2006 / xxx + 198 / illus. / ISBN: 0-88920-500-0 / ISBN-13: 978-0-88920-500-0

The Social Origins of the Welfare State: Québec Families, Compulsory Education, and Family Allowances, 1940–1955 by Dominique Marshall, translated by Nicola Doone Danby • 2006 / xx + 280 pp. / illus. / ISBN: 0-88920-452-7 / ISBN-13: 978-0-88920-452-2